Irish Winners of the Vi

Irish Winners
of the
Victoria Cross

Richard Doherty & David Truesdale

FOUR COURTS PRESS

Set in 10.5 on 12.5 Ehrhardt for
FOUR COURTS PRESS LTD
Fumbally Lane, Dublin 8, Ireland
e-mail: info@four-courts-press.ie
and in North America by
FOUR COURTS PRESS
c/o ISBS, 5804 N.E. Hassalo Street, Portland, OR 97213.

A catalogue record for this title
is available from the British Library.

ISBN 1–85182–491–x hbk
1–85182–442–1 pbk

Printed in Ireland
by ColourBooks Ltd.

In memory
Colonel Desmond G.C. Whyte DSO, MD, FRCP, FRCS, FRCR
Royal Army Medical Corps
Officer Commanding 111 Field Ambulance (Chindits) 1944
recommended for the Victoria Cross but denied the award

Contents

	Acknowledgements	8
	Introduction	11
1	A Proposed New Military Order ...	15
2	The Crimea	21
3	The Indian Mutiny	42
4	The Small Wars of Empire	66
5	The Dark Continent	81
6	1914-19	102
7	1920-45	141
8	Recommendation Rejected	174
	Postscript	184
	Appendix 1: Alphabetical List	189
	Appendix 2: Forfeited Awards	235
	Appendix 3: Irish VCs and Poetry	237
	Notes	241
	Bibliography	247
	Index	251

Acknowledgements

Writing a book on a subject as diverse as the Irish Victoria Cross winners was never going to be a simple task. The authors' original aim was to produce, in narrative form, as accurate a picture of Ireland's contribution to the history of the Victoria Cross as was possible. Both authors were also aware that a number of Irishmen who had won the coveted gallantry award had never been acknowledged as Irish and they wanted to rectify that situation.

The base line for the research for this book was the excellent compilation of Irish-born Victoria Cross winners produced by the late Lieutenant-Colonel Brian Clark MC, GM, for the *Irish Sword*, the journal of the Military History Society of Ireland. Indeed it could be said that Brian Clark's work was also the inspiration for this book, especially as Doherty attempted, unsuccessfully, to persuade Clark to continue with his work to produce a book. Sincere acknowledgement is therefore made to Brian Clark, to his widow Brenda, his daughter Shanny and to the *Irish Sword*.

While researching the book the authors had the willing and enthusiastic support of many individuals and bodies. Our thanks are therefore due to: the Military Historical Society, custodians of the Lummis Files, for access to those files; Hancocks & Co (Jewellers) Ltd, the manufacturers of the Victoria Cross, for their co-operation; the National Army Museum, Royal Hospital Road, London, especially the staff of the Reading Room for their invaluable assistance and courtesy; the Public Record Office, Kew, Surrey, and the staff of the Reading and Search Rooms for their efficiency and helpfulness; Major George Stephens MBE, and the staff of the Royal Inniskilling Fusiliers' Museum, Enniskillen; Major Mike Murphy, Royal Ulster Rifles' Museum, Belfast; Mrs Amanda Moreno and the staff of the Royal Irish Fusiliers' Museum, Armagh; Cheshire Military Museum, especially Major John Ellis; Royal Engineers' Museum, Chatham, Kent, especially the Curator, Mr J.H. Rhodes; The Fusiliers' Museum of Northumberland, especially Captain (Retd) P.H.D. Marr; Queen's Royal Lancers' Museum, Grantham, Lincolnshire, especially Captain J.M. Holtby; King's Own Royal Regiment Museum, Lancaster, especially Peter Donnelly; King's Own Royal Border Regiment Museum, Carlisle, especially Stuart Eastwood; The Duke of Wellington's Regimental Museum, especially Philipa McKenzie; Queen's Lancashire Regimental Museum, Warrington, Cheshire; RHQ The Royal Scots, especially Major R.P. Mason; Regimental Museum, The Royal Green Jackets, especially Major K. Gray; Light Infantry Office (Durham), especially Major Randal Cross; Gordon Highlanders Regimental Museum, Aberdeen; Regimental Museum, the Cameronians (Scottish Rifles), Hamilton, Museum XX The Lancashire Fusiliers, Bury; Airborne Museum, Oosterbeek, The Netherlands, especially Drs Adrian Groeneweg; Reverend F.J. Turner SJ, Archivist, Stonyhurst College, Clitheroe, Lancashire; Reverend Brian Keenan SM, Provincial, Marist Fathers, Milltown, Dublin; Reverend Brother J.P. McGowan FMS, Marist Brothers, Clondalkin, Dublin; The Royal School, Dungannon, especially Norman Cardwell, School Archivist; Portora Royal School, Enniskillen; Athy Heritage Centre, County Kildare, especially Mark McLaughlin; THCL Books, Blackburn, Lancashire, especially Henry L. Kirby and R. Raymond Walsh FZS; the staff of the Central Library, Foyle Street, Londonderry; the staff of Newtownards Public Library, especially Joan Thompson; the Linen Hall Library, Belfast; Derby City Council's Military Collection, especially the curator, Angela Kelsall; Roy McCullough and Leslie Beattie, Homer Graphics, Belfast; David Orr, Blood and Roses Publishing; David Rountree, .357 Publishing; Bob Phair and Matt Dillon, Antrim; Jim Fraser, Scotland; Ellis Williams, for information on Thomas Grady VC; Mr John Kirwan, Kilkenny, for information on the family of W.R.P. Hamilton VC and on Robert Johnston VC; Tony Crowe, Londonderry, for information on Robert Johnston VC; David and Florence Walker, Strathfoyle, Londonderry for information on Druminargal House; Paul Rea, Belfast; Paul Clark, UTV; James Durney, Athy, County Kildare; Dennis Pillinger, Military Historical Society; Miss V.C. (Peggy) Emerson, Drogheda; Mrs Anne Mayne, Groomsport, County Down and the Misses Dorothy and Evelyn Podesta, Bangor, County Down.

We would also like to thank Michael Adams and his staff at Four Courts Press for their support and encouragement and their professionalism in the final production of this book.

Acknowledgements are also made to all those who allowed us to use illustrations in the book. Their kindness is appreciated and details of copyright holders are included on the next page. In some cases in spite of our best efforts it has not been possible to trace copyright holders but the authors and the publishers are prepared to make the necessary arrangements to rectify this at the earliest opportunity.

Finally it would be remiss of us not to express our thanks to our wives and families – Carol, Joanne, James and Catríona Doherty and Sharon and Nathan Truesdale – for their support and patience during the researching and writing of this book.

PHOTOGRAPH CREDITS

1, 2 & 11 The King's Own Royal Border Regiment Museum; 3, 5, 6, 7, 10, 12, 13, 16 & 21 The Royal Green Jackets Museum; 4 The Royal Scots Museum; 8, 9 & 38 The Fusiliers Museum of Northumberland; 14, 15, 22, 36, & 39 THCL Books/Stonyhurst College. The portraits of the Stonyhurst VC winners currently hang in Stonyhurst College, Clitheroe, Lancashire; 17 Cranston Fine Arts; 18, 23 David Truesdale; 19, 25, 26 & 47 The Royal Fusiliers Museum; 20 Stephen Sandford; 24 The Cheshire Regiment Museum; 27, 31, 32 & 33 The Royal Inniskilling Fusiliers Museum; 28 Athy Heritage Centre; 29 The Lancashire Fusiliers Museum; 30 Miss V.C. Emerson, Drogheda; 34 Mrs Anne Mayne, Donaghadee; 35, 40 & 42 Chaz Bowyer; 37, 41, 43 & 44 Imperial War Museum; 45, 46 & 47 David Orr; 48 & 50 Richard Doherty; 49 Colonel Desmond Woods, MC & Bar; 51 Stonyhurst College

Introduction

In producing a history of Irish VCs the authors faced a problem of definition: what is an Irishman? The purists would argue that only someone born in Ireland may be considered Irish. But this would exclude many sons of Irish parents who were born elsewhere while including the sons of non-Irish parents who happened to be living in Ireland when those sons were born. Since the Victoria Cross was instituted at a time when the British Empire was at its zenith, there were many Irish soldiers, administrators and traders living throughout that Empire. Their sons could be defined as Indian, African, Canadian, Australian, or any one of a multitude of nationalities, but it seems most sensible, and reasonable, to consider them as Irish. Likewise, since all of Ireland was part of the United Kingdom until 1922, with many English, Scots and Welsh soldiers, civil servants and members of the professions domiciled in Ireland, their sons may have been born in Ireland but, like Irishmen born elsewhere, they would generally have considered themselves to have the same nationality as their parents.

It appeared to the authors that the most acceptable definition – which is really a compromise – is what we have termed the 'Jack Charlton rule': if one or other of a VC's parents were Irish-born, then he is regarded as Irish. Those born in Ireland of non-Irish parents are not excluded from this book, but it is made clear that they were, perhaps, not as Irish as some of those born outside the island.

Corporal George Edward Nurse of the Royal Field Artillery won the Victoria Cross during the Boer War. Nurse was born in Enniskillen in April 1873, but that is his sole connection with Ireland. His parents were Channel Islanders, whose home address was the Cobo Hotel, Guernsey, and Nurse was educated in Guernsey. He was Irish only by the accident of birth. By contrast, Drummer **William Kenny**, of the Gordon Highlanders, was born in Malta in 1880. His father was a soldier and a native of Drogheda, County Louth, as was his mother. When the announcement was made in February 1915 that Kenny had won the VC near Ypres in the previous October, Drogheda had no doubt that he was one of their own. On Saint Patrick's Day 1915 he was given the Freedom of the Borough, and the Mayor of Drogheda and the Corporation processed to High Mass with Kenny and his parents. In March 1999 the *Drogheda Independent* carried a full-page feature on the dedication of a headstone to his memory in Brookwood cemetery in Surrey. Was Kenny, therefore, Irish or Maltese?

In February 1942 Lieutenant-Commander **Eugene Esmonde** DSO, of the Fleet Air Arm won a posthumous Victoria Cross for his gallantry in an attack on the German ships *Scharnhorst, Gneisenau* and *Prinz Eugen*. Esmonde was born in Yorkshire in March 1909 where his Irish father was practising as a doctor. The family returned to Ireland later that year and Esmonde grew up at the family home in Tipperary. Yet his birth certificate would define him as English. **David Lord**'s birth certificate defined him as Irish since he was born in Cork in 1913 where his father was serving in the Army. But Lord spent most of his childhood in Wrexham where he was an altar boy in Saint Mary's Cathedral. At Arnhem in 1944, he won RAF Transport Command's only Victoria Cross when he remained at the controls of his stricken Dakota aircraft in an effort to allow his crew to bale out safely. Although born in Cork, Lord is claimed by Wales and Wrexham. Was he Irish or Welsh? As he left Ireland at a very young age, it seems reasonable to suggest that Lord would have regarded himself as Welsh.

In previous works on Irish Victoria Cross winners, Lord and Nurse have been defined as Irish, because of their places of birth, while Esmonde and Kenny have either been omitted or defined as VC winners with Irish town or county connections. It seemed invidious to the authors to omit the latter pair while including the former; hence our decision to look as closely as possible at the parents of VC winners with known Irish connections.

Until research began on this book the accepted number of Irish Victoria Cross winners was 166 individuals; none of the three double-VC winners was Irish although there is an Irish family connection for **Captain Noel Godfrey Chavasse** VC and Bar. This figure was established by the late Lieutenant-Colonel Brian Clark MC, GM in an article in the *Irish Sword*, the journal of the Military History Society of Ireland; he noted that there were a further 56 VC winners who were born of Irish parents abroad, or were officers and men of Irish regiments. Colonel Clark's work provided an invaluable foundation for the present book.

That figure of 166 Irish winners represents 12 per cent of the Victoria Crosses awarded to date. It is a surprisingly high proportion when one considers that the Cross could be won by any member of the British, Dominion or Empire forces for most of its existence. (Indian officers and men became eligible from 1911, on the orders of King George V.) Even in the Second World War, when Irish VC winners totalled eight, the proportion is still high, at almost 4.5 per cent of all VCs won in that conflict, whereas the Irish element of the British, Commonwealth and Imperial war effort in manpower represented just over one per cent. This book raises the number of Irish VC winners to over 200 and suggests that there may be some others with Irish connections that are sufficient to define them as Irish VCs.

The Lummis Files of the Military Historical Society, held in the National Army Museum in London, were another invaluable source for the authors and provided much useful information. Although initiated many years ago by the late Canon E.M. Lummis MC, the files are regularly updated through the painstaking efforts of the Society's custodian, Mr Dennis Pillinger.

Many Victoria Cross winners rose from obscurity to win the decoration and returned to the same obscurity. This is especially true of those VC laureates of the nineteenth century; in many cases very little is known about them. By contrast those who won the Victoria Cross in the two world wars of this century, and especially the Second World War, have been much better researched in terms of background and subsequent career than their predecessors. This was clear to the authors in their own research and is illustrated by the amount of information and detail that is included in this book on the Irish VCs of the Second World War.

Some Irish VC winners have been the subject of biographies, or have been included in anthologies of the Victoria Cross, but the majority remain obscure. It is the intention of this book to try to raise the majority above that obscurity and to restore to their rightful place in Irish history those who have been the 'forgotten Irish' by dint of their birthplaces.

I A Proposed New Military Order ...

On Sunday 21 May 1995, the chapel at Stonyhurst College, near Clitheroe in Lancashire, was the setting for a unique occasion in Irish history. On that day the college was celebrating the life of one of seven former pupils who had won the Victoria Cross. Five of those seven were either Irish-born or born into Irish families. **Harold Marcus Ervine Andrews** was Stonyhurst's sixth VC winner, and the last to die. His death also marked the end of Ireland's last VC holder, and yet the event passed with but little mention in the Irish media.[1]

The processional hymn that Sunday morning was 'O, God, our help in ages past', while the Mass concluded with what might once have been regarded as the anthem of the Catholic Church in Ireland – 'Faith of our fathers'. At the beginning of Mass, Andrews' sword was presented to the college and the soldier's life was recalled throughout the service. The passing of the college's last holder of the Victoria Cross was an especially poignant occasion, not only for the college but also for his friends and former Army comrades.[2] However, little note was made of the fact that, with Andrews' death, a milestone had been reached in Ireland's long and special connection with the Victoria Cross, In fact, history may well record him as the last Irish VC winner to die.

The Victoria Cross has long had a reputation as the world's premier gallantry award, with its only rival being the United States' Medal of Honor, another decoration that has been won by many Irishmen. Instituted by Queen Victoria in 1856, the decoration that bears that monarch's name was first awarded for gallantry in the Crimean War and the proto-winner of the award was an Irishman, **Charles Davis Lucas** of the Royal Navy.[3] Thereafter Irishmen have provided a number of 'firsts' in the medal's history, including the Army's first VC, the first VC of the Great War, and the RAF's first VC of the Second World War, while Harold Marcus Ervine Andrews was the first person to be decorated with the VC by King George VI in that war. In addition, the first VC awarded to a military chaplain went to an Irishman, and many regiments of the British Army had Irishmen as their first-ever VC winners. The youngest-ever winner of the VC was Irish – indeed the next youngest was also Irish – and Wanderers Rugby Football Club, Dublin, is probably the only sporting club that can boast of having had three winners of the Victoria Cross in its membership.[4]

Prior to Queen Victoria's authorization of the Victoria Cross in 1856, there were few gallantry awards available to members of the British forces. Senior officers were eligible for orders of chivalry, including the Order of Saint Patrick, but their juniors, and other ranks, received no formal recognition for acts of gallantry, although rewards were often made in the form of promotions, or cash awards, while some officers had medals struck for presentation to outstandingly courageous members of their regiments. Such awards were, however, rare. The situation began to improve in 1854 with the institution of the Distinguished Conduct Medal, followed by the Conspicuous Gallantry Medal the following year. However, neither medal could be awarded to officers and each was specific to a service: the DCM was for the Army and the CGM for the Royal Navy. Both medals were instituted as a result of the Crimean war, as was the Victoria Cross, which became the first truly democratic award for gallantry.

Although it may have been Prince Albert who inspired the idea of the new gallantry decoration, that award was to bear the name of his wife and there is no doubt that Victoria took a very close interest in the design and naming of the award, as well as the detail of the royal warrant that authorized the medal. The first draft of that warrant proposed that there should be an Order with its own structure, although with a single degree of membership, reflecting the various orders of chivalry already in existence.

> ... it is proposed to institute a new Military Order, the insignia of which, though trifling in intrinsic value, shall be highly prized and eagerly sought after by the Officers and men in Her Majesty's Military services.
>
> The Order to be styled 'The Military Order of Victoria' motto *Pro Patria Mori* or *Mors aut Victoria* or *God defend the right.*

The Order was to consist of the Sovereign, as its head, a grand secretary and grand registrar, both of whom would be honorary, as well as a paid secretary and a paid registrar. It was proposed that the grand registrar should be 'the Secretary of State for War for the time being'.

The insignia of the Order was to be a cross of steel or bronze and no more detail is included in the first draft of the warrant.[5] However, Lord Panmure, the Secretary of State for War, submitted two drawings to the Queen on 4 January 1856 together with a piece of metal to show the size of the cross; it was noted that the final cross would not be as thick or as heavy as the sample.[6]

Victoria decided that the idea of an order was inappropriate and that there should be no formal structure along the lines of the various orders of chivalry. The final version of the warrant omitted all references to an order. Instead all persons were to be placed on a 'perfectly equal footing' and 'neither rank nor long service, nor wounds nor any other quality whatsoever, save the merit of conspicuous bravery' would qualify an individual for the award of the decoration.[7]

Such conspicuous bravery was further defined as 'some signal act of valour or devotion to their country' performed in the face of the enemy while serving the monarch. Should a personal act of bravery contribute to the successful outcome of a military or naval operation, then the individual performing that act would also be eligible for the award. The Queen's final decision on the form of the decoration was that it would be 'designated the Victoria Cross and ... consist of a Maltese Cross of Bronze with our Royal Crest in the centre and underneath which an Escroll bearing the inscription For Valour'. For the Royal Navy the Cross was to be suspended from a blue ribbon while that for the Army would use a crimson ribbon. (After the First World War, with the creation of the Royal Air Force, the crimson ribbon was adopted for all three services.) The Victoria Cross came into being, officially, on 29 January 1856 when Queen Victoria signed the royal warrant at Buckingham Palace.[8] On 5 February the *London Gazette* announced the institution of the new gallantry award, which was to be made retrospective to late-1854 to allow for awards to sailors and soldiers in the Crimean war.

In addition to the inscription 'For Valour', chosen by the Queen in preference to the proposed 'For the Brave', the Victoria Cross was also to carry the date of the act of gallantry for which it was awarded. This was to be inscribed on the reverse of the Cross – together with the name of the recipient – and was to lead to some confusion whereby claims were made that various VC winners were multiple laureates, or winners of a Bar to the Cross. In fact, there could be several dates for which an award was made and it was be 1915 before the first Bar to a Victoria Cross was awarded. However, the principle of further awards was catered for in the original warrant, and it may have been this clause (No. 4) that made some people believe that a VC with two or more dates inscribed on the reverse represented further awards of the medal.

The Victoria Cross differs from other nations' gallantry awards in this inclusion of both the recipient's name and the date of his act of gallantry on the medal's reverse. Only the United States' Medal of Honor when awarded to US Air Force personnel carries both the individual's name and the date on which he won his medal.[9] This is one of the factors that has led to the Victoria Cross being regarded as probably the premier gallantry award. Another factor is the relative scarcity of the Victoria Cross: since its inception only 1354 awards have been made, to 1350 individuals (three of whom have won it twice) and to the American Unknown Warrior of the Great War.[10]

The first medals were struck by the London jewellers Hancocks, who make the Victoria Cross to this day. Hancocks were supplied with bronze from which to make the medals, and this material is itself significant. The metal from which all Victoria Crosses have been made was taken from the cascables of Russian cannon captured at Sevastopol during the Crimean war. In turn the Russians had taken the cannon from the Chinese, so that the metal is originally from the Orient. Although some sources state that the original metal ran out in 1942, this is not so and the Cross continues to be made from that oriental bronze.[11]

The design of the medal is described as a Cross Pattée in some sources and as a Maltese cross in others. In the original warrant the description Maltese Cross is used. The manufacturers express no preference but note that 'it is generally known as a Cross Pattée'.[12]

The first Victoria Crosses were presented by Queen Victoria in Hyde Park on 26 June 1857. Sixty-two members of the Royal Navy and Army were present to be decorated by their Sovereign and a large crowd had gathered to witness the ceremony.[13] Among those decorated by Queen Victoria that day were the very first recipients of the Victoria Cross in the Royal Navy and the Army. Both were Irish: Lieutenant **Charles Davis Lucas**, Royal Navy, and Ensign **Luke O'Connor**, 23rd Regiment; both had also been commissioned as a result of their gallantry.

Lucas and O'Connor were not the only Irishmen decorated that day. By the date of that investiture, more than two dozen Irishmen had earned the VC. Such a large proportion of Irish VC winners reflected the large numbers of Irishmen in the British forces at that time and this situation would prevail for many years to come.

One other aspect of the Victoria Cross became evident from the comments made by the *Times* reporter who was present at that first investiture.

> Than the Cross of Valour nothing could be more plain and homely, not to say coarse-looking. It is a very small Maltese Cross, formed from the gun-metal of ordnance captured at Sebastopol. In the centre is a small crown and lion, with which latter's natural proportions of mane and tail cutting the cross much interferes. Below these is a small scroll which shortens three arms of the cross and is utterly out of keeping with the upper portions bearing the words 'For Valour'. But even with all the care and skill which distinguishes Mr Hancock the whole Cross is, after all, poor looking and mean in the extreme.[14]

The *Times* missed the essence of the new award completely: the Cross was intended to be simple and dignified in its design. On its own the metal from which the Cross was made was valueless; and it remains so. Each Cross with its ribbon and the engraving of the recipient's name and date, or dates, for which the award was made cost the War Office the princely sum of £1.[15] The true value of the Cross arises from the story of the individual who won the Cross. For its time, the idea was revolutionary, and egalitarian; other British medals that had been issued for campaigns and battles had been made of silver and the orders of chivalry and the other new awards, such as the Distinguished Conduct Medal, included precious metals and eye-catching designs. It has been suggested that the *Times* was really being mischievous as the newspaper was opposed to anything that Prince Albert was said to be involved in, and the reporter went on to suggest that Albert may have designed the Cross that bore his wife's name.

At first the VC could be awarded only to members of the Royal Navy – including the Royal Marines – or the Army who had performed their act of gallantry in the face of an enemy. On 29 October 1857 the warrant was amended to allow the award of the Cross to 'officers and men of the Naval and Military services of the East India Company' and then, on 10 August 1858, to cover acts of gallantry not in the face of the enemy.[16] The former amendment allowed the VC to be awarded to many officers and men of the East India Company's forces during the Indian Mutiny – but only to Europeans – and the latter amendment was to lead to six awards for valour that would include three Irishmen. In 1881 this amendment to the warrant was rescinded by a new warrant that specified an act of gallantry in the presence of the enemy. This revision of the conditions under which the Victoria Cross could be won led, eventually, to the institution of the George Cross to cover acts of gallantry not performed in the face of the enemy.

Although the initial warrant mentioned sailors and soldiers it made no mention of civilians. Thus when Mullingar-born **Thomas Henry Kavanagh**, a civil servant, was recommended for the Victoria Cross for his actions at Lucknow during the Indian Mutiny, the recommendation was rejected and he was given a cash award of £2,000 instead. However, that decision was appealed and Kavanagh was awarded the Cross. He was also allowed to keep his £2,000.[17] Kavanagh thereby gained the distinction of being one of the few civilians ever to win the Victoria Cross.

Throughout the history of the Victoria Cross, Irishmen have been prominent. Irish winners of the medal began with **Charles Davis Lucas** in the Baltic Sea in 1854 and their story continues until **James Magennis** won the last Irish VC in the Johore Strait off Singapore in the closing days of the Second World War. The chapters that follow tell the stories of those two men and all the other Irish VC laureates in between. It is a story that includes men from all levels of Irish society – the sons of poor farmers are represented alongside the sons of lords and generals. It is a story that also throws up stories of unruly men, indisposed to discipline, who rose to the demands of a particular occasion, but subsequently returned to their previous condition. And it is a story of paradoxes: what else could a member of the IRA, two Black and Tans and a B Special policeman have in common? Yet **Martin Doyle** VC, MM was also a member of the IRA in the period of the Irish war of independence, while **Robert Scott** VC served in the Ulster Special Constabulary – and was possibly the oldest commissioned officer in the UK forces in the Second World War – while two English VC winners, **James Leach** and **George Onions**, were both Cadets in the Auxiliary Division of the Royal Irish Constabulary, commonly referred to as Black and Tans.[18]

The story of the Irish winners of the Victoria Cross is a fascinating and very human story of some 206 individuals who left a special mark in the annals of the past century and a half. It is a chapter of Irish military history that deserves to be better known throughout Ireland, both on the broader level and on the more local level in those areas from where the Victoria Cross laureates hailed. Courage is a commodity that we can all salute, irrespective of class, creed or political beliefs. And the special courage that is needed to win a Victoria Cross is rare enough to elicit admiration for those who won the Cross.

2 The Crimea

The first awards of the Victoria Cross were made retrospectively to sailors and soldiers who had fought during the Crimean war. That conflict came to a close in March 1856, a month after the institution of the new gallantry award had been announced in the *London Gazette*.[1] However, the institution of the Cross was to be backdated to the autumn of 1854 so that servicemen who had fought in the Crimea would be eligible. But why had British forces been involved in the Crimea at all?

The apparent cause of the war was a dispute over the guardianship of the Holy Places in Palestine between the Orthodox and Latin Catholic Churches. In this disagreement the Russians, themselves Orthodox, supported the Greek Orthodox Church while France supported the claim of the Catholic Church. However, there were deeper, and much less noble, issues being considered by the French and Russian governments. Czar Nicholas was anxious to secure Russia's southern route to the sea and a warm-water anchorage; and this route was threatened by the Ottoman or Turkish Empire. Turkey dominated Russia's shortest route to the sea in the south; but Turkish power was in decline and Nicholas recognized the opportunity to dominate Turkey and destroy what was left of its Empire and power. In order to sustain the balance of power in the region he conceived the idea of sharing out Turkey's territories to the other powers: France, Austria and Britain were all to benefit from the Russian carve-up of the Ottoman Empire, with Britain receiving Egypt and Cyprus.[2]

Such a plan ignored certain realities. Britain was unlikely to be happy about Russia extending its power in a direction that might threaten the Indian Empire, and the country was indifferent as to whether Latin rite or Orthodox Catholics held the wardship of the Holy Places. Across the channel, the French Emperor Napoleon III was unlikely to agree to any suggestions from the country that had inflicted humiliating defeat on France in 1812. But Nicholas had made his decision and demanded recognition as the protector of Greek Christians in the Ottoman Empire.[3] As a demonstration of his determination, the Czar sent a Russian force to occupy two of Turkey's dependant states. Moldavia and Wallachia were taken into Russian control in July 1853.* Soon Russia and Turkey were at war, with the latter suffering a dev-

---

* Moldavia and Wallachia are part of modern Romania.

astating naval defeat at Sinope on 30 November when all but two ships of a Turkish squadron of frigates were sunk and three-quarters of their crew members died.[4] Russian use of exploding shells gave the Czar's ships a definite advantage over the Turks, who were firing solid shot. Through the victory at Sinope Russia gained control of the Black Sea.

In Britain the threat to imperial communications presented by this Russian victory was not recognized immediately. Much more concern was felt about the new steam-powered warships of the French Navy which, it was believed, could be used by Napoleon to launch a sudden attack on Britain. However, Lord Palmerston, who was to become British Prime Minister, had little doubt of the threat posed to British interests by Russia. Not until Palmerston threatened to resign from the cabinet did the government decide to take action. An ultimatum was sent to the Russians after the battle of Sinope and the two countries were on the road to war. On 27 March 1854 Britain and France declared war on Russia.[5]

At the outbreak of the Crimean War the British Army's strength was less than 140,000 men, of whom 65,000 were at home in the United Kingdom, a further 30,000 were in India and 40,000 were scattered around the globe in Britain's many colonies.[6] It was neither a well-equipped nor well-trained army, and its soldiers were subjected to poor living conditions and were badly paid. There is a common belief that the Crimean War was responsible for improving the British military establishment but, while this is true to an extent, the process of improvement had already begun in the years before the war. In many respects the army had changed little since 1815, the year in which Wellington defeated Napoleon at Waterloo. One of the factors in that situation was Wellington himself, who saw no need for change, actively opposed change when he was in government and continued to do so as Commander-in-Chief from 1842 until his death in 1852.[7] Among other things, the Iron Duke had ensured that British soldiers were still armed with smoothbore muskets rather than rifled weapons. The Minié rifled musket had been selected to replace smoothbore percussion musket in 1851, but issue of the new weapon was not general when the war began. (In December 1853 the Enfield rifle was selected to replace the Minié, but it was 1855 before any significant numbers of the muzzle-loading Enfield were in the hands of soldiers.)[8] That Britain was able to gather an expeditionary force to sail for the Crimea was a remarkable feat in the circumstances, although that force was to meet many difficulties.

Under the command of Lord Raglan* some 25,000 British troops embarked for the Crimea and were landed at Varna, on the western shore of the Black

---

* Raglan was 66 years old when he received this, his first independent, command.

Sea. Here, 300 miles from the Crimea, they were joined by a French force of about 30,000 men.[9] There was no immediate call to action as the Turks had already pushed the Russians out of the areas that the latter had occupied the previous July. It was fortuitous that there was no need to deploy the Allied force in the field: both British and French had suffered severely on the voyage out and sickness began to take its toll as soon as the troops disembarked. The greatest problem was cholera, which claimed more lives during the coming war than did enemy action. It was also a swift killer: a healthy soldier could be dead within twenty-four hours, such was the speed of the disease which spread easily in the less than sanitary conditions of contemporary camp life.[10]

While the soldiers waited and suffered around Varna, a British naval expedition had sailed into the Baltic Sea in a pre-emptive attempt to prevent Russian naval forces striking at Britain. Russia had a strong naval presence in the Baltic and, when Czar Nicholas sent his troops across the river Prut to invade Moldavia and Wallachia, the Baltic fleet in the Gulf of Finland included twenty-seven ships of the line and frigates as well as many smaller vessels. In addition there was a strong military force at Saint Petersburg. Such forces might menace the English coast if there was no available force to oppose them. Vice-Admiral Sir Charles Napier had drawn the attention of Aberdeen, the Prime Minister, to this threat as early as 5 July 1853, but the latter believed that the 'Eastern question' could be resolved peacefully.[11]

Only in early 1854 did the British government begin to look seriously at the northern threat. There were reports from ambassadors at Saint Petersburg and Copenhagen, as well as from the British Consul in New York, that Russian agents were buying steamers from the United States.[12] Thus was the government provoked into action and British and French vessels were ordered to sail for the Baltic. The British fleet had been gathered together during the previous winter under the command of Sir Charles Napier. Its mobilization was too late for proper training to take place, and it was also handicapped by a lack of experienced seamen, who preferred the better pay of the merchant service. The strategic aim of the fleet was to bring the Russian battle squadron at Revel, near the mouth of the Gulf of Finland, to battle and destroy it while the Russian squadrons at Sweaborg and Kronstadt were unable to leave port due to ice. Thus it was hoped that Sweden would enter the war on the Allied side and provide troops and a fleet of coastal craft, thereby enabling a Baltic land campaign to be pursued. Such a plan echoed that of Lord Nelson many years before. The Swedes refused to join in the war unless the Allies showed a clear and serious intention of defeating Russia, without which Sweden would have to face the subsequent wrath of the Russian bear.[13]

Lacking Swedish coastal vessels and soldiers, Napier could not take the war into Russia and was restricted to a blockade. When he entered the Baltic in March 1854, he found the harbour at Revel empty of Russian warships. The fleet carried out exercises and reconnoitred the Russian fortifications. The First Lord of the Admiralty, Sir James Graham, was still hopeful of the Swedes joining the alliance in exchange for the Åland Islands, the archipelago that dominates the Gulf of Bothnia, but the Swedish government was not interested. Thus Graham decided to abandon his Baltic strategy and concentrate on the Crimea, but Napier had now been joined by a French squadron and the cabinet had agreed to deploy 10,000 French soldiers to capture Åland. There was no sound strategic purpose behind this plan.[14]

In the meantime, Napier's ships raided Finnish harbours in the Gulf of Bothnia where they destroyed shipbuilding materials and sought out Russian vessels. On 20 June the British fleet was bombarding Bomarsund, the main fortress in the Åland Islands. Captain Hall, commanding HMS *Hecla*, formulated his own plan for an independent attack on the fortress and with his own ship plus two others under his command, HM Ships *Valorous* and *Odin*, he put his plan into operation at 10 a.m. on 21 June. Steaming into position some 500 yards from the principal fortress he opened fire at the Russian fortifications. At once there was answering fire from the fort, which mounted eighty guns, and the action became even more intense as other neighbouring forts began to fire on Hall's ships.[15]

A brisk and accurate fire was being returned by the Russian gunners and at the height of the action a live shell landed on *Hecla*'s upper deck. All hands were ordered to take cover, but the ship's twenty-year-old acting mate, Midshipman **Charles Davis Lucas**, showed great presence of mind and rushed forward to grab the shell which he hurled over the side of the ship; it exploded just before it hit the sea. None of the crew were killed or seriously injured. For his gallantry Lucas was promoted to Lieutenant on the recommendations of Hall and Napier. The former wrote to the Admiral on 22 June.

> With regard to Mr Lucas, I have the pleasure to report a remarkable instance of coolness and presence of mind in action, he having taken up, and thrown overboard, a live shell thrown on board the 'Hecla' by the enemy, while the fuse was burning.[16]

In forwarding Hall's report to the Admiralty on 28 June, Napier added his own comments.

> Their Lordships will observe, in Captain Hall's letter, the great courage of Mr C.D. Lucas, in taking up a live shell and throwing it overboard; and I trust their Lordships will mark their sense of it by promoting him.[17]

Lucas' promotion was dated from 26 June, two days before Napier wrote his report. Such a promotion for gallantry in action was not unusual. It was, in fact, a regular method of rewarding such gallantry in the absence of adequate gallantry decorations; a financial reward might also be made. Having had Lucas promoted, Napier might have been expected to forget the case, but the Irishman's action had obviously made an impression on him as it was Napier who subsequently recommended Lucas for the Victoria Cross when the decoration was instituted. Lucas was decorated by Queen Victoria on 26 June 1857, at the first VC investiture ceremony, held in Hyde Park.

Charles Davis Lucas had become the first-ever winner of the Victoria Cross. Most sources give his birthplace as Druminargal* in County Armagh, but his father, David Lucas, came from Clontibret in neighbouring Monaghan and was a member of the Lucas family of Castle Shane, County Monaghan. In a letter to the *Times* in 1948, Sir Shane Leslie pointed out that Lucas was a Monaghan man and not an Armagh man as most would claim. Certainly, Sir John Smyth VC, an authority on the medal and founder-chairman of the VC Association, wrote that Lucas was born in Clontibret in February 1834.[18]

Enlisting in the Royal Navy in 1847, Lucas first saw action in the Burmese War of 1852-3. He eventually rose to the rank of rear admiral. From 1873 to 1883, he commanded the Ballachulish Corps in Scotland, with the rank of brigadier general. He died on 7 August 1914, at Great Culverden, near Tunbridge Wells, Kent, at the age of eighty. Although there is a memorial to him in Saint Lawrence's Church, Mereworth, Maidstone, Kent, he is not commemorated in his native Ireland.

The senior service had earned the distinction of winning the first Victoria Cross (three were awarded for the Baltic campaign, which was abandoned in the autumn of 1854 after French troops captured and then abandoned Bomarsund). The army would take its first VC as a result of land operations in the Crimea; and the first soldier to win the coveted medal was a native of County Roscommon, **Luke O'Connor**, who, in 1849, had enlisted as a seventeen-year-old in the 23rd (Royal Welch Fusiliers) Regiment with whom he served in the Crimea as a sergeant.

On 7 September 1854 the Allied force that had landed at Varna – now 30,000 French, 27,000 British, and 7,000 Turks – re-embarked to sail for the Crimea, landing on the western coast thirty-five miles north of Sevastopol (Sebastopol). But the delay in reaching the Crimea had given the Russians time to prepare defences. Prince Menschikoff, the Russian commander, had used the months since July, when the Allies should have landed, to deploy troops and strengthen their positions. As the Allied force began its march

* Lucas lived in Druminargal house, near Poyntz Pass. The National Trust plan to mark the house with a 'blue plaque' commemorating its connection with Lucas.

towards Sevastopol, Menschikoff deployed his army along the heights overlooking the river Alma. In all he had almost 40,000 men, of whom the majority – some 33,000 – were infantry, supported by artillerymen with over 100
guns; there were also 3,400 cavalry. The stage was set for the first major clash
of the war – the battle of the Alma.[19]

The Allied force had finished landing all its troops on 18 September and
set off on the march to Sevastopol the next day in a mile-and-a-half-long
column with no forward patrols and little in the way of flank protection.
Knowing that the Russians had stationed troops along the Alma, the two
senior commanders, Frenchman Saint Arnaud and Raglan, devised a plan
whereby the French, whose troops had suffered less from illness than their
British counterparts, would advance by the coast and then scale the cliffs overlooking the river to flank the Russians. The British would strike at
Menschikoff's centre where the bulk of his force was stationed, although the
theory of the plan was that Saint Arnaud's command would engage the major
part of the Russian army.[20]

Both commanders left much to be desired: Saint Arnaud was so ill that
he died soon afterwards and Raglan appears to have had little grasp on reality; he was so disoriented that he took up an observation position behind the
Russian front line at one point. However, this had the unexpected benefit of
making the Russians believe that the bulk of Raglan's army must be nearby
and no attempt was made to capture him.[21] Raglan's troops were marching
into battle much as British soldiers had done under Wellington and, long
before him, Marlborough. They went forward in parade-ground formation,
led by their senior officers on horseback with swords drawn and raised, and
exhorting their soldiers to follow. It was probably the last demonstration of
war as it had been fought heretofore: within weeks the British and French
troops would be in trenches, enduring bombardment by enemy artillery. The
Crimea would usher in the age of technological warfare.

As the British troops advanced on that September day, Luke O'Connor
was one of the centre sergeants advancing between the officers carrying the
colours of the 23rd. Although Russian gunners were seen to be limbering up
and withdrawing, heavy fire continued to pour into the attacking soldiers.
Lieutenant Anstruther, who was carrying the Queen's Colour, sprang on to
the Russian parapet and rammed the butt of the colour-staff into the ground
while he paused to regain his breath. While doing so he was struck down and
fell dead with the colour. Luke O'Connor immediately gathered the flag up
but he, too, then fell wounded.

> Private Evans forthwith accepted the sacred charge with eagerness; but
> O'Connor would not allow it. He was wounded, but he could still

stand. He was sergeant, and would suffer no one of inferior rank to take the colours. And so the brave fellow struggled on to the end of the hard day. Several times he was pressed to hand over his charge to some uninjured man and retire to have his wound dressed; but he fiercely refused. He had his reward in the praises and thanks of his general on the field, and the promise of a commission.

O'Connor was rewarded with a commission and the subsequent award of the Victoria Cross. The citation for his award included his actions during the assault on the Redan a year later where he again showed great courage in spite of gunshot wounds to both thighs. O'Connor also saw considerable service in the Indian Mutiny, where he was one of 32 survivors of Colin Campbell's relief of Lucknow, and in the Ashanti expedition of 1873.

The commission earned on the battlefield of the Alma was the beginning of a rise to the highest ranks of the army for Luke O'Connor. In this he paralleled Lucas' career in the Royal Navy. Eventually O'Connor became a major-general and was also knighted. He was also appointed Colonel of the Royal Welsh Fusiliers. He died in London on 1 February 1915 and was buried in Saint Mary's Roman Catholic Cemetery, Kensal Rise, London. His portrait hangs in the officers' mess of the Royal Welch Fusiliers at Caernarvon. O'Connor also appears to have been a very devout man who cared much for those who were less fortunate in life. In his will he left a total of £10,528 to charities, including the Sisters of Charity in Boyle, County Roscommon, and Elphin, County Roscommon – O'Connor's birthplace – 'for the very poor', the Catholic Blind Asylum, Merrion, Dublin, and the Poor Clares in Galway and Notting Hill, who each received either £500 or £300; and the Catholic Soldiers' Association, which received £200. The residue of his property was to distributed 'to such deserving charities as his executors may think fit'.

On that same day Captain **Edward William Derrington Bell** of the 23rd also earned the Victoria Cross. Bell was the first to capture one of the Russian guns as it was being limbered up, ready to be taken out of action. He later took command of the regiment after all the senior officers had been wounded and remained in command until the battle was over. Bell was the son of Lieutenant-General E.W. Bell, who fought at Vittoria, and his mother was the sister of Sir Thomas Chapman of County Westmeath, who had previously been married to Captain Battersby, who had commanded the ship that took Napoleon to Saint Helena.

Luke O'Connor was the first of many soldiers to win the Victoria Cross in the Crimean War. Before the year was out, another eight of his fellow countrymen would be numbered among those ranks. The first of this octet was **Thomas Grady**, from Galway, who served in the ranks of the 4th Foot, The

King's Own Regiment* and was one of those who volunteered to repair the Sailors' Battery on the left flank of the British position on 18 October. By this time the Allied armies were at Sevastopol and the siege of that port had begun. Grady carried out his task under the very heavy fire of the Russian artillery. Later, on 22 November, although severely wounded, Private Grady refused to leave his position, and his example lent such encouragement to others manning the post that all enemy assaults were beaten off. He was commended for the VC by Captain Lushington of the Royal Navy.†

Apart from the Victoria Cross, the first awarded to the 4th, Thomas Grady was also awarded the Distinguished Conduct Medal during the Crimean War. He left the Army with the rank of sergeant and emigrated to Australia where he died in 1891. There is a memorial to him in Melbourne General Cemetery and in the Priory, Lancaster, England. He is also one of the few Victoria Cross winners to have had a poem dedicated to him, although he himself was illiterate.

Two days after Grady's first action at the Sailors' Battery, another Irishman won the VC. Once again this was the first of two deeds by **William Mawhinney** that merited the award. Born in Bangor, County Down, in 1837 Mawhinney is believed to have spent his formative years in Newtownards before enlisting in the Army. In the Crimea he served as a sergeant in the 44th (East Essex) Regiment. His Victoria Cross was awarded for actions at the position known as the Quarries – a line of interconnected Russian rifle pits – on 20 October 1854.

A private soldier of the regiment, John Keane, had been seriously wounded and was lying in the open exposed to enemy fire. Sergeant Mawhinney ran forward, took the injured man on his back and carried him to safety, all the time being shot at by the Russians. On 5 December Mawhinney again showed the same brand of bravery, when he carried a wounded sharpshooter – Corporal Courtney – to safety from under enemy fire. This time he was not able to come back to British lines immediately due to heavy enemy fire, but had to dig a shallow scrape with his bayonet to give some cover until darkness fell. On 18 June 1855 he volunteered for the advance guard in the Cemetery position, close to the enemy lines, and maintained a listening post

---

* Grady originally enlisted in the 99th (Lanarkshire) Regiment on 18 June 1853, transferring to the King's Own on 13 February 1854.

† Another Irishman, Michael Regan, also volunteered to repair the embrasure and was recommended with Grady for the Victoria Cross. However, a bureaucratic mix-up meant that the citation was written for Patrick Regan instead. The latter died before the award was authorized, but the error was discovered and a new claim, supported by eyewitnesses, was submitted for Michael Regan. Unfortunately, this claim was not allowed.

for the remainder of the action. The January 1911 edition of the *Essex Regimental Gazette* refers to him as a 'Triple VC'. He was the first member of his regiment to be awarded the Victoria Cross which he received from Queen Victoria in Hyde Park in 1857.

William Mawhinney was also decorated with the Distinguished Conduct Medal and the French Medaille Militaire. He went on to serve for many years in the army and fought in China at the Taku forts; his service was rewarded with the Long Service and Good Conduct Medal. Such a record gives the lie to the allegation from Corporal Courtney, in a letter to the duke of Cambridge, the commander-in-chief, that it was not Mawhinney who rescued him. However, Courtney had originally testified that Mawhinney was his saviour and the account had been supported by Private George Finch.

Mawhinney died in Dover, Kent, on 17 May 1866, and while there is a memorial in Saint James' Cemetery, Dover, he is all but forgotten in his hometown. A local newspaper suggested that his medal was pawned, possibly in Smithfield Market, Belfast.[22] It was later offered for sale at Smithfield and bought by a Mr J. Forsyth of 288 Ravenhill Road, Belfast who subsequently sold it to a collector from Cork for £25. All trace of the medal was lost until it came up for auction at Sotheby's, London, in February 1911. It was sold to a 'gentleman' from Cheltenham for £90.

Mawhinney is one of a number of Irish VC winners whose name is recorded inaccurately in both Army records and published material on the Victoria Cross. The north Down man is generally referred to as McWheeney, or McWhiney.

Although the Russians retreated from the Allies at the Alma, the opportunity for a decisive victory had not been seized by the Allied commanders. British and French cavalry were not used to any effect and Menschikoff was able to withdraw men and artillery to Sevastopol. The Great Battery was taken twice before the road to Sevastopol was fully open and, had the Allied commanders but known it, the campaign could have been brought to a swift end. Menschikoff did not believe that Sevastopol could withstand an attack and so ordered his troops to pull out, leaving a skeleton garrison of militia and sailors. Although the town was wide open, the Allied commanders debated whether to attack Sevastopol or move to the little fishing village at Balaclava Cove, where they could establish a naval and supply base. They opted for the latter, and as the Allied army moved south it crossed the tail of the Russian army as it, too, moved to open country. Both sides were equally surprised and only minor skirmishes occurred, but the advantage had been surrendered to the Russians who returned to Sevastopol and were well placed to harass the British lines.[23]

Menschikoff had another great advantage in the engineering genius of a young Russian officer called Todleben. Only twenty-six years old, and a junior field officer, Todleben used the lull that occurred in the fighting to build a system of defensive works around Sevastopol. To the north was the Star Fort, which he surrounded with outworks and trenches in less than two weeks, to add to the menace of the 47 guns already deployed in the fort. (One of the artillery officers commanding a battery in the defences designed by Todleben was a young man from Tula province who was destined to become one of the most famous literary figures in Russian history: Leo Tolstoy.) To the south-west, Todleben was working on the Malakoff redoubt and the Redan; the latter was to become synonymous with the fighting around Sevastopol. In the meantime, the Russians decided to move to the offensive and attack the main Allied supply base at Balaclava.[24]

That decision was to lead to one of the most famous episodes in British military history. The Balaclava base was protected by a battalion of Scottish highlanders, two understrength cavalry brigades and 3,000 Turks. A Russian force that outnumbered the Allies four-to-one attacked the base and drove the Turkish troops from the outer defences. All that stood between the Russian cavalry and the harbour was the 'thin red streak tipped with a line of steel' of the 93rd Highlanders, part of the Highland Brigade under Sir Colin Campbell. The 93rd ought to have been ridden into the ground by the cavalry but the Highlanders fought off the charge and the British Heavy Brigade of cavalry was launched at the Russians. Although outnumbered and charging uphill, the Heavy Brigade forced the Russians to retreat. Then came an order from Raglan to prevent the Russians removing the Turkish guns they had taken in the redoubts that morning. Thus was launched the charge of the Light Brigade.[25]

On 25 October the Light Brigade, consisting of 13th Light Dragoons and 17th Lancers in the first line, and 4th Queen's Own Light Dragoons, 8th (King's Royal Irish) Hussars and 11th Prince Albert's Own Hussars in the second line, charged the Russians and rode not only into 'shot and shell', but immortality. The despatch with the order to carry out this fateful action was delivered to the Light Brigade by Captain Lewis Edward Nolan whose family lived at Kyleballuhue House, Carlow; his father was Babington Nolan, major in the 70th Foot and later British consular agent in Milan.

Sergeant **John Farrell**, from Dublin, of the 17th Lancers was one of the 'six hundred'* and among the first cavalrymen to win the Victoria Cross. Having had his horse shot from under him, he stopped to assist two other men of the brigade in the rescue of a severely wounded officer. Although they were able to move him out of range of the enemy guns, the officer subse-

---

* The Light Brigade's strength was closer to 700 men.

quently died. Both Farrell and the other two men, Sergeant Major Berryman, 17th Lancers, and Trooper Malone, of 13th Light Dragoons, a Mancunian whose name indicates Irish roots, were awarded the Victoria Cross. John Farrell became Quartermaster Sergeant of his regiment in India on 10 March 1857 but was reduced to private soldier on 18 January 1860. On the same day he was promoted again to sergeant. On 30 November 1864 he volunteered for the 18th Hussars but did not serve with that regiment, moving instead to 2nd Light Cavalry, an Indian regiment, with which he was serving when he died at Secunderabad on the night of 3/4 August 1865 of an abscess of the liver. The cause of death might also be an indicator as to why Farrell was reduced in rank in January 1860.

An officer of the 11th Hussars also won the VC on what became known as Balaclava Day. Lieutenant **Alexander Roberts Dunn** saved the life of a sergeant in his regiment who was being attacked from the rear by a number of Russian lancers. Dunn rode into the Russians and cut down two or three of them, thereby eliminating the danger to the NCO. Later in the action he also despatched a Russian hussar who was attacking a British trooper. Dunn wrote his own special entry in the annals of the Victoria Cross by becoming the first Canadian-born winner of the award. But there was also an Irish connection as both his parents were Irish immigrants into Canada. Colonel Alexander Dunn VC, died in Abyssinia in 1868 and is buried in the military cemetery at Senafe. His body was found sitting against a rock. He had been shot with both barrels of his own shotgun at close range. There were suspicions that he had been murdered, but nothing was ever proved.[26]

On 26 October, the day after the charge of the Light Brigade, another Irishman won the Victoria Cross. Lieutenant **John Augustus Connolly**, born at Cliff, Ballyshannon in County Donegal,* of the 49th (Princess of Wales's) Hertfordshire Regiment was commanding a company engaged in piquet duty that morning. During a surprise attack by the Russians,

> Outside Sebastopol during the 'great sortie', on October 26, 1854 ... Lieutenant Conolly was in command of his company on outlying picket. The Russians hurled themselves on the Second Division. They were met, in the first instance, by the 49th, resolutely led by Connolly in frequent short, sharp charges, he himself engaging several of them in hand-to-hand fight, one after another, till at length, from loss of blood, he fell insensible, and had to be borne off the field. His gallant behaviour, no less than that of his men, elicited a General Order, in which all were

* His father, Edward Michael Connolly, was a lieutenant-colonel in the Donegal Militia and MP for the county.

deservedly praised. Soon afterwards he was promoted Captain into the Coldstream Guards as part reward for his bravery and devotion.

Connolly's courage was observed by Lord Raglan and resulted in the award of the Victoria Cross. After his military service, Connolly served in the Dublin Metropolitan Police.

Corporal **James Owens**, also 49th Regiment, was awarded the Victoria Cross for his distinguished conduct in rescuing Connolly after the latter was severely wounded on 26 October. Connolly was surrounded by enemy soldiers when Owens came to his assistance. After a brief but bloody skirmish, Owens was able to escort his company commander back to the British lines. Curiously the VC citation for Owens gives the date of his deed as 30 October; but this is impossible as Connolly was severely wounded on the 26th and could not have recovered within four days. Owens ended his military service as a sergeant and after leaving the Army served as a warder at the Tower of London. A native of Baileyboro', County Cavan, he died on 20 August 1901 and was buried in Christ Church cemetery, Brentwood, after Requiem Mass celebrated by Father T.H. Burnett. Owens was one of those to receive the VC from Queen Victoria at the first investiture. His VC was sold in London on 15 October 1903.

On 26 October 1854, at the Little Inkerman position, Sergeant **Ambrose Madden**, from County Cork, led a small party of men in an attack on a Russian unit. At this time Madden's regiment, 41st (The Welsh) Regiment, was hotly engaged in a series of hit-and-run raids against the enemy. In this action a Russian officer and fourteen privates were taken prisoner, Sergeant Madden capturing three of them. For this he was awarded the Victoria Cross and was later commissioned. He died in Jamaica on 1 January 1863, aged forty-three.

John Byrne, from Kilkenny, was another soldier to receive the Victoria Cross for two actions in the Crimea. The first was at Inkerman on 5 November 1854, where over 40,000 Russians attacked the British positions, taking the latter by surprise; the Russian columns were hidden by mist and rain. Private Byrne's regiment, the 68th (Durham Light Infantry), was forced to retreat in the ensuing confusion. As the regiment fell back, some wounded men were left behind, but Byrne returned to the abandoned position and, at the risk of his own life, rescued one of the wounded from under very heavy fire. On 11 May 1855, John Byrne was stationed on the parapet of the regimental camp. During the hours of darkness the enemy attempted to rush the position, but Byrne engaged the attackers in hand-to-hand combat and prevented them crossing the wall.

John Byrne also earned the Distinguished Conduct Medal for gallantry in action at Te Ranga in New Zealand on 1 June 1864, when his life was saved by Sergeant John Murray who received the VC for his actions that day. Byrne left the army as a corporal and died on 10th July 1879, at Caerleon, Monmouthshire, at the age of 47. His was the first Victoria Cross awarded to the Durhams. His headstone was re-dedicated on 4 November 1985.

General Sir **Mark Walker** is remembered on two memorials, neither in his native Ireland. The first is at Cheriton Road Cemetery, Folkestone; the second, in Canterbury Cathedral. Mark Walker, the son of Captain Alexander Walker, a distinguished Peninsular War officer, was born in County Westmeath and enlisted in the 30th (Cambridgeshire) Regiment with whom he served as a lieutenant in the Crimea. During the attack on the Alma he was wounded and his horse was shot from under him. On 5 November 1854, at Inkerman, two battalions of Russian infantry attacked his regiment. As the enemy advanced, Walker realized that, in this case, the best defence was a swift counter-attack. Leaping over the wall that his men were using for shelter, he advanced towards the Russians. This act so inspired the remainder of the regiment that they followed him, and their spirited charge broke both enemy battalions, sending them reeling back. Walker's action illustrates the nature of the confused battle at Inkerman, which became known as the Soldiers' Battle due to the absence of higher command. After six hours' fighting, the British, with some French reinforcement towards the end of the battle, pushed the Russians back with about 10,000 casualties against some 2,000 British losses.[27]

Walker was again wounded at Sevastopol, as a result of which his right arm was amputated. He served in the China War of 1860 as a brigade major, was Mentioned in Despatches and promoted to brevet lieutenant colonel in 1861, becoming brevet colonel in 1863. In later life he was promoted to general and was also knighted.

The eight Irish VCs of 1854 were followed by no fewer than eighteen in 1855. These were all won in the shadow of Sevastopol, indicating the manner in which the war had become a static campaign of siegecraft and endurance. There were many gallant acts on both sides and all combatants suffered great deprivations during the siege.

Siege warfare makes heavy demands on engineers and gunners and among the Irish VCs of 1855 can be found an engineer and two gunners, one of whom was a shore-based naval gunner. The first Irishman to win the VC in 1855 was an engineer, **William James Lendrim** of the Corps of Royal Sappers and Miners, later the Royal Engineers. On 14 February 1855, Corporal Lendrim supervised a party of 150 French Chasseurs in the rebuilding of No. 9 Battery on the Allied left flank. The roof of the battery magazine was set on fire by Russian artillery on 11 April. Lendrim climbed onto the roof and extinguished the flames, all the time under enemy shelling. On

20 April he was one of four volunteers who destroyed a screen erected by the Russians to protect the construction of their rifle pits. For these actions he was awarded the Victoria Cross and promoted to sergeant major. The French government also awarded him the Medaille Militaire and Legion d'Honneur.

John Sullivan, a Cork man, enlisted in the Royal Navy and served in the Crimea as a member of the Naval Brigade, with the rank of boatswain's mate. The Naval Brigade was a force of sailors who fought on land, usually as gunners manning naval cannon, or, occasionally, as infantry. On 25 April 1855, coincidentally his twenty-fifth birthday, Sullivan was acting as captain of a gun in Greenhill Battery. A volunteer was called for to place a flag on a mound forward of the British gun positions to act as a range marker. Sullivan carried this out under a very heavy fire from the Russian guns, thus allowing accurate artillery fire to be delivered on hitherto concealed enemy positions. With the award of the Victoria Cross he also received the Legion d'Honneur from France, while Sardinia awarded him the Al Valore Militari. By the end of his military career he held the rank of chief boatswain's mate and had also been awarded the Royal Humane Society's Silver Medal and a Conspicuous Gallantry Medal. For a time he worked in the dockyard at Portsmouth. Sullivan died at Kinsale in 1884.

Daniel Cambridge came from County Antrim, where he had been born in 1820. At the age of eighteen, bored with life as a labourer, he enlisted in the Royal Regiment of Artillery on 24 June 1839, having attested at Lisburn four days earlier. On 8 September 1855 he volunteered for a spiking party at the assault on the Redan, the purpose of which was to disable enemy artillery pieces. Sergeant Cambridge was severely wounded during this attack but refused to be taken to the rear until the raid was successfully concluded. Despite his wound he went out under heavy enemy fire later that same day to rescue another injured gunner and was himself severely wounded a second time. After the war Cambridge was promoted to master gunner, serving for a time at Tarbert Fort, and later became a Yeoman of the Guard. He died in London on 12 June 1882 and is buried in the old churchyard at Plumstead. Sotheby's auctioned his medals on 1 December 1943 for £50. As well as the VC, these included the British Crimean Medal with Inkerman and Sevastopol clasps, the Long Service and Good Conduct Medal (awarded in 1861), the Sardinian Al Valore Militare and the Turkish Crimean Medal.

The other Irish VCs of 1855 were all infantrymen with one exception, a Royal Navy officer who was born in Dublin, the son of Field Marshal Sir John Fox Burgoyne. On 29 May 1855 Lieutenant **Hugh Talbot Burgoyne** was aboard HMS *Swallow* in the Sea of Azov. In company with Lieutenant Buckley of HMS *Miranda* and Gunner Robarts of HMS *Ardent*, Burgoyne volunteered to carry out a raid on a beach known to be heavily defended by the Russians. Landing unnoticed, they set fire to corn stores and ammunition dumps, and destroyed an enemy emplacement with explosives before returning safely to their own lines. All three were subsequently awarded the Victoria Cross. Burgoyne was promoted to captain and awarded the Legion d'Honneur by France and the Imperial Order of the Medjedic by Turkey. Captain Burgoyne drowned after the capsizing of HMS *Captain* off Cape Finisterre on 7 September 1870. There is a memorial to him in Saint Paul's Cathedral and at the family grave in Brompton Cemetery, London.

The infantry decorations were won for acts typical of siege warfare: officers and soldiers involved in storming parties; who showed great presence of mind in hurling unexploded missiles from their positions; were outstanding in defensive actions against attacking enemy troops; or who rescued wounded comrades under the guns of the Russians. Private **Alexander Wright**, a Ballymena man, of the 77th (East Middlesex) Regiment fell into at least two of these categories. He displayed great courage throughout his service in the Crimea, and his Victoria Cross was awarded for three particular feats of bravery, the first of which occurred on 22 March 1855, when he distinguished himself in repelling an enemy sortie against the regimental position. On 19 April he took part in the capture and holding of some Russian rifle pits under very heavy fire, and on 30 August he again showed complete disregard for his own safety while in action with the enemy. Wright never returned to live in his native land; he died in Calcutta on 28 July 1858.

Sergeant **George Gardiner**, of the 57th (West Middlesex) Regiment, was awarded the Victoria Cross for his actions at Sevastopol on 22 March 1855 when a sudden attack by the Russians against the regiment's outlying piquets sent the men retreating in disorder. Gardiner rallied the men, reformed a firing line and beat off the attack. During the attack on the Redan Gardiner again showed great courage and leadership. He was later promoted to colour sergeant and also received the Distinguished Conduct Medal. Born near Warrenpoint, County Down, he died in Lifford, County Donegal, on 17 November 1891, and is buried in the local churchyard. A memorial was erected shortly after his death.

Wright and Gardiner were the first members of their respective regiments to be awarded the Victoria Cross. In 1881 their regiments were amalgamated to form the Middlesex Regiment and their names headed the VC roll of the new regiment.

William Coffey, born at Knocklong, County Limerick, on 5 August 1829, served with the 34th (Cumberland) Regiment in the Crimea, although he had originally enlisted in the 82nd (The Prince of Wales's Volunteers) Regiment. On 29 March 1855, during a Russian bombardment, a live shell fell into the trench occupied by Private Coffey. With complete disregard for his own safety he lifted the shell and threw it over the parapet where it exploded without causing any casualties. As a result of this he was awarded the Victoria Cross, the first of four to be awarded to the 34th in the Crimea. He was later promoted to corporal and subsequently to sergeant. He also served in the Indian Mutiny and was discharged on 21 December 1860, although he re-enlisted in the 75th Regiment on 19 June 1861 before transferring to his original regiment, the 82nd, where he quickly attained his old rank of sergeant. During his military service, which totalled 21 years and 36 days, Coffey was also awarded the Distinguished Conduct Medal and the French Medaille Militaire. He was finally discharged from the Army on 25 August 1868, suffering from chronic bronchitis, and died at Chesterfield, Derbyshire, on 13 July 1875. The regimental museum at Carlisle holds his VC.

John Park's service in the Crimea was one of continuous valour. Born in Londonderry in 1835, he served in the 77th (East Middlesex) Regiment throughout the war and was cited for bravery at the battles of the Alma and Inkerman. On 19 April 1855 he displayed exceptional courage in an attack on the Russian rifle pits situated on the forward slopes of the Redan, where he was badly wounded. His VC was gazetted on 24 February 1857. The medal is held in the Leicester Museum and Art Gallery and bears three dates: 20 September 1854, 5 November 1854 and 19 April 1855; these mark his gallantry at the Alma, Shell Hill, Inkerman and the Russian rifle pits respectively. His VC citation also includes acts of gallantry at the Redan on 18 June and 8 September 1855. John Park died in Allahabad, India, on 18 May 1863.

Joseph Bradshaw came from Dromkeen in County Limerick and served with distinction throughout the war in the 2nd Battalion, Rifle Brigade. Rifleman Bradshaw's Victoria Cross was awarded for his actions on 22 April 1855 at a Russian rifle pit situated on the Woronzoff road between the Third Parallel on the right flank and the Quarries. As well as the Victoria Cross he was promoted to corporal and awarded the Medaille Militaire by France. He served during the Indian Mutiny, being severely wounded in action at Rampore Kussiah on 3 April 1858. Bradshaw died on 21 March 1875, at Woolwich. His name is inscribed on the Rifle Brigade memorial in Winchester Cathedral.

On 11 May Captain **Thomas de Courcy Hamilton** led a small force from the 68th (Durham Light Infantry) in a sortie intended to recapture a battery that had been taken by the Russians. Such was the ferocity of the charge that the Russians abandoned the position and the battery was secured against further enemy attacks. Hamilton was awarded the Victoria Cross and the Legion d'Honneur. Born in Stranraer, Scotland on 20 July 1826, Thomas de Courcy Hamilton was the son of James John Hamilton of Ballymacoll, County Meath. He later became a major general.

Captain **Henry Mitchell Jones** served in the 7th (Royal Fusiliers) and received the Victoria Cross for his actions at Sevastopol on 7 June 1855 when he led a storming party in a night attack against the Quarries. Despite being wounded early in the attack, Jones refused to be evacuated, and continued to lead his men throughout the night's bitter fighting. As well as his much deserved Victoria Cross, France awarded him the Legion d'Honneur. At the end of his military service he enjoyed a career in the diplomatic service and, after retiring, died in Eastbourne, Sussex, at the age of eighty-five.

Private **John Lyons** of the 19th (1st Yorkshire, North Riding) Regiment was born in County Carlow in 1823. He was a man to whom personal safety seemed to mean little. On 10 June 1855 Lyons was part of a guard detachment in a forward trench. During an enemy bombardment a live shell landed in the trench. Lyons lifted the shell and threw it over the parapet where it exploded without causing any injuries. For this action he was awarded the Victoria Cross and also received the Legion d'Honneur from France. Promoted to corporal, he survived the war and returned to Ireland where he died on 20 April 1867 at Naas, County Kildare.

Joseph Prosser, born in Monegal, King's County, enlisted in the 1st or Royal Regiment and served with their 2nd Battalion in the Crimea. On 16 June 1855, the battalion was occupying trenches before Sevastopol where Prosser pursued and apprehended a British soldier in the act of deserting to the enemy. This whole episode was carried out under heavy Russian fire. On 11 August he assisted in the rescue of a wounded comrade, again under enemy fire. He was awarded the Victoria Cross for his courage and also received the Turkish Crimea Medal, as well as the British Crimea Medal with Sevastopol Clasp. Although obviously a courageous man, he was not the most amenable to discipline and was recorded in the regimental defaulters' book forty-three times as well as being court-martialled on four occasions. Hepatitis led to his discharge from the Army and he returned to Ireland to become a customs officer. Although it is generally believed that he died in Tipperary in 1869, research carried out by Maurice Rigby of Anfield proves that he is buried in Liverpool's Anfield cemetery and so would appear to have moved to England, possibly with the customs service.

Corporal **Philip Smith** served in the Crimea with the 17th (Leicestershire) Regiment. Born in Lurgan, County Armagh, in 1825, he was awarded the Victoria Cross on 18 June 1855 for the rescue of wounded soldiers from the trenches in front of the Redan. His was the first VC awarded to his regiment. Philip Smith was later promoted to sergeant and received the Medaille Militaire from France. He was decorated with his Victoria Cross in Montreal, Canada on 1 August 1857. On his discharge he returned to Ireland and died at The Hospice, Harold's Cross, Dublin, on 16 January 1906; he is buried in

Glasnevin cemetery. Smith's actions in winning the Victoria Cross have been recorded by the artist Terence Cuneo.

Private **John Alexander** was also awarded his Victoria Cross for rescuing wounded soldiers under enemy fire. He enlisted in the 90th Perthshire Light Infantry and was in their ranks during the attack on the Redan on 18 June 1855, after which he left the safety of the trenches to rescue a number of wounded men while under heavy enemy fire. The following August he again came under notice, this time for the rescue of Captain Buckley of the Scots Fusilier Guards, who had been dangerously wounded. Alexander was killed in action at Alum Bagh, on 24 September 1857 while serving with his regiment during the Indian Mutiny.

Also on 18 June 1855, Tipperary-born Captain **Thomas Esmonde**, of the 18th (Royal Irish) Regiment, was awarded the Victoria Cross for his actions during the attack on the Redan. Between 18 and 20 June Esmonde repeatedly assisted, at great personal risk, in the rescue of British wounded from the front of the Redan, at all times under enemy fire. On 20 June, while commanding a covering party, he was instrumental in extinguishing an incendiary shell, hurled by the enemy, before it revealed the position of his men. He was later promoted to lieutenant-colonel. Esmonde subsequently returned to Ireland and joined the Royal Irish Constabulary as an assistant inspector general. On 8 May 1865 he was promoted to deputy inspector general and spent the next two years in the Belfast area, retiring from the force in 1867. Thomas Esmonde died in Bruges, Belgium, on 14 January 1873.

Private **Charles McCorrie**, or McCurry, of the 57th Regiment, was awarded the Victoria Cross on 23 June 1855, for having the presence of mind to throw from his trench a live shell before it exploded. A native of County Antrim, he died in Malta on 9 April 1857.

On 5 September 1855 Lieutenant Colonel **Frederick Francis Maude**, of the Buffs, led a ladder party against the walls of the Redan in the final assault of the siege. Having successfully entered the fortress his party, now reduced to nine men, held their position until all hope of support had gone. Only then did Maude order a retreat, during which he was severely wounded. For his gallantry and leadership, Maude was awarded the Victoria Cross. He also received the Legion d'Honneur and was mentioned in despatches. In later life Maude was promoted to general, appointed CGB and, then, KCB. From 1867 to 1873 he was the Inspector-General of Militia in Ireland. The son of the rector of Lisnadill and, later, Enniskillen, Maude died in Torquay, Devon, in 1897. There is a memorial to him in Brompton Cemetery, London. He was a cousin of Colonel Francis Cornwallis Maude, another VC laureate. His son, Lieutenant General Sir Stanley Maude, commanded the British forces in Mesopotamia during the Great War.

Joseph Connors also served in the 3rd (East Kent – The Buffs) Regiment and received the Victoria Cross 'for his conspicuous courage and devotion during the assault on the Redan' on 8 September 1855.

> He got inside the Redan at great personal risk, and seeing an officer of the 30th Regiment surrounded by the enemy, he rushed to his assistance. He immediately shot one of the Russians, ran his bayonet through another, and then for some time carried on a hand-to-hand encounter against great odds until support came.

Connors was also selected by the men of his company – C Company – to receive the French Medaille Militaire. A native of Listowel, County Kerry, he fell to his death from the battlements of Port Neuf on Corfu on 22 August 1858. He is buried in the British cemetery on the island under a headstone erected 'by the Officers of his Company and his comrades as a token of their esteem and regret at his untimely death'. His effects, including his VC, were sent to his widow in Galway.

Another Irish VC was won on 8 September by Sergeant Andrew Moynihan of the 90th Perthshire Light Infantry. He too was involved in bitter fighting on the walls of the Redan and was also instrumental in the rescue of a wounded officer, Captain Swift, from within the defences. Although Andrew Moynihan was born in Wakefield, Yorkshire, on 1 January 1830, the family originated in Templemore, County Tipperary. After his service in the Crimea he was promoted to the rank of ensign in the 8th (The King's) Regiment. He saw action in the Indian Mutiny and the Oude campaign of 1858-59. Moynihan died from illness on Malta on 19 May 1867 and was buried in the International Cemetery, Ta Braxia, Malta. Apart from the Victoria Cross, he was awarded the Turkish War Medal, French War Medal, and a Mention in Despatches.

In September 1855, as the British assaulted the Redan, the French stormed the Malakoff redoubt. Although the British force entered the Redan they had insufficient manpower to hold it and were forced to withdraw. But the French attack on the Malakoff was successful, the strongpoint was taken and the Russians abandoned Sevastopol, setting fire to the town as they did so.[28] The war was over, although it was March 1856 before the Treaty of Paris finally brought it to a close.

The Crimean War was an important one for the British Army. It accelerated the reform process that had begun shortly before the war and ensured that many reforms that might not otherwise have occurred were put into effect. One reason for that was the presence of war correspondents in the

Crimea – chief among whom was the Irishman William Howard Russell – whose reports told the public at home how their soldiers were suffering, not only from the enemy but from the failings of their own administration. And photographs also conveyed something of the reality of war to those who lived far from the clamour of battle. Thus was born Army nursing, while the medical services generally were changed out of all recognition; support services were improved; the artillery, engineers and ordnance came under War Office control rather than that of the Board of Ordnance; training camps were established – one of them at the Curragh – and a Staff College was established. Almost everything to do with the Army was improved and modernized as a result of the lessons so brutally learned during the war.[29]

The war was significant also as the first in which Britain and France were allies rather than enemies. It was both the last old-fashioned war and the first modern war. Taken in conjunction with the American Civil War in the next decade, the Crimean War proved a bridge between the Napoleonic and the modern.

Another lasting effect was the institution of the Victoria Cross. This was the first major war of Queen Victoria's reign; and it was her desire to mark the courage of her servicemen that led to the introduction of the medal that bears her name and which was to become the most respected of all gallantry awards. Following the institution of the new award there were many unsuccessful citations for the Victoria Cross, some of which included Irishmen. Private John Fisher of the 89th Regiment was commended for his gallantry in the siege of Sevastopol. However, the recommendation was rejected. Fisher had been given a cash reward of £a and this may have influenced the decision not to award him the VC.[30]

The commanding officer of the 55th Regiment, Colonel C. B. Daubeney, submitted recommendations for members of his regiment in January 1857, none of which was successful. When he saw the *London Gazette* entries for those citations that had led to the award of the Cross, Daubeney decided to try again. On 7 January 1858 his regiment was stationed in Dublin's Ship Street Barracks when he wrote to Horse Guards in London with recommendations for what he described as 'the Order of the Victoria Cross' for thirty soldiers of his regiment; he forwarded a separate recommendation for himself. His justification for these fresh submissions was that the earlier recommendations for members of his regiment had either been 'informally drawn up, or not sufficiently particularized, on the lists sent by me to the Horse Guards in January 1857'.

Daubeney's fresh submission bore no more fruit than his first. The individual citations bear the scribbled annotation 'rejected'. It may be that some of them might have been successful had Daubeney taken the same trouble with writing the original citations a year earlier. It may also be that his decision to commend himself prejudiced the official eyes that studied the other citations; or it may have been his suggestion that some of the deeds already rewarded with the Victoria Cross did not match those of his soldiers. Whatever the reason, Daubeney seems to have ensured that the 55th Regiment did not receive the full credit that it deserved for its service in the Crimea. He also ensured that a number of Irishmen in his regiment would not join the ranks of their fellow countrymen in the annals of the Victoria Cross.[31]

Among those recommended by Daubeney were Quartermaster-Sergeant John Egan, who had saved the life of Colour Sergeant Furphy at Sevastopol, Sergeants James Ryan and Dan Donohue and Privates Jeremiah Whelan and James Dunn. Reading the citations for each of these men, it is not difficult to concur with their commanding officer that their deeds equalled those of many of the first VC laureates.[32] As it transpired they were fated to be among the first of many who performed VC-worthy deeds but were never awarded the Cross.

3 The Indian Mutiny

In May 1857 there began what is known in British history as the Indian Mutiny. Today the people of India are more inclined to call it the first war of independence. But that latter title suggests an element of planning, of conspiracy between those involved; but no evidence has ever been found that indicates that the mutiny was anything other than a reaction to the poor treatment of Indian soldiers –sepoys – in the army of the East India Company.[1]

Over the years the officers of John Company's army, as it was known, had grown more and more out of touch with their men, and the Company itself regarded the army as a large and, to some extent, unnecessary expense. As a result, allowances to soldiers, and officers, were often withheld, and resentment grew among the rank and file of the Bengal army.[2] (At this time, India was divided into three presidencies: Bengal, Madras and Bombay, each with its own army.)

With the Crimean war scarcely over, the strength of British crown forces in India was at its lowest for many years. News of British reverses in the Crimea, and of military disasters in Afghanistan, had reached the ears of the soldiers of the 150,000-strong Bengal army. The opportunity to overthrow the British in India seemed to be beckoning. Even so, there may have been no mutiny but for an example of the breakdown in trust between the British officers of the army and their sepoys.[3]

In 1857 the new Enfield rifle was introduced to the East India Company's army. In this weapon the cartridge had to be rammed down and, to make the ramming easier, it was greased. But it seems that no one had considered the religious sensibilities of the Indian soldiers, who were either Hindu or Muslim. The cartridge grease was a mixture of cow and pig fat and, as the cartridge had to be bitten before ramming, this meant that a Hindu soldier would taste cow, and a Muslim soldier would taste pig. In each instance the flesh of the animal concerned was forbidden by the soldiers' religions. A rumour began to spread that the British were trying to force the sepoys to become Christians.[4]

Had there been trust and understanding between sepoys and officers, as there had been in years gone by, the matter could easily have been resolved by discussion. However, things had gone beyond that; although orders were issued immediately to change the grease and to discontinue the practice of biting the cartridge, the damage had already been done.

In March 1857, near Calcutta, there was a mutiny in the 19th Native Infantry. The regiment was disbanded, as was the 34th after a sepoy called Mangal Pandy, apparently under the influence of a narcotic drug, shot his adjutant in full view of the quarter-guard, who did nothing.[5] Tension was exacerbated by the great heat of the pre-monsoon season, which was even greater that year than usual.

On Sunday 10 May 1857, at Meerut, a town near Delhi, British troops were parading for church for Evensong. The local garrison included the Carabiniers, a British cavalry regiment, and 60th Rifles, a British infantry regiment, as well as 3rd Light Cavalry and two battalions of Native Infantry; the proportion of British to Indian troops was higher in this area than virtually any other location in the subcontinent.[6]

As usual for a church parade, the British soldiers had left their weapons in barracks. The Indian troops quartered close by waited until their own officers were unarmed and off their guard. At a given signal those officers, their wives and children, were attacked and massacred. Shortly after this the mutineers, about 2,000 in number, made their way to Delhi where they enlisted the assistance of the Indian garrison. A period of looting, arson and murder followed. (Although many accusations of rape were made against the mutineers, there is no evidence to substantiate those claims.)[7] A strong body of mutineers intent on gaining control of the city made a concerted attack on the Red Fort. This fortress, midway between Delhi and the river Jumna, had been the headquarters of the Mogul emperors and was still a major military installation with one of the largest arsenals in India.[8]

On the morning of 11 May 1857 the fort was defended by Lieutenant Willoughby with eight other officers, NCOs and a company of Indian troops. At the first sign of attack the sepoys deserted. Willoughby immediately ordered all available guns loaded with grape shot and aligned on the gates leading into the magazine courtyard.[9]

Escape might still have been possible for the defenders, via a small gate at the rear leading down to the river, but, rather than allow the store of ammunition to fall into the hands of the mutineers, Willoughby's little group decided that they would blow it, and themselves, up. With the faint hope that help might arrive, the garrison put up a determined resistance. As mutineers broke through the gates, they were met with blast after blast of grapeshot that cut them down in droves. Then the attackers attempted to cross the walls using scaling ladders, only to be met with accurate rifle fire. The action lasted for over five hours, until only two defenders were left unwounded. With mutineers about to overrun his position, Lieutenant Willoughby gave the order to fire the magazine. The explosion was so great that the forty-foot high wall surrounding the courtyard collapsed, burying as many as a thousand of the attacking mutineers. Miraculously four defenders survived the explosion. One was a fifty-seven-year-old Dublin man, Lieutenant **George Forrest**, of the Bengal Veteran Establishment. Although badly wounded he managed to make his way to safety. Promoted to captain, Forrest died two years later at Dehra Dun on 3 November 1859. Forrest and two others – John Buckley and William Raynor* – were awarded the Victoria Cross. Forrest had thus become the first Irish VC winner of the Mutiny. In 1996, the auctioneers Phillips sold Forrest's medal to an unknown buyer for £31,050. His name is commemorated on a tablet over the gateway to the Delhi magazine.

Peter Gill, another Dubliner, was serving with an Indian unit, the 15th Ludhiana Sikhs and earned the VC for a series of deeds. At Benares, on the night of 4 June 1857, Sergeant Gill volunteered with Sergeant Major Rosamund, 37th (North Hampshire) Regiment, to bring Captain Brown and his family into the regimental area. The family was in Brown's bungalow some distance away, and the area in between was swarming with mutineers. Under cover of darkness Brown and his family were brought in safely. During this period Sergeant Gill was twice responsible for saving the life of Major Barnett of the 27th Native Infantry, when that officer was attacked by sepoys of his own regiment. Earlier in the evening of 4 June he had also saved the life of the Quartermaster Sergeant of the 25th Bengal Native Infantry by cutting the head off a sepoy who had just bayoneted him. Sergeant Gill died at Morar, Central India, on 26 July 1868, aged thirty-seven.

General Anson, the Commander-in-Chief in India, was in Simla, in the Himalayan foothills, but had begun assembling a field force at Amballa to deal with the mutineers at Delhi. The lengthy period of peace in India had allowed the supply services to be run down and matters were made worse by the fact that the Governor-General, Lord Canning, was in Calcutta – which made it impossible for him to liaise with Anson on plans to recapture Delhi. A speedy recovery of the city was vital, and might even stop the mutiny from spreading. On 27 May, Anson, an old and tired man, died and General Sir Henry Barnard took command of the field force. It was not until 7 June that Barnard's small force arrived outside Delhi. It met and forced back a superior force of mutineers at Badli-ki-Serai and then encamped on the low ridge overlooking the city.[10]

Henry Hartigan from Drumlea, Enniskillen, County Fermanagh, was a cavalryman, serving in the 9th (Queen's Royal) Lancers. On 8 June, at the battle of Badli-ki-Serai, Sergeant Helstone, also of the 9th, became unhorsed while engaged in a mêlée with the enemy. Sergeant Hartigan came to his

---

* At 61 years and 10 months, Raynor was even older than Forrest and is thought to be the oldest winner of the VC

rescue and, at great risk to his own life, carried the wounded man to safety. The battle of Badli-ki-Serai marked the beginning of the British siege of Delhi. The failure to take the city allowed the mutiny to spread through the Bengal army from Calcutta to Peshawar. Fortunately for the British, the mutiny did not spread to the Madras army, which remained loyal throughout; the Bombay army suffered some mutinies but was able to maintain control without recourse to British Army assistance.[11]

On 10 October, Henry Hartigan was again responsible for saving a comrade's life. During the fighting at Agra, Sergeant Crews was in hand-to-hand combat with four sepoys when an unarmed Hartigan went to his assistance. In the ensuing fight one sepoy was killed and the remainder wounded, Hartigan himself receiving a severe wound. During this time Sergeant Hartigan also assisted in the raising of Mead's Horse, a light cavalry unit. His actions were subsequently recognized with the award of the Victoria Cross. Henry Hartigan never returned to Ireland; he died in Calcutta, India, aged 60 years.

John Purcell, from Oughterard in County Galway, was also serving in 9th Lancers. On 9 June an artillery battery, commanded by Major Scott, was being brought into position to assist in the siege of Delhi. As the gunners rode into position they were attacked by enemy cavalry and during the ensuing skirmish an ammunition wagon was set on fire and exploded, unhorsing Brigadier Grant, who was accompanying the battery. He was saved from death only by the intervention of Troopers Purcell and Hancock and Sowar Roopur Khan. Hancock was wounded and Purcell had his horse shot from under him as they fought to save Grant. Meanwhile Sowar Roopur Khan of the 4th Irregular Cavalry came forward and dragged the Brigadier to safety. As a result of this action both Purcell and Hancock were awarded the Victoria Cross. There is no record of any award to Roopur Khan. Three months later, on 14 September, Trooper Purcell was seriously wounded during the siege and died five days later. His Victoria Cross was not gazetted until 15 January 1858, some four months after his death. This makes Purcell the first posthumous Victoria Cross, although the award would not have been considered to be posthumous: it could be made after death if the awardee had been informed that he was to receive the Cross. In the strictest military sense the use of the word posthumous indicates that the medal winner died in the act of earning the VC, or expired from wounds shortly thereafter.

Another Galwegian, **Cornelius Coughlan** – he was born at Eyrecourt – fought at Delhi with the 75th Regiment.* On 8 June Coughlan, with three companions, entered an enemy compound and, in the thick of heavy fight-

* Later the Gordon Highlanders.

ing, the four were able to rescue Private Corbett, also of the 75th. On 18 July Colour Sergeant Coughlan led a party down a narrow lane in Subzee Mundee, a suburb of Delhi. Despite being raked by a murderous cross fire they were able to enter the enemy position at the end of the lane and completely wipe out the enemy. Later that day Coughlan collected stretchers to assist in the removal of the wounded. This action was carried out under a heavy enemy fire. He died on 14 February 1915 in Westport, County Mayo. His VC, which was gazetted on 11 November 1862, is held by the Scottish National Museum in Edinburgh.

Stephen Garvin from Cashel, County Tipperary, served in the 1st Battalion, 60th Rifles who were part of the force investing Delhi. On the morning of 23 June an advanced battery of heavy guns came under sniper fire from an enemy position known as the Sammy House, a local Hindu temple. Colour Sergeant Garvin volunteered to lead a small party of riflemen to deal with this threat. After a short sharp fight they succeeded in silencing the snipers and returned to their own lines. Throughout the remainder of the siege Colour Sergeant Garvin was recommended for his gallant conduct on many occasions and was subsequently awarded the Victoria Cross. He died in Chesterton, Oxfordshire, on 23 November 1874.

John McGovern, or McGowan, from County Cavan, served with the 1st Bengal Fusiliers, an East India Company regiment that recruited in Ireland. Private McGovern was awarded the Victoria Cross for his actions during the operations before Delhi in June 1857. On 23 June he carried a wounded comrade from an enemy battery back to his own lines in spite of heavy enemy fire. He moved to Canada after his army service and died at Hamilton, Ontario, on 22 November 1888.

John Duane served during the Mutiny in the 1st Battalion, 60th Rifles. On 10 September 1857, Private Duane led a successful charge by loyal Baluchi and Sikh troops against the enemy trenches that surrounded Delhi. As he mounted the top of the enemy breastworks he was shot and badly wounded but the charge was a success. As a result of this action he was elected by the men of his regiment for the award of the Victoria Cross. This process was authorized by Clause 13 of the royal warrant that instituted the VC. Duane's VC was gazetted on 20 January 1860. The citation forwarded to Whitehall bears the pencilled note, presumably inserted in Whitehall, that 'This seems to have been easily a case for election under the 13th Clause'.[12]

Until his distinguished action at Delhi John Duane had been one of those soldiers known to officers and NCOs as 'a bad bargain'. Enlisting in April 1854, a year later he was imprisoned by his commanding officer for fourteen days. Court martialled on 5 June 1855, he received another seven days' detention. In March 1856 a total of 156 hours' detention came his way. This pattern continued with another fourteen days' detention, plus a forfeiture of a penny per day from his pay for three calendar months. In November he again received 168 hours' detention but, paradoxically, received his third good conduct badge on 7 February 1857, in which month he was also ordered to forfeit a penny a day from his pay. On 1 January 1858 he was invalided to Ferozepore and thence to England in April. This brought his career in the army to an end.

John Duane never returned to live permanently in Ireland and died in Penzance, Cornwall, on 1 December 1888 where he was buried in a pauper's grave in the Catholic section of the Penzance cemetery. In official records he is shown as John Divane, which led to some confusion when Duane wrote to the War Office about the VC that he had been told he had won. Duane's letter, written by an amanuensis, was dated 23 February 1860, almost five weeks after the announcement of his VC in the *London Gazette*. Giving his name as John Duane, No. 2820, formerly 60th Rifles, he referred to an earlier letter of 4 February to the General Officer Commanding in Chief.

> relative to the decoration of the Victoria Cross which I was informed it was the intention of Her Most Gracious Majesty to confer on me with others for service in India and before Delhi.[13]

The response to Duane's letter was that it

> Could not be entertained on the claimant's own account of his valour, or without the recommendation of such of his superiors, as could either testify to the act of gallantry, or answer for the veracity of other witnesses thereof.[14]

A simple check on Duane's number would have shown that he was the soldier who had already been awarded the VC under the name John Divane. On 9 November 1860 Queen Victoria presented the Victoria Cross to John Duane at Home Park, Windsor. However, the name on the medal was Divane and this error has continued to be perpetrated ever since. In August 1995 Duane's regiment's successors, the Royal Green Jackets, had a memorial unveiled over their hero's pauper's grave. It, too, reads John Divane VC.

Patrick Green from Ballinasloe, County Galway, was awarded the Victoria Cross for his actions at Delhi on 11 September 1857, while serving with the 75th Foot. On this date a piquet of the 75th was stationed at the Koodsia Bagh. Shortly after daybreak they came under attack and were soon being hard pressed by the enemy. In the confused close-quarter fighting Private Green was responsible for the rescue of a wounded comrade and carrying him to safety. Sir Colin Campbell issued a general order in which he announced that Green was to receive the VC. Patrick Green was presented with his Victoria Cross in India in February 1859, and later attained the rank of colour sergeant. He died on 19 July 1889 in Cork. In May 1926, his medal was sold to an unknown buyer for £26.

On 14 September the British No. 3 Column attacked the Kashmir Gate on the west wall of Delhi. Lieutenant Salkeld of the Royal Sappers and Miners led a storming party of nine men to lay gunpowder charges against the gate. During the attack Salkeld suffered severe wounds and burns. Bugler **Robert Hawthorne**, 52nd (Oxfordshire Light Infantry) Regiment, a native of Maghera, County Londonderry, who was one of the storming party, did his utmost to bind his injuries and carry him to safety. Despite all his efforts the lieutenant later died. Hawthorne was awarded the Victoria Cross.

While Bugler Hawthorne was winning his Victoria Cross at the Kashmir Gate, a short distance away two other Irishmen were also in the process of gaining the award. Sergeant **James McGuire** and Drummer **Miles Ryan** were involved in the assault on the Kabul Gate. As members of 1st Bengal Fusiliers they formed part of the attacking brigade. The brigade was formed up, the officers awaiting their final orders, and the men refilling their ammunition pouches, when three ammunition boxes caught fire, possibly from sparks blown from burning buildings. Within a few seconds two exploded and others also began to burn. McGuire and Ryan at once ran to the pile of burning boxes and began throwing them over the parapet into the water-filled ditch below. As a result of their coolness and daring, many lives were saved. Miles Ryan, a Derryman, continued his military service and died in Bengal, India, in 1887.

James McGuire returned home to Fermanagh after his military service. In December 1862, his medal was forfeited as the result of a court case. It was reported that McGuire lent money to a relative to buy a cow. When it became time to repay the money, none was forthcoming. McGuire then took the cow in lieu, but was apprehended by the constabulary, charged with theft and received a month in jail. As a result of this he was stripped of his right to bear the post-nominal letters VC and lost the pension of £10 per year.[15] Although he made strenuous efforts to have his VC restored, enlisting the support of a number of prominent individuals, including the magistrate who had convicted him, McGuire was unsuccessful. The secretary of state for war's office would not submit the case to Queen Victoria, who was permitted, under the VC Warrant, to authorize the restoration of a VC.[16] Subsequently McGuire disappears from the public records and no note of his later life, or of his death, has been found. It is possible that he may have joined the Army under an assumed name.

Delhi was the seat of the Mutiny and its other main centre was at Lucknow, which city's name is probably more generally associated with the Mutiny than any other.[17] A number of Irishmen also gained Victoria Crosses at Lucknow. **William Dowling**, from Thomastown, County Kilkenny, served in the 32nd (The Cornwall) Regiment at Lucknow where he distinguished himself on three separate occasions, any one of which deserved the Victoria Cross. The first occurred on 4 July 1857, when, with two others, he spiked two enemy artillery pieces. He was the only survivor of the raid. Five days later Dowling again led a party to spike enemy cannon and again was the sole survivor. On 27 September he went out alone and spiked an 18-pounder gun. His return journey to the British line was made under very heavy fire from the enemy. Like many other retired soldiers he did not return to Ireland, but lived out his remaining days in Liverpool, where he died on 17 February 1887, in his sixty-second year.

Samuel Hill Lawrence came from Cork and was also a member of the 32nd Regiment, which was part of the Lucknow garrison. On 7 July 1857, Major Lawrence learned that a house held by the enemy might be used as a base from which a mine might be driven under the town walls. He at once put together a storming party to attack the house. Lawrence led the attack up a scaling ladder, which had been placed against a first-storey window. As he attempted to enter the room he was attacked by a rebel sepoy and had his pistol knocked from his hand. Nevertheless, the house was captured, and all occupants killed or taken prisoner, before it was destroyed by fire to prevent its further use by the mutineers. On 26 September Major Lawrence with two members of his company captured an enemy 9-pounder gun. Samuel Hill Lawrence was the cousin of Lieutenant Thomas Cadell, another Victoria Cross winner of the Mutiny. Lawrence died in Montevideo, Uruguay, on 17 June 1868.

Private **Patrick Mylott** was also a member of the Lucknow garrison, serving with the 84th (York and Lancaster) Regiment. He was elected for the award of the Victoria Cross by the other members of his battalion for his actions between 12 July and the relief of the Lucknow garrison. Mylott was also promoted to sergeant.

Abraham Boulger, from County Kildare, was a lance-corporal in the 84th Regiment. An extract from Major General Havelock's Field Force Orders, dated 17 October 1857, reads: 'For distinguished bravery and forwardness, as a skirmisher in all twelve actions fought between 12th July and 25th September 1857.' This outstanding service earned him the Victoria Cross. Boulger later became a lieutenant-colonel. After his military service he returned to Ireland and died at Ballymore, County Westmeath, on 23 January 1900 where he was buried in the Catholic cemetery.

James Travers, previously Colonel of the 2nd Bengal Native Infantry, was commanding the Bhopal Levy at Indore when rebel sepoys attacked the Residency there on 1 July. The assailants were closely supported by artillery, which soon began to cause casualties among the defenders. It was these guns which were charged by Colonel Travers and just five other men. This surprise attack drove off the enemy gunners, thereby buying valuable time for European fugitives to enter the safety of the Residency. James Travers was later promoted to general and was made a CB. He commanded the Central India Horse in 1861, the Sangor District in 1865 and the Mirat Division in 1869. He died in India on 1 April 1884. His Victoria Cross was not gazetted until 1 March 1861, the delay being due to General Sir Hugh Rose 'requiring ocular proof of Travers' act of gallantry' before he would sanction the award. Rose's demand suggests that there may have been some rivalry between the two men.

Private **Denis Dempsey**, from Bray, County Wicklow, was serving with the 1st Battalion 10th (North Lincolnshire) Regiment. In July 1857, during the retreat from Arrah he was one of those who assisted in carrying the wounded Ensign Erskine to safety. On 12 August of that year he was the first man to enter the village of Jugdispore under the most galling fire. Later, on 14 March 1858, he assisted with mining operations at Lucknow, on one occasion advancing through a burning village carrying a bag of gunpowder, despite the risk of it exploding from the heat of the flames. He was also shot at on numerous occasions during this journey. All of these actions earned the Bray man the Victoria Cross. Dempsey died on 10 January 1896, in Toronto, Canada.

With Lucknow under siege a relief force under Sir Henry Havelock was despatched to the city. On 29 July Havelock's small force was engaged with mutineers at the small town of Unao.[18] The British force achieved victory and among the men who distinguished themselves that day was Sergeant Major **George Lambert** of the 84th (York and Lancaster) Regiment, who had been born in Markethill, County Armagh. However, Havelock was forced to turn back towards Cawnpore when he learned that some 4,000 rebels at Bithur were menacing that town.[19] In the subsequent battle with that rebel force on 16 August, Lambert again showed great courage when the mutineers were put to flight by a bayonet charge. When the Lucknow relief force at last reached the city in late September, Lambert was prominent in the fighting to reach the Residency. His VC was awarded for these and other actions, including the storming of Hiran Khana. In addition to receiving the VC, George Lambert was also commissioned. He died in Sheffield on 10 February 1860. A local newspaper reported that his death was 'caused by the breaking of a blood vessel … whilst on the parade ground of the Barracks. He had been somewhat unwell for several weeks.'[20] There is a memorial to Lambert in Mullaghbrack Church in County Armagh.

Captain **Henry George Gore-Browne**, of the 32nd Regiment, was stationed within the Lucknow Residency and, on 21 August, led a party out on a raid against the enemy lines. The purpose of this sortie was to spike two enemy guns that had been causing great damage to the town's defences. Gore-Browne was the first man into the battery and in the ensuing mêlée some one hundred of the enemy were killed. The raid was judged a complete success and Browne was awarded the VC. In later life he rose to the rank of colonel and after his military service he became Deputy Governor of the Isle of Wight and President of the Isle of Wight Agricultural Society. He was very proud to be the great-grandson of Arthur Browne, in whose arms Wolfe is said to have died at Quebec.

William Olpherts, from County Armagh, was awarded the Victoria Cross while serving as a captain in the Bengal Artillery. *Hell-Fire Jack* Olpherts was a descendant of the Dutch General Olpherzen who had settled in County Donegal and built the family home, Ballyconnell House. Another branch of the family moved to County Armagh and made their home at Dartry Lodge, Blackwatertown. William was educated at the Royal School, Dungannon, and Addiscombe, the East India Company Cadet College. He enlisted with his cousin Henry, who would later rise to the rank of lieutenant-colonel before his death in 1860. Both joined the Bengal Artillery and William went on to serve in Burma and the First Sikh War. During a spell of leave he volunteered for service in the Crimea where he was given command of a unit of Turkish troops and, later, a body of Bashi Bazooks.[21]

On 25 September 1857, as the 90th Perthshire Light Infantry, under Sir Colin Campbell, penetrated into the town of Lucknow, Captain Olpherts, acting in support of the 90th, charged forward in the face of intense fire to capture two enemy guns. Using horses and limbers from his own battery he carried off the enemy ordnance. As a result of these actions the other members of his regiment elected him for the award. Olpherts later became a general and was also knighted. He became Colonel Commandant of the Royal Artillery in 1888 and the city of Armagh presented him with a Sword of Honour.

Also engaged in the attempt to relieve Lucknow was another highland regiment, the 78th (Highland), the Ross-Shire Buffs. This regiment so distinguished itself during the fighting that 'The VC was conferred on [it] as a body ... To enable it to be worn the Regiment had to nominate one individual to wear it, as its representative. A vote was taken, and it was almost unanimously agreed that it should be given to Assistant Surgeon McMaster for the intrepidity with which he exposed himself to the fire of the enemy, in bringing in and attending to the wounded on 25 September at Lucknow.'

Born in Trichinopoly, India on 16 May 1834, **Valentine Munbee McMaster** was the son of Irish parents; his mother was a member of the

Munbee family of County Londonderry, who had a close connection with Saint Columb's Cathedral in the nearby city.[22] His father may have been a Belfast man. McMaster had already served in the Persian War and had received the Persian Medal with Clasp. During the Mutiny he served with Havelock's column in the recapture of Cawnpore, in the advance into Oudh, during which he was wounded, then with Outram's force at the Alambagh until the capture of Lucknow. Subsequently he saw service in the Rohilcund campaign and the capture of Bareilly.

In 1864 McMaster was stationed at Mhow as medical officer of 6th Inniskilling Dragoons, which had at that time two other VC officers, the quartermaster, Wooden, and the riding master, Malone. McMaster returned to the 78th with whom he was serving at North Queen Street Barracks in Belfast when he died of congestion of the lungs on 22 January 1872. The *Belfast Newsletter* reported a 'vast assemblage of people of all ranks [who] congregated along North Queen Street and at the top of Donegall Street to witness the mournful cortege'. Relatives present included McMaster's father and Mr W.H.L. Cogwell, both stated to be 'of Belfast'. Valentine Munbee McMaster is buried in Belfast City Cemetery and is remembered on a memorial in Saint Columb's Cathedral in Derry.

The battle at Lucknow continued on 26 September when the 90th forced their way into the Residency. **William Bradshaw**, from County Tipperary, Assistant Surgeon of the 90th, with Surgeon Home, also of the 90th, organised the native dhoolie bearers (stretcher-bearers) in the collection of those wounded during the advance. Despite the close proximity of the mutineers, both Home and Bradshaw, now wounded, continued their work, at one time becoming separated from the main force and having to reach the safety of the Residency via the riverbank. Both men were awarded the Victoria Cross for their actions. After leaving the Army, Bradshaw returned to Ireland and after his death a memorial was raised in Saint Mary's Church, Thurles.

Private **Thomas Duffy**, 1st Madras Fusiliers, was also awarded the Victoria Cross at Lucknow on 26 September. Early that morning it was discovered that mutineers had captured a 24-pounder gun that had been left unattended overnight. Duffy, with two other soldiers, managed to crawl to the gun, attach ropes, and drag the piece back to their own lines, all the time under heavy enemy musket fire. A native of Athlone, Thomas Duffy died in Dublin on 23 December 1868.

On 21 September, at the village of Mungulwar, the 1st Native Infantry, a unit of mutineers, was in action against a British volunteer cavalry troop. Serving as a volunteer with the cavalry was Sergeant **Patrick Mahoney**, 1st Madras Fusiliers. During a fierce and bloody fight through the streets of the village, Mahoney was able to capture the colour of the mutineers, despite receiving a severe sabre slash to his right hand. The taking of a colour by a cavalryman from an infantry unit was a rare thing indeed and considered well worthy of the Victoria Cross. Sergeant Mahoney was killed on 30 October at Lucknow. His VC was gazetted after his death.

In the maze of alleyways and narrow streets that make up Lucknow two more Irishmen earned Britain's highest award. On 26 September, Private **John Ryan**, 1st Madras Fusiliers, and Private **Peter McManus**, Northumberland Fusiliers, were fighting side by side along one of Lucknow's narrow streets when they saw Captain Arnold of the Madras Fusiliers lying wounded on a stretcher. As they carried Arnold to a house held by the relief column he was hit again by musket fire. Despite their efforts he died of his wounds. Throughout the remainder of the day Ryan made repeated excursions into the streets to rescue wounded men. Both men were awarded the Victoria Cross and were later promoted to sergeant. McManus had already been a sergeant but had been reduced to private on 22 April 1857 and imprisoned for four days. Sergeant Ryan, a native of Kilkenny, died at Cawnpore the following year, while Sergeant McManus, from Tynan, County Armagh, died of smallpox two years later at Allahabad.

Bernard Diamond from County Antrim, served during the Mutiny with the Bengal Horse Artillery as a sergeant. On 28 September 1857 his battery was involved in the attack on the rebel held town of Bolandshahr. The British guns came under very heavy counter-battery fire and all the guns, except Diamond's, were knocked out. Nevertheless, both Diamond and Gunner **Richard Fitzgerald**, from Cork, continued to keep up a steady fire on the enemy. Both men were subsequently awarded the Victoria Cross. After his military service Bernard Diamond emigrated to New Zealand. Fitzgerald disappeared from War Office records after 1886 and is believed to have died in India about that time. The War Office records were themselves destroyed by enemy action during the Second World War as was his Victoria Cross which was held by a museum in Bristol that was destroyed by bombing.

During the action at Bolandshahr, 9th Lancers made a charge in column through the town, not a tactic that endears itself to cavalry troops. However, the Lancers' commanding officer, frustrated by the apparent timidity of the infantry, decided on the charge. Following this daring action no less than five Victoria Crosses were awarded, one of which went to Private **Patrick Donohoe**, from Tipperary, who saved the life of an officer who was unhorsed during the action. As a result of their service in the Mutiny the 9th earned the nickname 'The Delhi Lancers'.

On 2 October 1857, the rebel Ramgurh Battalion was ensconced at the village of Chota Belhar, a strong position supported by artillery. The responsibility for attacking the position fell to the 53rd (Shropshire) Regiment. The mutineers' guns had caused approximately one-third casualties to the 53rd, when Sergeant **Denis Dynon**, from Kilmannon in Queen's County, led a party of men forward and shot the gunners. As a result of Dynon's leadership the battery was successfully taken.

There is an interesting footnote to Dynon's award of the VC which echoes that of John Duane. On 7 August 1861 the office of the Secretary of State for War wrote to the staff officer of the Tullamore pensions' office stating, in response to a letter from the latter dated 27 July, that 'the Victoria Cross has not been awarded to Denis Dynan, a pensioner from the 53rd Regiment'.[23] Dynon's VC was not gazetted until 25 February 1862 and the Secretary of State for War's office was apparently unaware of the fact that an award was being processed, although Dynon appears to have been told by someone. The difference in the spelling of his surname of one letter is unlikely to have been responsible for this bureaucratic hiccup. It would seem that Denis Dynon is another Irish VC whose medal bears an incorrect spelling of his name.

Patrick McHale, from Killala, County Mayo, served in the Northumberlands at Lucknow. He had enlisted in the regiment at Parkhurst Barracks on the Isle of Wight on 18 December 1847. On 2 October 1857 he was the first man to capture one of the guns of the enemy-held Cawnpore Battery. Three months later, on 22 December, his company was engaged in skirmishing to the front of an enemy battery and was receiving casualties from grapeshot. By a daring rush he once again became one of the first men to take possession of an enemy gun. His great height – six feet two inches – would have made him a leader even though he could neither read nor write. His Victoria Cross was gazetted on 19 June 1860.

Four days after McHale captured his first gun, a Wexford man became another Victoria Cross winner. On 6 October Lieutenant Gibaut and Lance Corporal **John Sinnott** were attempting to extinguish a fire on their parapet, when the lieutenant was shot and his body fell outside the defences. Lance Corporal Sinnott, along with Sergeants Glinn and Mullins, and with the assistance of Private Mullins immediately went out from cover and brought the body back. John Sinnott was wounded twice during this time. He was elected by his regiment, the 84th (York and Lancaster), for the VC.

Thomas Henry Kavanagh, from Mullingar, County Westmeath, joined the Indian Civil Service in 1849 and was in Lucknow in company with Sir Henry Lawrence when the Mutiny started. His wife was wounded early in the siege and the youngest of his nine children killed. On 9 November Kavanagh volunteered to take information to the relief force. Although over six feet tall and with bright red hair, he was disguised as an Indian and was able to slip through the mutineers' lines and join up with the relieving troops, under the command of Colonel Sir Colin Campbell. He was presented with the Victoria Cross by the Queen on 4 January 1860, one of four to be awarded to civilians during the Mutiny. For the remainder of his life he was known by the nickname Lucknow Kavanagh, partly because he was prone to boasting about his achievement. When he proposed to write a book on his exploits, the Secretary of State for War's office refused to give him copies of the correspondence relating to his award.[24]

In November 1882 Kavanagh was taken ill on the P and O ship *Khedive* off Gibraltar and was landed for medical treatment. He died in Old Station Hospital, North Front, Gibraltar shortly afterwards. There are three dates for his death: the *Gibraltar Chronicle* stated that he died on 12 November, while most other records indicate the previous day; his memorial states that he died on 13 November.

Between 14 and 22 November 1857 two Irish members of the Bengal Artillery were awarded the Victoria Cross. The other members of their battery elected Rough Rider **Edward Jennings**, from Ballinrobe, County Mayo, and Gunner **Thomas Laughnan**, from Gort, County Galway, for their actions at the Relief of Lucknow. During this period Jennings was acting as a despatch rider and, as he rode between posts, he heard the cries of a wounded officer, who had fallen between the opposing forces. Jennings spurred his horse forward and leapt a stone wall into a group of mutineers who were sheltering behind it. Calling 'they're coming' in the vernacular, he scattered the mutineers, cutting down several of them with his sabre. He then carried the wounded officer to safety on his horse. Later the officer presented Jennings with a gift of 1,000 rupees and he was also offered a commission, which he declined as he could neither read nor write. Jennings later worked as a corporation street labourer in North Shields, where he died on 10 May 1889. His grave was refurbished in September 1997 and a service of rededication was held at which 101st Regiment, Royal Artillery fired a salute. His VC is held by the Royal Artillery.

Laughnan's name may actually have been Laughlin, making him yet another Irish soldier to have his name misspelt, and his VC citation simply indicates that he 'acted with conspicuous gallantry' during the period from 14 to 22 November. He died in County Galway on 23 July 1864. His Victoria Cross was held by 148 (Meiktila) Battery, Royal Artillery.

Corkman **John Dunlay** served with the 93rd Highlanders at Lucknow. On 16 November, during the regiment's assault on the Secundra Bagh, Lance Corporal Dunlay accompanied Captain Burroughs as he entered one of the breaches in the enemy defences. For a short time they were the only two British troops in the breach and had to fight hand to hand until relieved by other members of the regiment. Dunlay is another VC winner whose name may have been misspelled; it is also shown as Dunley or Dunlea. He died in Cork on 17 October 1890.

Private **Peter Grant**, also of the 93rd Highlanders, earned the second Secundra Bagh VC. When the Highlanders' commanding officer captured an enemy colour he was set upon by a number of rebel sepoys. Grant, having no ammunition for his musket, took an enemy sword and killed five of them in short order. He was elected by the private soldiers of the regiment for the Victoria Cross. He died in Dundee on 10 January 1868.

Private **Charles Irwin** of the 53rd (Shropshire) Regiment was the third recipient of the VC for this action. He received a serious gunshot wound to his right shoulder as his regiment forced its way into the defended buildings. A native of Manorhamilton, County Leitrim, Irwin was also elected by the private soldiers of the regiment for the award. He survived the war and later transferred to the 87th (Royal Irish Fusiliers) with whom he served from January 1860 to 30 June 1863. Irwin was not an exemplary soldier in peacetime and received many punishments for various transgressions during those three years. He seems to have taken his discharge in 1863 and died in Newtownbutler, County Fermanagh, on 8 April 1873.

The fourth Irish Victoria Cross won during the attack on the Secundra Bagh was awarded to Sergeant **Samuel Hill** of the 90th Perthshire Light Infantry, who was born in Glenavy, County Antrim. On the night of 16 November 1857, as the 90th stormed over the mutineers' defences, Hill was responsible for saving the life of Captain Irby, also of the 90th. Later that same night he rescued two wounded comrades who were lying under heavy enemy fire. His gallant conduct throughout the relief of the Lucknow garrison was inspirational and he was elected by the non-commissioned officers of the regiment for the award of the Victoria Cross. Samuel Hill died at Meerut, India, in 1863.

A Royal Navy VC was also won on 16 November 1857. Leading Seaman **John Harrison**, from Castleborough, County Wexford, was serving in the Naval Brigade during the attack on Lucknow. A battery of guns from HMS *Shannon*, under the command of Captain William Peel, was emplaced near the Shah Nujeff mosque and a volunteer was called for to act as an observer for the guns. Leading Seaman Harrison was able to climb a tree near the outer wall of the mosque and direct accurate fire onto the enemy positions. As a result of these actions, both he and Captain Peel were awarded the Victoria Cross. He was later promoted to petty officer and today lies in an unmarked grave in London's Brompton cemetery.

The next day, 17 November, Private **Patrick Graham**, a Dublin man, was elected by the private soldiers of his regiment, the 90th Perthshire Light Infantry, for the award of the Victoria Cross. This came about as a result of Graham's efforts in rescuing a wounded comrade from under enemy fire during the attack on Lucknow. He died in his native Dublin on 3 June 1875.

On 18 November there was further fighting around the Secundra Bagh and a fifth Irish Victoria Cross was earned. Tipperary-born Lieutenant **Thomas Bernard Hackett**, of the 23rd (Royal Welch Fusiliers), led a rescue party that recovered a fellow wounded officer of the 23rd from certain death. The officer had been lying in the open exposed to enemy fire and Hackett and his men arrived just in time to save his life. Later that day Hackett climbed onto the roof of a bungalow his men were defending and cut away the thatch to prevent it being set alight by the mutineers. Eventually rising to the rank of lieutenant-colonel, he returned to Ireland after his military career. His younger brother, Robert Henry, served in the Zulu War of 1879 and was wounded in action serving with the 90th. As a result of that wound, Robert was left blind and Thomas devoted a lot of his time to looking after his brother. It was therefore a double tragedy when Thomas died as the result of a shooting accident near his home at Arrabeg, King's County, in 1890. There is a memorial to him at the Marshall family vault, Lockeen Churchyard, Borrisokane, County Tipperary.

Also serving at Lucknow with Hodson's Horse was **Charles John Stanley Gough**, a member of a distinguished Irish military family. Gough was awarded the Victoria Cross for no fewer than four acts of gallantry during the Mutiny. In the first, during an action at Khurkowdah, near Rohtuk, on 15 August 1857, he saved the life of his brother, Hugh, who was wounded, killing two enemy soldiers in the process. The next incident occurred three days later when he lead a troop of the Guides Cavalry in a charge and cut down two enemy sowars, with one of whom he had a hand-to-hand clash. On 2 January 1858 he took part in a charge at Shumshabad, during which he attacked one of the mutineers' leaders and pierced him with his sword. However, Gough's sword was pulled from his grasp in the heat of the clash and he then had to defend himself with his revolver, with which he shot two enemy soldiers. The final deed mentioned in his citation occurred at Meeangunge on 23 February 1858 where he went to the aid of Major O.H. St George Anson.

His brother **Hugh Gough**, whom he had rescued at Khurkowdah, also won the Victoria Cross during the Mutiny, for two deeds of bravery at Lucknow. On 12 November 1857, while commanding a troop of Hodson's Horse near the Alambagh, he charged across a swamp to capture two enemy guns that were defended by a numerically superior force. During this action his horse was wounded in two places and his own headdress was cut through by sword cuts. At Jellallabad, near Lucknow, on 25 February 1858, he again distinguished himself 'by showing a brilliant example to his regiment when ordered to charge the enemy's guns, and by his gallant and forward conduct, he enabled them to effect their object. On this occasion he engaged himself in a series of single combats, until at length he was disabled by a musket ball through the leg, while charging two sepoys with fixed bayonets'. During the course of the day, Gough lost two horses that were killed under him, had a shot through his helmet and another through his scabbard, before receiving the wound that disabled him.

The Gough brothers were born in India, although the family home was at Rathronan House, Clonmel. Charles later married Harriette Power, also known as de la Poer, of Gorteen La Poer, County Waterford. He died at Inislonagh, Clonmel on 6 September 1912. Hugh died at the Tower of London, where he was the Keeper of His Majesty's Regalia, on 18 May 1909 and was buried at Kensal Green cemetery in London. Both brothers had achieved general officer rank and were knighted. Charles Gough's son, John Edmund, would win a third VC for the family in Somaliland in 1903, thus creating the situation of the VC being held simultaneously by father, son and uncle.

One other Irish VC was won before the end of 1857. On 28 November the 64th (2nd Staffordshire) Regiment charged an enemy artillery battery. In the ranks was Drummer **Thomas Flinn**, a native of Athlone. The attack was a success, but not before the regiment, including Drummer Flinn, was engaged in fierce hand-to-hand fighting. He was decorated with the Victoria Cross at Karachi in March 1860, at the age of 15 years and 3 months, making him one of the youngest winners ever. Flinn died in Athlone on 10 August 1892. There is a memorial to him in the Garrison Church, Whittington Barracks, Lichfield.

On 1 January 1858, the 95th (Derbyshire) Regiment was involved in the attack on Rewa.* This town was held strongly by the mutineers with extensive trenches and street barricades. Private **Bernard McCourt**, from County Armagh, was one of the first men of his regiment into the town and was engaged in close-quarter fighting for most of the battle. At the end of the day the regimental surgeon treated him for no less than five sabre cuts and a bullet wound. He survived the Mutiny and died in 1888. McCourt was probably illiterate, which accounts for the fact that his name appears as the highly-improbable McQuirt in the VC records, although he was shown as McCourt when he enlisted in the 95th, and he was buried as McCourt.

One of the best known military figures of the nineteenth century won the Victoria Cross the following day. Lieutenant **Frederick Sleigh Roberts** of the Bengal Artillery was destined to become Field Marshal Earl Roberts of Kandahar and Waterford, known to the soldiers as 'Bobs', and Commander-in-Chief of the British Army. His great grandfather, John Roberts of

---

* Incorrectly spelt in the citation as Rowa.

Waterford, was the architect responsible for the rebuilding of Waterford Cathedral in 1774. John and his wife had twenty-four children, one of whom, the Reverend John, was the father of Abraham Roberts who joined the East India Company's Army in 1803, having served in the British Army beforehand. Abraham was destined to become General Sir Abraham Roberts. He was also the father of Frederick who was born in India on 30 September 1832 and followed his father into the East India Company's army on 12 December 1851.[25]

At Khodagunge on 2 January 1858 Roberts joined in a cavalry charge during the pursuit of mutineers. He attached himself to a squadron commanded by Major Younghusband which came to close quarters with the enemy when the mutineers turned about and fired into the squadron at close range. In that initial outburst of fire, Younghusband was fatally wounded. Lieutenant Roberts engaged and killed a sepoy who was lunging at a sowar with a bayonet, thereby saving the sowar's life. Seeing two sepoys making off with a standard Roberts spurred after them and overtook the pair as they were about to enter a village. He despatched one with his sword and took the standard from him. The other sepoy fired his musket at Roberts at close range but the weapon misfired and the young officer was not hurt. He rode back to his unit with the standard. For these two actions Frederick Roberts was awarded the Victoria Cross. It was to be the first of many distinctions that he gained in the course of a long military career.

The fighting at Lucknow was continuing. On 11 March 1858 the 2nd Battalion, Rifle Brigade, was attacking across the Iron Bridge. Captain Wilmott's Company was engaged in heavy fighting with a large body of mutineers in the streets across the bridge. A small party consisting of Wilmott, Corporal **William Nash**, a Limerick man, Private Hawkes and an unnamed private found themselves cut off from the remainder of the company at the end of one of the narrow streets. The unnamed soldier was shot in both legs and Nash and Hawkes decided to try to carry him to safety, despite Hawkes himself receiving a serious wound a few seconds later. After a difficult journey over some distance, all the time under enemy fire and protected by the accurate shooting of Captain Wilmott, they made it back to their own lines. Wilmott, Nash and Hawkes were all awarded the Victoria Cross. Nash was later promoted to sergeant and lived until 1875 when he died in Hackney.

Richard Harte Keatinge, who was born in Dublin on 17 June 1825, joined the Bombay Artillery and in March 1858 was a Political Officer with the 2nd Brigade of the Central Indian Field Force. In the assault on Chandairee, Captain Keatinge led an attacking column through a protected breach under heavy and accurate enemy crossfire. The column would have suffered even more casualties had it not been for Keatinge's knowledge of a small path across the ditch which he had discovered the previous night during a personal reconnaissance. Having cleared the breach, Captain Keatinge led the column into the fort only to be felled by a gunshot wound. His actions earned him the VC. He recovered from his wound and rose to the rank of lieutenant general. He died in Horsham, Sussex, on 25 May 1904.

By 3 April 1858 the war was in its final phase and the British were assaulting the fort at Jhansi. Private **James Byrne**, from Wicklow, was serving in the 86th (Royal County Down) Regiment during this attack. As the regiment stormed the mutineers' positions Lieutenant Sewell was badly wounded and fell to the ground. Byrne, assisted by Captain Jerome, managed to pick him up and, fighting their way through a crowd of mutineers, the pair carried the wounded officer to safety. Both received the Victoria Cross. Byrne was badly wounded by a sabre cut during this action, but survived. After his army service he returned to Ireland and died in Dublin in 1872.

A further Victoria Cross was awarded to a member of the 86th at Jhansi. Private **James Pearson**, from Queen's County, showed great courage in defeating three mutineers in hand-to-hand combat, despite being badly wounded himself. Later, at Calpee, he rescued Private Michael Burns from an exposed position that was under heavy enemy fire. Private Burns subsequently died of his wounds. James Pearson, later promoted to sergeant, never returned to Ireland and died in India in 1900.

The third Irish VC won at Jhansi was awarded to Corporal **Michael Sleavon**, from Fermanagh, who served with the Royal Sappers and Miners. During the attack on the fort, Sleavon worked continuously at the head of a sap as the Sappers dug towards the wall. Throughout the assault he was at all times under heavy and accurate fire. He survived the Mutiny and died at his home in Fermanagh aged 72 years.

Born in Belfast in 1832, Private **Patrick Carlin** served in the 1st Battalion 13th (1st Somersetshire) (Prince Albert's Light Infantry) Regiment. During the attack at Azimgurh, on 6 April, Carlin was instrumental in rescuing a wounded naik, or corporal, of the 4th Madras Rifles. As he was carrying the wounded man back towards the regimental lines he was attacked by a mutineer. As his musket was slung over his shoulder at this time, Carlin drew the naik's sword and, after a brief flurry of blows, killed the mutineer before safely returning to his own lines. Some sources state that he was presented with his medal by General Sir Colin Campbell, Commander-in-Chief, East India at Allahabad on 29 June 1858, some days before Campbell was created Baron Clyde, but the *London Gazette* did not carry the announcement of Carlin's award until 26 October 1858. What actually happened is that Campbell issued a general order in which he stated that Carlin and Patrick Green were to be awarded the Victoria Cross and Carlin was honoured almost on the spot. Carlin received the medal itself at Gorakphur in Oudh during February 1859; Clyde, as Campbell had become, signed a receipt for the Cross on 9 February 1859.

Patrick Carlin returned to Ireland and lived at 47 Ward Street, Belfast, until his death, following an illness, in the Union Infirmary (the former workhouse) on 11 May 1895 at the age of sixty-three. He is believed to have been buried in an unmarked pauper's grave adjoining the Infirmary. On 28 November 1907* his Victoria Cross was sold by Sotheby's for £63 to a buyer called Weight.

Michael Murphy from Cahir, County Tipperary, enlisted in the 17th Lancers in 1855, but served with the 2nd Battalion, Military Train during the Mutiny. On 15 April 1858 the British were in pursuit of Kooer Singh's army as it fled from Azimgurh. In one of the many skirmishes that made up the pursuit, Lieutenant Hamilton, Adjutant of the 3rd Sikh Cavalry, was unhorsed, wounded, and surrounded by mutineer horsemen. Farrier Murphy charged into the fray, cutting down several mutineers and, despite receiving a severe wound from a sword cut, put the remainder to flight. He remained with the injured officer until help arrived and only then agreed to have his own wound attended to. In 1872, while serving with 7th Hussars as a blacksmith he was sentenced to nine months' hard labour for the theft of horse fodder. His Victoria Cross was rescinded by Royal Warrant and he left the Army in 1875, being discharged as medically unfit. He worked as a labourer in Darlington, until his death on 15 April 1893. After he was given a pauper's funeral, Sir Henry Havelock-Allen, also a Victoria Cross holder, paid for a headstone for his grave. The Royal Corps of Transport continued to count Murphy in its Roll of Honour as a VC winner, and named a troop of their Junior Leaders' Regiment after him. The conveniently mislaid VC, purchased by a quartermaster sergeant of the Army Service Corps for £44, remains on display in the Royal Logistic Corps Museum. In 1985 the Royal Corps of Transport refurbished Murphy's overgrown grave and held a service of rededication.

Lieutenant **Harry Hammond Lyster**, 72nd Bengal Native Infantry, was awarded the Victoria Cross on 23 May 1858. As the rebel army retreated from Calpee, Lyster 'came upon a unit of enemy skirmishers which had formed square. He at once charged and singly caused the square to break, killing a number of sepoys in the process'. Lyster, from Blackrock, County Dublin, later became a lieutenant general and died in London in 1922. He was the uncle of Captain H.L. Reed vc.

The next month, on 17 June, 8th (The King's Royal Irish) Hussars were awarded four Victoria Crosses for their gallant charge at Gwalior. One went

---

* This is the date given in the Lummis File. Sir O'Moore Creagh in his work on the VC and DSO gives the date of sale as 1903.

to Sergeant **Joseph Ward**, originally from Cork. With the Irish Hussars ably supported by the Bengal Horse Artillery and the 95th Regiment, the enemy was put to flight and two guns captured. After the action the men of the regiment elected Ward for the Victoria Cross. He died in Longford in 1872.

Patrick Roddy was born near Dublin* on Saint Patrick's Day, 1827 and later enlisted in the Bengal Artillery. He served throughout the Mutiny and was in Sir James Outram's force at the first relief of Lucknow in September 1857, subsequently taking part in the defence of Lucknow where he distinguished himself at the Baillie Guard Gate and the Alambagh. He was present at the second relief of Lucknow in November. Until the final suppression of the Mutineers on the Oudh frontier in 1860, Roddy was in virtually every engagement. In February 1858 he was commissioned as an ensign in the Bengal Army and was later – December – promoted to lieutenant.

Roddy was frequently mentioned in despatches and received the thanks of the Indian government. On 27 September 1858, near Kuthirga, he earned the Victoria Cross while returning with the Kapurthala Contingent, which had been pursuing Beni Madhu, a powerful and influential Indian leader. As the contingent was returning from Kuthirga, it was engaged by the enemy. One mutineer seemed to be a deterrent for most of the cavalry

> as each time they attempted [to approach him] the rebel knelt and covered his assailant; this, however, did not deter Lieutenant [*sic*] Roddy, who went boldly in, and when within six yards the rebel fired, killing Lieutenant Roddy's horse, and before he could get disengaged from the horse the rebel attempted to cut him down. Lieutenant Roddy sized the rebel until he could get at his sword, when he ran the man through the body. The rebel turned out to be a subadar [officer] of the late 8th Native Infantry – a powerful man and a most determined character.[26]

It seems that Roddy was subsequently offered a Bar to his Victoria Cross but said that he preferred to take a step in promotion. This may have been the reason for his rapid promotion to lieutenant. If this story is true – and it is difficult to find evidence to support or reject it – then Roddy would have been the first double-VC. As it was such a distinction was not conferred on anyone until the Great War. Roddy went on to have a most distinguished military career, retired as a colonel after almost forty years' service, and died in Jersey on 21 November 1895.

George Richardson was born on 1 August 1831, at Derrylane, Killashandra, County Cavan, the son of John, a linen weaver, and Anne Richard-

* Some sources give his place of birth as Elphin, Roscommon.

son. He enlisted in late 1855 in the 34th (Cumberland) Regiment and served with them in the Mutiny. On 27 April 1859, the 34th were engaged with rebel forces at Kewanie, Trans-Gogra. During the action Private Richardson, although severely wounded in one arm, was able to close with an enemy sepoy who was armed with a loaded revolver and took him prisoner. As a result of this wound he was discharged and admitted as an out-pensioner of the Royal Military Hospital, Chelsea, on 31 July 1860. He was awarded a pension of 8*d.* per day, increased to 14*d.* in May 1891. In 1862 he emigrated to Canada where he died on 28 January 1923, while a patient in Westminster Hospital, Westminster Township, London, Ontario. He was buried with full military honours in a soldiers' plot in the Veterans' Section of Prospect Cemetery, Toronto. The Colonel Sydney Lambert Chapter of the Imperial Order of Daughters of the Empire in Toronto had a memorial stone made and this was dedicated on 10 November 1939. His medals were sold in January 1975 by his great-nephew, Herb Kippax of Parliament Street, Toronto, to Mr Ian Hardcastle. The medals, according to a press cutting from the *Toronto Star* of 17 January 1975, were replacements, which Richardson received after a house fire destroyed the originals. The medals are today thought to be in the hands of a private collector in Canada.

On 18 June 1858 the *London Gazette* carried the announcement of the award of the Victoria Cross to Captain **Dighton McNaghten Probyn** of 2nd Punjab Cavalry. Probyn's citation covered many actions during the period 1857-58 and was one of the earliest of what would later be described as periodic awards of the VC. It was noted that Probyn performed many 'gallant and daring acts'. Typical of these was an incident during the battle of Agra when his squadron charged the rebel infantry. Probyn was separated from his men and surrounded by five or six mutineers. He defended himself doughtily and had cut down two of his opponents before his own men reached him. Probyn was later to give his name to a famous regiment of Indian cavalry, Probyn's Horse (5th King Edward VII's Own Horse) which is now 5th Horse of the Pakistan army and retains the title scroll Probyn's Horse on the regimental badge.[27] Probyn's mother was an Irishwoman, a member of the County Antrim McNaghten family. His father was a Royal Navy officer.

At the beginning of the Mutiny the Victoria Cross could only be awarded to members of the Royal Navy or the British Army; seamen or soldiers of the East India Company did not qualify. On 29 October 1857 a second VC warrant permitted the Cross to be awarded to the officers and men of the naval and military services of the Company. No Indian, or colonial servicemen could qualify, nor, contrary to the evidence of, among others, the Purcell case, could the award be made posthumously.[28] (Indian soldiers of all ranks could receive the Indian Order of Merit.) In all 182 Victoria Crosses were awarded during the Mutiny, a number that equals the awards made during the Second World War. This comparison suggests that the criteria on which a VC is recommended has become much stricter over the years, especially when it is remembered that colonial servicemen qualified for the award after 1867 and Indian servicemen after 1911, while posthumous awards were officially authorized in 1902.

However, it must also be remembered that many more gallantry awards existed during the Second World War in contrast to the mid-nineteenth century. Until 1854 only two awards could be won for bravery: the Order of the Bath for high-ranking officers – an award that could also be given for long service – and the Distinguished Conduct Medal for sergeants and, later, other NCOs. The institution of the VC fulfilled the need for a supreme gallantry award and, in turn, its existence proved the need for a graduated system of gallantry awards which was in place by the Second World War. Many nineteenth-century VC-winning actions might have qualified for the Military Cross, Military Medal (or their naval or air equivalents) or a Mention in Despatches had they been performed between 1939 and 1945. But those who recommended them and those who approved the awards did not have the benefit of the experience of twentieth-century warfare by which to guide their decisions. They made those decisions in the light of their own experiences and the realities of warfare in their own days. Those early awards of the VC were all made in good faith and no-one would see fit to suggest that some were undeserving of the medal.

The fact that not all recommendations for the Victoria Cross led to the award of the distinction is evidence that there was a system of assessing the validity of each citation. This was true in both the Mutiny and the Crimean War. A number of those whose citations failed to bring them the VC were Irish. Some had even recommended themselves. James Kellon, residing at 4 Silver Street, Dublin, in 1864, was under the impression that he had been recommended for the VC and wrote to claim his award and the annual pension of £10, only to receive a letter stating that 'it does not appear that your name has ever been submitted to The Queen for the Victoria Cross, and you are consequently not entitled to the Victoria Cross annuity'. Kellon had served in the Bengal Artillery during the Mutiny.[29] Two years later Daniel McLaughlin, of Cahirciveen, who had been a colour-sergeant with the 82nd Regiment during the Mutiny, sought the VC for himself, only to be informed that no claims had been considered for such awards for some time. Although McLaughlin later wrote again, enclosing testimonials, his case was not considered and he was further told 'that his age, and the loss of his right arm, render him ineligible for employment under this Department as a Clerk or as a Labourer in the Military Store Department'.[30] In 1872 John Dillon of

Longford, who had served in the Mutiny in the East India Company's Army, was also told that a claim submitted by him was too late.[31]

The last personal submission by an Irishman for a VC as a result of his service in the Mutiny may have been that of Patrick Brennan, who had served in the 10th Regiment, which was refused in May 1898.[32] A month later the submission of testimonials on behalf of Denis Neill, who had served in the 86th during the Mutiny, was stated to be 'now too late' as the claim ought to have been made at the time. Neill was commended by the Reverend William Sherrard 'and others' at the castle of Fermoy and their submission was made through an MP, W. McCarthy Downing.[33]

The end of the Indian Mutiny also brought the end of the East India Company's authority as control of India passed from the Company to the Crown, thereby beginning the period known as the Raj, when India was the jewel in the crown of the British Empire. With the demise of the Company's Army its units were taken into the British Army. Some of the infantry regiments, which had recruiting associations with Ireland, were given recruiting areas in Ireland and, when the Army underwent a period of re-organization between 1873 and 1881, those regiments took on full-blown Irish identities as the Royal Munster Fusiliers and the Royal Dublin Fusiliers as well as the 2nd battalions of both the Royal Inniskilling Fusiliers and the Leinster Regiment.[34]

4   The Small Wars of Empire

The 'little' Persian War of 1856-7 occurred between the Crimean war and the Indian Mutiny and resulted from the Shah of Persia's attempt to seize the disputed Afghan province of Heart while Britain was distracted by the Crimean War and its immediate aftermath. To prevent this the Indian government declared war on Persia on 1 November 1856 and Britain sent a contingent from Bombay. On 10 December the Royal Navy bombarded Bushire on the Gulf coast and 4,000 men of the Bombay army were landed.[1] The following January, Sir James Outram arrived with a second force of two divisions. The horse element of this force consisted of 14th Light Dragoons, a detachment of Scinde Irregular Horse, 3rd Bombay Light Cavalry and the Poona Irregular Horse. Of the four units, only the latter two saw any action of note.

That action occurred at Koosh-ab on 8 February 1857 and for once British cavalry did their job in a thorough and competent manner. After a forced march of forty-six miles in pouring rain, the British force arrived on the field of battle. Outram's men, 4,500 in number, faced some 6,900 Persians, only a few of whom were European-trained regulars, under Shooja-ool-Moolk. Although Outram's force consisted of infantry, cavalry and artillery, the ensuing battle was fought almost exclusively by a small number of cavalry supported by artillery.[2]

The Irish Victoria Cross won on that day went to Lieutenant **Arthur Thomas Moore**, from Carlingford, County Louth. Moore was serving in 3rd Bombay Light Cavalry which formed up in close column of squadrons facing the enemy. The enemy at this point was the Kashkai Regiment, an élite infantry unit which formed square as the cavalry charged at them; the square was the classic infantry defence against cavalry. As the 3rd charged the square, Lieutenant Moore and his brother Ross leapt the ranks of waiting infantry and landed inside the square. Both horses were killed in the process, and soon the two brothers, along with Lieutenant Malcolmson, another 3rd Bombay Light Cavalry officer who had also made the jump, were fighting for their lives. The elder Moore, 6 feet 7 inches tall and 18 stones in weight, cut his way out on foot while Malcolmson, still on horseback, picked up the younger Moore and crashed through the square making a breach that was quickly exploited by the remainder of the attacking cavalry. As a result of this action Lieutenant Malcolmson was also awarded the Victoria Cross. Moore eventually reached the rank of major-general. He died of heart failure after a bout of influenza at his Dublin home – 18 Waterloo Place – on 25 April 1913.

Britain first became involved with Burma during the latter half of the eighteenth century. The First Burma War began on 5 March 1824 after an attack by Burmese forces against British positions at Shahpuri Island on the Chittagong frontier in September the previous year. The war lasted until February 1826, when Burma was forced to cede the Arakan to Britain, renounce its claim to Assam and various other border regions, and pay an indemnity.[3]

In March 1852, as a result of transgressions of the treaty of 1826, the British once again went to war with Burma. This, the Second Burma War lasted until January 1853, with the annexation of the province of Pegu to the Crown, and the warning to the Burmese King, Pagan, that further resistance would mean the total destruction of his kingdom.[4] Pagan was dethroned the following month by a revolt, and his successor, Mindon, although not a favourite with the British, caused little trouble. Mindon died in 1878, and his son, Thibaw, immortalized by Rudyard Kipling, succeeded him. Thibaw caused internal unrest and the British Resident was withdrawn in 1879. Although Thibaw cultivated friendship with France and Italy, it was his imposition of a huge fine on the Bombay-Burma Trading Company that caused most consternation to Britain. Then, in November 1885, Thibaw instructed his people to throw the British into the sea, an exhortation that was almost guaranteed to provoke war between Britain and Burma.[5]

Following Thibaw's proclamation, the British assembled three brigades under the command of Major General Harry Prendergast VC, with instructions to remove Thibaw from his throne. The British advanced with such speed that the Burmese had little chance to organise effective resistance. Using a fleet of over fifty vessels, courtesy of the Irrawaddy Flotilla Company, they pushed up the river, engaging and neutralising Burmese shore batteries with consummate ease. On 17 November a Burmese force of infantry and artillery was dispersed at Minha, and on the 26th an offer of surrender was received from Thibaw. The war was over in less than a fortnight.[6]

Two Irish VCs were won in Burma during what was known as the pacification process following the Third Burma War.[7] On New Year's Day, 1889, Lieutenant Tighe, 27th Bombay Infantry, was witness to the exploits of Surgeon **John Crimmin** as he won his Victoria Cross. Crimmin, born in Dublin on 19 March 1859, decided to follow a medical career and enlisted in the Indian Army. When his unit was sent to Burma, Surgeon Crimmin was attached to the Mounted Infantry. On 1 January there was fierce skirmishing near the village of Lwekaw, in eastern Karenni. Lieutenant Tighe saw Surgeon Crimmin surrounded by Karen irregulars as he treated a wounded man but just as they closed in a Sepoy rode to the Surgeon's assistance and between them they beat off the enemy attacks. John Crimmin finished his military service as a colonel, he retired to Somerset and died at Wells on 20 February 1945. In addition to the Victoria Cross he was also a Companion of the Bath (CB), Commander of the Order of the Indian Empire (CIE), and a holder of the Volunteer Decoration (VD).

The second Burma VC was also won by a doctor, **Owen Edward Pennefather Lloyd**, who was born in County Roscommon on 1 January 1854. Educated at Fermoy College, Edinburgh University and the Royal Irish University, Lloyd was a surgeon major in operations against the Kachins. On 6 January 1893 Kachins attacked the position known as the Sima post. The officer commanding the garrison, Captain Morton, was on his way back from a visit to one of the outlying piquets when he was shot and wounded. Surgeon Major Lloyd ran to assist the fallen officer accompanied by Subadar Matab Singh. As Lloyd examined the fallen officer he saw that the wounds were serious and sent Subadar Singh back for assistance. Singh returned with five men of the Magwe Battalion of Military Police, and between them they carried Morton back to the camp. Their efforts were in vain as the captain died a few minutes later. The native officer and all five Sepoys were awarded the Indian Order of Merit. Lloyd received the VC and was later to become Sir Owen Edward Pennefather Lloyd VC, KCB. He died at Saint Leonards-on-Sea, Sussex on 5 July 1941.

Burma became part of the Indian Empire, that vast area of land that was coloured red on atlases and marked the extent of British domination of the region. But there were many times when that domination was challenged and the mettle of the soldiers of the British and Indian armies was put to the test. On India's North-West Frontier there was tension with Afghanistan and this boiled to the surface in a number of wars between Britain and the Afghans. The Second Afghan War began on 20 November 1878 when a British ultimatum expired. This war also followed the course of the First Afghan War in many other ways with the British invading in three columns. The first, led by Sir Donald Stewart, comprising some 12,000 men, moved from Quetta in the south towards Kandahar; the second, under Sir Sam Browne, advanced through the Khyber pass for Kabul; the third, led by Lord Roberts VC, advanced up the Kurram valley.[8]

Stewart's column met little opposition and Brown easily defeated an Afghan position at Ali Masjid by a skilful flanking movement but Roberts did not have things so easy. As he marched up the Kurram valley he found his way blocked at a high ridge named Peiwar Kotal. Afghan troops were well positioned on the heights, and a frontal assault was ruled out. On 1 December Roberts decided on a night outflanking move. This attack, together with a push from the troops left in the British camp against the Afghan centre, sent them fleeing the field.⁹ War would continue until May 1881 and six Victoria Crosses were won by Irishmen in its course. The first went to Lieutenant **Reginald Clare Hart**, Royal Engineers, from Scarriff, County Clare. On 31 January 1879 Hart was with a supply convoy which came under attack while crossing a river on its way up the Peshawar valley. A sowar of 13th Bengal Lancers was wounded and fell into the river. Hart returned to the crossing on foot and, braving a storm of enemy fire from both flanks, rescued the sowar, but not before putting to flight another band of the enemy who were attempting to advance along the dry river bed. Decorated with the VC by Queen Victoria at Windsor Castle on 9 December 1879, Hart had an illustrious army career, reaching the rank of general and receiving a knighthood. He died in Bournemouth on 19 October 1931 and is buried at Netherbury in Dorset.

The second Irish VC of the war was another Royal Engineer. Captain **Edward Pemberton Leach**, born in Londonderry, was acting as Assistant Superintendent of Surveys when, on 17 March, he became involved in a skirmish at Maidanah. The survey team, with a detachment of 45th Sikhs as escort, was retiring from the village, bringing with them the mortally wounded Lieutenant Barclay. Realizing that the enemy was going to close before the survey team got clear, Leach led a party of the 45th in a desperate counter charge. In the ensuing skirmish Leach killed three of the enemy in single combat before being seriously wounded by a sword cut to the left arm. Leach was decorated at the same investiture as Hart and he, too, went on to achieve high rank, retiring as a general with two knighthoods. He died in Italy on 27 April 1913.

A month after Leach won his VC, the Guides Cavalry were in action at Futtebad. On 2 April Major Wigram Battye, one of four brothers who would die fighting for the Empire, led the Corps of Guides Cavalry in a charge against superior numbers of enemy horsemen. At a critical moment in the action Battye was mortally wounded and command of the unit fell on Lieutenant **Walter Pollock Hamilton**, son of a well-known Kilkenny family. Hamilton at once cheered his men on to avenge the major's death. In the fight that followed, Lieutenant Hamilton saw Sowar Dowlut Ram fall from his horse and attacked by three enemy soldiers. Leading a few of his men forward Hamilton cut his way through to rescue the sowar. The Guides soldiers were each awarded the Indian Order of Merit, while Hamilton received the VC.

Walter Hamilton had arrived in Rawalpindi in the autumn of 1874 and, by 1876, had enlisted in the Corps of Guides. Three months after winning the Victoria Cross, Lieutenant Hamilton was in charge of the escort that accompanied Sir Louis Cavagnari to Kabul to act as British agent. By September Kabul was full of Afghan soldiers who had not been paid, a responsibility they laid at the door of the British. When, on 3 September, they received only one month's pay, they attacked the British Residency and killed Cavagnari, his staff and the seventy-five men of the Guides. The attack succeeded because of the effect of the attackers' artillery. Although the defenders made several attempts to capture these cannon, and drove off the gunners, the Guides had no way of either spiking the guns or of bringing them back inside the Residency. In the Guides' final charge, Hamilton was killed while once again driving off the enemy gunners. A surviving sowar of the Guides later told Hamilton's father that, with the Residency ablaze, the Irishman collected the handful of survivors in the courtyard and said to them: 'Now lads, we have only a few moments to live. Let us make the most of them. Open the gate and follow me'. Today the names of those who died are engraved on the Cavagnari Arch at Mardan.

At the time of his death, Hamilton knew that he had been recommended for the Victoria Cross and the announcement appeared in the London Gazette two days after he was killed. However, it appears that some bureaucrat decided that his death nullified the award 'as the VC was a decoration conferred only on the recipient in person, and at the hands of the Sovereign'. Walter Hamilton's father pointed out that his son had been recommended for the award six months before his death and that, since he continued to serve in Asia, there had been no opportunity for personal decoration. The controversy between Alexander Hamilton and the War Office continued for several months before the latter conceded Hamilton's point and gave him his son's medal.[10]

On 21 April 1879 a two-battalion force, under the command of Captain **O'Moore Creagh**, Bombay Staff Corps, was sent from Dakka to protect the village of Kam Dakka. County Clare-born Creagh would later rise to the rank of general and receive a knighthood. The following morning an overwhelming number of enemy attacked Creagh's force of 150 men. The villagers aided the assailants by attacking from within the village, and Captain Creagh was forced to retire to a position a short distance away. A defensive works was quickly thrown up using anything available, including the pack animals and the dead bodies of comrades. The defenders held off repeated assaults until 3 p.m., when a relief force arrived from Dakka. The enemy was finally put to flight by a charge of 10th Bengal Lancers. Creagh received the Victoria Cross for his actions that day, his very first day in action. He died on 9 August 1923, having begun work on what was then a definitive book on the Victoria Cross and the Distinguished Service Order.

At the beginning of the winter of 1879, British troops were in action at Charasiah, a fortified hilltop. On 6 October a two-company attack was launched against the flank of the position after sustained artillery fire had failed to dislodge the enemy. Major **George Stuart White**, 92nd (Gordon Highlanders)

Regiment, a native of Broughshane, near Ballymena, County Antrim, led the attacking force. As they arrived at the top of the adjoining hill, Major White and his men, exhausted by their climb, suddenly came upon a body of enemy infantry. It was a time for immediate action. Taking a rifle, White shot the enemy leader dead. This forced the enemy to flee and White's men immediately occupied the position. George Stuart White was an outstanding leader: in September the following year at the battle of Kandahar, he charged an enemy artillery battery, capturing one gun and forcing the remaining gunners to flee. White was decorated with the Victoria Cross by the marquess of Ripon, Viceroy of India at Simla on 4 October 1881. He would later rise to the rank of field marshal. Sir George White died at the Royal Hospital, Chelsea, on 24 June 1912 and is buried in Broughshane. He is commemorated in Broughshane Presbyterian Church and by a statue in Portland Place, London.

Throughout the period that soldiers have been eligible for the Victoria Cross, men of the cloth have earned their fair share. On 11 December 1879 the Reverend **James William Adams** of County Cork, attached to the Bengal Ecclesiastical Department, performed an act that won the first VC ever awarded to a military chaplain. At the village of Killa Kazi, 9th Lancers were in action when a number of them rode into a hidden nullah, a wide, deep, water-filled ditch, which formed part of the village defences. With the enemy closing on the floundering horsemen, the Reverend Adams rushed forward and, leaping into the waist-deep water, began to help the men out of the ditch. As the last Lancer was pulled from the water the enemy closed in on the Reverend Adams and he was unable to remount his horse. Steady fire from some of the other Lancers held the Afghans off long enough to allow him to escape on foot. Adams died at Ashwell Rectory, near Oakham in Rutlandshire, on 20 October 1903

On 27 July 1880 Sergeant **Patrick Mullane** of the Royal Horse Artillery won the last Irish VC of the war at Maiwand. Mullane's battery was about to retire with the enemy within ten or fifteen yards of the gun positions when Mullane ran back to rescue a wounded driver. He lifted the injured man and placed him on a gun limber, thus saving him from certain death at the hands of the Afghans. During the retreat that followed, Mullane volunteered to obtain water for the wounded men and did so by going into one of the enemy villages in which many men had lost their lives. Patrick Mullane later became a regimental sergeant-major. He was born in Ahmednuggar, India, in October 1858 and died in Plaistow, Sussex on 20 November 1919. It is believed that his Irish father was a soldier.

Britain first came into contact with China in 1757, when a trading post was set up at the port of Canton. By 1839, Britain and China were at war as the

British tried to force the Chinese to buy more opium from the East India Company, much to the detriment of many tens of thousands of ordinary Chinese people. This, the Opium, or First China, War, lasted from 1839 to 1842. It was not a time of continuous combat, but one of sudden outbreaks of violence and ambush. British troops had most of their successes under the command of that able Irish soldier, Sir Hugh Gough.[11]

By 1854 the treaty that had ended the Opium war came up for revision, but the Chinese were in no mood to relent. In December 1857, a combined British-French force captured the port of Canton. This was followed, in May 1858, by an attack on the Taku Forts situated at the mouth of the river Peiho. These forts were large earthen structures, well defended by cannon and trenches filled with sharpened bamboo stakes.[12]

When British and French ships attempted to sail up the river, against the terms of the treaty, the forts opened fire. Allied attempts to take the forts were unsuccessful, six gunboats were damaged and an attempted landing by infantry was foiled by deep mud that was exposed by the low tide.

Following the arrival of reinforcements from Europe and India, the attack was resumed. In August 1860 a small army of some 11,000 British and Indian troops under the command of General Sir Hope Grant, with 6,000 French troops led by General de Montauban, landed about eight miles upriver from the forts. The Allies marched inland and decisively beat an Imperial Army on 12 August. They then turned and made their way downstream to attack the forts from the rear.[13]

The Taku forts complex consisted of two large emplacements on either side of the river with a smaller position to the rear and further inland. On the morning of 21 August the attack began with a bombardment of forty guns from the landward side, while British ships standing off the coast rained shells down from their guns. The approach to the inland fort was along a narrow causeway and the attackers, mostly men of the 44th (East Essex) and 67th (South Hampshire) Regiments, found themselves hampered by mud flats and swamps. Reaching the outer defences of the fort they were met with repeated volleys of small arms fire and cannon. As they began scaling the walls, the Chinese successfully pushed away many of the scaling ladders. In a desperate attempt to climb the outside of the fort, officers stuck their swords into the mud walls to make climbing easier. Four Irishmen won the Victoria Cross that day. Lieutenant **Nathaniel Burslem** and Private **Thomas Lane**, both of the 67th, and Lieutenant **Robert Montressor Rogers**, of the 44th, earned their awards during the fighting to secure a foothold on the fort's walls. Burslem, a Limerick man, and Lane, from Cork, earned their VCs for 'distinguished gallantry in swimming the ditches of the North Taku Fort, and persevering in attempting during the assault, and before the entrance of the Fort had been effected by anyone, to enlarge an opening in the wall, through which they eventually entered, and in doing so were both severely wounded'. Rogers, a Dublin man, performed a similar deed together with a private of his own regiment and a lieutenant of the 67th. Burslem drowned five years later during an attempt to rescue a comrade in the Thames river, New Zealand, while Lane, from Cork, died in South Africa in 1889. Rogers, who was later promoted to major-general, died in Berkshire in 1895. Lane was one of the eight VC winners whose VC was forfeited; the warrant for the forfeiture was dated 7 April 1881.

The fourth Irish VC that day was won by a hospital apprentice of the Indian Medical Establishment. **Andrew Fitzgibbon**, who was attached to a wing of the 67th Regiment in the assault, was one of the youngest ever winners of the Victoria Cross. At 15 years and 3 months, he was the same age as Thomas Flinn who had won the Cross during the Indian Mutiny. Fitzgibbon accompanied his wing of the 67th when it took up position within 500 yards of the fort. Under heavy fire from the Chinese, he then went to the assistance of a dhoolie bearer who had been wounded and began to bandage the man's wound. As the 67th advanced under enemy fire, Fitzgibbon dashed across open ground to tend to another wounded soldier. During this mission of mercy he was himself severely wounded. Andrew Fitzgibbon was born in India on 13 May 1845, the son of William and Elizabeth Fitzgibbon, of Cork. William Fitzgibbon enlisted at Cork on 6 November 1826 and served in the Bengal Artillery. At the time of Andrew's birth William was quartermaster of the Kumaon Battalion, later 3rd Gurkha Rifles.

Andrew Fitzgibbon's military career came to an ignominious end in 1880. By then he had been promoted to apothecary but was dismissed for dereliction of duty at Jammu in the Khyber Pass during the Afghan War of 1878-80. He died in Delhi in March 1883 and it is believed that his VC was buried with him. His daughter claimed that he had also been awarded the Legion d'Honneur by France but had been refused permission to wear it.

Between 18 March 1861 and 21 June 1864, Irishmen won seven Victoria Crosses in what became known as the Fire in the Fern. While the United States of America was deciding its future through a civil war, Britain was once again embroiled in one of its many bush-fire wars. From 1840, there had been conflict with the Maoris in New Zealand. Increased immigration of white settlers, the dubious progress of European diseases, liquor and prostitution, and the general lawless nature of the settlements all gave rise to tension. The Maori were a proud people and the offer of British 'protection' did not sit well with many of their chiefs.[14]

In 1845 the First Maori War began; it lasted until May 1846 when the Maoris abandoned conventional warfare and turned to 'the fire in the fern'.

No sooner was an outbreak of fighting beaten down in one place than it spread across country and flared up again elsewhere. On the afternoon of 18 March 1861 skirmishers of the 40th (2nd Somersetshire) Regiment were on the right flank of regimental redoubt No. 7 and close to a Maori position in the Huirangi Bush. At approximately 4 p.m., a heavy and well aimed fire came from the Maori position and three of the 40th's skirmishers fell wounded, two mortally. Reinforcements were sent for to evacuate the wounded to the rear. As these men arrived one of them was also wounded along with Lieutenant Rees, the officer in command. Colour Sergeant **John Lucas**, from Carlow, immediately went to his aid and ordered one of the unwounded men to take him to the rear. Lucas then took charge of the remainder and held the position until relieved some time later. Lucas showed great courage and presence of mind at all times during the action and was subsequently awarded the Victoria Cross.

The next Irish VC (gazetted on 16 Januray 1864) was won on 7 September 1863. The 65th (2nd Yorkshire, North Riding) Regiment was in action near the town of Cameron. Captain Swift of that regiment was mortally wounded in a skirmish with a Maori war party. Lance Corporal **John Ryan**, together with Privates Bulford and Talbot, recovered Swift's body and remained with it during the night, therefore preventing any mutilation by the enemy. They spent a long tiresome night surrounded by the war party, but escaped detection. Ryan, originally from Tipperary, drowned three months later, on 29 December, at Tuakan while attempting to rescue a comrade.

Drummer **Dudley Stagpoole**, born in Killunan, County Galway, saw distinguished service with the 57th (West Middlesex) Regiment in New Zealand. On 25 September, while the regiment was in action near Kaipakopako, he was awarded the Distinguished Conduct Medal for the rescue of several wounded men, in spite of being badly wounded himself. On 2 October 1863, at Pontoko, he earned the Victoria Cross when he volunteered to go with an ensign to rescue a wounded soldier. Although under heavy enemy fire from short range, Ensign Down and Drummer Stagpoole succeeded in bringing in the wounded man who had been lying about fifty yards from their positions. On retirement, Stagpoole went to England and died in Herefordshire in 1911.

Assistant Surgeon **William Temple** was attached to the Royal Artillery during the Maori War. On 20 November 1863 an assault was launched on a Maori position at Rangiriri. Temple accompanied the assault and was able to treat wounded men in the very midst of the action, especially in the area of the enemy gate. He and Lieutenant A.F. Pickard exposed themselves to great personal danger by crossing and recrossing the entrance to the Maori keep 'at a point upon which the enemy were concentrating their fire'. Both Pickard and Temple received the Victoria Cross for their courage that day.

Originally from Monaghan town, William Temple died in Tunbridge Wells in 1919.

In April 1864 the Royal Artillery supplied a battery to support an attack on a Maori Pah, or strongpoint, near Tauranga. Assistant Surgeon **William George Nicholas Manley**, from Dublin, volunteered to accompany the storming party into the Pah. He then risked his own life to save those of several wounded men. He attended a mortally wounded naval officer who was carried out from the Pah and then volunteered to return to 'see if he could find any more wounded'. He was one of the last officers to leave the Pah. Manley later became a surgeon general and was appointed a CB. In the Franco-Prussian War of 1870-71 he served with the British Ambulance Corps, treating the wounded of both sides, and was awarded the Prussian Iron Cross (2nd Class), the Bavarian Order of Merit, and the Geneva Cross. He was also a Knight of the Order of Saint John of Jerusalem. Manley died in Cheltenham in 1901.

The following June the 68th (Durham Light Infantry) attacked Maori rifle pits at Tauranga. Sergeant **John Murray**, of Birr, assaulted one pit single-handed and killed or wounded all ten of the occupants. Later in the attack he again fought with extreme bravery and as a result of this was awarded the Victoria Cross. He returned to Ireland and died in Offaly in 1911.

While Sergeant Murray was assaulting one group of Maoris, Captain **Frederick Augustus Smith** of the 43rd (Monmouthshire Light Infantry) was also engaged in a similar attack involving hand-to-hand combat in the rifle pits. Although wounded before reaching the rifle pits, Smith continued to encourage and lead his men throughout the battle, 'setting a fine example' to them. Smith had seen previous service in the Crimea in the ranks of the 1st Regiment, which he had joined in 1849. He exchanged as a captain into the 43rd in 1861 and was later promoted to lieutenant-colonel. A native of Dublin, he died in Duleek, County Meath, in 1887.

Formed in 1858 in the United States, the Fenian Brotherhood, a name derived from the anglicization of Fianna, the ancient war-band of Finn MacCool, had as its aim the independence of Ireland from Britain. The Brotherhood was at its strongest during the American Civil War, with branches being formed in nearly every Irish regiment on both sides, although meetings were always held in secret.

By 1866 the Brotherhood had organized itself into battalions of the Irish Republican Army,* issued with ex-American Army uniforms and arms. The uniforms were quite often decorated with green stripes to the trousers and green cuffs to the jackets, with an Irish harp adorning the headgear. This

---

* This was the first time that this title was ever used.[15]

army was well-equipped and trained and lacked only cavalry to make it complete. Canada became aware of the threat of invasion in early 1866, and by June had mobilized some 20,000 militia, all volunteers.

On the night of 31 May 1866, General John O'Neill, a Civil War veteran, led an IRA force of 800 men across the Niagara River into Canada. He was met on 2 June by a Canadian force of 850 men, commanded by Lieutenant Colonel Alfred Booker, at the town of Ridgeway. After a brief skirmish, in which the Canadians were thrown back, O'Neill advanced to Fort Erie where further skirmishing took place. However, with the arrival of British reinforcements, O'Neill retreated back across the border.[16]

One of the units coming to Booker's aid was 1st Battalion, Rifle Brigade, in which Rifleman **Timothy O'Hea**, from Bantry, County Cork, was serving. On the evening of 9 June 1866 the battalion was travelling on a troop train along the Grand Trunk Railway between Quebec and Montreal when an alarm was raised: a fire had broken out in a wagon containing almost a ton of ammunition. When the train was stopped at Danville Station, the fire was burning fiercely. The burning wagon was disconnected and while 'the sergeant in charge was considering what to do, Rifleman O'Hea took the keys from his hand, rushed to the [burning] car, opened it and called for water and a ladder'. The blaze was extinguished, thanks to O'Hea's quick thinking. For his actions at Danville, Timothy O'Hea was awarded the Victoria Cross. His was the first Cross to be awarded for bravery other than in the face of an enemy.

After his military service O'Hea went to New Zealand where he served in the police force for a time. In June 1874, he arrived in Australia, where he joined up with a group who were to search the desert of Western Queensland for a supposed survivor of the 1848 Leichardt expedition. With Andrew Hume and Lewis Thompson, Timothy O'Hea went into the desert of south-western Queensland in November 1874. It was the last anyone ever saw of him. O'Hea and Hume died of thirst some fifty miles west of the Wilson River, leaving Thompson to stagger back to civilization.

A year after Timothy O'Hea won his Victoria Cross, three Irishmen won the decoration in unusual circumstances. In May 1867 troops of the 24th (2nd Warwickshire) Regiment were sent by steamer from Rangoon, in Burma, to the island of Little Andaman in the Bay of Bengal. Their task was to ascertain the fate of members of the crew of the ship *Assam Valley*. When that vessel had put in at the island earlier, some of the crew had gone on shore and were not seen again. It was believed that they 'must have been set upon and murdered' by the islanders.

On 7 May a party of the 24th landed on Little Andaman and were attacked by the inhabitants, thus confirming the fate of the crew members from *Assam Valley*. At much the same time a storm blew up 'and turned the surf into a raging sea'. Those soldiers on shore were now in very great peril. Realizing this, Assistant Surgeon Douglas and four men of the 24th volunteered for a rescue mission. Manning a gig, the five made for the shore but their boat began to fill with water and they were forced to return. A second attempt was made and this was successful: the gig reached the shore, five men were taken off and brought to safety on board the steamer. Thereupon Douglas and his party made a further trip through the raging sea to rescue the remainder of the shore party. As a result of this, all five were awarded the Victoria Cross. Three of the five were Irish: Private **David Bell** from County Down, Private **Thomas Murphy** from Dublin and Private **William Griffiths** from Roscommon. Bell died in England in 1920 while Murphy went to live in America, dying in 1900. William Griffiths did not survive his military service; he was killed by the Zulus at the battle of Isandhlwana on 22 January 1879.

The *London Gazette* praised the rescuers, stating that Douglas accomplished his trips through the surf 'by no ordinary exertion': 'He stood in the bows of the boat and worked her in an intrepid and seamanlike manner, cool to a degree. The four privates behaved in an equally cool and collected manner, rowing through the roughest surf when the slightest hesitation or want of pluck would have been attended with the gravest results. Their bravery and devotion were the means of saving seventeen men from an awful fate.'[17]

In November 1879, on the eastern frontier of India, Captain **Richard Kirby Ridgeway** of the Bengal Staff Corps, but serving with 44th Gurkha Rifles, was awarded the Victoria Cross for his actions during the attack on Konoma. This village had been made into a fortress by the defenders and during the assault Ridgeway tore at the barricades with his bare hands in an attempt to gain entry. During this time he received a severe gunshot wound to the shoulder, but his leadership and courage was mainly responsible for a successful attack. Ridgeway was a native of Oldcastle, County Meath. Colonel Ridgeway retired from the army in 1906 and died at Harrogate in Yorkshire on 11 October 1924. He was cremated four days later at Lawnswood crematorium in Leeds and his ashes were scattered in the cemetery copse. There is no known memorial to him.

Fenton John Aylmer, a Royal Engineers officer, won the Victoria Cross on the North-West Frontier in the Hunza campaign of 1891. Hunza was a state on the north-west tip of Kashmir, which paid an annual tribute to Kashmir. Together with Nagar, also in the same area, Hunza's leader – the Thum was the title used by both leaders – regarded himself as being outside the jurisdiction of any supreme ruler, such was the inaccessibility of the region. Unfortunately for them, Britain was concerned with the possibility of Russian expansion and sought to secure the border area. In 1889, the Gilgit Agency was established and Colonel A.G.A. Durand, the agent, secured an agreement with both thums, in return for an annual subsidy to be paid by the British and Kashmiri governments, that Hunza and Nagar would cease their practice of raiding.[18]

The agreement did not last long. In order to secure the border, better communications were vital and construction of a road began. Both Hunza and Nagar regarded this road-building programme as an attack on their independence, which was based on the isolated nature of the region, and the two tribes began attacking the construction parties. Retaliation was soon forthcoming: Durand led a punitive expedition of some 1,000 soldiers, the bulk of whom were Kashmiri, and captured the fort at Nilt on 2 December, the day after the campaign began.[19] It was during this operation that Aylmer won his VC.

Nilt fort stood on a ledge overlooking Nilt nullah and was protected by a precipice and an abattis, a thick fence of cut branches. Since the mountain guns of the expedition could not be brought to bear on the fort, it was decided to take it by storm. Aylmer's engineers, supported by a hundred Gurkha soldiers under Lieutenants Boisragon and Badcock were assigned the task. The Gurkhas hacked at the abattis with their kukris to make an entrance through which Aylmer, Boisragon – who was also to win the VC – and Badcock passed to force the gate of the outer wall. Under heavy fire Aylmer went forward to place a guncotton charge against the main gate and was shot in the leg as he lit the fuse. He retreated to await the explosion but the guncotton failed to explode. Aylmer went forward again to relight the fuse. This time he was severely injured by a rock that was dropped on him from the fort but the charge exploded and the Gurkhas dashed into the fort. After desperate close-quarter combat the defenders were driven out of the fort.[20]

In spite of his injuries, Aylmer took part in the fighting and killed several enemy soldiers before he passed out through loss of blood. He survived the brief campaign and later rose to the rank of lieutenant-general. Although he was born in Hastings, Sussex, he was the heir to an Irish baronetcy and is remembered by a memorial in Kilcock Church in County Kildare.

By the end of the month both states had been pacified and Safdar Ali Khan, Thum of Hunza, had fled to China. His half-brother, Nazim Khan, took his place. The Thum of Nagar, Zafar Khan, was permitted to remain on his throne.[21]

Lieutenant **Edmund William Costello**, of the 22nd Punjab Regiment, won the last Irish VC in India of the nineteenth century at Malakand on 26 July 1897. Costello, a former Stonyhurst pupil, had been born in India of an 'old and distinguished Irish family'. His parents were Colonel Charles Peter Costello, Indian Medical Service, and Mrs Bessie Costello (*née* Harkan). Commissioned into the West Yorkshire Regiment in 1892, he subsequently transferred to the Indian Army and 22nd Punjab Regiment.[22]

In 1897 Costello was attached to 24th Punjabis at Malakand on the North-West Frontier. The Malakand pass was vital to the defence of the frontier region. In 1895 the British outpost at Chitral in the Hindu Kush mountains had been besieged by hostile tribesmen and a relief operation had been mounted. Subsequently the policy of forward defence led to the extension of the British presence into the Swat valley, north of Peshawar, and the establishment of fortified camps at the Chakdara and Malakand passes.[23]

In 1897 the Malakand post was garrisoned by three infantry battalions, supported by a mountain battery of Indian Artillery, with a sapper company and medical and commissariat staff. The atmosphere in the area was uneasy and there was considerable tension that was exacerbated by the presence of many fakirs and mullahs who were hostile to the British. Even so, the rising that broke out in the Swat valley that July did so suddenly and without real warning.[24]

On 26 July there were reports that a 'Mad Fakir' was moving through the valley and preaching jihad, or holy war, against the infidels. It was reported that 'he claimed to be invisible at night; he promised immortality to those who might be killed in the [jihad] and he told his followers that on the outbreak of war a mighty army would descend from the clouds and secure victory'.[25]

The war began that very day. The 'Mad Fakir' and his followers were advancing towards Malakand. The brigade commander made his dispositions, troops were sent out to try to cut off the 'Mad Fakir's' advance, reinforcements were sent for and defensive positions were taken up at Malakand. The attempt to intercept the advance was successful; the attacking tribesmen were denied the opportunity to strike at Malakand's most vulnerable area, the southern side of the post. Instead the Swati tribesmen took to the hills to descend on the camps within the perimeter covered by the forts at Malakand.[26]

Lieutenant Costello was commanding a company of 24th Punjabis in the crater camp where the attack began at 10 o'clock that night. Between the crater camp and the bazaar lay a soccer pitch, which became a battleground as the Swatis took possession of the bazaar and were then attacked by a company of 24th Punjabis who forced them out at bayonet point. Although the Punjabis held the bazaar for almost an hour they were forced to withdraw into an inner defensive line within the crater camp.[27]

So many casualties had occurred that Costello and his men set up a new enclosure to protect the injured, the hospital having been within the crater area. By midnight this was one of three distinct defensive areas within the Malakand central camp; the others were the engineers' and commissariat park and the cup of the crater itself. Battle raged for three hours and the tide of action ebbed back and forth.[28]

At about one o'clock Costello's company was lining the crater's eastern face when cries for help were heard during a lull in the battle. A wounded lance-havildar (lance-sergeant) was lying some fifty yards away on the soccer pitch, having been left for dead by the enemy who had given him three deep sword cuts in an earlier attack on the bazaar. The ground on which the havildar lay was swept by crossfire from both sides and dominated by enemy swordsmen. In spite of this, Costello, accompanied by two Indian soldiers, left the comparative safety of his position and worked their way to the injured man under cover of the darkness. The three reached the wounded man and were able to bring him back to the safety of the hospital area. 'It was an act of great bravery and leadership. It demonstrated the strength of loyalty that exists between soldiers, regardless of rank, and was undertaken in the highest traditions of a great regiment.'[29]

The fighting continued for several days, through the day of *Jumarat*, 29 July, on which the prophet was believed to watch over with special interest those of his followers who died for the faith. It was the day on which the 'Mad Fakir' promised victory. Twice during the fighting, Costello was seriously wounded; either of his wounds could have proved fatal but he survived. At much the same time as Costello received his second wound on 29 July, the 'Mad Fakir' was hit and the attack collapsed.[30]

With the Fakir's departure the spirit went out of the attackers and the most dangerous part of the Swat uprising had passed. Thereafter steps were taken to ensure that the area was brought back under control and the Malakand Field Force was despatched to secure the Malakand and Chakdara passes before moving into the Swat valley.[31]

In his subsequent despatch on the operations Brigadier-General Meiklejohn made special reference to the work carried out by Lieutenant Edmund Costello and recommended that he be awarded the Victoria Cross. On 9 November 1897 the *London Gazette* carried the announcement of the award and Costello received the Cross from Queen Victoria at Windsor Castle on 2 December 1897.[32]

Costello was also the first of seven former pupils of Stonyhurst College to win the Victoria Cross. Of the seven, five were Irish, either born in Ireland or born of Irish parents in Britain or India. Costello lived until 1949, during which time the other six Stonyhurst VCs were won. He rose to the rank of brigadier-general and, in addition to the Victoria Cross, was awarded the Order of Saint Michael and Saint George, the Royal Victorian Order, the Distinguished Service Order, the Indian General Service Medal (1895-1902), the Indian General Service Medal (1908-36), the 1914-15 Star, the British War Medal, the Victory Medal and Coronation Medal, 1937. The French government also awarded him the Croix de Guerre (avec palmes). All his medals, except the Coronation Medal, are held by the National Army Museum at Chelsea.

5   The Dark Continent

In 1864 Britain had again become involved in one of her many colonial police actions. At this time Abyssinia was ruled by the self-crowned King Theodore III, who had initially been on friendly terms with Britain and willing and anxious to receive material aid. Theodore sent a British consul, Captain Cameron, to England with a letter of friendship for Queen Victoria. Foreign Office incompetence meant that no reply was sent. Cameron, ignorant of this slight, returned to Abyssinia; and made a visit to Kassala in neighbouring Sudan. This was perceived by Theodore as part of an Anglo-Islamic plot and, coupled with the contempt with which his letter had been treated, caused him to imprison Cameron and all his party, as well as many European missionaries.[1]

In March 1866 Britain sent an envoy to secure Cameron's release. This failed and the envoy was also imprisoned.[2] As a result, gunboat diplomacy was employed. General Sir Robert Napier was given command of an Abyssinian Field Force of 14,214 British and Indian troops, plus their logistic support.[3] One of the regiments involved was the 33rd (Duke of Wellington's) Regiment,* commanded by Colonel **Alexander Dunn** VC. At this time the *Havercakes* – the regimental nickname – contained a large number of Irishmen, so many in fact that the *New York Herald* correspondent† frequently described them in his despatches as the 'Irish Regiment'. Even the commanding officer, Dunn, was of Irish descent, having been born in Canada of Irish parents. He was also the first Canadian-born VC winner.

By early December the Field Force had landed at Annesley Bay, near Massawa, on the Egyptian-controlled Red Sea coast and after many months of effort reached Theodore's capital at Magdala. On 10 April there was a brief skirmish with the enemy, which cost Theodore some 800 killed and 1,500 wounded. The assault on Magdala was launched on the morning of 13 April, Easter Sunday. Eighteen guns and the rockets of the Naval Brigade detachment supplied the preliminary bombardment.[4]

Magdala was situated on a hilltop, with the only approach a steep rock-strewn track, best suited to goats. The town's gates were of heavy wooden timbers flanked by a stone archway and surrounded by sharpened stakes and

* The only British regiment named after a non-royal, in this case the Dublin-born Arthur Wellesley, first duke of Wellington.
† The *New York Herald* correspondent was Henry Morton (later Sir Henry) Stanley, the Welsh explorer and journalist, who later found Livingstone.

thick prickly thorn hedges. The 33rd, in the van of the attack, bypassed the gate and made their way to the right of the main gate. There they climbed the cliff to a ledge just below the thorn hedge in which Private **James Bergin**, from Queen's County, cut a gap with his bayonet. Drummer **Michael Magner**, from Fermanagh, then climbed onto Bergin's shoulders and pushed his way through the gap, turning to pull Bergin after him. Both men then maintained a steady fire on the enemy as other members of the regiment made their way through the enemy defences. When enough men were in position they stormed the gate from the rear, drove off the enemy and opened the gates. The attackers then charged up to an inner gate which was stormed before it could be shut. Within minutes the regimental colour was flying from the parapet. Bergin and Magner were both subsequently decorated with the Victoria Cross. Bergin died in Poona, India, in 1880, while Michael Magner died in Melbourne, Australia, in 1897.

In 1877 the Ninth Cape Frontier War broke out as a result of conflict between two African tribes, the Fingoes, long standing allies of the British, and the Galekas. Both tribes were involved in skirmishing along their respective borders when the British interceded on behalf of the Fingoes. Initially the Government deployed only local forces, the Frontier Armed Mounted Police (FAMP), but it was quickly realized that imperial troops would have to be used.[5] One of the regiments involved was the 94th, later 2nd Battalion, Connaught Rangers. On 29 December the regiment was in action against the Galeka near Komgha. A unit of FAMP was skirmishing to the front of the 94th when they were forced to retreat before a charge of overwhelming numbers. As this happened Major **Hans Garrett Moore**, from Dublin, saw Private Giese of the Mounted Police knocked from his horse. Quickly riding out, Major Moore rode among the tribesmen, using his revolver in an attempt to hold them off until Giese could escape. Unfortunately he was unable to do so and Giese was killed. When Major Moore returned to his own lines it was discovered he had received a severe assegai wound to the arm. His efforts to save Giese gained him the Victoria Cross. The son of Captain Garrett Moore of the 38th Regiment, his mother was Charlotte Butler of Drum, County Tipperary, and the family could claim descent from Rory O'Moore, the Irish chieftain who fought against Henry VIII and forced that Tudor monarch to sign a peace treaty. Hans Garrett Moore returned to Ireland after his Army service and died in Tipperary in 1889.

Greed for land in South Africa led Britain to instigate a war with the Zulus in 1879. Making near-impossible demands and giving little time for the Zulus to respond, the British invaded in January of that year.[6] The invasion force, under Lord Chelmsford, crossed into Zululand in three columns, each widely spaced to begin with, but coming closer each day until they were due to meet at Ulundi, the Zulu capital. This tactic meant they were in a better position to support each other as they neared Ulundi; but it weakened the force prior to a junction and made each column liable to defeat in detail.[7]

At 2 a.m. on 22 January Chelmsford received news that contact had been made with a Zulu force to the east and, two hours later, he led part of the centre column out of the camp at Isandhlwana towards Ulundi. Remaining at Isandhlwana was Colonel Henry Pullein, commanding 1st Battalion 24th (2nd Warwickshire) Regiment. At his disposal were five companies of his own battalion, one of the 2nd, two guns of N Battery, Royal Artillery and four companies of native troops, plus another one hundred Imperial soldiers of supplementary units. The record shows a total of sixty-seven officers and 1,707 other ranks present in the camp. Twelve hours later all that remained at Isandhlwana were the dead as 20,000 Zulus overran the garrison.

As the battle neared its end an attempt was made to save the regimental colour. Lieutenant Teignmouth Melvill, Adjutant of the 1st/24th, was given the responsibility of carrying the flag to safety. As he rode out of the camp he was joined by Lieutenant **Neville Coghill**, a twenty-seven-year-old Irishman from Drumcondra, County Dublin, whose Army service had begun in the Irish Militia. When they reached the Buffalo river, the border with Natal, they found it a raging torrent, but Coghill at once galloped into the water and crossed quickly. Melvill, burdened by the colour, came off his horse in mid stream and clung to a boulder, but lost his grip on the flag, which was swept away. Coghill returned to the river to attempt to rescue his comrade. A shot from a Zulu rifle killed his horse and both men barely managed to swim to the Natal bank. With their backs to a large boulder they made their last stand. When their bodies were found some time later, Melvill's watch had stopped at 2.10 p.m. The spot where they died is known as Fugitives' Drift.

Both men were awarded the Victoria Cross in what are, chronologically, the first official posthumous awards of the medal. Although it had been awarded after death previously, this only occurred when the winner had been told *before* his death that he would be decorated. However, the awards to Coghill and Melvill were not gazetted until 1907, after considerable pressure had been brought on the authorities to recognize the gallantry of the pair. The two men were buried where they fell. Coghill, the eldest son of Sir John Joscelyn Coghill, fourth baronet, and Katherine Frances, second daughter of John third Baron Plunket, is commemorated in Drumcondra Church, while the South African War Graves' Board erected a memorial in Natal in 1974.

The right 'horn' of the Zulu army, 4,500 strong, had been largely unengaged during the battle, with the exception of cutting down some of those survivors who attempted to escape back to Natal. These warriors, determined to 'wash their spears', crossed the Buffalo river and made for the nearest British outpost, the mission station at Rorke's Drift, a supply store on the road to Ulundi, which was defended by B Company, 2nd/24th. Many of the men in the ranks were Irish.

The fight at Rorke's Drift began in the late afternoon and lasted until the early hours of the following day. Of eleven Victoria Crosses awarded for the action, one went to Surgeon Major **James Reynolds** of the Army Hospital Corps, who was also Mentioned in Despatches. Reynolds, a native of Dun Laoghaire, then Kingstown, County Dublin, went on to become a lieutenant colonel and died in Surrey in 1932. His father was a Longford man, the only county in Ireland that does not have a native-born Victoria Cross winner. The citation for Reynolds' VC notes 'his conspicuous bravery during the attack at Rorke's Drift, on Jan 22 and 23, 1879, which he exhibited in his constant attention to the wounded under fire, and by his voluntarily conveying ammunition from the store to the defenders of the hospital, whereby he exposed himself to a cross fire from the enemy both in going and returning'.[8]

Reynolds was buried at Kensal Rise Cemetery in London, the final resting place of a number of VC winners. In 1997 Lieutenant Mike Ryan, the officer commanding an Army Cadet Force detachment affiliated to the Royal Army Medical Corps, discovered Reynolds' grave which, by then, was in a sad state. The headstone was worn and the inscription almost invisible. Ryan set about a project involving his cadets to restore the grave as a fitting tribute to the memory of James Reynolds.

B Company's commander, and the second-in-command of the post at Rorke's Drift, Lieutenant **Gonville Bromhead**, had an Irish mother, although he had been born in Paris. Bromhead also received the Victoria Cross for his 'fine example and conducting himself with great gallantry in most trying circumstances'.[9]

After Isandhlwana, Chelmsford retired to Natal, with the other columns also being forced to withdraw. The right-hand column split, part retiring to Natal, while the remainder encamped at Eshowe which effectively put them in a state of siege. The left-hand column, under Colonel Evelyn Wood VC, had engaged part of the Zulu army at Hlobane on 21 January. In this action the Zulus were defeated, but Wood was forced to break off the fight on hearing the news from Isandhlwana.[10]

In March, Chelmsford led a force into Zululand to relieve the forces trapped at Eshowe and ordered Wood to make a diversionary attack to draw off the Zulus. Wood made his attack on 28 March, again at Hlobane but the attack failed due to a surprise counterattack from unexpected Zulu reinforcements.[11] In the confusion of this battle two more Irish Victoria Crosses were won. Private **Edmund Fowler**, a Waterford man, serving in the 90th (Perthshire Light Infantry) was responsible, with several other men, for driving a number of Zulu snipers out of caves on the side of the mountain. Queen Victoria invited him to Windsor and he was decorated there in May 1882.

Although Fowler took his discharge from the Perthshire Light Infantry, he was soon back in uniform. He re-enlisted, this time joining the Royal Irish Regiment and becoming a sergeant in its 1st Battalion. However, in 1882, by which time he was serving with the regiment's 2nd Battalion, Private Fowler was sentenced by court martial to lose all his medals and decorations, including his Victoria Cross. Her Majesty declined to approve of his being deprived of his VC, which was then restored to him, as were his other medals and decorations. Perhaps Queen Victoria felt that it would be unjust to deprive Fowler of his decoration so soon after she had personally bestowed it on him. Fowler seems to have felt less attachment to his VC: in 1906 it was sold at Sotheby's for £42.

Dalkey-born Major **William Knox Leet** was with 1st Battalion, 13th (1st Somersetshire) (Prince Albert's Light Infantry) Regiment during the battle. In the course of the British retreat, Leet saw Lieutenant Smith, of the Frontier Light Horse, fall from his mount. As the Zulus closed in Leet rode into the enemy and, with his pistol, kept them at bay until Smith was able to climb up behind him. Both rode to safety. Leet received his VC from Queen Victoria at Windsor on 9 December 1879. He later commanded 1st Somerset Light Infantry and exchanged to the 2nd Battalion, which he commanded in action in Burma. He retired from the Army in July 1887 and died on 27 June 1898.He is buried at Great Chart in Kent.

In July 1879, Chelmsford had his revenge for Isandhlwana. Leading a force of 5,000 men into Zululand, he advanced on the Zulu capital, his men formed in a large hollow square.[12] Scouting ahead of Chelmsford's force was a detachment of 9th Lancers and some mounted infantry from 1st Battalion, 24th Regiment. As this party was reconnoitring a way across the White Umvolosi river, it was attacked by a Zulu war party. In the mêlée Sergeant Fitzmaurice of the 24th fell to the ground as his horse stumbled. Captain Lord **William Leslie de La Poer Beresford**, on leave from his job as ADC to the Viceroy of India, was with 9th Lancers and at once went to assist. The injured Fitzmaurice took some time to mount up behind Beresford, but the latter kept the Zulus at bay with well-aimed pistol shots and both men reached safety. Beresford, who had been born in Mullaghbrack, County Armagh, was awarded the Victoria Cross. He survived the war and later became a lieutenant colonel. He died at Dorking, Surrey, on 28 December 1900.

The last African Irish VC of 1879 was won by Private **Francis Fitzpatrick** of the 94th Regiment on 28 November, the day an attack was launched on King Sekukuni's capital in the Transvaal.[13] Among the units involved were the 94th and 1st Dragoon Guards. During the attack Private Fitzpatrick along with Private Flawn came across the badly wounded Lieutenant Dewar of the 1st Dragoons being carried from the field by a party of native stretcher-bearers. Suddenly about thirty of the enemy appeared some forty yards away, whereupon the stretcher-bearers fled. Fitzpatrick and Flawn at once picked up the wounded lieutenant and, alternately carrying him and turning to fire at the pursuing enemy, managed to return to the main force. Both men were awarded the Victoria Cross. Fitzpatrick, born in Tullycorbet, County Monaghan, returned to Ireland after his military service and died on 10 July 1933.

The Transvaal, or First Boer, War began on 16 December 1880 and within days hostilities against the scattered British garrisons began. The first of these was the besieging of two companies of the 2nd Battalion, 21st (Royal Scots Fusiliers) Regiment at the small town of Potchefstroom. Responsibility for restoring order was given to Sir George Pomeroy-Colley, the commander of troops in Natal and the Transvaal. The first in a series of British disasters occurred on 20 December 1880, when a commando of some two hundred Boers attacked a column of the 94th Regiment between Lydenburg and Pretoria. In an action lasting no more than fifteen minutes the 94th were destroyed by Boer marksmanship; the survivors were ordered to surrender by their commander, Lieutenant Colonel Anstruther, who later died of his wounds.[14]

Colley gathered a force of 1,200 men to march into the Transvaal and relieve the besieged outposts. When, on 28 January 1881 he found his advance blocked by a force of 2,000 Boers at a hill called Laing's Nek, Colley decided to make a frontal attack which was easily beaten off by the Boer riflemen. This also the last occasion when a British battalion, the 58th (Rutlandshire) Regiment, carried their colours into action. Colley would lose again at Majuba Hill on 27 February in a battle that cost him his life. A truce was declared on 6 March and peace terms were concluded on 21 March.[15]

The Victoria Cross was awarded to three Irishmen in this war. The first two were awarded to Trooper **John Danaher**, of Nourse's (Transvaal) Horse, and Lance Corporal **James Murray** of the 2nd Battalion, 88th (Connaught Rangers) Regiment on 16 January 1881. Danaher's unit, in conjunction with the Connaughts and Royal Scots Fusiliers was engaged with a Boer force at Elandsfontein. When a private of the Scots Fusiliers was observed lying wounded in front of the Boer positions, Danaher and Murray advanced some five hundred yards over open ground to rescue the wounded man and bring him back to the British lines. Danaher, a native of Limerick, was later promoted to sergeant. He returned to Ireland after his military service and died on 9 January 1919. Murray, a Corkman, also returned to Ireland and died in Dublin on 19 July 1942. Twelve days later the third Irish VC was awarded. Private **John Doogan** serving in the ranks of 1st King's Dragoon Guards took part in a cavalry charge at Laing's Nek on 28 January 1881.[16] Doogan was batman to Major Brownlow, and when that officer's horse was shot from under him the Irishman at once rode to his rescue. Despite being severely wounded himself, Doogan dismounted, helped Brownlow into the saddle, and the pair made their escape. As they rode away from the Boers, Doogan received another wound but managed to reach safety. John Doogan, who had been born in County Galway in 1853, survived the war in South Africa and died in Folkestone, England, in 1940, aged eighty-seven.

His VC was bequeathed to his old regiment but appears to have been lost after being lent out by the regiment.

The next Irish VCs in Africa were won far to the north in the closing years of the century in what had been the Turkish province of Sudan. In August 1881 a boatbuilder's apprentice called Mohammed Ahmed, a devout Muslim who had become a religious teacher, issued a proclamation that he would free the oppressed people of Sudan from the yoke of Turkish rule. The 'Mahdi', or guide, as he was called by his followers, declared that he would then establish true Islam throughout the world, starting with Egypt.[17]

The Mahdi quickly overran Turkish garrisons in Sudan and the Turkish viceroy in Egypt appealed for British help. Gladstone was reluctant to go to Turkey's assistance as he wanted to pull British troops out of Egypt, except for a small garrison in Alexandria. He advised the evacuation of Sudan and sent out General Charles 'Chinese' Gordon to organize the withdrawal. Unfortunately, Gordon managed to get himself trapped in Khartoum and pressure grew for a British force to be sent to his rescue.[18]

Inevitably a British force was despatched to Gordon's aid but it was too late, as the general was killed in Khartoum. Nonetheless British forces were now committed to a campaign in the region against Osman Digna (Uthman Diqna), a capable Sudanese commander, but this was ended in March 1885 when Gladstone ordered a withdrawal. Three months later the Mahdi died and Khalifa Abdullah el-Taaishi assumed his mantle. The Khalifa claimed that the Mahdi's dying wish, to be considered an order, was for an invasion of Egypt. This was fought off and the Khalifa's men remained relatively quiet, save for some border skirmishes, for the next decade.[19]

In 1896 the Italians tried to invade Abyssinia from Eritrea but were decisively defeated at the battle of Adowa. Concern mounted in Cairo and London that this might encourage the Khalifa to mount an invasion of Egypt, or seize the Sudanese port of Suakin. To prevent any such move by the Khalifa,

London readily agreed to an Italian request for a diversionary operation on the Nile that would ease pressure on their outpost at Kassala, on the Eritrean–Sudanese border. A force under the Kerry-born General Herbert Kitchener was despatched in June with orders to reclaim the province of Dongola.[20]

This expedition was successful and Kitchener began preparations for further operations, although the government refused to provide funds or troops for such operations until the end of 1897. In April 1898 the Khalifa's army suffered defeat near Berber on the Atbara river. However, the Khalifa was not present himself. He was waiting at Omdurman, across the Nile from Khartoum. And it was towards Khartoum that Kitchener then directed his force.[21]

The two armies met at Omdurman on 2 September when the Khalifa launched his troops against the British in the dawn's early light. Against the disciplined rifle fire – still known as musketry – of the British infantry, and the devastating steel hail of their machine guns, the poorly-equipped Dervish soldiers had little chance. One correspondent described the result as an 'execution' rather than a battle. Defeated in their efforts to reach the British infantry, the Dervishes turned their attention to Kitchener's right flank, which was manned by Egyptian troops. As they did so, the British troops began to advance from their positions. In the van was the cavalry and leading them were the 21st Lancers.[22]

The regiment moved at the walk with its forward patrols some distance ahead. As one patrol passed Surgham, they discovered a body of some 700 blue-clad Dervishes crouched close to a shallow dry watercourse. Colonel Rowland Hill Martin, the commanding officer, wheeled the 21st to the left to bring them up on the flank, but as the cavalry crossed the front of the Dervishes, they opened a rapid fire, which brought down several lancers.

The order 'Right wheel into line' sounded from the regimental trumpeter and Martin led sixteen troops in extended line, with lances levelled, against the tribesmen. The distance between them was only about two hundred yards and, given the odds, it seemed that the Dervishes would simply be ridden down. But the situation was not quite what it seemed to be. As the Lancers reached the midway point of their charge, Martin saw that he had been fooled. His men were not riding towards a shallow depression holding a few riflemen but a deep twenty-feet-wide gully packed from end to end with 2,000 white-clad spear and swordsmen. It was too late to stop; at full gallop the 300 met the 2,000. In the initial impact some thirty lancers and two hundred Dervishes were toppled over. As the remaining cavalrymen struggled to stay in the saddle the Dervishes, commanded by Osman Digna, were everywhere, hamstringing horses, cutting at reins and stirrups. The Lancers fought back with sword and lance, all the time trying to stay in the saddle: to be unhorsed was certain death. One of those who was unhorsed owed his life to a stocky, red haired, ex-farmer from Dublin. Trooper **Thomas Byrne** of A Squadron saw Lieutenant the Honourable R.F. Molyneux fall to be immediately surrounded by the enemy. Although severely wounded, Byrne managed to turn his horse in the whirling throng and make his way back to the fallen officer. In the ensuing mêlée Byrne was again wounded, but managed to get Molyneux up behind him and ride on through the mass of warriors to reform with those of the regiment who had made it to the other side. Winston Churchill, who was experiencing his first battle, was riding with 21st Lancers as a war correspondent and described Trooper Byrne's rescue as the bravest act he had ever seen. Byrne was awarded the Victoria Cross.

The cost to 21st Lancers had been dear. From a regimental strength of 300, five officers, sixty-five men and 119 horses had been killed or wounded. The Dervishes had lost only thirty dead and about one hundred wounded. There was no thought of a second charge; the regiment had gained three Victoria Crosses in as many minutes, had proved there was no lack of courage or discipline in its ranks, but had failed in its original objective, a thorough reconnaissance of the ground towards Omdurman. But the Khalifa's army had been defeated in detail and he himself was on the run. Fourteen months later he was tracked down and killed at Kordofan.[23]

Thomas Byrne survived the war and on retirement went to live with his wife, Bridget, in Canterbury, Kent, where he died on 14 March 1944 at the age of seventy-eight. He had begun his military career in the 8th (King's Royal Irish) Hussars and when he finally retired from the Army he had an impressive collection of medals to show for his service. These included the Victoria Cross, the Queen's Sudan Medal 1896-97, the Queen's South Africa Medal with clasps Cape Colony, Orange Free State and Transvaal, the British War Medal 1914-18, the Long Service and Good Conduct Medal, the Jubilee Medal 1935, George VI Coronation Medal 1936, and the Khedive's Sudan Medal 1896-98 with clasp Khartoum. His original VC was stolen and an official replacement was issued after his death. His medals were sold at Spinks in November 1996 for £9,800.

One of the other two VCs won by 21st Lancers that day went to another Irishman, Captain **Paul Aloysius Kenna**, the second son of James Kenna of Ballinakill House, County Meath. Born at Oakfield House, Lancaster, Kenna was educated at Stonyhurst College and then served as a lieutenant in a militia battalion before entering the Royal Military College, Sandhurst in 1884. After commissioning he served in the West India Regiment and transferred to 21st Hussars in 1889. He served with the regiment in India until 1895 when he returned to Ireland. In that year he received the Royal Humane

Society's testimonial on vellum for saving the life of a man who jumped into the river Liffey near O'Connell (then Carlisle) Bridge.[24]

The following year, Kenna's regiment arrived in Egypt and on 2 July received orders to become part of Kitchener's expedition.[25] By the time of the battle of Omdurman the regiment's title had been changed from 21st Hussars to 21st Lancers.* Kenna took part in the same charge as Thomas Byrne and earned his Victoria Cross in similar circumstances. Lieutenant de Montmorency had turned back to recover the dead body of Lieutenant Grenfell. However, his horse bolted when de Montmorency lifted the corpse on to the animal. The unfortunate de Montmorency found himself on foot, cut off in the midst of hordes of Dervishes; he was armed only with a revolver. Kenna saw his plight and, with Corporal Swarbrick, fought through the mass of enemy to reach their comrade. Swarbrick caught the frightened horse and brought it back to its master who remounted as Kenna fought off the Dervishes. All three men fought their way to safety. Kenna had earlier gone to the aid of Major Crole Wyndham whose horse had been shot, leaving its rider alone in the midst of screaming Dervishes.[26]

Paul Kenna later commanded 21st Lancers. He fought in the Boer War, where he earned the DSO as well as being twice Mentioned in Despatches. By a quirk of circumstances – he was taking part in a riding exhibition in Brussels when the Great War broke out – he received the 1914-15 Star with August-November Bar. Brigadier-General Paul Kenna was killed at Gallipoli on 30 August 1915 and is buried at Lala Baba cemetery, Suvla Bay. His VC is held by the Queen's Royal Lancers, the modern successor regiment of the 21st Lancers.[27]

The discovery of gold in the Transvaal in 1886 was to lead to another war against the Boers. Lured by that gold, many fortune-seekers made their way to the Transvaal; large numbers of these newcomers were British. Such an invasion of gold-hunters was resented by the Boers and friction between them and the *Uitlanders* increased to the point where the Boers restricted the legal rights of the newcomers. In turn some of the *Uitlanders* planned to overturn the Boer government and this led to the Jameson Raid of 1896, in reprisal for which the Boers imposed further restrictions on the *Uitlanders*.[28]

The ingredients for outright strife were all present and the spark was applied to the powder keg when a Boer policeman killed an *Uitlander* in dubious circumstances and was acquitted by the courts. A petition was sent to the Queen from the *Uitlanders*, asking that Transvaal be brought back under full

---

* It had begun life as 21st Light Dragoons in 1759 but had been disbanded after Waterloo. In 1862 the regiment was reborn in India out of 3rd Bengal European Cavalry.

British control. The high commissioner in South Africa was told to approach the Boers, who, angered by the British attitude, declared war on 11 October 1899.[29]

This conflict was not to be short-lived and it stretched the British Army to the limit, compelling the government to call upon the militia to relieve regular units for service in South Africa and to ask the dominions to assist by sending troops to South Africa. The war lasted until May 1902 and during those years the tiny Boer republic, with a population of about 100,000, challenged the might of the greatest empire the world has ever seen and did so with remarkable success.[30]

When war began in October 1899 there were fewer than 22,000 British troops in South Africa and this gave the Boers an initial advantage in numbers. Realizing that British reinforcements were on the way, the Boers were not slow to exploit their numerical advantage and invaded Natal, repulsing the subsequent British counter-offensive, commanded by Sir George White VC, who was forced to retire to his advanced base at Ladysmith, where he was besieged by the Boers.[31] Not until February 1900 would Ladysmith be relieved, after three attempts to do so had failed.

Also under siege within days of the outbreak of war were Mafeking and Kimberley, on the western border of the Orange Free State.[32] On 14 October 1899 an armoured train left Mafeking on the western railway for Kimberley. Shortly afterwards it was ambushed and a relief force was sent out to effect a rescue. This force consisted of a squadron of the Protectorate Regiment, partly-trained men with no experience in action, commanded by Captain FitzClarence. **Charles FitzClarence** was born at Bishopscourt, County Kildare, on 8 May 1865 and had been commissioned into the Royal Fusiliers in November 1886, subsequently serving with the regiment in South Africa. For the men under FitzClarence this was to be their first time in action. When the squadron arrived at the train it found itself greatly outnumbered and in danger of being either beaten off or captured. FitzClarence exhibited such efficiency in the deployment of his troops that not only were the Boers forced to break off the action but they were also forced from the field, leaving behind fifty dead and many wounded. Two weeks later, on the night of 27 October, Captain FitzClarence led his men out of Mafeking on a raid against the Boer trenches. For the next two hours there was fierce hand-to-hand fighting before the enemy were driven out with heavy losses. When the British returned to the town just before dawn their casualties were six killed and fifteen wounded. On 26 December FitzClarence was severely wounded in action at the Game Tree position near Mafeking. He was recommended for the Victoria Cross, which was gazetted on 6 July 1900 and presented by Earl Roberts VC on Church Square, Pretoria on 25 October of that year.

On 12 November 1914 Brigadier-General Charles FitzClarence was killed in action at Polygon Wood, Zonnebeke, Belgium, on 12 November 1914 while commanding 1 Guards Brigade during the first battle of Ypres. He has no known grave but is commemorated on the Menin Gate Memorial. On 8 February 1990 his medals were sold by Sotheby's to a regular VC purchaser for £38,000.

Captain **Robert Johnston** was awarded the Victoria Cross for his actions in the cavalry charge at Elandslaagte on 21 October 1899, one of four VCs gained that day. This action was part of Sir George White's response to the Boer attacks on the area known as the Natal Wedge. White, an Irishman recently arrived from India, ordered fellow Irishman Major-General Johnnie French, later Lord French of Ypres, to attack the Boers at Elandslaagte. French did so in a surprise dawn attack, forcing the Boers to withdraw to Hog's Back Ridge.[33]

French's attacking force included D Squadron, 5th Royal Irish Lancers, a squadron of 5th Dragoon Guards and a detachment of Imperial Light Horse, Captain Johnston's unit. Johnston and another Imperial Light Horse officer, Captain Charles Herbert Mullins, 'at a most critical moment of the advance, when the attack had been checked by very severe fire at point-blank range, … rushed forward and rallied their men, thus enabling the flanking movement which decided the day to be carried out. Captain Mullins was wounded in this action.'[34]

The leadership shown by the two officers had been most important in steadying the men under their command. Johnston's VC was gazetted on 12 February 1901, three weeks after the death of Queen Victoria, and he was decorated by King Edward VII at Saint James's Palace on 25 July. Johnston had been born at Laputa House, Ballyshannon, County Donegal, on 13 August 1872. Surviving the war in South Africa, he was commandant of a concentration camp at Middleburg in 1902 and district commissioner in the Eastern Transvaal from 1903 to 1911, after which he returned to Ireland and joined the prison service. He died in County Kilkenny on 25 March 1950. Johnston was an Irish international rugby player and one of three VC winners who played for the Dublin club Wanderers RFC.

Among the early reinforcements to reach South Africa from Britain was a corps under General Redvers Buller, which included three infantry and one cavalry divisions. Buller arrived at Cape Town on 31 October, in time to hear the news of the withdrawal to Ladysmith, which had happened only hours before, and set about making operational plans for his troops. Among these plans was the relief of Ladysmith.[35]

Buller himself led the expedition to relieve Ladysmith. But he met the Boers at Colenso on the Tugela river on 15 December and his attack was repulsed. In that same week, two other British forces had been defeated – an attempt to relieve Kimberley and another to prevent Boer forces striking out from the southern Orange Free State. This series of defeats led to that December week becoming known as 'Black Week'.[36]

At Colenso the attack consisted of three distinct phases. On the left flank, Major-General Hart's Irish Brigade advanced towards the Bridle Drift: they were to cross the river and take the Boers in the flank. On the right, Colonel the Lord Dundonald would advance with his brigade of mounted infantry and seize Mount Hlangwane. In the centre, Major General Hildyard's 2 Infantry Brigade would deliver the main attack. This force was to have support from artillery under Colonel C.J. Long, Royal Field Artillery but, instead of waiting for the infantry, Long galloped forward leading the six guns of 14 Battery, a further six of 66 Battery and six naval 12-pounders.

As the twelve 15-pounders unlimbered at a range of one thousand yards from the hidden Boer positions, the naval guns, pulled by oxen, had fallen about six hundred yards behind. When the Boer artillery and small arms opened fire, the naval guns, at extreme range from the enemy suffered few casualties. The same cannot be said for the two 15-pounder batteries; they found themselves in the main zone of fire, a killing ground in which both horses and gunners fell with monotonous regularity. One of the first to fall was Long, shot through the lung.

Within a short time one third of the detachments were down and the survivors were forced back into the shelter of a small rocky hollow, leaving the twelve guns abandoned to enemy fire. In the meantime the naval guns had unlimbered and were returning fire. Later in the day Buller rode up the sheltering gunners and asked for volunteers to try to rescue the guns. One of those who volunteered was Corporal **George Edward Nurse** of 66 Battery. Nurse, who had been born in Enniskillen, County Fermanagh, on 14 April 1873, enlisted in the Royal Artillery in January 1892. His birth in Fermanagh appears to be his sole connection with Ireland as his parents were Channel Islanders and returned to Guernsey soon after George was born.

As Corporal Nurse and six other men prepared for the rescue attempt they were joined by three officers from Buller's staff to make up the numbers, one of whom was Lieutenant Freddy Roberts, son of Lord Roberts of Kandahar and Waterford. With the necessary number of men available, two teams were assembled and set off at a canter for the abandoned guns. Through a storm of fire they made it to the battery position and, after a few short minutes, both teams managed to hook up to a gun and made it back to shelter, but not without loss: Lieutenant Roberts was mortally wounded.

A second attempt was made, but was brought to a standstill by the weight of enemy fire. A third attempt, by a team from 7 Battery, which had been supporting Dundonald's attack on the right also failed, but resulted in a second Irish VC being awarded. Captain **Hamilton Lyster Reed** had been born in Dublin on 23 May 1869 and was serving in 7 Battery. His attempt to rescue three of the guns resulted in the loss of twenty horses, one man killed and thirteen wounded, Reed himself suffering a severe gunshot wound.

After this Buller refused to sanction any further attempts to recover the guns and they were left to the Boers who removed them after the battle. All that remained to be done was to withdraw the troops and recover the wounded, a task which was carried out by some two thousand volunteer stretcher-bearers. Eight hundred of these were members of Natal's Indian community and were led by a 28-year-old barrister who would become more famous than all the soldiers who fought in Africa. His name was Mohandas K. Gandhi, later known as the Mahatma Gandhi.

Nurse's VC was gazetted on 2 February 1900 and he was decorated by Buller at Ladysmith on 18 March. He was commissioned during the Great War. His grandson, Staff-Sergeant Charles George Colenso Nurse, was serving in the Royal Signals when that Corps mounted guard on Buckingham Palace in February 1973. A great-grandson, Bombardier Stuart Colenso Nurse, served in the Royal Artillery in the Gulf War of 1991.

Reed's VC was also presented to him by Buller on 18 March 1900. He had been gazetted on the same day as Nurse. Hamilton Lyster Reed was also Mentioned in Despatches three times during the war. The only son of Sir Andrew Reed KCB, CVO, Inspector-General of the Royal Irish Constabulary, Reed achieved the rank of lieutenant-colonel before retiring from the Army. He died in London on 7 March 1931. On 29 May 1940, the *Daily Mirror* reported the death in action of his son, twenty-year-old Andrew Patrick Reed, Royal Ulster Rifles and Flying Officer, RAF.

A third VC of that action at Colenso can be claimed as Irish and was a posthumous award. The Honourable **Frederick Roberts** was the son of Lord Roberts of Kandahar and Waterford. Although born in India, Roberts was of Irish stock. His VC was significant in that it created the official precedent for further posthumous awards. Although there had been previous instances of the Cross being awarded *after* the death of the winner, it was held that this had happened only when the individual concerned had been told that he was to receive the VC. Roberts was killed in action and is thus, officially, the first posthumous VC for whom the recommendation was made after his death. The Cross was posted to Lady Roberts by Queen Victoria who included a note stating that 'here is something that I have tied up with my own hands'. Freddy Roberts' headstone bears the inscription: *Blessed are the pure in heart for they shall see God.* Lord Roberts' grandson, Lieutenant F.R.A. Lewin of the Irish Guards, was also killed in action – in France in 1940 while serving with his regiment, of which Roberts was the first Colonel.

Robert Scott was born in Haslingden, Lancashire, on 4 June 1874. His father had left the family home at Ballinran, County Down, to work in the cotton mills in England. Having secured a job he brought over his wife and eight children to live in Haslingden and Robert was born shortly afterwards. He followed his father into the cotton mill for a time until, on 2 February 1895, he joined the Manchester Regiment with whom he continued to serve for the next 28 years, until his discharge on 2 February 1923.

During the siege of Ladysmith Private Scott and two other soldiers occupied a sangar on the position known as Caesar's Camp on the town perimeter. On 2 January 1900 they were attacked by a strong Boer force and within a short time all the officers were either killed or wounded. For the next sixteen hours, without food or water, Scott and his comrades held their position. They were relieved at 7 o'clock next evening.

Robert Scott was wounded during this action; but after receiving hospital treatment he returned to duty and continued to serve through the next four months of the siege without once being absent from duty. On 26 July 1901 the *London Gazette* announced the award of the Victoria Cross to Private Robert Scott. During the First World War he served with the Manchesters as a quartermaster sergeant. On discharge he returned home to Ballinran and worked as a clerk with the Ulster Special Constabulary, stationed in Newtownards. A post with the civil service followed this until he retired aged sixty-five. When the Second World War broke out, Scott lied about his age and managed to enlist in the Royal Air Force. He served on the embarkation staff until after D-Day.

Four days after Scott earned his VC, there was a brisk and bitter engagement at Waggon Hill, near Ladysmith, in which three VCs were gained. One of these was won by Lieutenant **James Edward Ignatius Masterson** of 1st Devonshire Regiment, who had joined the Army as a private in Princess Victoria's (Royal Irish Fusiliers) at Armagh in 1881. A descendant of the Sergeant Masterson of the 87th (Prince of Wales's Irish) Regiment who had captured the first French Eagle to be taken in battle by the British Army at Barrosa on 5 March 1811, the later Masterson has not hitherto been acknowledged as Irish. However, his christian names and education – by the Marists – as well as his choice of regiment, all point to his having been Irish-born; there is no evidence to suggest otherwise.*

During this engagement Trooper Herman Albrecht, Imperial Light Horse, and Lieutenant Robert James Thomas Digby Jones, Royal Engineers, were outstanding in the close-quarter struggle that followed the re-occupation of

---

* Neither the Lummis Files nor the *Register of the Victoria Cross* indicate a place of birth for Masterson. The family came originally from County Roscommon.

the top of Waggon Hill. The pair had led the assaulting force that arrived at the summit just as the Boers reached it. Jones shot the Boer leader and Albrecht brought down the next two. It was the prelude to a murderous battle in which Masterson, although shot in both thighs, displayed great courage and leadership. The Devons, who had been held in reserve, charged and captured a ridge that the Boers had held.

> No sooner were they installed there than they were swept by a terrific fire from the right and left front. Rather than abandon the ground they had taken, Lieutenant Masterson volunteered to carry a message to the Imperial Light Horse, who were holding a ridge some 100 yards behind, to fire to the left front and endeavour to check the enemy's fire in that direction. The space he had to traverse was swept by very heavy cross-fire, and there was not an atom of cover. He was shot in both thighs, but picking himself up, he managed to crawl and deliver and deliver his message before falling exhausted into the ILH trench.

Masterson's courage was undoubtedly instrumental in saving many lives that day. His VC was gazetted on 4 June 1901. He was decorated with the Cross in India.

Before the year, and the nineteenth century, ended there were two further Victoria Crosses won by men with strong Irish connections. The first of these was Major **Edward Douglas Brown**, 14th (King's) Hussars, who, during an action at Geluk on 13 October, carried to safety on his horse a sergeant whose own horse had been shot. He did this under heavy fire. Later he assisted a lieutenant to mount his horse under similar attention from the Boers; the horse was very restive and the other officer would have been unable to mount unaided. Finally, Major Brown carried a wounded lance-corporal to safety. Brown, who later changed his name to Browne-Singe-Hutchinson, was of Irish descent although born in India. Less than a month later, on 7 November 1900, Sergeant **Edward James Gibson Holland**, Royal Canadian Dragoons, won the Victoria Cross for saving a field gun from the Boers. He kept the enemy away from two 12-pounders with his revolver and when he saw that they were too close for him to escape with the gun carriage – his horse was blown – he removed one of the barrels, placed it under his arm and rode away. Holland was born in Ottawa but of an Irish family that hailed from Athy in County Kildare. He died in Ontario, Canada, on 18 June 1948.

The tenth Irish Victoria Cross of the Boer War – and the first of the twentieth century – was awarded to Private **John Barry** of 1st Royal Irish Regiment, who was decorated for his actions during the attack on Monument Hill on the night of 7/8 January 1901. The Royal Irish were dug in on the slopes of the hill and came under very heavy attack from the Boers. Barry was a Maxim machine gunner at the time and, as his position was overrun, he remained behind to disable his weapon by smashing the breechblock. In retaliation for his doing so, he was shot and mortally wounded by the Boers. General Smith-Dorrien later wrote of this action

> I would especially call attention to the heroic conduct of No. 3733 Private J. Barry, Royal Irish, who seeing the machine gun surrounded by Boers seized a pick and began to smash the action, which he completed in spite of the threats of the Boers. I regret to say that the Boers in retaliation shot him dead, or I would have recommended him for a V.C.[37]

However, Barry was to receive the VC as one of the first posthumous awards; the proclamation permitting such awards came into effect on 9 August 1902. Issued by the secretary of state for war it noted that

> The King has been graciously pleased to approve of the Decoration of the Victoria Cross being delivered to the representatives of the under-mentioned officers, non-commissioned officers and men who fell during the recent operations in South Africa, in the performance of acts of valour, which would, in the opinion of the Commander-in-Chief of the Forces in the Field have entitled them to be recommended for that distinction had they survived.[38]

On 30 August 1902 the Victoria Cross was sent to his widow, Mrs Catherine Barry at the family home at Greenwood Street, Ballyraggct, County Kilkenny, together with a personal letter from Lord Roberts. John Barry was a native of Kilkenny, having been born at Saint Mary's on 1 February 1873. He is buried in South Africa.

A month later Ireland's next Victoria Cross of the Boer war was won by Sergeant **William Bernard Traynor**, 2nd West Yorkshire Regiment, at Bothwell Camp. William Traynor was born in Hull on 31 December 1870, the son of Frances Traynor, a flax dresser from County Monaghan and his Hull-born wife, Rebecca. Educated at Pryne Street Catholic School, Traynor enlisted in the Army and had been promoted to sergeant by the time he won his VC.

On the night of 6 February 1901, Traynor ran out of a trench to help a wounded man in spite of intense enemy fire. As he ran to the aid of the injured man, he was struck by an enemy round and his wound meant that he was unable alone to carry the wounded man. He called for help and a lance-corporal came to his assistance. The two men then managed to carry their wounded comrade to safety. Disregarding his own wound, Sergeant Traynor remained in command of his section, giving encouragement to his soldiers until the action had ended. His VC was gazetted on 17 September 1901. William Traynor died in Dover on 20 October 1956.

It was not until five months later that the next Irish VC was won. On 3 July British positions at Valkfontein came under attack. The right of the position was held by a party of five men of 2nd Scottish Horse, under Lieutenant John English. During the attack, two of English's men were killed and another two were wounded but

> the position was still held, largely due to Lieutenant English's personal pluck. When the ammunition ran short he went over to the next party and obtained more; to do this he had to cross some fifteen yards of open ground under a heavy fire at a range of from twenty to thirty yards [from the Boer riflemen].

On 1 July 1902 he was decorated with the VC by General HRH the Prince of Wales at the inspection of the Colonial Contingents at Horse Guards' Parade in London.

John English, who was born in Cork on 6 October 1882, was educated at Harvey Grammar School, Folkestone, between 1894 and 1898 and then at Campbell College, Belfast. He served in the Merchant Navy before joining the Army as a private soldier. In March 1901 he was commissioned in 2nd Scottish Horse. After the war, English remained in the Army, as a trooper in 2nd Dragoon Guards (Queen's Bays) and was subsequently appointed lance-corporal. On 17 October 1906 he was again commissioned, this time into the Army Service Corps, and posted to Dublin the following year. In February 1908 he was posted to South Africa.

On the outbreak of war in August 1914, John English was promoted captain and served with the Army Service Corps during that conflict. He was promoted major in November 1924 when he was serving in Belfast; his second wife Mary Isabel Pyper, whom he married in 1922, was a native of that city. (His first wife had died in 1918.) In 1928 he transferred to the Indian Army Service Corps and retired some time later to become the Northern Ireland organizer for the National Association for Employment of Regular Soldiers, Sailors, and Airmen. When hostilities began again in 1939 he was back in uniform, as a lieutenant-colonel with the Royal Ulster Rifles. On 4 July 1941, Lieutenant-Colonel John English VC, died at sea, 'near Egypt'. Among the decorations he was entitled to wear was that of Officer of Agricultural Merit from the French government.

In August 1901 **Alexander Young**, a Galwegian, was awarded the Victoria Cross for his capture of a Boer Commando leader. On 13 August a unit of the Cape Mounted Police, South African Forces, was in action at Ruiters' Kraal. As the action came to a close a party of about twenty Boers was spotted on a small kopje close by. One of them was recognized as Commandant Erasmus, a well-known commando leader. Sergeant Major Young immediately charged the hill.

> On reaching these kopjes, the enemy were seen galloping back to another kopje held by Boers. Sergeant-Major Young then galloped on some fifty yards ahead of his party, and closing with the enemy, shot one of them and captured Commandant Erasmus, the latter firing at him three times at point-blank range before being taken prisoner.

Young's Victoria Cross was gazetted on 8 November 1901 and he was decorated by Sir Alfred Milner GCMG, KCB, Governor and Commander-in-Chief, Cape Colony, in South Africa on 9 August 1902.

Alexander Young's skill as a horseman approached legendary proportions and he was said to be one of the finest rough riders in the Army. Born at Ballinona, Clarinbridge, County Galway, on 27 January 1873 Young was educated at Galway Model School and joined 2nd Dragoon Guards (Queen's Bays) at Renmore Barracks, Galway, in 1890. Following an injury he retired from the Army and emigrated to South Africa, where he joined the Cape Mounted Police with whom he served throughout the Boer War. He later resumed his military career and was commissioned in the South African Scottish Regiment. While serving with that regiment on the Somme, Lieutenant Alexander Young was killed on 19 October 1916. He has no known grave and is commemorated on the Thiepval Memorial as well as on the Bulwer War Memorial in Natal.

The last Irish VC of the Boer War was awarded to a doctor. **Thomas Joseph Crean** was born in North Brook Road, Dublin on 19 April 1873, the son of Thomas Crean, a barrister. A keen sportsman, he was one of the three VC winners to play rugby for Wanderers RFC; he was capped nine times for Ireland. Educated at Clongowes Wood College and the Royal College of Surgeons in Dublin, Crean enlisted as a trooper in the Imperial Light Horse on the outbreak of the war. In March 1900 he was commissioned captain and took command of a squadron. He gave up that command in June 1901 to become a surgeon-captain and was gazetted captain in the Royal Army Medical Corps on 3 September 1902.

Crean took part in the battle of Elandslaagte, where he was wounded, and served through the siege of Ladysmith, participating in most of the engagements during that siege. He later took part in operations in the Transvaal, Orange River Colony and the relief of Mafeking. It was in the action against the Boer commander De Wet's forces at Tygerskloof on 18 December 1901 that Crean won the Victoria Cross.

> This officer continued to attend to the wounded in the firing line, under a heavy fire at only 150 yards' range, after he had himself been wounded, and only desisted when he was hit a second time, and, as it was first thought, mortally wounded.

The *London Gazette* of 11 February 1902 announced the award of the Victoria Cross to Crean and he was decorated by King Edward VII at Saint James's Palace on 13 March. In 1903 Crean was awarded the Arnott Memorial Gold Medal as the Irish medical graduate who had 'performed or accomplished the most conspicuous act of heroism or distinguished service whether in civil life or in naval or military service at home, on the high seas, or abroad'. Although he retired from the Army in 1906 to practise as a civilian doctor, he returned to the military life in 1914 and served in France where he was twice Mentioned in Despatches and won the DSO.

Discharged as medically unfit in October 1918, Tommy Crean's health did not permit him to resume a full practice. He was declared bankrupt in 1922 and died in London on 25 March 1923. Major Thomas Joseph Crean VC, DSO, LRCP, FRCS is buried in Saint Mary's Catholic Cemetery, Kensal Rise, London.

Two years after the Boer war ended, an incident in British Somaliland led to the award of a third Victoria Cross to the Gough family. Brothers Hugh and Charles had each won the VC during the Indian Mutiny. On 22 April 1903, it was the turn of Charles' son, John, to win another VC for the Tipperary family. **John Edmund Gough** was born at Murree, near Rawalpindi on 25 October 1871, his parents having returned to India from Tipperary the previous year. Johnnie began his Army career as a second-lieutenant in the Westmeath Militia on 12 April 1890. The Westmeaths were one of a number of Irish militia regiments that were not affiliated to Irish regiments; the official post-1881 title of the Westmeaths was 9th Rifle Brigade. He subsequently followed his older brother Hubert, born in London, into Sandhurst and was commissioned into the Rifle Brigade on 12 March 1892.[39]

Arriving at Berbera on the Red Sea coast in November 1902, John Gough was appointed staff officer of a flying column being formed under the command of Captain A.S. Cobbe VC, who held the local rank of lieutenant-colonel. The flying column's task was to undertake operations against the forces of

Mohammed-bin-Abdullah Hassan, known as the 'Mad Mullah', which had been raiding into British territory.[40]

By April 1903 Gough was commanding the Bohotle column as it pressed Hassan. On 22 April, days after a small force of British and native troops had been all but wiped out, Gough's men moved to battle at Daratoleh. They were outnumbered and found that the enemy was better equipped than had been expected – many of the Mullah's men were using captured Lee-Metford rifles, taken from dead British soldiers. Eventually Gough was forced to order his command, which had formed square, to retreat.[41]

The rearguard fell some distance behind the main body in the retreat and, as they did so, Captain C. M. Bruce, Gough's staff officer, fell wounded. Learning of this Gough dismounted and ran back to meet Captain George Rolland, his intelligence officer, who told him that Bruce was badly injured and that a camel was needed to carry him. Ordering the column to halt, Gough went to the assistance of Captain Bruce while Rolland obtained a camel. However, he discovered that Bruce was practically dead already, not responding to Gough's placing a finger in his eye.[42]

Bruce was hit again while his comrades were struggling to get him on the camel and it was probably at that point that he died. This was virtually the last action of the battle at Daratoleh as the Mullah's forces melted away when the square reached more open country. For his actions Gough received the Victoria Cross as did Rolland. A third VC was awarded to Captain William George Walker.

John Gough was appointed brigadier-general in October 1913.[43] He went to France with the BEF in August 1914 and soon established himself as one of the finest brains in the Army. It was all the more tragic, therefore, that this outstanding officer fell to a sniper's bullet near Fauqissart in France on 20 February 1915. Two days later he died at Estaires. Unusually, he was posthumously knighted on 22 April 1915, twelve years to the day after he won his Victoria Cross.[44] He is buried at Estaires communal cemetery.

6   1914-19

The first shot fired by a British soldier in the Great War came from the car-
bine of Corporal Edward Thomas, a drummer, of C Squadron, 4th (Royal
Irish) Dragoon Guards on 22 August 1914, just a day before the first VCs of
the war were won.[1] Thomas was a native of Nenagh, County Tipperary.[2] The
distinction of being the war's first VC winner also went to an Irishman,
Lieutenant **Maurice James Dease**, of the Royal Fusiliers.

Born in Gaulstown, Coole, County Westmeath, on 28 September 1889,
the only son of Edmund Fitzlawrence Dease JP and his wife Katherine,
Maurice Dease was educated at Stonyhurst College and the Royal Military
College, Sandhurst. The third of Stonyhurst's five Irish VC winners, Dease
was commissioned into the Royal Fusiliers (City of London Regiment) in
May 1910. Promoted to lieutenant on 19 April 1912, he was commanding 4th
Battalion, Royal Fusiliers' machine-gun section of two weapons when the regiment moved to Belgium as part of the British Expeditionary Force in August
1914.[3]

The first exchange of fire between British and German troops in what was
supposed to be the war to end all wars took place on 22 August. But the
BEF's II Corps was at a distinct disadvantage, placed in a salient, surrounded
on three sides by Germans and liable to attack at any moment. At dawn on
Sunday 23 August the Germans fired the first shots of the battle of Mons.[4]

Fourth Royal Fusiliers were part of 9 Brigade of 3rd Division and had
reached the outskirts of Mons on 22 August. After some changes in position
they found themselves defending the line of the canal and the Nimy and
Ghlin bridges across it. On their right flank was 4th Middlesex Regiment and
on the left 1st Royal Scots Fusiliers.[5]

The first enemy infantry attack was launched before 9 a.m.[6] On the northern side of the canal the Germans were screened by small fir plantations, from
which their machine guns could pour withering fire into the defenders at the
bridges. The firs also provided cover for the massing of infantry units to attack
the bridges. In the first attack, six German battalions advancing in close order
were stopped in their tracks by concentrated machine-gun fire and rapid firing
riflemen. The enemy withdrew and half an hour later tried again, this time
in open order with the support of their own machine guns and artillery. Four
battalions attacked the Nimy bridge, on the north-west corner of the canal

loop, which was defended by a single company of Royal Fusiliers, under Captain Ashburner, with a machine gun section under Lieutenant Dease.

During this assault the Fusiliers were under great pressure with the machine-gun section taking very heavy casualties. Maurice Dease was wounded no less than five times, but refused to leave his guns, ensuring that they stayed in action to bring effective fire to bear on the enemy. When Dease was hit for the last time it was about 3.30 p.m., after the remainder of the infantry had withdrawn.[7]

For his part in the action at Mons, Lieutenant Maurice Dease was posthumously awarded the Victoria Cross, the very first VC of the conflict. One of Dease's machine-gunners, Private Sidney Frank Godley, was also awarded the VC for this action and there was some uncertainty as to which of the two was the first winner. The matter was resolved by the War Office in 1926; in response to a request from Stonyhurst College, Major A.F. Becke, historical secretary at the Committee of Imperial Defence, wrote that

> Dease might be considered as primus inter pares; although it is no doubt true that, as battalion machine-gun officer, he had trained Pte Godley and formed in him that military character which at the opening of the first action vindicated the worth of the training that he had received.[8]

Godley was taken prisoner and survived the war. He lived until 1957[9] and is believed to have been the inspiration for Bruce Bairnsfather's character *Old Bill*, the embodiment of the British soldier of the Great War.[10]

The practice of awarding posthumous VCs was still relatively new in 1914 and was administered in an apparently offhand fashion. On 11 January 1915 the War Office sent Dease's VC to his family by post. This practice continued until King George V instituted the practice of holding investitures at which the VC could be presented to the next of kin of the winner. Maurice Dease is buried in Saint Symphorien military cemetery, close to where he died. He is also commemorated on memorials at Stonyhurst College, Westminster Cathedral, London and at Nimy bridge. His medals, including his VC, are held in the Royal Regiment of Fusiliers (City of London) Museum in the Tower of London.

The soul of an infantry battalion rests in its colours and there were many occasions when last stands were made around a tattered flag, or death-defying actions carried out to save the colours. Although the Royal Artillery does not carry colours in the same fashion as the infantry, gunners regard their guns as their colours and will defend those weapons with the same tenacity as infantry defending their colours; on many occasions gun detachments gave their lives while defending their guns.

On the day after Dease won his posthumous Victoria Cross, a German corps attacked the flank of the BEF at Elouges. In the desperate fighting that ensued an artillery battery was in danger of being overwhelmed but was saved by the cool thinking and decisive leadership of its commander, Major **Ernest Wright Alexander**. His gunners had suffered so many casualties that it seemed as if Alexander's 119 Battery, Royal Field Artillery, would have no hope of escape. But Alexander called on the assistance of the nearby survivors of 9th Lancers and, with the aid of those volunteers, he and his surviving gunners were able to manhandle 119 Battery's guns and limbers out of the line of enemy fire so that the horse teams and their drivers could gallop up and remove the guns to safety. Both Alexander and Captain Francis Grenfell of 9th Lancers were later awarded the VC. Alexander was the son of Robert Alexander, a shipowner and director of the Suez Canal Company; his mother was Annie Alexander, *née* Gregg, of Belfast.

After the action at Mons, the Allies retreated towards Paris. On the morning of 1 September 1 Cavalry Brigade, part of the British rearguard, was in position at the village of Nery. Thick mist had delayed the start of a move by L Battery which formed part of the brigade with 2nd Dragoon Guards, 5th Dragoon Guards and 11th Hussars. The soldiers had breakfasted and the horses were being watered when the first German shell screamed out of the morning mist. Within minutes hundreds of shells fell among the cavalry and artillery horses.[11] Added to this was a near constant rain of rifle and machine-gun fire.

When the mist began to clear it became apparent that the British position was under fire from three German batteries, a total of twelve guns. L Battery and 2nd Dragoons were receiving the worst of the fire, those units on the flanks suffering fewer casualties. In the initial enemy salvo, L Battery lost three of its six guns but efforts were made to bring the remaining three into action. After only a few rounds had been returned two of those weapons were also put out of action. An ever-changing gun detachment kept the last gun in action as men were killed and injured by German shells. One of those who served the gun was Sergeant **David Nelson** who, although wounded, continued to act as range finder until the final round was fired.[12] David Nelson was born at Deraghland in County Monaghan on 3 April 1886, enlisted in the Royal Field Artillery in 1904 and later transferred to the Royal Horse Artillery. He was promoted to bombardier with L Battery on 18 May 1910. With a first-class gunnery certificate from the School of Gunnery at Shoeburyness, Nelson was promoted to sergeant on 5 August 1914. Hospitalized after the action at Nery and taken prisoner by the Germans two days later, he managed to escape after some days in captivity and made his way back to his own lines. Four VCs were awarded for L Battery's action at

Nery, one of which went to David Nelson. In addition, he was commissioned as a second-lieutenant in the Royal Field Artillery on 15 November, the day before his VC was gazetted.

Subsequently Nelson was posted as an instructor to the School of Gunnery and promoted lieutenant in June 1915, by which time he was an acting-Captain Instructor. On 12 October 1916 he was appointed Temporary Captain and was promoted to major on 1 March 1918. He was appointed to command D Battery, 59th Brigade, RFA with whom he went into action again in France. Wounded while commanding D Battery on 7 April 1918, David Nelson succumbed to his injuries at No. 58 Casualty Clearing Station, Lillers. He is buried in the Lillers Communal Cemetery.

By October 1914, 2nd Gordon Highlanders were in position between Kruiseecke and Zandvoorde in Belgium. The regiment was part of 20 Brigade, 7th Division, and was tasked with defending a line running south east of the Menin Road and the village of Gheluvelt. What became known as the first battle of Ypres began on 19 October; the town was soon under determined attack. The ardour and morale of the attackers had been badly underestimated by both the British and French commands and it took every effort to retain a fingertip hold on Ypres and the surrounding area. On 21 October the German XXVII Corps attacked both 21 and 22 Brigades of 7th Division, but no attack was pressed home on 20 Brigade. Instead the enemy dug in close to the front of the lines and brought down accurate shellfire and sniping.[13]

On 23 October Drummer **William Kenny** was awarded the Victoria Cross for the rescue of no fewer than five wounded men, all of whom were brought to safety through heavy enemy fire. Added to this were two incidents in which he recovered abandoned machine guns while, on numerous occasions, he carried vital messages across the battlefield. All of these actions were undertaken at great personal risk over machine-gun-fire-swept ground.

Kenny's award was announced in the *London Gazette* of 18 February 1915. At the time, he was in hospital at Newton Abbot, having been invalided home suffering from a broken wrist, sustained in a fall on the battlefield. He was thus a prime target for newspaper reporters looking for a story of heroism. But Kenny was a modest man who had not told anyone of his exploits until the announcement of his award was made. One newspaper quoted him as saying: 'There were men lying about wounded, and I simply brought them in. The Maxims [machine guns] had to be fetched, and I did it, that's all'.

Although William Kenny was born in Malta on 24 August 1880, where his soldier-father was stationed, his parents were both natives of Drogheda, County Louth, and the young Kenny was educated in Drogheda and joined the Army as a teenager, serving in the Boer War.

Drogheda did not hesitate to honour its soldier son. On Saint Patrick's Day, Kenny was at home in the town with his parents and the mayor of Drogheda, Luke J. Elcock, and the corporation processed to High Mass with the Kennys. Subsequently, at a public meeting in Saint George's Square, Kenny was made a freeman of the borough and presented with a cheque for £120, an enormous sum at the time which would have represented more than six years' pay for an ordinary soldier.

The King presented Lance-Corporal Kenny with his VC on Glasgow Green, Glasgow on 18 May 1915 and he was subsequently promoted sergeant and appointed drum major. He was also the subject of a presentation by the Musicians' Company on whose behalf the Lord Mayor of London presented him with a gold watch.

Sergeant Kenny was discharged in 1919 and joined the Corps of Commissionaires. He lived in the Corps barracks in London until early in 1936 when he was taken ill and died on 10 January, at Charing Cross hospital. He was buried in the Corps' plot in Brookwood Cemetery, Woking. Although he has no identifiable grave, a headstone was erected by the Gordon Highlanders' Association in March 1999. A standard Commonwealth War Graves' Commission stone, it is engraved with the Victoria Cross, Kenny's details and the words 'buried near this spot'. His VC is in the Gordon Highlanders' Museum in Aberdeen, together with his other medals, which include the Queen's South Africa Medal with four clasps, King's South Africa Medal with two clasps, 1914 Star (Mons Star), British War Medal, Victory Medal with Mention in Despatches, Delhi Durbar Medal 1911 and Russian Cross of the Order of St George (Third Class).

Six days after Kenny won his VC, the assistant adjutant of his battalion won a posthumous VC. Lieutenant **James Anson Otho Brooke**, a Scottish-born member of the Fermanagh Brooke family, was carrying a message from his commanding officer during a determined German attack. As he made his way to his destination, Brooke saw that the Germans had broken through part of the Gordons' line and he set about organizing a counter-attack. Gathering together about a hundred men, all he could muster, he led them in an assault on the enemy's newly-won positions and forced a German withdrawal. Brooke then left the trench to bring up reinforcements and was killed while doing so. He was thirty years old. Educated at Wellington, he had gone on to Sandhurst where he won the Sword of Honour and was a good sportsman as well as an officer with considerable potential.

At Cuinchy, south of Bethune on the La Bassée canal, as dawn broke on 1 February 1915, a German raiding party overran a position held by a unit of the Coldstream Guards. Lieutenant Blacker-Douglass and his No. 4 Company, 1st Battalion Irish Guards – the Micks – were ordered to assist the

Coldstream make a counter-attack. During the attack all the officers were either killed or wounded, and command passed to CQMS Carton. The position could not be retaken that night, but the Guardsmen held on until morning when artillery fire was brought down on the Germans. When the bombardment lifted, a second attack was launched, with thirty Irish Guardsmen led by Lieutenants Graham and Innes. An enemy-held railway embankment overlooked the trenches at this point and threatened the Micks' advance but Lance Corporal **Michael O'Leary**, Innes' batman, rushed forward along the top of the embankment, killing five enemy riflemen and a three man machine-gun team. Then, for good measure, he captured some prisoners. All this O'Leary did in full view of both the enemy and his own company. Eyewitnesses reported that 'he did his work quite leisurely and wandered out into the open, visible for any distance around, intent upon killing another German to whom he had taken a dislike'.¹⁴ O'Leary was a Reservist who was recalled to the Army when war broke out. He had enlisted initially in the Royal Navy before being discharged as a result of rheumatism in his knees. After a spell working as a farm labourer at home, he was restored to full health and joined the Irish Guards. In 1913 he left the Army on completion of his term of enlistment and went to Canada where he joined the Royal North-West Mounted Police with whom he served until war broke out and he returned to Britain to rejoin the Micks.

Born in Inchigeela, Macroom, County Cork on 29 September 1888, Michael O'Leary was awarded the Victoria Cross and was subsequently commissioned into the Connaught Rangers with whom he served in Salonika. He ended the war as Major O'Leary, served in the Second World War, with the Middlesex Regiment and the Army Pioneer Corps, and died in London on 2 August 1961. As well as the VC, he held the 1914 Medal with 5 August to 22 November clasp, the British War Medal, Victory Medal with Mention in Despatches oak leaf, 1939-45 Defence Medal, 1937 Coronation Medal, 1953 Coronation Medal and the Russian Cross of St George (Third Class). O'Leary always insisted that he was entitled to the 4 August to 22 November Clasp to his 1914 Medal as he was adamant that he arrived in France on 22 November and therefore qualified for what became known as the Mons Star. Official records show that he arrived on 23 November 1914 but there is every likelihood that O'Leary was correct as the official documentation may indicate the day he arrived on the strength of 1st Irish Guards rather than the day on which he landed in France.

As with William Kenny in Drogheda, Michael O'Leary was received as a hero in his native Cork when he returned home in June 1915. The *Times* reported that he arrived in Cork ... and was received by the Lord Mayor, the Cork Sheriff, and the Town Clerk, attended by the sword and mace bearers and many prominent citizens, including members of the Cork Reception Committee, by whom the reception was arranged.

A number of officers and men of the Cork Corps of the National Volunteers, under Lt-Col. Donegan, formed a guard of honour on the platform, while the band of the Leinster Regiment struck up as the train steamed in.

The Lord Mayor cordially welcomed Sergeant O'Leary to Cork, and he having been presented to the High Sheriff, was congratulated by him and others on the well deserved honour conferred on him. He was then taken to a motor-car in waiting, and accompanied by the Lord Mayor and High Sheriff, a procession was formed and marched through the principal streets to the Imperial Hotel, where he was entertained to luncheon. Thousands had collected on the footpaths en route and a very cordial reception was given to the young Cork hero.

In the evening O'Leary went by motor to his father's home at Inchigeela.[15]

At the first battle of Messines on 12 April 1915 the Royal Irish Fusiliers – the Faughs – gained their first Victoria Cross. That day the 1st Battalion was due to be relieved in the trenches to prepare for its part in a planned offensive in May. Although the morning and afternoon passed without serious incident, the Germans began to bombard the Faughs' positions at about 5 p.m. with heavier shells than those to which the battalion had become accustomed.[16]

At first the enemy rounds fell behind the trench line but German artillery observers on the Messines ridge soon corrected their gunners' fire and shells began to fall among the Faughs, 'churning the trench into a terrible debris of men and earth'. Many were killed, either blown to pieces or buried alive.

A quiet, undemonstrative boy from D Company, Private Robert Morrow, left the support trench where the survivors were sheltering and returned to the front trench, where the shells were still pumping down. He came back dragging one of his comrades who had been buried in the debris, then returned again and again to the smitten line, each time rescuing a wounded man. It was one of those moments on the Western Front when the individual seemed to reassert himself triumphantly in the face of all the horrors of mass warfare; for, miraculously, Morrow was unharmed on this occasion, though he was to be killed only a fortnight later.[17]

A native of New Mills, near Dungannon, in County Tyrone, **Robert Morrow** had already shown great courage in earlier episodes in the trenches, although 'in peace time he was not conspicuous as a soldier'.[18] He was recommended for the Victoria Cross but did not live long enough to learn that it had been awarded: he was killed in the Ypres salient on 26 April, four weeks before his VC was gazetted. By now the practice of presenting posthumous VCs to next of kin had been established and King George V handed Robert Morrow's Cross to his widowed mother, Mrs Margaret Jane Morrow, at Buckingham Palace on 26 November 1916. On 15 October, the King had written to Mrs Morrow to tell her that 'It is a matter of sincere regret to me that the death of Private Robert Morrow deprived me of the pride of personally conferring upon him the Victoria Cross, the greatest of all distinctions'. In 1919 Mrs Morrow gave the Cross to the Royal Irish Fusiliers and it remains in the Regimental Museum to this day. Morrow's company commander recommended him for a Bar to the VC, but this was not awarded. He was also awarded the Russian Cross of St George (Third Class).

On 20 April 1915, 1st Battalion, East Surrey Regiment was in position on Hill 60, south of Sanctuary Wood on the Ypres Front. Throughout the day the battalion positions had been under severe enemy fire, that of Lieutenant George Roupell being especially hard hit. Although wounded on several occasions, Roupell refused to leave his men and remained with them to repel an enemy attack. During a brief lull in the fighting he had his wounds dressed, but insisted on returning to his trench and his soldiers. As dusk drew on, and his company was severely depleted by deaths and injuries, he went back to battalion headquarters to seek reinforcements. With the extra men he was able to hold the position until the battalion was relieved at 2 o'clock the next morning. He was recommended for the VC and the award was gazetted on 23 June 1915. On 12 July **George Patrick Rowland Roupell** was decorated by King George V at Buckingham Palace.

Roupell was born in Tipperary on 7 April 1892. He survived the war, entered the Staff College at Camberley in 1921 and later attained the rank of brigadier. In 1954 he was appointed Colonel of the East Surreys and later recalled his earliest days in the regiment, which he joined as a second-lieutenant at Kinsale in 1912. '[I] did my time on the square and eventually with considerable pride took over my first command, No. 4 Platoon of A Company'.[19] George Roupell died in Shalford, Surrey, on 4 March 1974.

Ireland's next Victoria Cross was won four days after Roupell's deed by a soldier of the Canadian Expeditionary Force. **Frederick William Hall** was born in Kilkenny on 8 February 1885. His father, also Frederick, had been a soldier and became the bandmaster of 2nd Volunteer Battalion, South Lancashire Regiment. As did many young Irishmen of his generation he emigrated to Canada* and appears to have taken his widowed mother with him, or brought her to Canada subsequently since Mrs Mary Ann Hall is buried in Toronto. When war broke out in 1914, Hall was working in Winnipeg, Manitoba where he enlisted in the 106th Battalion of the Canadian Army and was later posted to the 8th Manitoba Battalion, the Little Black Devils, with whom he went to France.

In 1915, the Manitobas were in position at Saint Julien on the Ypres Front. On the afternoon of 24 April, a wounded man was heard calling from no man's land about fifteen yards in front of the battalion's positions. Colour Sergeant Hall and two others attempted a rescue, but the enemy fire was too heavy and both Hall's companions were wounded. Frederick Hall then made a solo effort and, despite fierce enfilading machine-gun fire, he reached the wounded man. As he lifted the casualty onto his shoulder another long burst from a German machine gun arced towards him and he was hit in the head. Mortally wounded, Hall died the next day in a field hospital at Gravenstafel, near Sanctuary Wood. He was recommended for a posthumous VC, which was gazetted on 23 June. The VC was sent to Canada and presented to Mrs Hall in Winnipeg. Hall has no known grave and is commemorated on the Menin Gate Memorial and on the family grave in Saint Helen's Borough Cemetery in Lancashire, where his father is buried.

On the day that Frederick Hall died at Gravenstafel, Allied troops were landing in the Gallipoli peninsula in an operation that was intended to force the passage of the Dardanelles strait and eliminate Turkey from the war. The Gallipoli landings and subsequent operations were to become synonymous with courage, suffering and incompetence. The incompetence was on the part of those who planned the operations; the courage and suffering were shown and endured by the soldiers who took part. Needless to say, many of those soldiers earned the Victoria Cross.

The first Irish VC of the campaign went to Private **William Keneally**, 1st Battalion, Lancashire Fusiliers. Keneally was born at 38 Parnell Street, Wexford on 26 December 1886, the son of former Colour-Sergeant John Keneally of the Royal Irish Regiment. Keneally senior later settled in England where he became a weighman at a Wigan colliery. William was educated at Saint John's School, Wigan and Saint Oswald's, Ashton-in-Makerfield before following his father into the colliery. However, in September 1909, he enlisted in the Lancashire Fusiliers and served in India, whence his battalion came to England to join the expeditionary force for Gallipoli. William Keneally was one of six brothers who served in the Great War; two would not come home.

* Canada's VCs suggest that Hall was born in Belfast.

At dawn on 25 April three companies and the headquarters of 1st Lancashire Fusiliers stormed ashore on W Beach on the Gallipoli Peninsula to the west of Cape Helles. They were met by a storm of Turkish machine-gun fire and, within a few yards of the waterline, became enmeshed in a broad belt of barbed wire. Nonetheless, the surviving members of the company managed to cut their way through and establish a foothold on the beach.

> Probably hundreds of officers and men in this most gallant regiment performed deeds that, singly, would have been rewarded by the V.C.; but when all are so brave how shall the King decide upon whom to pin the Cross?
> So it was left to the battalion to select three super-heroes, and they chose, as the War Office announced last night, a captain, a sergeant and a private.[20]

The private soldier was William Keneally. Six VCs were won by Lancashire Fusiliers that day and their achievements have become one of the enduring legends of the Victoria Cross. However, the battalion paid a heavy price: 533 men were killed or wounded.[21] Of the six men who won the Victoria Cross that day Private Stubbs was killed in action while William Keneally, who had been promoted to sergeant, died of wounds on 29 June. One obituary suggests that he died in hospital on Malta but most sources indicate Gallipoli. The fact that he is buried at Lancashire Landing Cemetery at Gallipoli (grave no. C.104) would support the latter contention.

The second Irish Victoria Cross at Gallipoli went to Corporal **William Cosgrove** of 1st Battalion, Royal Munster Fusiliers. Born on 1 October 1888, at Aghada, County Cork, he won his award a day after Kencally's deed, on 26 April 1915. The battalion had landed at V-Beach at Sedd-el-Bahr, on the Cape Helles peninsula, from the converted collier *River Clyde* on 25 April and had suffered heavily as they did so. Their comrades of 1st Royal Dublin Fusiliers and 1st Hampshire Regiment had also sustained heavy losses and the two Irish battalions effected a temporary and unofficial merger, calling the result the *Dubsters*. In spite of their losses they fought on and sought to gain their objectives.[22]

On 26 April the advance continued, through the village of Sedd-el-Bahr. A hour before noon the attackers were through the village and poised to attack Hill 141. At about 1.30 p.m. Captain Stoney, King's Own Scottish Borderers, moved the troops under his command up on the flank to support the Irish attack and it was in the subsequent action that Corporal Cosgrove won his VC. As he led his section towards the Turkish positions Cosgrove found the way barred by a barbed wire fence. Using his bare hands he tore the fence down, thus allowing his men to make a successful attack and thereby contributing to the clearing of the heights above the beach. After Sergeant-Major Bennett was killed, Cosgrove took command and led the charge on the Turkish positions. One eyewitness recorded the event thus

> An Irish giant, with his officers and brother Tommies dying and dead around him, continued a task he had set himself of clearing a way through the Turkish wire. Though under heavy fire, he continued at his task, and eventually aided by his exceptional strength, succeeded in wrenching a stanchion out of the ground. The others had failed to cut the wire. The manner in which the man worked out in the open will never be forgotten by those who were fortunate enough to witness it.[23]

Cosgrove was later promoted sergeant. His VC was gazetted on 23 August 1915 and was presented to him by George V at Buckingham Palace on 4 November 1916. After the disbandment of his regiment in 1922 he transferred to the Northumberland Fusiliers. He was posted to the Indian Unattached List as a staff-sergeant instructor and served with the Kolar Gold Fields Battalion Auxiliary Force in India. By the time he left the Army he had been awarded the Long Service and Good Conduct Medal and the Meritorious Service Medal to add to his VC, 1914-15 Star, British War Medal and Victory Medal. All of his medals were bought by an American collector in 1966. William Cosgrove died at Millbank, London, on 14 July 1936, and was buried at Aghada, his birthplace.

Three months passed before the next Irish Victoria Cross was won at Gallipoli. Captain **Gerald Robert O'Sullivan**, born at Douglas, County Cork on 8 November 1888, volunteered to lead a bombing party of 1st Royal Inniskilling Fusiliers to recover a section of trench that been lost to the enemy. This operation was successfully carried out on the night of 1/2 July and the trench section retaken.

> He advanced in the open under a very heavy fire, and, in order to throw his bombs with greater effect, got up on his parapet, where he was completely exposed to the fire of the enemy occupying the trench. He was finally wounded, but not before his inspiring example had led on his party to make further efforts, which resulted in the recapture of the trench.
>
> On the night of June 18-19, Capt. O'Sullivan saved a critical situation in the same locality by his great personal gallantry and good leading.[24]

These two incidents were included in the citation for O'Sullivan's VC, the first awarded to an Inniskilling Fusilier.* Captain O'Sullivan did not survive the war, being killed at Suvla Bay the following month. His VC was sent by post to his mother on 27 September 1916; she was then living in Dorchester.

The Inniskillings' second Victoria Cross was won that same night by Sergeant **James Somers**, a native of Belturbet, County Cavan, where he had been born on 12 June 1894. Sergeant Somers, who was also serving in 1st Inniskillings, held out alone in a forward sap throughout the night after the men who were supposed to hold it withdrew. As dawn approached, reinforcements brought up a supply of grenades. Using these, Somers led an attack against the Turkish positions and captured a section of their trench. This position was held throughout the day, with Somers making frequent trips back to the rear to obtain fresh supplies of ammunition and water. James Somers survived Gallipoli and was decorated with the VC at Buckingham Palace on 14 October 1915. His family was then living at Cloughjordan in County Tipperary and he was hailed as the county's first Victoria Cross winner when he was welcomed home and congratulated by the Lord Lieutenant for County Tipperary, Lord Dunalley. Somers was also given a civic reception in Derry in early October where he drove through the city in an open carriage with the mayor.

James Somers subsequently served in France where he suffered from gas poisoning. He was so badly effected that he was medically discharged from the Army and returned home to Cloughjordan. He died there from the effects of the gas on 7 May 1918 and was buried in Modreeny Church of Ireland churchyard, where his father was sexton.

Back on the Western Front, Second-Lieutenant **George Arthur Boyd Rochfort** of the Scots Guards, earned the Victoria Cross in the same manner as the very first Irish winner some sixty-one years previously. By a strange coincidence Boyd-Rochfort, who had originally been rejected by the Army on medical grounds but accepted following an operation for varicose veins, was the first Guards' officer to win the Victoria Cross since the Crimean War. On 3 August 1915, 1st Scots Guards were entrenched between Cambrin and La Bassée and Lieutenant Boyd-Rochfort was supervising a small working party at a junction of the communication trench. At 2 a.m. a German mortar

---

* Field-Marshal Sir George Stuart White won the VC in the Afghan War in 1879. Although commissioned into the 27th (Inniskilling) Regiment, White had transferred to the 92nd (later the Gordon Highlanders) by the time he won his VC. During the South African War, Lieutenant Edgar Thomas Inkson, the Medical Officer of 1st Royal Inniskilling Fusiliers, won the VC for rescuing two Inniskillings' officers under fire.

bomb landed on the parapet. Boyd-Rochfort shouted a warning to his men and, rushing forward, hurled the bomb over the edge of the trench where it exploded without causing any casualties. The citation for his Victoria Cross states that 'this splendid combination of presence of mind and courage saved the lives of many of the working party'.

Boyd-Rochfort was born at Midleton Park, Castletown, County West-meath, the son of Major R. H. Boyd-Rochfort of 15th Hussars. He returned to his native Westmeath on 3 September 1915 and was given a hero's wel-come. The *Daily Express* reported that he 'had an enthusiastic reception. Crowds thronged the railway station, many having driven in decorated cars from all parts of the county, and as he alighted he was received with ringing cheers'. On 6 September Boyd-Rochfort was decorated with the Victoria Cross by George V at Windsor Castle. He was promoted to captain, survived the war and died in a Dublin nursing home on 11 August 1940. He is buried in Castletown-Geoghan churchyard, County Westmeath. His two brothers also served in the Army, one earning the DSO and the other the Croix de Guerre avec Palme. Three cousins were also decorated soldiers but all failed to sur-vive the war: Colonel H. Rochfort-Boyd DSO, Royal Horse Artillery, was killed at Cambrai in November 1917; Colonel H. Cheape DSO, who commanded the Warwickshire Yeomanry in the advance to Jerusalem, drowned following the torpedoing of the ship in which he was travelling in August 1917; and Major Leslie Cheape was killed in Egypt in August 1915.

The battle of Loos began on 25 September 1915 with an Allied gas attack, followed by the infantry some forty minutes later at 6.30 a.m. One of the best-known images of the battle is that of the London Irish Rifles dribbling a football across no man's land. But the battle was far from a walkover and it cost many lives and saw many acts of gallantry, among which the courage of a London-born Irishman earned the Victoria Cross. Private **Henry Edward Kenny**, 1st Battalion, Loyal North Lancashire Regiment, rescued six wounded men who had been lying in the open. Kenny went out on his missions of mercy under heavy shell-, rifle- and machine-gun fire and was himself wounded in the neck as he handed the last wounded man over the parapet to safety. His VC was gazetted on 30 March 1916 and he was decorated by King George V at Buckingham Palace on 20 May.

Born in Hackney in 1888, Kenny was the son of an Irish couple who had left County Limerick in search of a better life. The young Kenny enlisted in the Loyals in October 1906 and passed to the Reserve in 1911. Recalled to the Colours in August 1914, he was one of the relatively few veterans of Mons, the retreat from that town, the Marne and the Aisne to survive as a front-line soldier until the end of the war. Later promoted to sergeant, he was demobilized in 1919 but joined the Home Guard during the Second

World War. Kenny died in Surrey in 1979 and is buried in Saint John's Cemetery, Woking.[25]

Among the most underrated soldiers on any battlefield have been the medical orderlies and stretcher-bearers, men who qualify for the description 'unsung heroes'. On a cold wet afternoon on 16 November 1915, the men of 2nd York and Lancaster Regiment watched from their trenches at La Brique as one of their number earned the regiment's second Victoria Cross of the war. A soldier of the West Yorkshire Regiment was observed lying wounded in no man's land, about 350 yards from the enemy trenches. Corporal Stirk, Royal Army Medical Corps, and Private **John Caffrey** attempted to cross the open ground, but were driven back by shrapnel from German artillery fire. A second attempt was made and the two volunteers managed to reach the wounded man, in spite of enemy machine-gun fire and the close attention of snipers. Corporal Stirk lifted the injured soldier onto Caffrey's shoulders and they started back to their own lines. Almost immediately the medical orderly was hit in the head and fell to the ground. Private Caffrey put the wounded man down and dressed Stirk's wound before helping him back to safety. He then made a third journey into no man's land and brought Stirk back to safety. John Caffrey was decorated by King George V at Buckingham Palace on 23 February 1916. He was promoted to lance corporal and received the Cross of the Order of St George (Fourth Class) from the Tsar.

Although born in Birr, King's County, on 23 October 1891, John Caffrey was raised in Nottingham. He survived the war and returned to live in England for the remainder of his days, dying in Derby on 26 February 1953.

The Royal Navy had been engaged actively in the war since its outbreak but there had been no large-scale battle between the main fleets of Britain and Germany as had been expected by many. Instead there had been small actions such as the battles of Coronel, the Falkland Islands and the Dogger Bank early in the war. That changed on 31 May 1916 when the British and German fleets, under Admirals Jellicoe and Scheer respectively, met in action at Jutland in the largest naval battle of the war. Jutland remained the only great naval battle of the Great War and the last of its kind in European waters. On that day four VCs were won by the Royal Navy and Royal Marines. In the course of the battle, British ship losses were three battle-cruisers, three cruisers and eight destroyers against German losses of one battleship, one battle-cruiser, five destroyers and four light destroyers. The German losses in men were also lighter than the British: 3,039 German sailors were lost against 6,784 British.[26] Based on that analysis the battle was a victory for the German Navy but in strategic terms the Royal Navy was the victor as the German High Seas Fleet never sought battle again.

Of the four Jutland VCs, one was awarded to an Irishman. Commander the Honourable **Edward Barry Stewart Bingham** was also the only one of the four to survive the battle. Born at Bangor Castle, Bangor, County Down, on 26 July 1881, Bingham was the third son of the fifth Baron Clanmorris and joined the Royal Navy in 1897. At Jutland, Bingham was commanding a division of destroyers which closed with the enemy in the late afternoon.

The main bodies of the opposing fleets were some six to ten miles apart when Bingham led his destroyers towards Scheer's ships with the aim of launching a torpedo attack. As they sped towards the enemy fleet Bingham's ships – HM Ships *Nestor*, *Nicator* and *Nomad* – met a flotilla of German destroyers, two of which were sunk after a fierce engagement. The British destroyers then attacked the German battle-cruisers and met heavy and sustained fire as they did so. Finally, Bingham, in HMS *Nestor*, sighted the enemy capital ships and,

> followed by the one remaining destroyer of his division (Nicator), he closed in with dauntless courage to within 3,000 yards of the enemy in order to attain a favourable position for firing his torpedoes. Whilst making this attack Nestor and Nicator were under the concentrated fire of the secondary batteries of the High Seas Fleet. Nestor was sunk and Comdr Bingham was picked up by the Germans.[27]

Bingham was initially reported dead and it was some months before his wife learned that she was not a widow after all. On 15 September the *London Gazette* announced the award of the Victoria Cross to Commander Bingham who, by then, was known to be a prisoner of war. Bingham finally received his VC from the King in the ballroom of Buckingham Palace on 13 December 1918. On his repatriation in November 1918 he was given a hero's welcome in Bangor and was carried shoulder-high to the castle and later conveyed to the Dufferin Hall in a torchlight procession. Bingham returned to naval service after the war and achieved flag rank before retiring in 1932. Rear-Admiral Bingham died in a London nursing home on 24 September 1939, three weeks after a new war broke out in Europe.

A month after the battle of Jutland, one of the land battles that is synonymous with the Great War began on 1 July 1916, a date that is instantly recognizable to even casual students of military history. To the people of Ireland that date, the beginning of the battle of the Somme, represents the sacrifice of a generation. Irish losses were heavy on that fateful day and four Irishmen won the Victoria Cross.

The first Irish VC of the battle of the Somme was awarded posthumously to Private **William Frederick McFadzean**, 14th Battalion, Royal Irish Rifles. Born in Lurgan, County Armagh on 9 October 1895, Billy McFadzean later moved to Belfast with his family who lived in the Cregagh area. Private McFadzean was detailed as a bomber in his company, one of those who went over the top carrying canvas buckets full of hand grenades. His physique marked him out for such a role: he stood six feet tall, weighed thirteen stones and had been an enthusiastic junior rugby player, lining out for Collegians RFC. As his battalion prepared for its attack near Thiepval Wood on the morning of 1 July, grenades were being primed in the concentration trench. Men were crowded around the ammunition box that fell to the ground. Two safety pins were seen to fall out. McFadzean, knowing what was about to happen, immediately threw himself on top of the box just before the explosion. He was killed instantly, yet only one other man was wounded. McFadzean's prompt action had saved many lives. One wonders just how many of those men who survived the explosion survived the rest of the day? His VC was gazetted on 9 September 1916 and the King presented the Cross to his father, also William McFadzean, at Buckingham Palace on 28 February 1917. Billy McFadzean has no known grave and is commemorated on the Thiepval Memorial, as well as in Newtownbreda Presbyterian Church, Belfast, First Lurgan Presbyterian Church, Collegians RFC and by Castlereagh Borough Council.

Later that same July day the Royal Inniskilling Fusiliers won their third VC. Captain **Eric Norman Frankland Bell** of 9th Battalion (Tyrone Volunteers) was commanding the battalion's trench mortar battery, which advanced with the infantry to provide close support when required. Shortly after the advance began, enfilading fire from a German machine gun held the Inniskillings up. Bell crept forward and, with several well-aimed shots, killed the machine-gun crew. Throughout the remainder of the day he led several bombing attacks against enemy positions, all of which were successful. He used mortar shells as bombs and when he ran out of bombs he employed a rifle to deadly effect. He was killed while attempting to organise a counter attack with scattered parties of infantry who had lost their officers. Bell, born in Enniskillen on 28 August 1895, was the son of an Inniskilling Fusilier and had been living and working in Liverpool when war broke out, whereupon he returned to Ireland to join the Inniskillings.

Bell's VC was gazetted on 26 September 1916 and was presented to his father, Captain E.H. Bell, by the King at Buckingham Palace on 29 November. Eric Norman Frankland Bell has no known grave and, in common with Billy McFadzean, is commemorated on the Thiepval Memorial.

The third Irish VC was won by Private **Robert Quigg** of 12th Royal Irish Rifles. Quigg had been born at Cornkirk, near the Giant's Causeway in

County Antrim on 28 February 1885. His father, also Robert, was a boatman and a tourist guide at the Giant's Causeway, which attracted many visitors even in those days. Robert Quigg junior was educated at Giant's Causeway National School where he was described by the principal, David McConaghy, as 'a diligent and reliable pupil'. Quigg went to war as a batman (servant) to Sir Harry Macnaghten, Bt, by whose family he had been employed as a farm labourer before the war.

On the morning of 1 July, Quigg advanced to the assault with his platoon three times. Having survived that day on which so many of his comrades perished, he learned next morning that Sir Harry had been wounded and was lying out in no man's land. Throughout the day Quigg made seven journeys in search of Macnaghten, each time bringing back a wounded man. His final rescue of the day failed to find the officer, but brought back another casualty, this time dragged on a ground sheet. After seven hours, all under enemy shell- and machine-gun fire, exhaustion forced him to give up. Sir Harry Macnaghten was never found and was posted as 'missing believed killed'. Robert Quigg was recommended for the Victoria Cross which was gazetted on 9 September 1916 and presented to him by George V at York Cottage on the Sandringham estate on 8 January 1917. On that occasion, Quigg is reputed to have been told by the King that he was 'a brave man', to which he responded: 'You're a brave wee man yourself, Sir.' The use of the term 'a brave man' in rural Ulster did not refer to physical courage but to the individual being a decent sort of person. Quigg's comment to the King has often been misunderstood by many commentators on the VC. His own misunderstanding of the King's compliment also poses a question about Quigg's IQ. That comment that he was a 'diligent and reliable pupil' was surely a teacher's diplomatic comment on a not-very-bright pupil who later achieved fame. One of the authors was struck by the similarity between Quigg's VC-winning exploit and that which gained the eponymous hero the Medal of Honor in the Tom Hanks film *Forrest Gump*. Was Gump a latter-day Quigg?

Robert Quigg later saw service in Mesopotamia and Egypt and remained in the Army until he was medically discharged, as a sergeant, in 1934, but continued to work in the Royal Ulster Rifles' depot in Armagh as a civilian worker. In 1926 he fell fifty feet from a third-storey window of a soldiers' home in Belfast, narrowly escaping being impaled on railings. He was 'so severely injured that little hope [was] entertained of his recovery'.[28] But he did recover and, in 1934, followed in his father's footsteps as a guide at the Giant's Causeway. He died in Dalriada Hospital, Ballycastle, on 14 May 1955, aged seventy. He was given a full military funeral and is buried in Billy Parish Churchyard, near Bushmills, County Antrim. As well as the Victoria Cross, Quigg was awarded the 1914-15 Star, British War Medal, Victory Medal,

General Service Medal with clasp, Silver Jubilee Medal 1935, Coronation Medals for 1937 and 1953, and the Medal of the Order of St George of Russia (Fourth Class), all of which are in the Royal Ulster Rifles' Museum, Belfast. Sir Harry Macnaghten's younger brother, Douglas, succeeded to the baronetcy on Harry's death but was himself killed in action when leading his platoon of 8th Rifle Brigade near Delville wood on 15 September 1916.

The Royal Irish Fusiliers also gained a Victoria Cross on the opening day of the Somme campaign. This medal, the fourth won by 36th (Ulster) Division that day, was earned by Lieutenant **Geoffrey St George Shillington Cather**, who was killed in the course of the deeds that led to his VC. Born in London of Irish parents, Cather joined the Army shortly after war broke out in 1914, enlisting in 19th Royal Fusiliers (2nd Public Schools Battalion). When he received a commission it was in the Royal Irish Fusiliers, the regiment most closely associated with his mother's birthplace of Portadown: that town's Shillington Bridge is named for her family. A quiet young man, Cather was described as 'brave and fearless' and a man 'ready at all times to extend a kindly hand'.

On 1 July 1916 Lieutenant Geoffrey Cather was serving as adjutant to 9th Royal Irish Fusiliers in 108 Brigade which was charged with assaulting German positions in the area of Beaumont Hamel. As it advanced, the battalion came under intense enemy machine-gun fire and wave after wave of Faughs were simply mown down. It took the Germans only an hour to restore the position on the battalion's front. Only the reserve was left from 9th Faughs: only eighty men were left unwounded; nine officers and 235 men were dead or died of wounds; all the other officers in the assault were wounded. There were many injured Faughs lying in no man's land and among those who made valiant efforts to help them was Geoffrey Cather. He went out that evening to try to bring in wounded men. Although there was heavy fire from the enemy, he managed to bring three men to safety over a five-hour period before midnight. He resumed his efforts the following morning at 8 o'clock when he

> brought in another man, and gave water to others, arranging for their rescue later. Finally, at half-past ten, he took out water to another man and was proceeding further on when he was himself killed. All this was carried out in full view of the enemy and under direct machine gun fire and intermittent artillery fire.[29]

Cather's Victoria Cross was gazetted on 9 September 1916 and was presented to his widowed mother by King George V at Buckingham Palace on 31 March 1917. In 1979, Geoffrey Cather's brother, Captain Dermot Cather

RN (Retd), presented the VC and Geoffrey's other medals to the Royal Irish Fusiliers' Museum.

There was an Irish connection with another VC won in July 1916. Lieutenant-Colonel **Adrian Carton de Wiart** was already a holder of the DSO and had been Mentioned in Despatches when he won the Victoria Cross while commanding 8th Gloucestershire Regiment on 2/3 July. Carton de Wiart had previously lost an eye and his left hand in action in the Great War; and he had been twice wounded in the Boer war. In the course of the First World War he was wounded a total of eight times, seven of which occurred on Sundays.

On 2/3 July Adrian Carton de Wiart displayed dauntless courage and inspiration in averting what might have been a serious reverse for his brigade. When the three other battalion commanders of 57 Brigade had been killed or wounded, Carton de Wiart took control of their battalions and ensured that none of the ground gained by the brigade was lost to the enemy.

Adrian Carton de Wiart was born in Belgium on 5 May 1880. His Irish connection was through his grandmother and he chose to retire to live in County Cork where he died on 5 June 1963 at the age of eighty-three years. He also served during the Second World War when he was taken prisoner by the Italians after the aircraft in which he was flying was shot down off the Libyan coast.

For generations Irishmen had been leaving their native land in search of work and settling in many countries around the world. Many of them joined the armed forces of their adopted countries when war broke out and returned to Europe to fight. We have already seen how Frederick Hall won a VC with the Canadian Expeditionary Force in 1915. In the summer of 1916 an Irishman serving with the Australian Imperial Force in France also won the Victoria Cross. Private **Martin O'Meara**, 16th (South Australia and Western Australia) Battalion, who had been born in the parish of Lorrha, County Tipperary, on 31 December 1882,* had emigrated to Australia as a youth and had found work as a labourer and sleeper-cutter at Bowling Pool, near Collie, Western Australia. He enlisted in the AIF on 19 August 1915 and completed his initial training at Black Boy Hill Camp. He left Freemantle as part of a group of reinforcements for 16th Battalion aboard HMAS *Ajana* on 22 December 1915.

On 6 August 1916, 2nd Australian Division captured the Pozieres Heights on the Somme Front and were then relieved by 4th Division, which included

---

* The Lummis Files give his birthplace as Lorrha, Rathcabbin, near Birr in County Offaly and his year of birth as 1885. The *Australian Dictionary of Biography* gives his birth date as 6 November 1885.

O'Meara's battalion, with orders to continue the advance northwards towards Mouquet Farm. On 9 August, 16th Battalion moved into the front-line trenches. At midnight the battalion assaulted Point 78 and captured it after fierce fighting. Two days later the battalion advanced again, starting at 1 a.m. At first all went well but, as day broke, enemy shelling brought the attack to a halt. Shortly after 2 p.m., the Germans counter-attacked, but, as they approached 16th Battalion, they were met by a withering fire and, within fifteen minutes, they retreated. During the four days' heavy fighting around the area of Mouquet Farm, Martin O'Meara, acting as a stretcher bearer, went out time after time to bring in the wounded from no man's land, even at the height of enemy bombardments. On at least four occasions he carried forward water and supplies and brought back injured men, once volunteering to carry forward bombs and ammunition to a part of the trench that was under particularly heavy attack. He was wounded on three occasions between 12 August 1916 and 31 August 1918. His VC was gazetted on 5 September 1916, the citation noting that he had shown 'utter contempt of danger' and he was decorated at Buckingham Palace by George V on 21 July 1917.

As well as visiting Buckingham Palace to receive his VC, O'Meara also returned to Ireland to visit his native Tipperary. He was accorded a hero's welcome, even though this was after Easter 1916. Money was raised as a testimonial for him but, in his will, he asked that this, and any other money collected, be used for the restoration of Lorrha Abbey. On 13 March 1918 O'Meara was promoted to corporal and later, on 30 August, to sergeant. He left France to return home to Australia on 15 September 1918, and was demobilised on 30 November at Perth. Shortly after returning home his mental health broke down completely and he spent his remaining days in a psychiatric hospital at Claremont. He died on 20 December 1935, and was buried with full military honours in the Catholic section of Karrakatta Cemetery, Perth. He had never married and had no family in Australia. Three other VC laureates were mourners at his funeral. The 16th Infantry Battalion at Perth today holds his Victoria Cross while the money in his estate was used for repairs to Lorrha parish church, the sum bequeathed having been insufficient to restore the ancient monastery.

On 3 September 1916, the village of Guillemont was captured after a number of attacks that were part of the Somme offensive that had started in July. Two Irish Victoria Crosses were won during the battle. The first went to Private **Thomas Hughes** of 6th Connaught Rangers, a native of Coravoo, near Castleblaney in County Monaghan. Although wounded in the initial attack, the thirty-one-year-old Hughes returned to his unit after being treated by a medical orderly. Later in the afternoon he single-handedly captured an enemy machine-gun position, killing the gunner and capturing the remainder of the crew in spite of having been wounded twice more. Hughes survived those wounds and the remainder of the war and died in Carrickmacross on 8 January 1942. His VC was gazetted on 26 October 1916 and he was decorated by George V in Hyde Park on 2 June 1917. His Cross was purchased by the Connaught Rangers Association in 1959 and presented by them to the Sandhurst Military Museum. It is now in the National Army Museum in London.

On the left flank of the Connaughts, 7th Leinster Regiment gained another Victoria Cross through the actions of the battalion bombing officer, Lieutenant **John Vincent Holland**, who was born in Athy, County Kildare, on 19 July 1889. At Guillemont, Holland led a party of twenty-six men into the village, each man a trained bomber with a supply of hand grenades. The group advanced with great courage, not stopping for anything, even their own artillery bombardment, which fell around them. By the end of the day they were reduced to the lieutenant and five men but had destroyed many enemy bunkers, cleared a large part of the village and captured fifty German prisoners. The *London Gazette* of 26 October 1916 carried the announcement of Holland's VC, which he received from the monarch at Buckingham Palace on 5 February 1917. The son of a veterinary surgeon, Holland was educated at Clongowes Wood College and Liverpool University and had travelled extensively before returning home on the outbreak of war to enlist in 2nd Life Guards. He was later commissioned into the Leinsters. He remained in the Army until 1920 when he transferred to the Indian Army from which he retired in 1922. John Vincent Holland died in Hobart, Tasmania on 27 February 1975. His requiem Mass at Saint Mary's Cathedral was attended by many ex-servicemen, after which he was buried in Cornelian Bay cemetery.

In September 1916, the Allies again attempted to capture the Thiepval stronghold. With the losses of July made up with fresh intakes, two divisions, 11th and 18th, were allotted the task. The latter division contained 54 Brigade within which was 12th Middlesex Regiment, commanded by Lieutenant Colonel Maxwell VC. Maxwell's battalion was given the task of capturing the village of Thiepval itself and made good progress, having had support from two tanks at the outset of the attack. It was during a critical phase of the attack later in the day that the next Irish VC was won. B Company, in which Private **Frederick Jeremiah Edwards** was serving, was held up by heavy machine-gun fire. All the officers had become casualties and it looked as if the line was about to fall back. In one of those decisive actions which determines the success or failure of an attack, Private Edwards charged forward alone towards the enemy machine gun and destroyed it with hand grenades, thus allowing the advance to continue. At the end of the day a successful attack had been carried out across a mile of heavily defended ground. Frederick Edwards' VC was gazetted on 25 November 1916. Born in Queenstown, County Cork, on 3 October 1894, the son of a soldier in the Royal Garrison Artillery, Edwards was educated at the Royal Hibernian Military School in Dublin and enlisted in the Royal Garrison Artillery in 1908, subsequently transferring to the Middlesex Regiment as a drummer. Edwards was promoted to corporal, transferred to the Royal Fusiliers with whom he was promoted to sergeant and survived the war, having been captured in March 1918. He died in the Royal Star and Garter Home at Richmond, Surrey, on 9 March 1964.

On 4 October 1916, Second Lieutenant **Henry Kelly**, 10th Battalion, Duke of Wellington's Regiment, earned the Victoria Cross for his bravery in an attack on the village of Le Sars which had been captured by the Germans two days earlier. The regimental journal of the Duke of Wellington's Regiment suggests that the action for which Kelly gained the VC actually took place on 3 October. Disagreements over the exact date do not detract from the gallantry of Henry Kelly, who was to end the war as one of the most decorated of Irish officers.

In the attack on Le Sars, two understrength companies of 10th Duke of Wellington's had to cross a hundred yards of mud and mire under heavy rifle and machine-gun fire. The attackers reached the enemy barbed wire where two officers were killed and the attack stalled. The artillery had been unable to deal with the wire and it seemed as if the assault was doomed. Notwithstanding this setback, Henry Kelly twice rallied his company under the heaviest fire

> and finally led the only three available men into the enemy trench, and there remained bombing until two of them had become casualties and enemy reinforcements had arrived.
>
> He then carried his Company Serjeant-Major, who had been wounded, back to our trenches, a distance of 70 yards, and subsequently three other soldiers.
>
> He set a fine example of gallantry and endurance.[30]

Henry Kelly was decorated with the ribbon of the VC by his corps commander in France and subsequently received the medal itself from the King. He went on to win the Military Cross and a Bar in Italy and was also decorated with the Belgian Croix de Guerre and the French Medaille Militaire. By the time of his discharge in 1920 he held the rank of major.

Kelly was born in Manchester on 10 July 1887, the son of Charles Kelly, a native of Sandyford, Dublin, and Jane, *née* McGarry, of Manchester. He was educated at Saint Patrick's School and Xaverian Brothers College, Victoria Park, Manchester before going on to the National University of Ireland at Dublin. When his father died in 1904, Henry became the head of the family and was employed in the Post Office. He was also a member of the Territorial Force. In 1914 he enlisted in the Cameron Highlanders, transferred to the Manchester Regiment and was then commissioned into the Duke of Wellington's Regiment.

After the war he spent some time in Ireland and became chief of staff for overseas operations of the Irish Free State Army in 1922 with the rank of major-general. He also married Eileen Guerin from County Kerry; they had a son and a daughter. In the Spanish Civil War he served as commandant-general of the International Brigade from 1936 to 1938 and was decorated with the Grand Laurelled Cross of San Fernando.

Henry Kelly rejoined the British Army on the outbreak of war in 1939 and was appointed a lieutenant in the Cheshire Regiment. In 1944 he was court-martialled for allegedly making fraudulent claims – for the use of public transport when he was travelling by War Office car – to the value of £2.50. He was severely reprimanded, resigned his commission and returned to work in the Post Office. In January 1960 he died after a lengthy illness and was buried in Southern Cemetery, Manchester; his grave has no headstone.

On 23 October 1916 Sergeant **Robert Downie**, 2nd Royal Dublin Fusiliers – the Old Toughs – won the Victoria Cross near Lesboeufs in France. Fourth Army was attacking German positions near Le Transloy and by nightfall on 23 October the Dublins had captured enemy gunpits east of Lesboeufs as well as a strongpoint beyond those pits. The citation for Downie's VC noted that he had displayed

> most conspicuous bravery and devotion to duty in attack. When most of the officers had become casualties, this non-commissioned officer, utterly regardless of personal danger, moved about under heavy fire and reorganized the attack, which had been temporarily checked. At the critical moment he rushed forward alone, shouting: 'Come on, the Dubs!' this stirring appeal met with immediate response, and the line rushed forward at his call.[31]

Downie was wounded early in the fight but continued to lead his company and captured a German machine gun, killing the crew. His inspiring leadership led to the fall of a German position that had already resisted four or five previous attacks.

Downie was born in Glasgow of Irish parents on 12 January 1894 and joined the Royal Dublin Fusiliers in February 1912. His father was a native of Dublin who had gone to Glasgow in search of work. As well as the VC, he earned the Military Medal – as did one of his brothers – was twice Mentioned in Despatches and was wounded five times. He also received the Russian Order of Saint George. Robert Downie died in Glasgow on 18 April 1968 at the age of seventy-four years.

Frederick Maurice Watson Harvey was born in Athboy, County Meath, on 1 September 1888, the son of the Reverend and Mrs Alfred Harvey, 8 Woodstock Gardens, Dublin. Frederick attended Portora Royal School, Enniskillen, where he was 'an excellent rugby player'.[32] He was the third of the VC winners who played for Wanderers RFC of Dublin. Harvey emigrated to Canada and, when war broke out, enlisted in Lord Strathcona's Horse, a Canadian cavalry regiment that had been raised for the Boer War and which recruited many of its men from the Royal North-West Mounted Police. The Strathconas sailed for Europe with the Canadian Expeditionary Force and Harvey was to become the first Canadian cavalryman to win the VC in the Great War.

On 27 March 1917, the Canadians were attacking the village of Guyencourt, a position well defended by both barbed wire and machine guns. In front of Lieutenant Harvey's position one particular machine gun was causing problems. With his men pinned down and the advance stopped, he ran forward alone, leapt across the wire and killed the machine-gun crew with his pistol, capturing the gun and putting the remainder of the defenders to flight. Harvey's actions ensured the attack was a complete success. He also earned the Military Cross in 1918[33] for conspicuous gallantry in an attack in which he engaged many of the enemy in hand-to-hand combat and was himself wounded. His VC was gazetted on 8 June 1917 and was presented to him by George V at Buckingham Palace on 21 July. Harvey later rose to the rank of brigadier. He died in Calgary, Alberta, Canada, on 24 August 1980 and is buried in Union Cemetery, Fort McLeod, Alberta.

The following month the Leinster Regiment added another Victoria Cross to its already impressive list. It was awarded to Corporal **John Cunningham**, a Lewis gunner in the 2nd Battalion. On 12 April, at Bois-en-Hache near Barlin, Corporal Cunningham's position came under attack from twenty German stormtroopers. After expending all his machine-gun ammunition he stood in full view of the enemy and kept them at bay with hand grenades. When these were exhausted he made his way back to his own lines. During this time he had received a fractured arm and several other bullet and shrapnel wounds. Despite hospital care he died four days later from these wounds. John Cunningham had been born in Thurles, County Tipperary, on 22 October 1880 and is buried in Barlin communal cemetery, near Noeux-les-Mines in the Pas de Calais. His posthumous VC was gazetted on 8 June 1917

and his mother received the Cross from George V at Buckingham Palace on
21 July, the same investiture attended by Frederick Harvey.

On 26 June another Victoria Cross winner succumbed to the wounds he
had received while winning the Cross. During the night of 24/25 June,
Second Lieutenant **John Spencer Dunville**, 1st Royal Dragoons, was in
charge of a party of scouts and sappers who had been assigned the task of
destroying the enemy wire. In the course of this operation, Dunville placed
himself in the direct line of fire between a Royal Engineers' NCO and the
enemy lines to enable the sapper to complete safely his work on the demoli-
tion of the wire. It was a rare example, even by Victoria Cross-winning stan-
dards, of cool and unselfish courage; and it was to cost the young officer his
life. Dunville was hit by enemy bullets and severely wounded, but he continued to direct his men until the raid was completed, 'setting a magnificent
example of courage, determination and devotion to duty'. His VC was gazetted
on 2 August and the Cross was presented to his father, Squadron-Commander
John Danville Dunville, RN, at Buckingham Palace on 29 August. The
Dunvilles were a well-known Belfast family, although John was born in
London, and owned one of the many Irish distilleries of the time. The family
name is still remembered in Dunville Park. John Spencer Dunville was buried
in Villers Faucon Communal Cemetery and his Victoria Cross is held by his
old regiment, now the Household Cavalry Regiment. When John Spencer
Dunville's mother died in 1943 she left estate valued at £196,569. In her will
she left £500 to Holywood Parish Church to found a John Spencer Dunville
VC Trust to make gifts on Armistice Day, as well as £500 to the Royal
Victoria Hospital in Belfast.

The next Irish VC was the third to an Irishman in the Canadian
Expeditionary Force, indicating the high level of Irish in that army. Private
Michael James O'Rourke, a Limerick man, was serving as a stretcher-bearer
in 7th Battalion, British Columbia Regiment. O'Rourke was quite old for a
soldier in an infantry battalion, having been born on 19 March 1878* but he
was to end the war with a record that was matched by few others. Not only
did O'Rourke win the Victoria Cross, the highest gallantry decoration, but he
also won the Distinguished Conduct Medal and the Military Medal.

Between 15 and 17 August 1917, he worked unceasingly to bring in
wounded men from no man's land. During the whole of this period machine-
gun and shellfire were sweeping the ground and, on several occasions, enemy
shells buried him and his helper. Throughout this time O'Rourke showed

---

* The Provincial Archives in Victoria, British Columbia, indicate that he was born in
Dublin rather than Limerick and that his date of birth was 3 March 1874, which would
have made him 43 when he won the Victoria Cross.

complete disregard for his own safety, his only thought being for the wounded men in his care. Gazetted VC on 8 November 1917 he received his Cross from George V at Buckingham Palace on 5 December. He survived the war and returned to Canada where he died on 6 December 1967. His funeral at Holy Rosary Cathedral was attended by many ex-servicemen and the pall bearers included seven VC winners – Lieutenant-Colonel C. C. Merritt, Lieutenant-Colonel Robert Shankland, Lieutenant-Colonel Harcus Strachan, Sergeants Ernest Smith, Robert Hanna (another Irishman, who was gazetted on the same day as O'Rourke and invested at the same ceremony in Buckingham Palace), John C. Kerr, and Charles W. Train.

The fourth Irish Canadian VC of the Great War was awarded for an action carried out on 21 September 1917, near the town of Lens, France, by a man from the fishing village of Kilkeel in County Down. **Robert Hill Hanna** was born at Aughnahoory, Kilkeel, County Down on 6 August 1887 and emigrated to Canada in 1905, where he settled in British Columbia. He worked as a lumberman until the outbreak of war in 1914, when he enlisted in the Canadian Army and was posted to 29th (Vancouver) Battalion, British Columbia Regiment, Canadian Expeditionary Force.

By September 1917, Hanna was a company sergeant major. During the attack on 21 September, 29th Battalion was pinned down by heavy machine-gun fire from a German strongpoint. After the third attack had failed, CSM Hanna collected a party of volunteers and made a rush through the barbed wire and into the position. In the ensuing mêlée Hanna personally killed four of the enemy, therefore silencing the gun and capturing the remainder of the crew.

Robert Hanna was subsequently commissioned and finished the war as a lieutenant. Returning to civilian employment he managed a logging camp until 1938, when he returned to farming. He died on 15 June 1967, at Mount Lehman, British Columbia, and is buried in the Masonic Cemetery at Burnaby. His Victoria Cross was still in the possession of his son in 1978. Hanna was also a member of the Orange Order – LOL 2226 – and, by the rules of that organization, should not have been present at O'Rourke's requiem Mass. However, the brotherhood of the soldier and the special brotherhood of the Victoria Cross took precedence over the rules of the Orange Order.

On 12 September 1917, 2nd Irish Guards were being heavily bombarded by German artillery all along the line of the Broembeek, a very marshy river. The bombardment was followed up by a skilful attack by two companies of German stormtroopers wearing body armour. The German raid overran the Guards' outposts with the exception of Ney Copse, which was held by Sergeant **John Moyney** and fifteen men. As the Germans settled into their new positions they positioned a machine gun to cover the ground between

Moyney's post and the battalion line, a distance of some five hundred yards. The enemy knew that there was an outpost still intact, but were not sure of its exact location and so the area was sporadically shelled for the next four days. Throughout this time Sergeant Moyney kept a tight rein on his command, not allowing them to open their iron rations as he had not been ordered to do so, and ensuring that each man took his equal share of guard duty and fatigues. At dawn on 16 September their position, now spotted by the Germans, was attacked by a full company. Moyney allowed them to close to within twenty-five yards before opening fire. The Lewis gun caught the Germans in the flank, while accurate bomb throwing forced the remainder of the enemy to ground. A charge was then ordered through the Germans towards the Broembeek and back into the Guards' main trenches. Moyney's men were bombed and machine gunned as they waded across the foul muddy water while he covered them with rifle fire. As they crossed the marshy ground Private Woodcock earned the Victoria Cross for his rescue of Private Hilley, who had been wounded in the charge. John Moyney's conduct over the four days of the action was exemplary and earned him a well-deserved VC,[34] which was announced in the *London Gazette* of 17 October 1917. He was decorated by King George V at Buckingham Palace on 9 March 1918.

John Moyney was a native of Rathdowney, County Laois, where he was born on 8 January 1895.* A teetotaller, he was illiterate when he enlisted for the Leinster Regiment. His attestation papers were amended to the Irish Guards with whom he carried out his war service. On discharge he returned to Ireland to work for the Great Southern Railway Company, and remained with the railways until he retired. He travelled to London regularly to receive his shamrock each Saint Patrick's Day. As well as the VC he had the 1914-15 Star, the British War Medal, Victory Medal, Coronation Medals 1937 and 1953, Queen's Silver Jubilee Medal 1977 and the French Medaille Militaire. His medals are held by the Irish Guards. John Moyney died in Roscrea, County Tipperary, on 10 November 1980, the last surviving Irish VC laureate of the Great War. In March 1999 a set of wire-cutters that Moyney had used in the engagement during which he won the VC, and which he had given to a friend, were presented, mounted on a 4,800-years-old piece of Irish yew, to the Guards' Museum in London.[35]

Hugh Colvin lies buried in a family grave at Carnmoney cemetery near Belfast, although most sources on the Victoria Cross suggest that he was buried in Bangor, County Down.[36] The fact that Colvin was Irish is also

---

* *The Register of the Victoria Cross* gives his date of birth as 1885, but his attestation form shows his apparent age on enlistment in 1915 as 20. His obituary in the *Irish Guards Journal* shows that he died at the age of 85 in 1980, which would support the later date of birth.

1 The Victoria Cross. A plain bronze cross 'trifling in intrinsic value' but regarded as probably the premier gallantry award in the world. It was the first democratic award for gallantry in the British forces (Museum of the King's Own Royal Border Regiment).

2 (top, left): Thomas Grady, the first VC winner of the 4th (King's Own) Regiment. He earned his Cross for bringing back into action a British gun the crew of which had been brought down by Russian fire during the siege of Sebastopol (Museum of the King's Own Royal Border Regiment). 3 (top, right): Joseph Bradshaw, Rifle Brigade. He also earned his Cross for gallantry during the siege of Sebastopol (Royal Green Jackets Museum). 4 (bottom, left): Joseph Prosser, pictured with his wife and children. A soldier of the 1st, or Royal, Regiment (later the Royal Scots), Prosser was another who gained the VC at Sebastopol. His was awarded for two acts of gallantry, on 16 June and 11 August 1855 (Royal Scots Museum). 5 (bottom, right): Stephen Garvin. A colour-sergeant in the 60th Rifles (later King's Royal Rifle Corps), Garvin won his VC at Delhi during the Indian Mutiny (Royal Green Jackets Museum).

"THEY LIFTED ARNOLD OUT, THE SEPOYS FIRING VOLLEY AFTER VOLLEY" (P. 153)

6 (top, left): John Duane. Elected by his comrades of the 60th Rifles for the VC, Duane has consistently been given the name Divane in books on the VC (Royal Green Jackets Museum). 7 (bottom, left): Robert Hawthorne. A bugler of the 52nd Regiment (later Oxfordshire and Buckinghamshire Light Infantry), Hawthorne won the VC for rescuing a wounded officer while under heavy enemy fire during the Indian Mutiny (Royal Green Jackets Museum). 8 (top, right): Peter McManus and John Ryan. Private McManus of the 5th (Northumberland Fusiliers) Regiment was another whose VC was earned in the rescue of an injured colleague. He and Private John Ryan, of the 1st Madras Fusiliers – later Royal Dublin Fusiliers – are seen carrying Captain Arnold of the Madras Fusiliers to safety (Fusiliers Museum of Northumberland).

9 (top, left): Patrick McHale. Another soldier of the 5th Regiment, McHale won his VC for a series of courageous actions during assaults in the course of the actions at Lucknow (Fusiliers Museum of Northumberland). 10 (top, right): William Nash was another Lucknow VC winner. A corporal of the Rifle Brigade he was one of two men who carried a badly-wounded comrade to safety after an action near the Iron Bridge when a group of four men of Captain Wilmot's company was engaged by a much larger body of mutineers (Royal Green Jackets Museum). 11 (bottom, right): The reverse of the Victoria Cross awarded to Private William Coffey of the 34th (Cumberland) Regiment in the Crimean War. At some stage someone has attempted to alter the date on the reverse of the medal (King's Own Royal Border Regiment).

12 (top, left): Frederick Augustus Smith. A captain in the 43rd (Monmouthshire Light Infantry) Regiment – later the Oxfordshire and Buckinghamshire Light Infantry – Smith won the Victoria Cross at Tauranga, New Zealand during the Maori Wars when he led an attack against a heavily-defended Maori position (Royal Green Jackets Museum). 13 (top, right): Timothy O'Hea. A soldier of the Rifle Brigade, O'Hea was one of the few men who won the Victoria Cross for an act of gallantry that was not performed in the face of an enemy. He won his Cross at Danville, Quebec, Canada in 1866 for extinguishing a fire in a railway wagon that was carrying ammunition (Royal Green Jackets Museum). 14 (bottom, left): Edmund William Costello. One of five Irish VC winners who attended Stonyhurst College, Lancashire, Costello won his Cross with the Malakand Field Force in July 1897. He was serving as a lieutenant in 22 Punjab Infantry of the Indian Army (THCL Books/Stonyhurst College). 15 (bottom, right): Paul Aloysius Kenna. Another Stonyhurst VC, Kenna took part in the charge by 21st Lancers at Omdurman in 1898, in the course of which he took part in two rescues. For these deeds he was awarded the Victoria Cross (THCL Books/Stonyhurst College).

17 (top, left): The Last Shoot at Colenso by Caton Woodville. Roberts with two other officers attempts to save the guns (Cranston Fine Arts). **16 (top, right):** The Hon. Frederick Hugh Sherston Roberts. Son of Lord Roberts of Kandahar and Waterford, Freddie Roberts served in the King's Royal Rifle Corps. He earned a posthumous VC at Colenso during the Boer War when he tried to save the guns of two batteries of the Royal Artillery (Royal Green Jackets Museum).

18 (top, left): Robert Scott. Born of Irish parents in Lancashire, Scott won the VC with the Manchester Regiment in Natal in January 1900. He later served in the Great War, then with the Ulster Special Constabulary and, finally, with the RAF during the Second World War. He retired to live in County Down (Truesdale). 19 (top, right): James Edward Ignatius Masterson. A former Royal Irish Fusilier. Masterson was serving with the Devonshire Regiment when he won his VC at Wagon Hill, Ladysmith in 1900 (Royal Irish Fusiliers Museum). 20 (bottom, left): William John English. A lieutenant with 2nd Scottish Horse, English won his VC at Vlakfontein in 1901 during the Boer War. He was responsible for the defence of a position that came under intense fire and heavy attack. English served in both world wars (Stephen Sandford). 21 (bottom, right): Johnny Gough. A member of the famous Tipperary family, Major John Gough, Rifle Brigade, won the VC at Daratoleh in Somaliland in 1903 (Royal Green Jackets Museum).

22 (top, left): Maurice Dease. A former pupil of Stonyhurst College, Dease was machine-gun officer with 4th Royal Fusiliers and won the first Victoria Cross of the Great War on 23 August 1914. Dease was fatally wounded during the action at Mons. 23 (top, right): Henry Kelly. Serving as a second-lieutenant in 10th Bn., Duke of Wellington's Regiment, Kelly won the VC at Le Sars, France on 4th October 1916. He later served in the Spanish Civil War and in the Second World War and was also an officer in the Irish Army. He is pictured with Captain William Archer Redmond, Irish Guards, son of John Redmond, leader of the Irish Party at Westminster. 24 (bottom, left): Hugh Colvin. A second-lieutenant in 9th Bn., Cheshire Regiment, Colvin's Cross was awarded for his courage in leading an attack near Ypres in september 1917 when all but one of the more senior officers of two companies had been killed or injured (Cheshire Regiment Museum).

25 (top, left): Robert Morrow. The first VC winner of the Royal Irish Fusiliers, Private Morrow won his Cross at Messines, Belgium in April 1915 when he rescued several men under heavy enemy shellfire (Royal Irish Fusiliers Museum). 26 (top, right): Geoffrey St George Shillington Cather. Also an Irish Fusilier, Lieutenant Cather won his VC at the Somme in July 1916 for his valliant efforts to rescue wounded men. Cather lost his own life while engaged on this work (Royal Irish Fusiliers Museum). 27 (bottom, left): Eric Norman Frankland Bell. Another Somme VC, Captain Bell was serving with 9th Royal Inniskilling Fusiliers on 1 July 1916 when he earned the posthumous award of the VC for his gallant and inspiring leadership (Royal Inniskilling Fusiliers Museum). 28 (bottom, right): John Vincent Holland. An officer of the 3rd Bn., Leinster Regiment, Lieutenant Holland won the VC in a daring attack on the Somme sector in September 1916. He led a party of 26 bombers who cleared most of a village of enemy troops and took 50 prisoners. Only five of Holland's men survived and he was also wounded (Athy Heritage Centre).

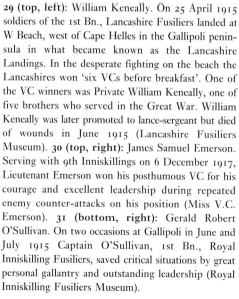

29 (top, left): William Keneally. On 25 April 1915 soldiers of the 1st Bn., Lancashire Fusiliers landed at W Beach, west of Cape Helles in the Gallipoli peninsula in what became known as the Lancashire Landings. In the desperate fighting on the beach the Lancashires won 'six VCs before breakfast'. One of the VC winners was Private William Keneally, one of five brothers who served in the Great War. William Keneally was later promoted to lance-sergeant but died of wounds in June 1915 (Lancashire Fusiliers Museum). 30 (top, right): James Samuel Emerson. Serving with 9th Inniskillings on 6 December 1917, Lieutenant Emerson won his posthumous VC for his courage and excellent leadership during repeated enemy counter-attacks on his position (Miss V.C. Emerson). 31 (bottom, right): Gerald Robert O'Sullivan. On two occasions at Gallipoli in June and July 1915 Captain O'Sullivan, 1st Bn., Royal Inniskilling Fusiliers, saved critical situations by great personal gallantry and outstanding leadership (Royal Inniskilling Fusiliers Museum).

32 (top, left): James Somers. Another Gallipoli VC winner of 1st Royal Inniskilling Fusiliers, Private Somers earned his Cross on the night of 1-2 July 1915 when his actions and leadership were instrumental in the recapture of a sap that had been taken by Turkish troops (Royal Inniskilling Fusiliers Museum). 33 (top, right): James Duffy. Serving with 6th Bn., Royal Inniskilling Fusiliers in Palestine, Private James Duffy, a stretcher bearer, saved the lives of two men by bringing them to safety while under heavy enemy fire (Royal Inniskilling Fusiliers Museum). 34 (bottom): William David Kenny. An officer in 4/39th Garhwal Rifles, Indian Army, Kenny won his VC at Kot Kai on India's North-West Frontier on 2 January 1920 when he ensured that his company was able to withdraw. Kenny was killed in action. He is photographed with his mother, Miriam, brother Gerald, sister Georgina, who died in the flu epidemic of 1919, and his father Joseph who was a senior officer in the RIC (Mrs Anne Mayne).

35 (top, left): Donald Edward Garland. The Royal
Air Force's first VC of the Second World War.
Flying Officer Garland earned a posthumous VC
when he led an attack on a heavily-defended bridge
over the Albert canal in Belgium on 12 May 1940
(Chaz Bowyer). 36 (top, right): Harold Marcus
Ervine Andrews. The first man to be presented with the VC in the Second World War.
Captain Andrews, who was educated at Stonyhurst College, won his Cross for his leadership
in the Dunkirk perimeter on 31 May–1 June 1940. He was the last Irish VC holder to die
(THCL Books/Stonyhurst College). 37 (bottom, right): Edward Stephen Fogarty Fegen.
Captain Fegen won a posthumous VC in November 1940 when he was commanding HMS
Jervis Bay, an armed merchant ship which was escorting convoy HX 84. When the convoy
was attacked by the German pocket battleship *Admiral Scheer*, Fegen took his ship into battle
against the German even though he was heavily outgunned. He bought the convoy time to
scatter to safety (Imperial War Museum).

38 (above): Captain James Jackman leads Z Company, 1st Royal Northumberland Fusiliers into action at El Duda (Fusiliers Museum of Northumberland). 39 (right): James Joseph Bernard Jackman. Captain Jackman was commanding a company of 1st Bn., Royal Northumberland Fusiliers during the breakout from Tobruk in November 1941. At El Duda on 25 November, the British attack was being hald up until Jackman brought his company into action and allowed the tanks to move forward again. He was later killed. Jackman was the last of the Irish VCs educated at Stonyhurst College (THCL Books/Stonyhurst College).

40 (top, left): Eugene Esmonde. On 12 February 1942 Lieutenant-Commander Esmonde DSO led 825 Naval Air Squadron in an attack on the German ships *Scharnhorst*, *Gneisenau* and *Prinz Eugen* which had slipped out of Brest and were making their way to Germany through the straits of Dover. Esmonde died in the attack and was posthumously awarded the VC (Chaz Bowyer). **41 (top, right):** Richard Kelliher. Private Kelliher was serving with 2/25th (Queensland) Bn., Australian Imperial Force in New Guinea when he won his VC on 13 September 1943. Kelliher rescued several wounded men under fire and knocked out a Japanese machine-gun position while doing so (Imperial War Museum). **42 (bottom, left):** David Samuel Anthony Lord. Flight Lieutenant Lord won RAF Transport Command's only VC at Arnhem in September 1944. He flew through intense enemy anti-aircraft fire to drop vital supplies to the airborne troops on the ground. Although his aircraft had been hit twice, he made a second run during and then ordered his crew to bale out. The plane then crashed in flames and Lord was killed (Chaz Bowyer). **43 (bottom, right):** Claude Raymond. Lieutenant Raymond, of the Royal Engineers, was operating with D Force in Burma in March 1945 when he earned a posthumous VC. He led his men in the successful attack on an enemy position during which he was wounded seriously. He refused medical attention until his men had been treated and died of his wounds next day (Imperial War Museum).

44 (top, left): James Joseph Magennis. The last Irish VC, Leading Seaman Magennis earned his Cross for his part in the attack on the Japanese cruiser *Takao* in the Johore strait on 31 July 1945. Magennis attached mines to the cruiser in very difficult circumstances and later left his midget submarine again to remove a limpet carrier that had not jettisoned (Imperial War Museum). **45 (top, right):** Bernard McCourt. Private McCourt is one of those unfortunate VC winners who have gone into posterity under a misspelt name. Official records show him as McQuirt and this memorial to him in his native Donacloney perpetuates that error (David Orr). **46 (bottom, left):** An unusual memorial to a VC winner can be seen at Enniskillen Castle where a German howitzer, captured during the Great War, stands as a memorial to Lieutenant James Anson Otho Brooke of 2nd Bn., Gordon Highlanders who won a posthumous VC near Gheluvelt, Belgium on 29 October 1914 (David Orr). **47 (bottom, right):** The medal group of Robert Morrow, VC at the Royal Irish Fusiliers Museum, Armagh. As well as his Victoria Cross, the group includes the 1914-15 Star, with Mons Clasp, the British War Medal, the Allied Victory Medal and the Russian Order of St George (bottom right) (Royal Irish Fusiliers Museum. Photo David Orr).

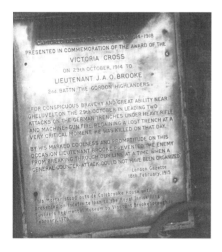

48 Desmond Whyte. Major Whyte was recommended for the Victoria Cross for his work with the wounded of 111 (Chindit) Brigade behind enemy lines in Burma in 1944. The award was denied and he received the DSO instead (Doherty). **49 (top, right):** Jimmy Barnes. Corporal Barnes of 2nd London Irish Rifles was recommended for a posthumous VC by his company commander, Major Desmond Woods MC, in May 1944. Corporal Barnes had led the remnants of his platoon in an attack on a German anti-tank gun that was holding up the tanks support-ing the Irish Rifles. No award was made. (Colonel Desmond Woods, MC). **50 (bottom, left):** Father Dan Kelleher MC. Brian Clark, then Adjutant of 1st Bn., Royal Irish Fusiliers, believed that Father Dan would have earned a periodic VC had he been serving with an English brigade. In the Irish Brigade, his courage was regarded as that expected from a chap-lain (Doherty). **51 (bottom, right):** Memorial Mass for Harold Marcus Ervine-Andrews – order of service (Stonyhurst College).

A. M. D. G.

Mass for Lt. Col.
Marcus Ervine-Andrews VC

Sunday 21st May 1995

missed by those same sources. Born in Burnley on 1 February 1887, he joined the 8th (King's Royal Irish) Hussars[37] and served in the ranks before he was commissioned into the Cheshire Regiment on 13 March 1917. He had only been on active service with the 9th Battalion of the Cheshires for a short time when he won the Victoria Cross near Ypres. During an attack on 20 September all the other officers in his company were killed or wounded and the battalion's leading company had also lost all but one of its officers. Second Lieutenant Colvin took command of both companies and led them forward in the face of heavy fire towards their objective. With two soldiers he approached an enemy dug-out, left the two men outside, entered the dug-out alone and emerged with fourteen prisoners. This was the first in a series of similar dug-out clearances; he entered most of the others either alone or with one soldier and captured machine guns, took many prisoners and killed a number of Germans who chose to resist rather than surrender.

Hugh Colvin survived the war and died in Chester on 16 September 1962. His sister, who lived in Bangor, had his remains brought to Belfast for burial in the family plot in the cemetery on Carnmoney hill overlooking the city on the Lagan.

In December 1917 the battalions of 36th (Ulster) Division were involved in that most difficult of military manoeuvres, a withdrawal in the face of a sustained enemy attack. The Germans had launched their most determined offensive since Verdun in early-1916 and British troops were falling back under the onslaught. It was in such circumstances that Second-Lieutenant **James Samuel Emerson**, of 9th Royal Inniskilling Fusiliers, won a posthumous Victoria Cross. On 3 December the Ulster Division came under command of III Corps and its brigades moved into the line the following day for a most difficult handover, as there was uncertainty about the exact locations of the British positions and the German artillery was in full cry. In the III Corps area the new British front ran from near Marcoing, in the north-east, to Villers Plouich in the south-east and was dominated by Highland Ridge to the north-west and Welsh Ridge to the south-east. The latter ridge was to be the responsibility of 9th Inniskillings who arrived at their new positions on the afternoon of 4 December.[38]

The Inniskillings came under bombardment as they arrived and also learned that German troops were bombing their way up the line and making good progress. The leading platoon of the Inniskillings was immediately pressed into service and fought off the attackers. Next day the battalion, supported by a platoon from 14th Royal Irish Rifles, made their own counter-attack to regain ground that had been lost before their arrival. That attack was too successful: the Germans retreated but the Inniskillings, instead of consolidating their gains, began pursuing the enemy and were ambushed by other German troops, who captured many of the leading attackers from 9th Inniskillings.[39] It was during the battle that followed that Emerson, born in Collon, County Louth, on 3 August 1895, won his VC.

The diminutive officer, he was little more than five feet tall, led his platoon in an attack that cleared 400 yards of trench. When the German counter-attack was launched he was wounded – an eyewitness recalled that there was a hole in the top of Emerson's steel helmet – but continued to organize the defence of his company position; he believed that most of the company had been wiped out. With eight men, he had left the trench to fight off the assaulting Germans, in which engagement a number of enemy were killed and six were made prisoner. Emerson was now the only officer left with the company and refused to leave his men for medical treatment. Instead he led the defence over a three-hour period, fighting off several more attacks. It was while repelling one of these attacks that he was mortally injured. The Germans had advanced with superior numbers and Emerson led his men out of the trench to meet the assault. He fell dead at their head but his heroic leadership inspired the remaining Inniskillings to hold out until reinforcements arrived.[40]

James Emerson's Victoria Cross was announced in the *London Gazette* of 13 February 1918. Unusually for a posthumous VC at this stage of the war, it was not presented to his family by the King at a Buckingham Palace investiture. Instead it was handed formally to his widowed mother in a ceremony at the Whitworth Hall in Drogheda by Brigadier-General Hackett-Payne before a packed audience that included 'the different classes of the Drogheda public'. Emerson has no known grave but is commemorated on the Cambrai Memorial and by an obelisk in Collon parish churchyard.

The first-ever Irish division to serve in the British Army was 10th (Irish) which fought in the Gallipoli and Macedonian campaigns. In early 1917 the division was sent to Palestine as part of XX Corps. At the third battle of Gaza 10th (Irish) Division attacked Beersheba, on the left flank of the Turkish positions. Following the capture of the town on 30 October, XX Corps went on to attack the remaining Turkish defences and by 7 November their part in the battle was over.[41]

Tenth (Irish) Division next saw action after the capture of Jerusalem and it was during this fighting in the Judaean hills that Private **James Duffy**, a stretcher-bearer with 6th Royal Inniskilling Fusiliers, won the next Irish VC. In the hard fighting that went on around Kereina Peak, Duffy performed several acts of cool bravery in the recovery of wounded men. When his fellow stretcher-bearer was hit, Duffy continued alone to bring in a wounded man before returning to rescue his partner. His VC was gazetted on 28 February 1918 and Duffy made a visit to his family home at Letterkenny, County

Donegal, at the time of his investiture. He received a hearty welcome from the people of the district. James Duffy was born at Thorr, near Crolly Bridge, Gweedore, County Donegal, on 17 November 1889, and was brought to his father's home at Bunagee, near Letterkenny when he was only months old; his mother had returned to her parents' home for his birth. After the war, James Duffy returned to Letterkenny where he lived for the rest of his days. Although 'a most unassuming man [who] did not wish to boast about his achievements', he was proud of the fellowship of the Victoria Cross and this made his life difficult in post-independence Donegal. He was kidnapped by the IRA in the early 1920s and received threatening letters, purporting to come from that body, when he attended VC celebrations in London in 1929. In spite of that, he was also present at the VC Centenary Review in London on 26 June 1956. James Duffy died on 8 April 1969 and is buried at Conwall cemetery, outside Letterkenny. A headstone was erected by the Royal Inniskilling Fusiliers' Association and includes an engraving of the Victoria Cross.

British forces were also engaged against the Turks in Mesopotamia – present-day Iraq – in a campaign that had brought much suffering to the British and Indian soldiers who served in that country. There were many calls on the medical services, which were not found wanting, and many of the medical officers were decorated for their courage and devotion to duty. One of them, Captain **John Alexander Sinton** of the Indian Medical Service, won the Victoria Cross.

Sinton was born in British Columbia, Canada on 2 December 1884, of parents who both hailed from Ireland. When their son was six years old, Walker and Isabella Sinton returned to their native soil and John Alexander was educated at Nicholson Memorial School in Lisburn, Royal Belfast Academical Institution and Queen's College, Belfast. He then studied tropical medicine in Liverpool and was, for a time, on the staff of the Royal Victoria Hospital in Belfast. In 1911 he joined the Indian Medical Service and in 1916 was serving with the Indian Expeditionary Force in Mesopotamia.

On 21 January 1916 a force of British and Indian troops was trying to reach the town of Kut el Amara, which was under siege by the Turks. The relief force was under the command of an Irish VC winner, General Sir Fenton J. Aylmer VC, and the action in which Sinton won his Victoria Cross took place on the banks of the river Tigris. At the Orah ruins Captain Sinton went to the aid of wounded soldiers under very heavy enemy fire. He was himself severely wounded – shot through both arms and the side – but refused to leave the injured men to go to hospital. All through the daylight hours he continued with his duties, constantly risking further injury or death as the enemy fire continued to be heavy and sustained. Eventually he was evacuated for treatment and recovered from his injuries. Sinton had displayed 'the utmost bravery' on three previous occasions and these, together with his courage at Orah, earned him the Victoria Cross which was gazetted on 21 June 1916. He was presented with his medal in Delhi by the Viceroy on 31 January 1918. Sinton was also awarded the Russian Order of Saint George.

Captain Sinton returned to duty as a medical officer and served until the end of the war. Returning to the Army, he served throughout the Second World War also, receiving a Mention in Despatches (his second), and retired from active life to spend his last years in Northern Ireland where he settled near Cookstown. He died there on 25 March 1956. John Alexander Sinton was also a Fellow of the Royal Society and, at the time of his death, was believed to be the only person entitled to the post-nominal letters, VC, FRS.

The only double Victoria Cross winner of the Great War was also a doctor, Captain Noel Godfrey Chavasse of the RAMC, attached to the Liverpool Scottish. Although Captain Chavasse was not Irish, the family has an Irish connection, with the Chavasse family of West Cork, three of whom served in the Second World War and earned three DSOs, and two DSCs as well as two Mentions in Despatches. Incidentally, the Irish branch of the Chavasse family was also related to the Coghills of Drumcondra, and therefore have a connection with another VC, that of Nevill Josiah Aylmer Coghill.

In the pre-dawn darkness and fog of 21 March 1918, at 4.40 a.m., a storm of German artillery fell on the Allied positions on the Western Front in France. Front-line trenches and rear areas were drenched in high explosive and gas shells. Units were decimated in those first few minutes and survivors fought to the death in the swirling smoke and fire. Operation MICHAEL, the German attempt to knock out Britain and France before significant numbers of American troops could arrive in Europe, had begun. The attack was made possible by the collapse of Russia, which allowed the transfer of large numbers of German divisions from the Eastern Front.

Thirty-sixth (Ulster) Division was hit at 9.40 a.m., with their front-line positions being overrun in short order. Three positions held out for some considerable time, the first at Le Pontchu, where 12th Royal Irish Rifles held on until 3.30 p.m. The second was on the Essigny Plateau, where a company of 1st Royal Irish Fusiliers held until 4.30 p.m. The third was at the Racecourse Redoubt near Groagie, where Second-Lieutenant **Edmund de Wind**, of 15th Royal Irish Rifles, earned a posthumous Victoria Cross for his actions in its defence. Despite being wounded twice, de Wind held his position for seven hours, until another section came to his aid. On two occasions with two NCOs he ventured forth under heavy machine-gun fire and cleared the enemy from the trench. He continued to repel attack after attack until he was fatally wounded. A posthumous VC for De Wind was announced in the *London*

Gazette on 15 May 1919 and the decoration was presented to his mother by King George V in the quadrangle of Buckingham Palace on 21 June 1919. His father had died in 1917. Edmund De Wind has no known grave but is remembered today on the Pozieres Memorial while in his home town of Comber, County Down, where he was born on 11 December 1883, a street bears his name. Mount De Wind in Alberta, Canada was also named in his honour. The Canadian connection is interesting as De Wind is also claimed as a Canadian VC, although he won his Cross with the Royal Irish Rifles. Educated at Campbell College, Belfast he worked in the Bank of Ireland in Cavan as a clerk before emigrating to Canada in 1910 where he was employed by the Bank of Commerce. In 1914 he enlisted in 31st Battalion (Calgary Regiment) CEF and served in its machine-gun section in France from September 1915 to April 1917, after which he was commissioned in the Royal Irish Rifles.

On 27 May 1918 at the river Aisne, Brigadier-General **George William St George Grogan** CMG, DSO was in command of the remnants of the infantry of a division and attached troops. The Germans were attacking with all their strength and it was due to the superb leadership of Grogan that the British line held.

> His utter disregard for personal safety combined with sound practical ability helped to stay the onward thrust of the enemy. He rode up and down the front line encouraging his troops under artillery, trench mortar, rifle and machine-gun fire and when one horse was shot under him, he continued encouraging his men on foot until another horse was brought.[42]

Grogan's VC was gazetted on 25 July 1918. His has not been recognized as an Irish Victoria Cross in previous works on the medal. However, the short-lived contemporary publication, the *Irish Soldier*, included an account of his VC in 1918.[43]

The newly-formed Tank Corps won four Victoria Crosses in the course of the war, the fourth of which was awarded to Lieutenant-Colonel **Richard Annesley West** for actions near Courcelles on 21 August and at Vaulx Vraucourt on 2 September 1918. Born in Cheltenham on 26 September 1878, West was the son of Augustus George West of White Park, County Fermanagh. His mother, Sara, was the daughter of Canon Richard Booth Eyre, rector of Eyre Court in County Galway. Richard West served in the South African War and on the outbreak of war in 1914 he joined the North Irish Horse. He transferred to the Tank Corps with the rank of major in 1917, by which time he was already a holder of the DSO. On 8 August 1918 he earned an immediate award of the Military Cross. Then, on 21 August, came the first of the

two actions that earned him the VC. He was also awarded a Bar to the DSO
for his actions on 21 August.

> during the attack on Courcelles, the infantry having lost their bearings
> in the dense fog, this officer at once took charge of any men he could
> find. He reorganized them and led them on horseback through the vil-
> lage on to their objective in face of heavy machine-gun fire. ...
> Throughout the whole action he displayed the most utter disregard of
> danger, and the capture of the village was in great part due to his ini-
> tiative and gallantry.[44]

West had two horses shot from under him during the action and was fortunate to escape unscathed himself. He was on horseback again on 2 September
when it was planned that a battalion of light tanks should exploit an initial
attack by infantry and heavy tanks. To keep himself appraised of the battle's
progress, West went forward to the front infantry positions. This would also
give him the advantage of being aware immediately of any enemy counter-
attack. When he arrived with the foremost infantry he soon learned that the
battalion had suffered severe casualties to its officers and that its flanks were
exposed. There was a very real possibility of the battalion giving way before
the Germans and, to prevent this, West rode out in front of the soldiers,
ignoring heavy rifle and machine-gun fire. He rallied the men and ordered
NCOs to take the place of the officers who had been killed or wounded. In
spite of the enemy pressure he restored the situation at the front.

Riding up and down in front of the battalion, West exhorted the men to
stand their ground, calling: 'Stick it men, show them fight, and for God's
sake put up a good fight'. Those were probably his last words. He was struck
by a burst of machine-gun fire and fell to the ground, dead.

There could be little doubt that West would receive a posthumous VC.
The award was gazetted on 30 October, and the Victoria Cross, the DSO and
Bar, and the Military Cross were presented to his widow in the ballroom of
Buckingham Palace on 15 February 1919. By that time, Maud Ethel West
had given birth to their daughter, Gertrude Annesley, on 17 November 1918.
Richard Annesley West is buried in Mory Abbey Military Cemetery.

The final Irish-Canadian VC of the war was won by Private **Claude Joseph
Patrick Nunney** DCM, MM, of 38th Battalion (Eastern Ontario Regiment)
CEF, on 1 September 1918. Born in Dublin on 24 December 1892,* Nunney

---

* *The Register of the Victoria Cross* shows Nunney's birthplace as Hastings, East Sussex,
but the Lummis Files and Sir John Smyth indicate Dublin, as does *Canada's VCs* (p. 140).
The three christian names that he bore certainly indicate Irish parentage.

had already won the DCM at Vimy Ridge in April 1917 and the MM at Avion on 28 June 1917.

On 1 September, Claude Nunney was at his company headquarters when 38th Battalion, which was preparing for an advance, was counter-attacked by the Germans under cover of a heavy artillery bombardment.

> Entirely on his own initiative [Nunney] went forward through the barrage to the company outpost line, going from post to post and encouraging the men by his own fearless example to stand fast. The enemy were repulsed and a critical situation was saved. During the attack next day he again displayed the same fearless leadership.[45]

Nunney was severely wounded in the attack on 2 September and succumbed to his injuries on 18 September. His brother Alfred, who was serving in 80th Battalion CEF, had been killed in action on 10 August. Claude Nunney is buried in Aubigny Communal Cemetery at Aubigny-en-Artois. His VC was gazetted on 14 December 1918.

On 2 September 1918 no fewer than eleven VCs were gained. The Allies were now advancing in what was to be the final phase of the war; the 'last hundred days' had begun. But, although the Germans were withdrawing on many sectors of the front, they continued to present a formidable opposition and following them up as they withdrew was frequently much more hazardous than fighting a defensive action. Such was the case near Reincourt on 2 September. As the advance reached Reincourt, a company of 1st Royal Munster Fusiliers suffered the loss of all its officers and command devolved on Company Sergeant Major **Martin Doyle** MM, a native of New Ross, County Wexford, where he had been born on 25 October 1894.* Doyle had earned the Military Medal in March 1918 and had been captured shortly afterwards but escaped when his battalion launched a counter-attack.

In the confused fighting around Reincourt, CSM Doyle realised that the enemy had surrounded part of his unit. Gathering together a rescue party he led a charge which drove off the Germans and recovered the missing men, including a wounded officer whom he carried to safety. The Munsters were being supported by tanks at this time and, later in the day, Doyle personally drove off a party of enemy who were swarming over one tank and trying to gain entry. A few minutes after this incident a German machine gun opened up on the same tank, preventing the removal of some of the crew who had

---

* The *Register of the Victoria Cross* shows Doyle's date of birth as 1891. An article in *An Cosantóir* in April 1991 indicates that he was born in 1894 but added two years to his age to enlist in the Royal Irish when he was 15.

been wounded. Doyle once again single-handedly rushed forward and knocked out the gun and captured three of its crew. That evening the Germans counter-attacked and the company was able not only to beat off this attack, but also to take a large number of prisoners, all due to the inspiration and leadership of Martin Doyle. On 31 January 1919 his VC was gazetted and he received the decoration from George V in the quadrangle of Buckingham Palace on 8 May 1919.

Martin Doyle was one of the very few regular soldiers from the pre-war Army who was still alive in 1918. He had joined the Royal Irish Regiment at Kilkenny in 1909 and served with them in India. In 1914 he returned to Ireland and by December was in France with the Royal Dublin Fusiliers with whom he reached the rank of sergeant. On promotion to CSM, Martin Doyle transferred to the Munsters and it was with the *Dirty Shirts* that he earned both VC and MM.

After receiving his VC from King George V, Martin Doyle returned home to a hero's welcome in New Ross. He was demobilized from the Army in July and married Charlotte Kennedy of New Ross on 25 November 1919. Doyle attended two VC functions in London during the 1920s as well as regimental reunions. However, he had also been an intelligence officer for the IRA's Mid Clare Brigade during the war of independence in 1920 and 1921. Working for the British Army at their garrison in Ennis, it is assumed that Doyle was passing on information on British activities to his IRA comrades. For these activities Doyle was posthumously decorated by the Irish government.[46]

In February 1922 Martin Doyle enlisted in the new Irish Army and fought in the ensuing civil war. He continued to serve in the Irish Army after the war and became a company sergeant. In 1937 he left the Army to work for Guinness as a security man although he remained a reservist until January 1939.

Retirement from uniformed service was short for Martin Doyle. He died in Sir Patrick Dun's Hospital in Dublin on 20 November 1940 and was buried in Grangegorman British Military Cemetery in Dublin. A headstone bearing the badge of the Munsters and the inscription 'Coy Sgt Major Martin Doyle, VC, MM; Royal Munster Fusiliers; died 20 November 1940' was erected by his old comrades of the Munsters.

As the war entered its final days two more Irish Victoria Crosses were won, one of which went to yet another member of the Irish diaspora. A veteran of the Boer War, Private **James Crichton** was serving in 2nd Battalion, Auckland Infantry Regiment of the New Zealand Expeditionary Force, which was in action at Crevecoeur, France during the advance on the German lines.

Two incidents led to the award. The first was the carrying of a message back to battalion headquarters which involved crossing a canal and a river, both of which were swept by enemy machine-gun fire. The second was, under his own initiative, the removal of explosive charges from a bridge; this was also carried out under machine-gun and sniper fire. During this time Crichton was suffering from a painful wound that he had received earlier that day. His VC was gazetted on 15 November 1918 and presented by the monarch in the ballroom of Buckingham Palace on 26 February 1919.

Born in Carrickfergus, County Antrim, on 15 July 1879, James Crichton survived the war and died in New Zealand at Auckland Hospital, Takapuna, on 22 September 1961. He is buried in Waitumette Soldiers' Cemetery, Auckland.

Martin Moffatt was the last Irishman to win the Victoria Cross on the Western Front in the First World War. At the time he was serving as a private in 2nd Leinster Regiment although his military career had begun with the Connaught Rangers as befitted a native of Sligo. On 14 October 1918 the battalion was advancing in the area of Ledgehem in Belgium and Private Moffatt was a member of a five-man working party which was crossing a stretch of open ground when they came under machine-gun fire from a nearby house. Running towards the house alone, through a hail of bullets, Moffatt threw bombs at the position and silenced the gun. Working his way around to the rear he killed two of the enemy and succeeded in capturing thirty more. The *London Gazette* of 26 December 1918 carried the announcement that he had been awarded the Victoria Cross and he was decorated in the quadrangle of Buckingham Palace on 12 June 1919.

Interestingly, in view of the political situation in Ireland in mid-1919, the town of Sligo came to a standstill when Moffatt returned from receiving the VC. The train carrying him to the shadow of Ben Bulben even had difficulty getting into the station, such was the size of the crowd that awaited Sligo's hero. On discharge Moffatt returned to Sligo, where he had been born on 15 April 1884, and became a harbour policeman until his death by drowning near Rosses Point on 5 January 1946.

The Great War saw the birth of aerial warfare and, from the slow, flimsy machines of 1914, aeroplanes developed into nimble fighters and bombers that presaged a new era in warfare. Nineteen airmen won the Victoria Cross during the war. One of them was an Irishman, **Edward Mannock**. Although born in England, Mannock was the son of Irish parents: his mother's maiden name was O'Sullivan and his father, also Edward, was a soldier, serving in 5th Dragoon Guards, although some sources suggest that Mannock senior was a corporal of the Royal Inniskilling Fusiliers. Edward Mannock was known in the service as Mick which indicates that his contemporaries had no doubt that he was Irish.

Edward Mannock was born on 24 May 1887 at Preston Cavalry Barracks, Brighton. He was not the healthiest of children and suffered from an astigmatism in his left eye that was so severe that he was effectively blind in that eye for most of his life. He did not appear to have the makings of one of the most successful fighter pilots of the Great War. Yet that is what he became, winning the DSO, with two Bars, and the MC, with Bar, as well as the Victoria Cross, which was gazetted posthumously.[47]

By the time of his death in July 1918 – which was caused by small-arms fire from German ground troops – Mannock had been credited with 73 aerial combat victories. After the war, many of his former comrades pressed for the award of the VC to Mannock and the Air Minister, Winston Churchill, lent his support. The award was gazetted on 18 July 1919, although the citation reduced his number of victories to fifty. On 26 November 1919, King George V presented the Victoria Cross and the other decorations to Mannock's father, who had abandoned his wife and four children when Edward was twelve years old.

Although English-born, **James Thomas Byford McCudden**, another air VC, was of Irish descent. Born on 28 March 1895, at Gillingham, Kent, his father was William Henry McCudden, a Scotsman and serving soldier and his mother was Amelia Byford, an Irish girl who had married William when he was stationed in Ireland. McCudden, therefore, provided that heady combination described by the Scottish poet Hugh Macdiarmid: 'Scots steel tempered wi' Irish fire is the weapon I desire.'

Between August 1917 and March 1918, McCudden served with No. 56 Squadron Royal Flying Corps on the Western Front. His behaviour during this time both in his aggressive patrolling and the protection of new members of the squadron was of the highest calibre. By March 1918, he had accounted for fifty-seven enemy aircraft destroyed, some single-handed, some while leading his flight. On 16 February 1918, he shot down a total of four aircraft, three on a dawn patrol and the fourth in the afternoon. McCudden flew an SE5, an aircraft type in which no less than four Victoria Crosses were won.[48]

James McCudden was killed in the air near Marquise, France on 9 July 1918. He was twenty-three years old. In addition to the Victoria Cross, he was awarded the Croix de Guerre by France. He had also found time to write *Five Years in the RFC*. His service career and that of Edward Mannock had crossed when McCudden helped train the latter to fly.

One other air Victoria Cross winner of the war who had Irish ancestry was the Australian Frank Hubert McNamara, a former teacher. However, no evidence has been found to indicate that his Irishness was sufficient to merit inclusion in this book.

The war that was supposed to end all wars came to an end on the Western Front at 11 a.m. on 11 November 1918, the eleventh hour of the eleventh day of the eleventh month, the hour at which it was agreed that an armistice would come into efect and the guns would finally fall silent after more than four years of dealing death and destruction. However, although the formal end to the war with Germany came in 1919, there were five VCs awarded in that year. All of those awards were for actions in north Russia, in support of the White Russians against the Bolsheviks, and one of them was won by Lieutenant **Augustus Agar** of the Royal Navy.* Born in Kandy, Ceylon in 1890, Agar was the son of John Shelton Agar of Woodmount, County Kerry.

On 17 June 1919, Agar was commanding HM Coastal Motor-Boat No. 4 which sank the Bolshevik cruiser *Oleg* in Kronstadt harbour. The coastal motor-boats were a new weapon in the Royal Navy's inventory: torpedo-armed, fast and with a very shallow draught that allowed them to pass over minefields in relative safety, they were ideally suited to operations close inshore such as attacking enemy vessels in defended anchorages. In the citation for Agar's Victoria Cross, published in the *London Gazette* on 22 August, it notes simply that the award was made 'In recognition of his conspicuous gallantry, coolness and skill under extremely difficult conditions in action'. That brief explanation was a product of the low-profile nature of the operations against the Bolsheviks. Agar had first penetrated a defensive screen of destroyers to reach the bay in which *Oleg* lay. CMB 4 had sustained hull damage from gun-fire and, as the vessel closed on its target, it broke down. Agar was forced to take the gunboat alongside a breakwater for twenty minutes while repairs were carried out, all under full view of the enemy. Once repairs were effected, the attack was resumed and *Oleg* was sunk, following which Agar made good his escape to the open sea under heavy fire.[50]

Agar went on to win the DSO in a further attack on Kronstadt harbour on 18 August in which the Bolshevik battleships *Andrei Pervozzani* and *Petropavlosk* were torpedoed. In 1941 he was commanding the cruiser HMS *Dorsetshire*, with its sister ship *Cornwall* also under his command, when the two ships were attacked by Japanese aircraft in the Indian ocean. Less than eight minutes later *Dorsetshire* slid below the waves. The survivors endured an appalling ordeal during which Agar's leadership was inspiring and helped many men to survive. His own health was destroyed by the experience of a night and a tropical day in the water before help arrived.[51]

---

* *The Register of the Victoria Cross* gives his forenames as Augustine William Shelton.

Augustus Agar reached the rank of commodore and commanded the Royal Naval College at Greenwich from 1943 to 1945. He died in Alton, Hampshire, on 30 December 1968.

And so the Great War had come to an end. But it was not a clean end. In the treaty of Versailles that ended formally the war with Germany the Allies sought to place a heavy burden of war reparations on the defeated German nation. This was to cause much resentment and, coupled with the belief that the German army had not been defeated in the field, was to provide a platform for the politics of Nazism. From the ashes of the German army in 1918 rose the commander-in-chief of German forces in a further war: Adolf Hitler. In the conflict against Hitler, Irishmen would again play their part and eight of them would win the Victoria Cross; a ninth Cross would be won by an Irish-born Welsh airman.

7 1920-45

Between the end of the First World War and the beginning of the Second five Victoria Crosses were won. One was gained in Mesopotamia and the remaining four in India's North West Frontier province. Of the four Crosses won in India, three were awarded posthumously, including one to an Irishman, Lieutenant William David Kenny, from Saintfield in County Down. General Sir John Smyth VC, MC, who was Kenny's brigade commander, described him as being 'as grand a young subaltern as any regiment could wish to have'.[1]

The North West Frontier province was an area that had been the source of much unrest over many years. There the power of the British Empire was at its weakest and the writ of the King-Emperor never truly ran. From time to time the frontier erupted into open warfare between the hill tribes and the imperial power and, at all times, soldiers stationed there were constantly on the alert.

Many years had passed since a VC had been awarded for an action on the North West Frontier of India. Then, on 22 October 1919, Captain John Henry Adams MBE, of the Indian Medical Service, was awarded a posthumous VC for his gallantry in an action in Waziristan. Adams' decoration was won near Khajuri post on the Shinki Pass, which was within 43 Brigade's area. The elderly medical officer died at the end of an action against a raiding party of some 100 Mahsuds, described by Sir John Smyth, 43 Brigade's commander, as 'the toughest of all North-West Frontier tribesmen'.[2]

Lieutenant **William David Kenny** was serving with 4th Battalion 39th Garhwal Rifles, of the Indian Army, in that same brigade. He gained the supreme award for gallantry for his actions at a small hilltop village called Kot Kai on 2 January 1920. By that stage troops on the Frontier were involved in operations against the Mahsuds, one of the most difficult campaigns in the long history of strife in the region.[3]

The Mahsuds proved doughty opponents, especially when equipped with modern rifles and a plentiful supply of ammunition, and fighting in the crags and valleys of their mountain homeland. They dogged the steps of the soldiers who fought them and they were especially effective and dangerous when they were following up a British withdrawal. In the nature of operations on the Frontier they had many opportunities for such action. And it was during a withdrawal near Kot Kai that January day in 1920 that Kenny lost his life and won the Victoria Cross.[4]

Smyth was organizing the withdrawal of men of 43 Brigade from the Kot Kai area and, while preparing the fire-plan for the withdrawal, went forward to visit Kenny's company, which held a critical position. For Smyth's plan to succeed, Kenny's men needed to hold their position until the rest of 4/39th Garwhalis had pulled out.

> It was a brute of a position, perched on a knife edge, which they had done wonders to hold, but from which, I knew, it would be equally difficult to withdraw. Kenny's broad smile was the last I ever saw of him.[5]

When the Garwhalis began their withdrawal, the Mahsuds attacked Kenny's company from all sides, pressing home their attack with vigour. But the young Irishman and his soldiers did not flinch. They fought stubbornly, refusing to concede any ground to the foe until the order to withdraw was received. At that stage, Kenny ordered three of his four platoons* to fight their way out in succession; he remained with the fourth platoon to provide covering fire. Finally, he gave the order for the last platoon to begin its withdrawal. As his men began their retreat, Kenny noticed that the other platoons had suffered casualties and that they were having problems removing the wounded to safety. Such was the cruelty of warfare on the frontier that wounded were never abandoned to the tender mercies of the hillsmen, or their women folk.[6] Kipling summed up the soldier's philosophy when he wrote 'When you're wounded and lying on Afghanistan's plains/ And the women come out to cut up what remains/ Just roll to your rifle and blow out your brains/ And go to your God like a soldier.'[7]

Kenny was not prepared to leave any of the Garwhalis to the mercy of the Mahsuds. Only one course of action was open to him: 'Without hesitation [he] ordered his small party to turn, fix bayonets and charge the pursuing enemy. This very gallant act enabled the wounded to be withdrawn but Kenny and his men were all killed.'[8]

Kenny was the type of officer who could inspire soldiers to such self-sacrifice. Smyth summed him up as 'tall, strong, red-haired, always smiling; his men would have followed him anywhere'.[9] His final action proved the truth of that assessment. He is listed on the Delhi War Memorial as well as the Donaghadee memorial. A member of the Kenny family is always given the honour of laying the first wreath on the Donaghadee war memorial on Remembrance Sunday each year.[10]

---

* Until 1937 infantry companies were composed of four platoons. After that date the number of platoons in a company was reduced to three.

After the Great War the British forces had been much reduced and returned to their principle peacetime tasks. For the Army that meant garrisoning India and the type of operations in which Kenny was killed. There was little investment in the forces and the ability to fight a major war was not a priority with the governments of the day. However, the political and strategic outlook in Europe began to change markedly in the early-1930s with the rise of Adolf Hitler and the Nazi party in Germany. By the middle of the decade the British government had been forced to begin a re-armament programme to match the rising power of Germany. In the early stages of that programme the principal beneficiary was the Royal Air Force, which received new monoplane bombers and fighters and formed new squadrons that began to train for a possible European war.

That war finally came in September 1939 and a British Expeditionary Force was sent to France to support the French army. An air element accompanied the BEF in the form of the Advanced Air Striking Force, which included ten squadrons of Fairey Battle light bombers from No. 1 Group.[11] The Battle was a single-engined daylight bomber with a crew of three, a modest bombload and negligible defensive power. It was already obsolete by the outbreak of war and its first encounters with German fighters were to prove how hopelessly outclassed the aircraft was. But it was a Battle of No. 12 Squadron that earned the Royal Air Force's first two Victoria Crosses of the war. The pilot of that Battle was **Donald Edward Garland**, born at Ballinacorr, County Wicklow, on 28 June 1918 and educated at the Cardinal Vaughan School in Kensington. He then applied to join the RAF, to fulfil a lifelong ambition, and was accepted for a short-service commission on 12 July 1937. He undertook elementary flying training at Hamble and was confirmed in rank as a pilot officer on 3 September before progressing to No. 2 Flying Training School for service training. On 7 May 1938 he graduated and was posted to No. 12 Squadron which was converting from Hawker Hind biplane bombers to the new Fairey Battle.*[12]

Flying Officer Garland moved to France with his squadron in September 1939 and flew on some of the missions that proved the vulnerability and obsolescence of the Battle. Garland's squadron deployed to Barry-au-Bac where it flew its first operational mission on 17 September, a reconnaissance overflight of the German border zone.[13]

---

* The Battle was a monoplane, powered by a 1,030 h.p. Rolls-Royce Merlin engine, the same powerplant as the new Hurricane and Spitfire fighters. However, with a crew of three and a bombload of 1,000 lbs (maximum) the Battle was hopelessly outclassed by the contemporary Luftwaffe fighter the Messerschmitt Bf109. By the time war broke out the Battle was already obsolete.

On 30 September five Battles of No. 150 Squadron were sent on a photographic reconnaissance mission over German territory. Engaged at first by anti-aircraft guns they were also attacked by fighters. Four of the five aircraft were shot down and the fifth machine was badly damaged. Following this incident, offensive operational flights by the Battles were stopped. In December No. 12 Squadron moved to Amifontaine, a satellite of Barry-au-Bac, although even practice flying was restricted considerably by very cold conditions. The lack of flying added to the image of phoney war. When a thaw set in, in March 1940, a regular routine of flying began. Battles were allowed to fly night operations, dropping leaflets, over Germany and No. 12 again carried out reconnaissance flights over German territory, although these generally followed NICKEL leaflet raids.[14]

On 9 April the Germans invaded Denmark and Norway. An Allied expeditionary force had already sailed for Norway and there was a short campaign there. However, life remained quiet on the western front and No. 12 Squadron's routine continued. That routine was shattered completely on the morning of 10 May when the Germans launched Operation SICHELSCHNITT (sickle cut), the invasion of France, Belgium, the Netherlands and Luxembourg.

No. 12 Squadron learned of the German attack that afternoon, and five aircraft deployed on a daylight-bombing mission, in spite of the Battles' shortcomings. One Battle returned. There could be no doubt that the Battle was truly obsolete. No missions were flown by Garland's squadron the next day although German bombers attacked Amifontaine.[15]

Early on the 12th, the crews of No. 12 Squadron were called to an emergency briefing where they learned that German troops had seized, intact, several bridges over the Albert canal. The bridges were vital to the Germans since they facilitated their advance into Allied territory. Already several unsuccessful attempts had been made by RAF aircraft to destroy the bridges but these had been foiled by intense opposition from fighter aircraft and anti-aircraft guns. No. 12 Squadron's briefing was to inform the crews that the squadron had been selected for a special mission to destroy the bridges at Veldwezelt and Vroenhoven.[16]

This was to be a mission for volunteers since those aircraft which had already attacked the bridges had suffered so heavily. Every member of No. 12 Squadron stepped forward at the call for volunteers, each man eager to take the risks involved in an attack on the bridges. A compromise was made whereby the six crews already detailed on the 'readiness' roster would be the strike force.[17]

Those crews and their machines were designated as two sections, each of three aircraft, and each assigned a bridge. Flying Officer Norman Thomas was selected to lead the section attacking the concrete bridge at Vroenhoven;

Donald Garland would lead the attack on Veldwezelt's steel bridge. Thomas decided to make a divebombing attack from high-level, while Garland opted for a low-level approach to his target.[18]

By 9 a.m. the Battles were ready for take off but just at that point one of Thomas' section discovered a fault that left his Battle unserviceable, thus reducing that section to two aircraft; the second machine was flown by Pilot Officer T.D.H. Davy. Garland's section had no problems and all three Battles flew off from Amifontaine towards their target. Eight Hawker Hurricane fighters of No. 1 Squadron were acting as escort to the light bombers, an escort that was to prove woefully inadequate.

Donald Garland's section also included Battles flown by Pilot Officer I. A. McIntosh and Sergeant Fred Marland. The Irishman's crew was Sergeant Thomas Gray, observer, and Leading Aircraftman (LAC) L. R. Reynolds, who manned the Battle's single Vickers K rearward-firing machine gun.*[19]

Thomas and Davy reached Vroenhoven and were met by fierce anti-aircraft fire and considerable fighter opposition. Dive-bombing attacks were made from 6,000 feet but both aircraft were hit. Thomas was shot down and captured but Davy, after ordering his crew to bale out, brought his damaged plane back to Allied territory. Their attack had caused some damage to the concrete bridge.[20]

After a low-level flight under the cloud base at 1,000 feet, Garland's section reached Veldwezelt where they met considerable opposition. The Germans had emplaced some 300 AA guns around the bridge area and there were swarms of fighters in the vicinity that pounced on the Hurricanes which had been intended to defend the Battles. These were left helpless as the RAF fighters fought desperately for survival.

From 1,000 feet Garland led his section in a shallow diving approach to the bridge and through a storm of anti-aircraft gunfire. Such powerful defences made it almost impossible for the Battles to get through. McIntosh's plane was struck before he could even begin his final run; the aircraft began to blaze, forcing its pilot to dump his bomb load and try to bring the Battle down. Incredibly, McIntosh managed to make a forced landing and survived the crash to be made a prisoner of war.[21]

As Donald Garland's aircraft swooped on the bridge the intensity of the AA fire inevitably told. The Battle was struck many times and 'blasted into the ground'. The Irishman and his crew perished as their aircraft fell to earth. Sergeant Fred Marland and his crew also died as German guns hit it repeatedly.[22]

---

* The Battle was also fitted with a .303 machine gun in one wing which was fired by the pilot.

When the smoke cleared it could be seen that the Battles had achieved the impossible: the western end of the Veldwezelt bridge was badly damaged; the planes had carried out their mission although almost all the crew members had perished. Although not conclusive, the evidence suggested 'that this damage had possibly been caused by Garland's cool attack'. It was, however, quickly repaired by the Germans.[23]

The tactics employed in the attacks had been seriously flawed. Too few aircraft attacked each target and such was the defensive strength that the attackers were bound to be overwhelmed. However, the AASF had insufficient modern aircraft to attack and overwhelm targets and it would be some time before the RAF was able to do so in daylight missions on mainland Europe. In spite of this, the courage of the men sent against the bridges was in no doubt while Donald Garland's cool and inspiring leadership was a vital factor in the little success that No. 12 Squadron did achieve.[24]

On 11 June the *London Gazette* carried the official announcement of the posthumous awards of the Victoria Cross to Garland and to Thomas Gray, his navigator. No award was made to LAC Reynolds, the third crew member.

A little over a year later Garland's mother, accompanied by her son Patrick, attended the investiture ceremony at Buckingham Palace, to receive the little bronze cross awarded to Donald – first of her four sons to die during the war. Donald Garland had become Ireland's, and the Royal Air Force's, first Victoria Cross winner of the Second World War.

An Irishman was also the first soldier of the Second World War to receive the Victoria Cross from King George VI. On the night of 31 May 1940, B Company of 1st East Lancashire Regiment was holding a line stretching about a thousand yards along the Canal de Bergues, about three quarters of a mile from Dunkirk. Commanding the company was Captain **Harold Marcus Ervine-Andrews**, born in Keadue, County Cavan. The battalion had been en route to the beaches when a staff officer arrived from Divisional HQ and, learning that the battalion was still a fighting force, albeit without transport, ordered the commanding officer to move back to the defensive perimeter and take up positions between 1st and 46th Divisions. The gap filled by 1st East Lancashires was 3,000 yards long and followed the line of the canal de Bergues, near the village of Galghoek.[25]

Ervine-Andrews was a character in the battalion. Thick set and heavily built, he was renowned as a first class shot, a skill that he had displayed from childhood. When his father was managing the Provincial Bank of Ireland in New Ross, County Wexford, the young Ervine-Andrews would, according to one writer, shoot pencils out of people's hands. His father was a keen outdoorsman, 'fond of ... fishing and shooting, and Marcus quickly inherited his gifts in this direction and became an excellent marksman'.[26]

Described by a Stonyhurst contemporary as 'a red-haired, hot-headed Irishman, more interested in devilment and mad pranks than in his studies' Marcus Ervine-Andrews, the army officer, was venerated by his men. Senior ranks were less sure of him. While stationed in Shanghai and Hong Kong in the 1930s he had become something of a legend for eccentricity, once hiking fifty-six miles for a five-pound bet, on another occasion going out into the jungle to shoot a buck for breakfast. He also served in India, including a spell in Waziristan on the North-West Frontier, where he was on loan to the Royal Air Force as a liaison officer and earned a Mention in Despatches.[27]

Ervine-Andrews' Victoria Cross was the only one awarded for an action within the Dunkirk salient. Sir John Smyth VC – the same Sir John who had witnessed Kenny's VC-winning exploit in far-off Waziristan – wrote of Ervine-Andrews' deed.

> It is printed indelibly on my own mind because the [1st] East Lancashires were in 126 Infantry Brigade, the sister brigade to 127 which I was commanding in the 42nd Lancashire Division at Dunkirk. I had been ordered to move 127 Brigade down to the beaches on May 31st and 126 Brigade were to go on the next day. As we moved off all hell seemed to be let loose in the rearguard position behind held by 126 Brigade – and this, as I afterwards discovered, was when Captain Ervine-Andrews won his VC. Had he and his company not been so steadfast in repelling the fierce German attacks at this critical time it might have been even more difficult than it was to embark the last divisions of the B.E.F.[28]

The actions of Ervine-Andrews and his company of 1st East Lancashires were remarkable and there is no doubt that the Stonyhurst-educated Cavan man earned the Victoria Cross. B Company was in action against a much stronger German force for over ten hours, during which they were subjected to intense artillery, mortar fire and machine-gun fire. Another East Lancs company, sent to provide protection for his flank, was unable to reach him. As a result, one platoon was in real danger of being overrun. By this time B Company was at little more than platoon strength, having been reduced to forty men. However, there had been a welcome resupply of ammunition when Second-Lieutenant Griffin arrived with three Bren-gun carriers.[29]

A barn that Ervine-Andrews' company had been holding was set alight. This was a crucial position, at a point where a small tributary met the Bergues canal, and a German attack threatened to over run the building. Instead of ordering a withdrawal, the Irishman told his soldiers that they were going to charge the Germans – less than forty men against some 500. As the enemy soldiers crossed the canal de Bergues at dawn on 1 June, Ervine-Andrews led his depleted company on what should have been a suicide mission. However, the Germans were so shocked by the sight of this charge that they fell back for a time.

> Despite the intense fire, Captain Ervine-Andrews, with a few men, ran across to the barn, and with complete disregard for his own safety he clambered to the roof and from the blazing rafters picked off, with a rifle, no fewer than 17 Germans in the leading wave. Such marksmanship took the steam out of the German attack, and the invaders took cover in folds and hollows in the ground which had not been flooded. Meanwhile with the machine-gun which was now useable, Ervine-Andrews was able to dominate the ground by a deadly fire which accounted for more of the enemy. All through this action, Captain Ervine-Andrews had to supervise the evacuation of his wounded, control his limited supply of ammunition, and still exercise overall command of his company.[30]

All the while German mortars and armour-piercing bullets were punching through the frail roof. When ammunition ran low Ervine-Andrews and his men laid into the Germans with bayonets, fists, feet and even teeth, as one survivor subsequently told the *Daily Telegraph*. Faced with such ferocity the Germans withdrew completely, giving Ervine-Andrews the opportunity to send his wounded back to safety on the company's sole remaining carrier. By this stage only eight men were left and, determined to lead them to safety, the big Irishman collected them 'from this forward position and when almost surrounded, led them back to the cover afforded by the company to the rear, swimming or wading up to the chin in water for over a mile'.[31] At dusk on 2 June the battalion was evacuated from Dunkirk on the destroyer HMS *Shikari* and arrived at Dover early on the morning of the 3rd. Although it was the last Victoria Cross of the campaign, Ervine-Andrews' award was the first Army VC to be approved in the Second World War and the first to be presented by the King.

Following the fall of France, Britain prepared for a possible German invasion. In the summer and early autumn of 1940 the RAF defeated the Luftwaffe in the battle of Britain and the immediate threat of invasion receded. But there was another danger facing the United Kingdom, the possibility of starvation through the campaign of submarine warfare being waged by the German Navy. In order to combat the U-boats, the Admiralty had reintroduced the convoy system, which had proved successful in the Great War. However, there were insufficient escort vessels and many ships were pressed into service in this role as a temporary expedient. These included battleships and the improvized armed merchant cruisers. The latter were merchant vessels that were converted into warships by providing them with some armament and carrying out some modifications to their structure to allow them to carry that armament. One such ship was HMS *Jervis Bay*, a 13,839 tons former liner built in 1922 and owned by the Aberdeen and Commonwealth Line which operated it on the Australian run until its requisition for war service. Although now fitted with seven 6-inch guns, *Jervis Bay* lacked the armoured skin of a true warship and could not hope to engage any major German warship with any chance of success.[32]

In March 1940 Captain **Edward Stephen Fogarty Fegen** took command of *Jervis Bay*. Although born in Hampshire, Fegen was an Irishman, the younger son of a serving naval officer, Vice-Admiral F.F. Fegen of Borrisoleigh, Ballinlanty, County Tipperary. The older Fegen's father had also been a Royal Navy officer. The young Fegen entered the naval college at Osborne as a thirteen-years-old cadet in September 1904 and served throughout the Great War. By the end of the war he was commanding a destroyer. In the inter-war period he earned two medals for lifesaving, one of them from the Dutch government, and commanded the Australian Naval College at Jervis Bay.[33]

When war returned to Europe in September 1939, Fegen was a much-respected officer with

> an unerring instinct to do the right thing. His command was no more than a projection of his own character. Moreover, he was always on the spot when decisions were due. Whether ships' boats were stove in or washed overboard in those months from September to March, he arrived on the scene first – somehow. In mid-Atlantic Fegen stood on the heaving deck of the *Emerald*, his breath caught at his throat, with scant regard for his own safety but much more for his men's.[34]

This was the man who became captain of HMS *Jervis Bay* in March 1940. Fegen was then forty-eight years old.

In November 1940 *Jervis Bay* sailed as the sole escort to convoy HX84, from Halifax to Britain. The convoy's thirty-eight merchant ships carried vital supplies, including fuel and food, for Britain's war effort. Soon after departure a Polish ship dropped behind with engine trouble. In the Atlantic the ships formed nine columns with *Jervis Bay* ahead of the main formation, flanked by *Empire Penguin* and *Cornish City*. The latter was the commodore's ship. This was the civilian officer in charge of the convoy, usually a retired senior naval officer; Admiral Maltby was commodore of HX84. *Cornish City*'s

captain was a forty-eight-years old Irishman, John O'Neill of Wexford, who
had first sailed as a fourteen-years-old deckboy.[35]

The morning of 5 November dawned fair and calm and Fegen went about
his business of shepherding his charges eastwards for Britain. Later that morning a British merchant ship, *Mopan*, sailing alone, overtook the convoy and
steamed on to an unexpected rendezvous with one of Germany's pocket battleships, *Admiral Scheer*, commanded by Kapitan Theodor Krancke. The latter
was aware of the presence of the convoy since it had been spotted by the battleship's floatplane but Captain Fegen was totally unaware of the danger that
lay just over the horizon.[36]

In mid-afternoon *Scheer* came suddenly on the unsuspecting *Mopan*.
Krancke's ship had sailed from Gdynia – present-day Gdansk – on 23 October
to prowl the Atlantic for targets of opportunity. *Mopan* was such a target.
The little banana boat was ordered to stop by a morse lamp signal from
Scheer; the captain was ordered not to transmit any radio signals, to put his
crew into the lifeboats and to make for *Scheer*. The battleship's anti-aircraft
guns then blasted the merchantman's hull below the waterline. As *Mopan* slid
below the waves, HX84 continued on its way, still unaware of the danger
ahead.[37]

That afternoon Midshipman Ronnie Butler was on watch on *Jervis Bay*.
He scanned the ocean for anything untoward while the ship's company were
having their tea. Some were settling down to the meal while others had just
finished. The sun was going down and the ocean's surface was totally calm.
It was a perfect evening. At 4.50 p.m. the peace was shattered as Butler spotted a ship on the horizon, to *Jervis Bay*'s port side. He reported his sighting
to Fegen who trained his binoculars on the distant vessel and identified it as
a German warship. He ordered 'Action Stations' to be sounded immediately
and directed the convoy to scatter and make smoke.[38]

The Admiralty was notified of the raider's presence and position as was
Cornish City; the German was twelve miles distant, on a bearing of 328° from
the *Jervis Bay*, steering a course on bearing 208°; its position was 53° N and
32° W. When that message reached the Admiralty in London, it was their
Lordships' first inkling that *Admiral Scheer* had slipped into the north Atlantic
via the Denmark Strait. Assisted by adverse weather conditions, *Scheer* had
escaped detection by naval surface vessels and Coastal Command aircraft.[39]

Fegen did not hesitate to order his ship to engage the *Scheer*, which was
now changing course for an attack. His first priority was the safety of the
convoy and this could best be assured by diverting the German from it. *Scheer*
opened fire from 17,000 yards range and the first salvo fell around *Cornish
City*. There were no hits. HX 84 was scattering in three dozen different directions, denying the German the opportunity to destroy all the vessels. But the

Scheer was not given the chance to concentrate on the fleeing merchantmen. Before Krancke could order a second salvo, Fegen's ship was steaming towards the *Scheer* and the puny *Jervis Bay* prepared to match its seven 6-inch guns and thin plating against the pocket battleship's six 11-inch main guns and thick armour plate.[40]

Although this was no contest, *Jervis Bay*'s attack meant that *Scheer* had to eliminate the escort before being able to turn attention to the convoy. Fogarty Fegen was buying vital minutes for the convoy with the most precious coin of all: his own life, his crew and his ship. Only one outcome was possible to this clash. HMS *Jervis Bay* was doomed.

As Fegen manoeuvred between the convoy and *Scheer*, an enemy shell burst in the water near *Jervis Bay*. *Scheer*'s captain was positioning his ship just outside the effective range of the merchant cruiser's guns so that he could pound the old liner to scrap while taking no damage in return. His second salvo aimed at *Jervis Bay* claimed at least one hit, damaging the bridge and striking the range-finder. The bridge area was ablaze and the forward steering gear disabled. Fegen had also been hit and severely injured, but he continued to direct operations. One arm hung useless by his side, having been virtually severed.[41]

From his gun position Able Seaman Lane saw the blood-soaked Fegen stagger to the second bridge. One of *Jervis Bay*'s rounds had struck *Scheer* but the German's next salvo scored a direct hit on Lane's position. Lane was the sole survivor as his gun and the rest of its crew were blown into the sea. Another shell struck *Jervis Bay* below the waterline. The ship was ablaze almost from bow to stern but continued to fight back, its crew manning its remaining guns, damage-control parties fighting to cope with the effects of the onslaught. Then the engine room was hit. Power for the pumps was knocked out and no water could be pumped up with which to fight the fires. *Jervis Bay* began listing.[42]

Fegen was still in command from the after bridge which was then shot away. By now his ship was an easy target for the German gun crews as it could steam only in a straight line. As Fegen made his way to what was left of the main bridge, *Jervis Bay* steamed straight for *Scheer*. In a show of defiance one crew member climbed the rigging to nail a fresh white ensign to the mast, to replace the ensign that had been shot away. Then another hit in the engine room stopped *Jervis Bay* in the water. Her forward guns were all out of action, the aft weapons could not be trained on *Scheer*, and, with the ship ablaze, there was the danger of her ammunition exploding. Crewmen threw burning debris overboard. They even tried to extinguish fires by stamping on them. But their efforts were in vain. *Jervis Bay* was now a dead ship, awaiting burial by the waves that washed over the decks as the list increased.[43]

The dying Fegen retained command to the very end. From the remains of the main bridge he gave the order 'Abandon ship!' but only one lifeboat was left. As *Jervis Bay* settled by the stern, the crew took to the boat and to life-rafts. The lifeboat was holed before it could be lowered and most of the seventy survivors leapt on to the rafts, although some remained with the lifeboat. Even as *Jervis Bay* slid beneath the waves, German shells continued to pound the old liner, until only the hull ribs were visible. Shrapnel shells were fired at the men on the liferafts.[44]

Edward Stephen Fogarty Fegen went down with his ship. Among the vessels in HX 84 was the Swedish ship *Stureholm* whose captain, Sven Olander, had stayed close by and witnessed *Jervis Bay*'s gallant fight. Olander later told of how, through his binoculars, he watched the British ship slowly sink below the waves with Fogarty Fegen standing on its remains, both arms hanging limp by his side. After nightfall, Olander mustered his crew on deck and the decision was made to return and pick up any survivors from *Jervis Bay*. In spite of a rising sea, the men were located and *Stureholm* picked up sixty-five survivors. Some were rescued from the lifeboat which was then manned by Swedish crewmen who rowed towards two of the life-rafts to take off survivors. When the crewmen were unable to row any more, Olander took his ship alongside the other two rafts and brought off the remaining survivors from Fegen's crew. The Swedish captain described the engagement between *Jervis Bay* and *Scheer* to the *Times*:

> 'There she rode like a hero,' said Captain Olander, speaking of the fight put up by the *Jervis Bay*. 'She was right into the guns of the battleship. She did not have a chance and we all knew it, but there she stayed to the last to give us all in the merchant ships a chance to run for it.'

John O'Neill, on *Cornish City*, also witnessed the initial stages of the action and described the uneven struggle to the *Wexford People* shortly after the war ended:

> Within 15 minutes of the epic encounter beginning, *Jervis Bay* was a raging inferno from stem to stern. Billows of smoke soared skywards from the slowly sinking cruiser, from which now and then a solitary salvo was returned in answer to the fire of the raider. As dusk was falling and the smoke ... exceedingly dense, it was difficult for the attacker to see the prey.[45]

The one-sided battle had lasted almost an hour before the weaker *Jervis*

Bay succumbed to the pocket battleship's greater power. Those sixty minutes proved invaluable to the ships of HX 84 which were able to scatter, thus denying Krancke a juicy, concentrated target. Having sunk *Jervis Bay*, *Admiral Scheer* turned the full fury of its heavy guns to the merchant ships, some of which it had already engaged with its secondary weapons. But, as darkness deepened, it could engage only a handful of vessels. Five ships were lost: *Beaverford*, *Fresno City*, *Kenbane Head*, *Maidan* and *Trewellard*. A sixth, the tanker *San Demetrio*, was set ablaze and abandoned by her crew but, that night one lifeboat's crew rowed back to the tanker, boarded her and extinguished the flames in spite of the proximity of the ship's lethal cargo of some 11,000 tons of petrol. *San Demetrio* made landfall off Ireland's north coast six days later and was escorted into the Clyde.[46]

Edward Stephen Fogarty Fegen had saved HX 84 from certain destruction. The naval official historian wrote: 'The result was a foregone conclusion but Captain Fegan's action gained enough time to save all the convoy except five ships.' His gallantry almost defied belief but was entirely in character for a man who had often shown that he was willing to risk his own life for others. One of his two brothers – both of whom also served in the Royal Navy and commanded warships – encapsulated his spirit when he said of that last battle: 'It was the end he would have wished.'

Admiral Scheer disorganized the convoy system for two weeks as major surface vessels were sent to hunt her. Regular convoys resumed with HX 89 which sailed from Halifax on 17 November. The next day the *London Gazette* announced the posthumous award of the Victoria Cross to Captain Edward Stephen Fogarty Fegen. On 26 November J. Piekarski, of the Polish steamer *Puck*, wrote to the *Times* to express his appreciation of the courage of the crew of *Jervis Bay* and to extend sympathy to the relatives of those who died, 'who may be proud for the role they have played in their fight for freedom'.

Fegen had become the third Irishman to be awarded Britain's highest decoration for gallantry in the war. All three services were now represented on the Irish VC roll. Fegen's Victoria Cross was presented to his sister, Miss M.C. Fegen, by King George VI at Buckingham Palace on 12 June 1941. At the same investiture, Donald Garland's Victoria Cross was presented to his mother.

A memorial to Captain Fegen and the crew of *Jervis Bay* was erected at Albuoys' Point, adjacent to No. 1 Dock, Hamilton Harbour, in Bermuda. It reads

REMEMBER

Captain E.S. Fegen, VC, Royal Navy, the Officers and Ship's Company of HMS *Jervis Bay* who cheerfully gave their lives in successful defence of their Convoy, fighting their ship to the last against hopeless odds. November 5th 1940.

'Be thou faithful unto death' Rev. II, 10

Ireland's next VC was won in North Africa just over a year after Captain Fegen's death in the Atlantic. In late-1941 the newly-created Eighth Army launched its first operation, codenamed CRUSADER, in Libya. One aim of the operation was to relieve the besieged port of Tobruk, the garrison of which was to strike out to link up with Eighth Army. During this operation Captain **James Joseph Bernard Jackman** won the Victoria Cross.

Jackman was born in Dun Laoghaire, County Dublin, on 19 March 1916, the only son of Dr J.J. Jackman, a Waterford man, and Mrs Jackman, of Glenageary. The young Jackman's early education was received at Saint Gerard's School, Bray, after which he went to Stonyhurst College. For some of the time that Jackman was at Stonyhurst, Ervine-Andrews was also a pupil and the two often travelled to Ireland together at holiday times. But they were very different individuals with Jackman being much more of an intellectual and a brilliant conversationalist.[47]

> His family and friends thought that Jackman would follow his father in medicine and it came as great surprise to many when he decided to make the Regular Army his career. There were some, on hearing this, who took the view that he would be wasted there, whilst others held the opinion that he might succeed in one of the army's more technical or administrative branches. Nobody could picture him as an infantry man charging into an enemy stronghold.[48]

In 1934 Jackman entered the Royal Military College, Sandhurst from where he passed out in July 1936 with a prize for military law. He was commissioned into the Royal Northumberland Fusiliers, one of the Army's oldest regiments, and one with an Irish origin.* Jackman was a popular officer whose life, it seemed, was devoted to one purpose: 'the welfare and efficiency of those under him, he took infinite pains to achieve this, and no man who served in his Company can but have known he served with a friend'.[49]

---

* The Northumberlands were descended from an Irish regiment of British auxiliaries in Dutch pay in 1674 commanded by Daniel O'Brien, viscount Clare. In 1675 this regiment was given to Sir John Fenwick and became an English unit but remained in the Netherlands until James II recalled it to England at the time of Monmouth's rebellion after which it went back to Holland and returned with William of Orange to become a permanent part of the English army. It served at the battle of the Boyne as Monk's Regiment and became the 5th Foot when numbers were later assigned to regiments.

In November 1941 Jackman was serving with 1st Royal Northumberland Fusiliers in 70th Division which had relieved the Australians in Tobruk. The Northumberlands were a machine-gun battalion whose role was to provide support for the division's infantry brigades. Typically, machine-gun battalions had three machine-gun companies, each with three platoons of four Vickers .303-inch medium machine guns plus an anti-tank company of four platoons, each with four 2-pounder weapons. Captain Jackman was the officer commanding Z Company, a machine-gun company.[50]

Plans were being finalised for the major offensive against the Italo-German forces in Libya with the objectives of destroying a large portion of those forces, occupying much of Libya and relieving Tobruk. As the main body of Eighth Army advanced from the Egyptian frontier the Tobruk garrison was to punch its way out and link up.[51]

Eighth Army attacked in the early morning of 18 November after a cold, wet night. For three days British armour engaged the German and Italian forces in one of the war's most confused battles while 70th Division waited for the order to break out from Tobruk. The division, commanded by Major-General Scobie, had been training for its breakout role for a month. Captain Jackman had trained his company rigorously to create an excellent mobile force that would achieve all that was expected of it. On the night of 20/21 November there was great activity in the south-eastern corner of the Tobruk perimeter. From there, 70th Division was to strike out to link up with 7th Armoured Division, the 'Desert Rats', at Sidi Rezegh; less than a dozen miles separated the two British divisions.[52]

At daybreak on 21 November Scobie's men opened their assault, accompanied by diversionary attacks from Tobruk by Polish troops and the British 23 Infantry Brigade. The opposition was stronger than expected and the attackers found themselves up against strong defensive positions manned by German and Italian soldiers who were determined not to give up ground. A two-mile wide breach was created in the enemy front line, and broadening attacks were launched, but there would be no speedy link up with 7th Armoured's tanks.[53]

The Northumberlands' machine-gun companies were ordered into action against four enemy strongpoints, codenamed 'Lion', 'Tiger', 'Jack' and 'Jill'. Of these 'Tiger' proved the toughest with 2nd Black Watch sustaining 75 per cent casualties in taking it. Jackman's Z Company deployed to support the Black Watch at 'Tiger', to prevent the highlanders being pushed out of their gain by an enemy counter-attack. Once 'Tiger' was consolidated, a platoon of Z Company moved off to help capture another enemy position. Z Company was under the operational command of 32 Army Tank Brigade, which also included a squadron of King's Dragoon Guards, an anti-tank battery and 1st

Essex Regiment. The brigade's objective was El Duda, a feature on the El Adem escarpment south of Tobruk.[54]

The following morning, two platoons of Z Company were sent to defend captured positions. Jackman was left with his company headquarters and 14 Platoon, which then deployed to assist 1st York and Lancaster Regiment and a squadron of tanks in an attack on a position flanking the approach to El Duda. This position was held in strength; most of an infantry battalion was supported by anti-tank and machine guns. That strength told as the British attack went in and the York and Lancasters were fought to a standstill.[55]

> Captain J.J.B. Jackman, on seeing this, made a quick and bold decision. He led No. 14 Platoon, under 2/Lieut F. Ward, off to the south and then swung away in a wide circle and came in on the enemy's right flank. Although they had to go through some heavy shell-fire, they got on to the objective and took some prisoners. The drill for getting into action off vehicles had been perfected and No. 14 Platoon were very soon firing hard from the captured positions while their vehicles were being driven away to safety.[56]

The German army's tactical doctrine dictated the launching of swift counter-attacks on positions that had just been lost so that the captors might be taken off balance before they could consolidate their gains. That doctrine was applied on this occasion. Supported by light tanks and heavy shellfire, lorried German infantry forced the British infantry out of the positions which they had not had time to consolidate. However, one machine-gun section of Jackman's company was ideally placed to meet the German attack and they began pouring sustained fire into the enemy, loosing off almost all their ammunition. Although they took considerable punishment from enemy fire, they drove off the attackers. Sergeant D. McKay, who commanded the section, was subsequently awarded the Distinguished Conduct Medal. Z Company then returned to 32 Tank Brigade's fold.[57]

The British advance had created a narrow wedge in the enemy position into which and X and Y Companies were ordered to provide a defensive base while Z Company moved forward for the assault on El Duda. But the enemy's determined resistance had delayed 70th Division and the attack on El Duda was postponed until the 26th. By that time the entire CRUSADER timetable had fallen forty-eight hours in arrears.[58]

Two tank regiments led 1st Essex in the assault on El Duda; Jackman's Z Company followed in open formation. The tanks were held up by heavy shelling and mortaring and, once again, James Jackman put his well-rehearsed tactics into operation. He led Z Company forward 'at a terrific speed, under heavy shell and mortar fire – taking no notice of anything but [the] objective'.[59] Reaching a pre-arranged line the platoons deployed for action and their vehicles withdrew. Since there were no radios with the platoons, Jackman and his company sergeant-major, CSM Hughes, supervised the deployment. Hughes followed Jackman's vehicle and, on the latter's signal, drove to a high point on the El Duda feature, left his own vehicle and waved a flag to order the platoons to break formation and drive to their positions. Each position was indicated by Hughes.[60]

From their positions the platoons enjoyed an excellent field of fire on to the Trigh Capuzzo, the main Axis supply route, and their Vickers guns wrought havoc among the enemy troops. They played a vital part in the fall of El Duda, which was taken for the loss of two I-tanks. However, the Essex Regiment later lost 40 men in a bombing attack by British aircraft; the pilots were unaware that the feature had changed hands.[61]

James Jackman distinguished himself throughout this period. He drove around the various positions, encouraging his men and co-ordinating their fire. At all times he was calm and cheerful and appeared to have a charmed life. But then his luck ran out. Fusilier R.J. Dishman later wrote an eyewitness account of the last moments of the gallant Irish officer.

> Captain Jackman came and lay down on the gun line, and began to observe through his binoculars. He then gave us the order to fire at [a] truck and [motor] cyclist. 'Give them a burst,' he said, and just as these words were said a mortar bomb dropped just in front of our left-hand gun, wounding three and killing Captain Jackman and Corporal Gare instantly.[62]

Only one mortar round struck that platoon's position, but a splinter from the bomb passed through James Jackman's neck. The splinter severed his jugular vein and he bled to death. Fusilier Dishman wrote that 'Captain Jackman was a fine leader and an inspiration to us all, and in losing him we lost a very young, and capable commander'. There can be little doubt of his leadership qualities: the awards subsequently made to Z Company prove that. James Jackman was posthumously awarded the Victoria Cross; his second-in-command, Captain Derek Lloyd, and 14 Platoon's commander, Lieutenant Ward, each received the Military Cross; both CSM Hughes and Sergeant McKay received the Distinguished Conduct Medal and another DCM and six Military Medals were awarded to Jackman's company. There are few examples of a company, especially one operating in a machine-gun role, receiving so many gallantry awards for one action. Those awards testify both to the training that James Jackman had carried out and to his personal leadership.[63]

According to some accounts, his own VC was awarded for his conduct during the action of 19/20 November although the citation specifies the 25th.

> On 25th November, 1941, at Ed Duda,* South East of Tobruk, Captain Jackman showed outstanding gallantry and devotion to duty above all praise ... His magnificent bearing was contributory in a large measure to the success of a most difficult and hard fought action. As the tanks reached the crest of the rise they were met by extremely intense fire from a larger number of guns of all descriptions: the fire was so heavy that it was doubtful for a moment whether the Brigade could maintain its hold on the position.
>
> The tanks having slowed to 'hull-down' positions, settled to beat down the enemy fire, during which time Captain Jackman rapidly pushed up the ridge leading his Machine Gun trucks and saw at once that Anti-Tank guns were firing at the flank of the tanks, as well as the rows of batteries which the tanks were engaging on their front.
>
> He immediately started to get his guns into action as calmly as though he were on manoeuvres, and so secured the right flank. Then standing up in front of his truck, with calm determination he led his trucks across the front between the tanks and the guns – there was no other road – to get them into action on the left flank.
>
> Most of the tank commanders saw him, and his exemplary devotion to duty regardless of danger not only inspired his own men, but clinched the determination of the tank crews never to relinquish the position which they had gained. [64]

The Northumberlands' historian can hardly be accused of exaggeration for his suggestion that there 'can be no instance of a more merited award of the Victoria Cross than that to this courageous officer of the Fighting Fifth'. James Jackman was the fourth Irishman to win the VC in the war; only one had survived to receive his award.

The fifth Irish VC winner was also to die in the action that earned him his award. Lieutenant-Commander **Eugene Esmonde** died in a courageous but vain attack on the German battlecruiser *Prinz Eugen* on a grey February day in the straits of Dover in 1942. Esmonde is one of those Irish VC-winners who is not always recognized as Irish, since he was born in Yorkshire in 1909

---

* The misspelling *Ed* Duda was used in the original citation and the Northumberlands' regimental history and is repeated in more recent publications, including John Laffin's *British VCs of World War 2 – a study in heroism* (Stroud, 1997)

where his doctor father was practising. The Esmondes returned to County Tipperary later that year when Eugene's grandfather died and Dr John Joseph Esmonde inherited the family home at Drominagh. Eugene Esmonde was the grand-nephew of Captain Thomas Esmonde, who won the Victoria Cross in 1855 during the Crimean War. Another ancestor, John Esmonde, was executed for his part in the 1798 rebellion.[65]

Eugene Esmonde joined the RAF in 1928, having decided that he was not cut out to be a priest – as was his older brother. He later became a pilot with Imperial Airways and flew with them for five years until 1939 when he was offered a regular commission as a lieutenant-commander in the Fleet Air Arm. He re-enlisted and, following refresher training, took command of No. 754 Squadron before being appointed commander of 825 Squadron, a torpedo-bomber unit equipped with Fairey Swordfish.[66]

By May 1941 Esmonde's was a highly-efficient squadron, with excellent morale, first-class leadership and considerable operational experience. No. 825 was operating from the aircraft carrier HMS *Victorious* in the Home Fleet pursuing the German battleship *Bismarck*. Esmonde led 825 Squadron through atrocious weather conditions in a strike intended to slow *Bismarck*'s progress and allow surface ships to engage it. Six of his aircraft returned safely and Eugene Esmonde was awarded the Distinguished Service Order. *Victorious*'s captain wrote of 'skilful and gallant' leadership and commended his unbounded enthusiasm, which inspired the whole squadron.[67]

Shortly afterwards, 825 Squadron transferred to *Ark Royal* to operate in the Mediterranean. In November *Ark Royal* was struck by a torpedo while returning from delivering fighter aircraft to Malta. Although great efforts were made to save the ship, fire broke out in a boiler room and stopped salvage efforts for two hours. As *Ark* listed to 35 degrees the 'abandon ship' order was given, and the last 250 men of the crew slid down ropes to the destroyer HMS *Laforey*.

Eugene Esmonde was the last to leave, except for the captain. The Irishman had volunteered to stay aboard and arranged food and refreshments for those who struggled to save their ship. After leaving the ship he 'continued to see to the welfare of his men, including their spiritual needs in the case of fellow Roman Catholics by arranging for a local priest at Gibraltar to attend them'. For his work on *Ark Royal*, especially during the carrier's death throes, Esmonde earned a Mention in Despatches that spoke of his 'courage, enterprise and resolution in air attacks on the enemy'.[68]

Most of 825 Squadron's crews were transferred to Lee-on-Solent and Esmonde remained in command as the squadron began to re-equip. He had commanded 825 for eighteen months, most of which had been on front-line operations. Had he been serving in the RAF, he would probably have been given a non-operational posting at this stage as a 'rest', but the Fleet Air Arm was short of pilots with his experience and rank and this probably played a part in his continuing to lead 825 Squadron.[69]

In January 1942 the squadron had only six aircraft, although there was no shortage of Swordfish. Only two of Esmonde's pilots and four of his observers had seen operational service, although all six telegraphists/air gunners (TAGs) had been on operations. This part-trained, half-strength unit was shortly to be sent on an impossible mission and most of them would not return.

The mission was against the German battlecruisers *Scharnhorst* and *Gneisenau*. These vessels had sunk about 115,000 tons of Allied shipping in the three months before they had docked at Brest in March 1941, where they were later joined by the heavy cruiser *Prinz Eugen*. These three major German surface units presented the Admiralty with a considerable headache since their presence at Brest threatened Atlantic and Africa-bound convoys and added to the overstretching of the Royal Navy's resources.[70]

RAF Bomber Command was asked to deploy bombers against the German vessels. Air Marshal Sir Richard Peirse (an Irishman), who was Bomber Command's supremo, issued a directive stating that, should they attempt to move, the ships would be attacked by surface vessels and aircraft by day, but that no aircraft would attack by night. Since the presence of the three ships at Brest caused considerable diversion of British naval and air effort, the German Navy was happy to keep all three there. However, Hitler, who was obsessed with the possibility that the Allies might invade Norway, issued an ultimatum to the Kriegsmarine commander, Admiral Raeder, to move *Scharnhorst*, *Gneisenau* and *Prinz Eugen* from Brest, or have the ships dismantled with their heavy guns being moved to the Norwegian coastal defences.[71]

Faced with this ultimatum, Raeder began to plan a move from Brest to Norway via a German port and gave the operational task to Admiral Otto Ciliax. In turn, Ciliax decided to sail from Brest after dusk on a moonless night, thus obtaining maximum cover for the first part of the voyage. The desired combination of current, moon and tide current conditions made 11 February the date chosen for Operation CEREBUS; *Scharnhorst*, *Gneisenau* and *Prinz Eugen* would slip their moorings at 7.30 p.m. and, with their escort force, sail through the night for the English channel, reaching the straits of Dover around noon on the 12th. Darkness would reduce the chances of detection and much of the route to Germany might be completed without being intercepted.[72]

The British planners expected any escape attempt by the German ships to be made in daylight although Air-to-Surface-Vessel (ASV) radar-equipped aircraft flew regular night patrols off the French coast. In early February,

Bomber Command dropped mines on the possible routes of a German dash from Brest. Three squadrons of Coastal Command Beaufort torpedo-bombers were held ready to attack the German ships, and were seen by senior naval and air officers as the principal weapon against Ciliax's force. Based on experience of the *Bismarck* attack, and the damage wrought by Swordfish torpedo-bombers on the Italian fleet at Taranto, it was considered that the Beauforts could damage the enemy ships sufficiently to leave them at the mercy of surface vessels. A force of Swordfish was later added to the attacking air units by Vice-Admiral Bertram Ramsay at Dover. Ramsay also believed that the Germans would quit Brest in daylight and sail through the Dover straits during the night hours. Darkness would provide cover for the Swordfish, and the Beauforts, to attack without a fighter escort. Ramsay's Swordfish 'force' was to be Esmonde's 825 Squadron which moved to RAF Manston in Kent to prepare for the operation.[73]

On 11 February Eugene Esmonde was at Buckingham Palace receiving his DSO for his part in the *Bismarck* operations and, later, was a guest of Admiral Somerville at dinner. In France, Admiral Ciliax had ordered his command to leave harbour for a night exercise between La Pallice and Saint Nazaire, returning to Brest the following day. That order was a cover for Operation CEREBUS: the breakout was about to begin.

An RAF bombing raid delayed the departure of the German ships by almost two hours. At 9.14 p.m. Ciliax ordered the ships to slip anchor. *Scharnhorst*, as the flagship, led the squadron out of harbour and, by midnight they sailing past Ushant, at best speed through thin haze on a clear, starlit night. A combination of circumstances allowed the Germans over twelve hours' undetected sailing before the alarm was raised at 11.35 a.m., an hour after a sighting had first been broadcast by a Spitfire pilot. Ciliax could not have asked for better luck.[74]

At 12.15 p.m. Esmonde and his crews climbed into their Swordfish to attack the German ships. A five-squadron fighter escort had been promised and Ramsay had told Esmonde that the decision to go was his and his alone. Esmonde was *not* being ordered to lead his squadron in a daylight attack.

With the promise of protection from five fighter squadrons, however, Esmonde made the decision to attack, having asked 'for the love of God' that the fighters be with 825 Squadron on time. At 12.25 p.m. he led his Swordfish off Manston's frozen grass runway to rendezvous with their escort. Seven minutes later, ten Spitfires from 72 Squadron met Esmonde's planes over Ramsgate. No other fighters appeared. Esmonde could have called off the attack at that point: he had accepted the daylight mission on the understanding that his highly vulnerable biplanes would have support from 60 fighters. Instead of taking his squadron back to base, Esmonde, with a wave of a gloved hand, led them to their rendezvous with Ciliax's force. His biographer, Chaz Bowyer, suggests that, since he had given his word to Ramsay that 825 Squadron would attack, Esmonde felt it his duty to carry out the operation as

> by his very nature [he] would have felt totally obliged to honour his word – honour and duty had been the lynchpins of the Esmonde family lineage and Eugene particularly exemplified those ideals throughout his life. His devout Catholic faith undoubtedly softened the all-too human fear of death and its aftermath. But, whatever his actual thoughts at that crucial moment, Esmonde's decision became instantly plain.[75]

The Swordfish made for their target at less than 100 m.p.h., flying only fifty feet above the waves. Overhead their escorts flew a weaving flightpath at about 2,000 feet altitude. Fifteen minutes later, as the biplanes flew on, the missing escorts arrived over Ramsgate in two separate formations, before heading across the Channel. Although they engaged enemy aircraft, no sighting was made of 825 Squadron.

Esmonde's squadron met their first enemy fighters ten miles out from Ramsgate when two *Staffeln* of Messerschmitt Bf109 fighters pounced on the biplanes with cannon and machine-guns blazing. Although they caused damage to most of the Swordfish, there were no injuries. Bf109s were beaten off by the Spitfires before they could make a second attack.

The German fleet was spotted at 12.50 p.m. So, too, was the swarm of fighters above it. As the Swordfish closed to within two miles of the battleships, German fighters swooped to the kill, having to drop flaps, and even undercarriages, to reduce speed sufficiently to engage their victims. The Spitfires dived to protect their charges.[76]

A number of Royal Navy motor torpedo boats had finished an attack on the German giants, each firing its two torpedoes in an unsuccessful effort to damage the enemy vessels. The MTBs remained close by, ready to rescue the Swordfish crews if needed. Esmonde reached the outer destroyer and E-boat screen with his aircraft trailing fabric torn by the German fighters' fire and flew on through a blizzard of tracer fire, and the huge, frightening spouts of water thrown up by the battleships' heavy armament. The other two aircraft of his sub-flight were close behind. Although a further fighter attack forced them to weave and dodge to avoid being shot down, they were soon back on a steady course, heading for *Prinz Eugen*.

Charles Kingsmill, flying the third machine in the sub-flight, watched Esmonde fly steadily on through tracer that laced the air. Kingsmill was so intent on watching Esmonde that he had no recollection of being aware of danger; and, save for one machine, hardly noticed the German fighters. He kept his gaze on Esmonde even when his own plane shook from the blows of cannon shells. Then Esmonde's plane lurched upwards and Kingsmill lost sight of it.[77]

This must have been the stage at which Esmonde's Swordfish was attacked by two Bf109s. When the Swordfish's tail caught fire, his TAG, Jack Clinton, crawled out along the fuselage, beat out the flames with his hands and returned to his machine gun. *Prinz Eugen*'s heavy guns blasted forth at the leading Swordfish and most of the port lower wing was torn away. The biplane dipped a wing seaward as it staggered from the force of a shell strike, but Esmonde regained control, came back on course, and kept flying towards the huge warship.

Then the two Bf109s attacked again from behind. Their bullets killed Clinton and the Observer, Lieutenant William Henry Williams, and struck Esmonde in the back and head. The Swordfish nosed up slightly as its torpedo fell away, presumably released by the dying Esmonde. The shattered aircraft dropped to the sea, disintegrating as it struck the surface. The other two Swordfish of the sub-flight were also shot down by fighters and *Prinz Eugen*'s captain changed course to avoid Esmonde's torpedo.[78]

All six Swordfish were shot down. Only five men survived to be rescued by the MTBs. At least three RAF pilots had witnessed Esmonde's last moments. When the sole unwounded survivor of 825 Squadron, Edgar Lee, returned to Manston, he was met by Wing Commander Tom Gleave. The latter had watched the Swordfish depart and had saluted each as it passed him for he had seen in Esmonde 'the face of a man already dead' and known that 825 Squadron would not return. Gleave then wrote a recommendation that Esmonde be posthumously awarded the Victoria Cross.

That recommendation – the first time a RAF officer had commended a naval officer for the VC – was supported by Admiral Ramsay. Concluding his own recommendation Ramsay wrote that Esmonde's

> high courage and splendid resolution will live in the traditions of the Royal Navy and remain for many generations a fine and stirring memory.[79]

However, Ramsay was highly critical of the many errors that had led to the deaths of Esmonde and so many of his squadron. Those deaths had been in vain: their efforts made no impression on the Germans' operations. But an impression had been made in another manner. The Germans had noted the gallantry of Esmonde and his crews who, in antiquated biplanes, had taken on the might of the Kriegsmarine and Luftwaffe and died in the act. Admiral Ciliax wrote of them that they were men 'whose bravery surpasses any other action by either side that day'. That comment reflects Admiral Ramsay's comment that it was 'one of the finest exhibitions of self-sacrifice and devotion that this war has yet witnessed' and Gleave's succinct summary of the Swordfish crews as 'courage personified'.[80]

There could be little doubt that Eugene Esmonde would be awarded the Victoria Cross. An announcement appeared in the *London Gazette* on 3 March 1942 and, on Saint Patrick's Day, his mother with two of his brothers – Owen, an RAF officer, and Patrick, an Army doctor – received the Cross from King George VI who had suggested that this posthumous investiture of an Irishman with the VC should take place on Ireland's national day. The Esmonde family had decided that Eily Esmonde, although infirm, should be the one to receive her son's award at Buckingham Palace.[81]

Although Eugene Esmonde died at sea, his body was later washed ashore at the mouth of the river Medway in Kent, from where it was taken to Chatham. A line of bullet holes marked his back from neck to waist. Eugene Esmonde VC, DSO was later buried with full naval honours in Woodlands Cemetery, Gillingham. Memorials were erected to him at the Royal Naval Air Station, HMS *Daedalus*, at Lee-on-Solent. At Kakamega in Kenya, his brother Donald, who was a missionary priest, and whom Eugene once wished to emulate, had a circular stained-glass window with a representation of the Victoria Cross, placed over the entrance of the new church of Saint Pius X in 1959.

Thus far in the war the Irish VC winners had all been officers, but the next Irishman to earn the Victoria Cross was an ordinary soldier, Private **Richard Kelliher** of the 2/25th Battalion, Australian Imperial Force. Kelliher, who was born in Ballybeggan, Tralee, County Kerry, on 1 September 1910, won his Cross in the jungles of New Guinea in September 1943. At the time Richard Kelliher was a thirty-three-year-old private in 2/25th (Queensland) Battalion.

The youngest of six brothers, Kelliher had emigrated to Australia in the '30s and was working as a labourer in Queensland when he volunteered for service with the AIF on 21 February 1941. On 26 June he was posted to 2/12th Battalion and embarked for the Middle East to join the battalion. He was transferred to 2/25th Battalion on 11 October at a time when that unit was carrying out garrison duties in Syria following the campaign against the Vichy French.

Japan's attack on Pearl Harbor in December 1941 brought war much closer to Australia and prompted the withdrawal of Australian troops from the

Middle East to meet the threat of attack on Australia. In March 1942 Richard Kelliher's 2/25th Battalion returned to Australia to prepare for a move to New Guinea.[82]

After Pearl Harbor the main thrust of Japanese aggression had been to the south-west of Japan itself, aimed towards Singapore. Japanese commanders, realizing that, ultimately, they would have to defend their gains from American attack from the east, began consolidating the island chains to the south, including the Marianas, Carolines, Solomons, and Marshalls. The establishment of this defensive belt of island fortresses brought war to Australia's mainland.[83]

Japanese troops landed unopposed in New Guinea in March 1942 but spent weeks preparing the base for an attack southwards thus allowing the Australians breathing space to build up their strength. Australian troops were despatched to Milne Bay, on the south-eastern tip of New Guinea and a further two battalions were ordered to push over the Owen Stanley mountains, by the Kokoda trail, to Buna on the north coast. An airfield was to be built there from which to attack the Japanese positions.[84]

Thus began a tough, bloody campaign. The Japanese were stopped on 25 August and a further landing at Milne Bay was repulsed. Evacuation followed on 6 September, the first time that the Imperial Japanese Army had been forced to retreat. Another repulse followed for the Japanese on the Kokoda trail. On 23 September General Sir Thomas Blamey took command of the Australian force to begin an offensive with two divisions – 6th and 7th – that had been concentrated on Papua. At the end of the campaign 7th Division was withdrawn to rest, re-equip and re-organize for further operations. By September 1943 Kelliher's battalion was making ready for another phase of operations against the enemy in New Guinea as the Australians moved against Japanese positions at Nadzab and Lae.[85]

Both 7th and 9th Divisions began to advance on Lae from different directions in early September. The leading troops of 2/25th Battalion, still in 7th Division, were more than one-third of the way to Lae before they met their first serious opposition, at Jensen's plantation, on 10 September. They overcame this and pressed on to reach Whittaker's plantation two days later. There Japanese marines were encountered, well entrenched in strong defensive positions, and fighting with the usual Japanese tenacity. But the Australians intensified the pressure and two companies of 2/25th reached high ground overlooking Heath's plantation, their next objective, by nightfall on the 13th, repelling several determined counter-attacks during the night. It was during that advance towards Heath's plantation that Richard Kelliher won his Victoria Cross.

On the morning of 13 September Kelliher's platoon of B Company came under sustained fire from a camouflaged machine-gun. The weapon was positioned on a slight rise about fifty yards away. Five soldiers were killed and three wounded by the machine-gun fire. One of the wounded was Corporal W.H. Richards, Kelliher's section leader. The Kerryman's reaction was to say to another soldier,

'I'd better go and bring him in', then [he] suddenly got up, rushed the post and hurled two grenades at it. When he ascertained that some, but not all, of the enemy had been killed he returned to his section, seized a Bren gun, and again dashed forward to within thirty metres of the post and with accurate fire completely silenced it. He then went forward again, through heavy rifle fire, and successfully rescued his section leader who had been wounded in the shoulder.[86]

The citation for Kelliher's VC states that his action

electrified everyone who saw it and his company as a whole, besides directly resulting in the capture of the enemy position, which was later found to contain one officer and eight other ranks enemy dead.[87]

Kelliher's version differs from the official account:

A party of Japanese marines – and well-fed they were too – occupied a small ridge in Heath's Plantation near Lae and were able to overlook our positions along the track. The opposition was pretty stiff, because it was apparently headquarters and we were held up. When we cut a telephone line leading from the headquarters, the Japanese became a bit demoralised. Our section leader, Cpl 'Billy' Richards, went down with a bullet through his shoulder, and appeared to be losing a fair amount of blood. Another man was shot through the ankle, and a third was wounded. All lay out in No Man's Land.

I wanted to bring Cpl Richards back, because he was my cobber, so I jumped out from the stump where I was sheltering and threw a few grenades into the position where the Japanese were dug in. I did not kill them all, so I went back, got a Bren gun and emptied the magazine into the post. That settled the Japanese.

Another position opened up when I went on to get Cpl Richards, but we got a bit of covering fire and I brought him back to our lines. I also helped the section to bring back the other two.[88]

The company went on to take its objective. The Japanese defenders left almost 300 dead behind. Thereafter 7th Division turned its attention to

Markham Point across the river which was subjected to frontal assault, mortar and machine-gun fire for some days until, one night, Australian patrols found that the enemy had abandoned the strongpoint and slipped away in the night. The fugitives were later mopped up along the coast.[89]

Kelliher fought at Markham Point, in actions in the Ramu valley and then at Balikpapan in Borneo. The *London Gazette* carried the announcement of his Victoria Cross on 30 December 1943. Richard Kelliher lived to learn that he had been decorated, survived the war and went to London in 1946 with the Australian contingent for the Victory parade. In 1956 he travelled to London again for the centenary celebrations of the Victoria Cross. He died in Melbourne as the result of a stroke in January 1963, aged fifty-two, and is buried in Springvale Cemetery.

Kelliher was married to Olive Margaret Hearn and they had two daughters and a son. In 1965 his widow, who had remarried, attempted to sell his Victoria Cross, but withdrew the sale after adverse reaction from many ex-servicemen. A successful appeal by the 2/25th Battalion Association raised sufficient funds to buy the medal and it was presented to the Australian War Memorial on 13 September 1966. Today it can be seen in the Hall of Valour.

One of the most memorable actions of the Second World War was the attempt to take the bridges over the Neder Rijn (Lower Rhine) river in September 1944. Known as Operation MARKET GARDEN, the best-remembered element was the struggle for the bridge at Arnhem. Although the north end of Arnhem bridge was seized by British airborne troops, the south end and the road to Nijmegen were held by the Germans. Allied ground forces, from the British XXX Corps, had made some progress driving up from the Belgian border, but the bridge at Nijmegen had yet to be captured.

Around the area of Oosterbeek in the Arnhem suburbs the survivors of 1st British Airborne Division were running short of food and ammunition by the fourth day of the battle. Some of the re-supply for the Division was delivered by aircraft from No. 271 Squadron, RAF Transport Command. Flight Lieutenant **David Samuel Anthony Lord** flew one of those aircraft, a Douglas C47 Dakota, one of the most versatile transport aircraft of the war. *Lummy* Lord had been born in Cork on 18 October 1913, of Welsh parents; his father was a warrant officer in the Royal Welsh Fusiliers, then stationed in the town. His connection with Ireland was brief as his father was posted to India where the young Lord was educated in a convent school in Lucknow. Prior to Arnhem, Lord had seen service in India and Burma, where he had earned a Distinguished Flying Cross. His soubriquet of *Lummy* was due to his use of that word where others might have sworn or blasphemed. A former altar boy at Wrexham's Saint Mary's Cathedral, David Lord had wanted to be a priest. Instead he enlisted in the RAF in 1936, began pilot training at Hamble in 1938 and was appointed sergeant-pilot on 5 April 1939. He was commissioned on 12 July 1942.[90]

On the afternoon of 19 September 1944, David Lord's Dakota approached the supply Dropping Zone (DZ) at Arnhem at a height of 1,500 feet. A hail of flak met it and the starboard wing of the aircraft was set on fire after receiving two hits. Although he would have been justified in abandoning the drop, Lord took his plane down to 900 feet to ensure an accurate drop on the DZ. On completing the first run he was informed that two containers remained. Although the wing was now well on fire, he turned, made another approach and, after successfully dropping the last of the containers, ordered his crew to bale out. The Dakota was now down to 500 feet. As Lord fought to hold it steady, the wing collapsed and the aircraft ploughed into a field below. There was only one survivor: Flight Lieutenant Harry King, the navigator, was thrown clear as he attempted to assist the other crewmen with their parachutes.[91] David Lord is buried in Oosterbeek War Cemetery, not far from where he crashed in 1944. His gallantry was rewarded with a posthumous Victoria Cross, the only such award to RAF Transport Command.

Two Irishmen won the Victoria Cross in the final year of the war. The first of these was a young officer in the Royal Engineers. **Claud Raymond** came from a Kerry family – his father was also a soldier and three of his uncles served in the Indian Army – although he was born at Mottistone on the Isle of Wight on 2 October 1923.* Educated at Wellington College, Raymond then went to Cambridge where he studied at Trinity Hall before joining the Army and being commissioned into the Corps of Royal Engineers.

In March 1945, Lieutenant Claud Raymond was attached to a patrol of D Force, a special force whose role was to obtain information and create a diversion in the Taungup area of the Arakan in Burma. The diversion was to be created by attacking and destroying isolated Japanese posts about forty miles ahead of an Indian infantry brigade that was advancing down the road from Letpan to Taungup.[92]

On 21 March the patrol, of two officers and eight men from 58 Company of D Force, landed south of Taungup, some forty miles ahead of the line of advance of 4 Indian Brigade from Letpan. As well as obtaining information the patrol was to create the impression of a landing in strength and thus draw off enemy troops who might otherwise deploy to oppose 4 Brigade's advance. Claud Raymond was second-in-command of the D Force patrol.[93]

---

* The Lummis Files suggest that he may have been born in India, but the Royal Engineers' Museum state that he was born at Mottistone.

The patrol was landed on the southern bank of the Thinganet chaung in an area that intelligence reports indicated was held by numerous enemy strongpoints and gun positions. From the chaung the patrol marched about five miles inland without hindrance but, as they approached the village of Talaku, they came under heavy fire from a detachment of Japanese who were well dug in on the slopes of a jungle-covered hill. There was little cover for the patrol as they were moving across open ground.[94]

Claud Raymond's immediate reaction was to take part of the patrol and charge in the direction of the fire, while the remainder made a flanking attack. As he began to climb the hill, Lieutenant Raymond was hit in the right shoulder but he ignored his wound and continued to advance, firing his rifle from the hip. A few yards farther on he was wounded again, this time by a Japanese grenade which exploded almost in his face. Raymond fell but 'in spite of loss of blood from his wounds, which later were to prove fatal, he still continued on, leading his section under intense fire'. As he did so he sustained a third wound with his wrist being shattered by an explosive bullet. At six feet three inches tall, Raymond would have been the most obvious target for the Japanese.[95]

In spite of his own terrible injuries, the young sapper officer led his men into the enemy position. In the close-quarter battle that followed he was largely responsible for killing two Japanese and wounding another. Faced with the ferocity of this attack, the Japanese fled, leaving their position in the patrol's hands. It was a well-equipped position, that was strongly fortified with bunkers and trenches and it would have proved a formidable obstacle had it not been for the determined and courageous leadership of Claud Raymond in charging the position rather than going to ground and seeking cover.[96]

Several other men from the patrol had been wounded during the action and Raymond refused any treatment for himself until all his soldiers had been attended to. In spite of his severe injuries he insisted on walking back to the patrol's landing craft in case a delay caused by treating his wounds and carrying him would endanger the withdrawal.[97]

> It was not until he had walked nearly a mile that he collapsed and had to allow himself to be carried on an improvised stretcher. Even then he was continually encouraging the other wounded by giving the thumbs up sign and thus undoubtedly helping them to keep cheerful and minimize the extent of their injuries until the landing craft was reached. Soon after he died of his wounds.
>
> The outstanding gallantry, remarkable endurance, and fortitude of Lieutenant Raymond, which refused to allow him to collapse, although mortally wounded, was an inspiration to everyone and a major factor in the capture of the strongpoint. His self-sacrifice in refusing atten-

tion to his wounds undoubtedly saved the patrol, by allowing it to withdraw in time before the Japanese could bring up fresh forces from neighbouring positions for a counter-attack.[98]

The last Irish Victoria Cross of the war was won in the closing days of the war against Japan. It completed a remarkable trio of naval VCs to Irishmen: the first was won on the surface of the north Atlantic by Captain Edward Fogarty Fegen in HMS *Jervis Bay* in 1940; the second went to Lieutenant-Commander Eugene Esmonde who led 825 Squadron into the maws of death in the air over the straits of Dover in 1942; and the third went to Leading Seaman James Magennis under the waters of the Johore Strait, Singapore, on 31 July 1945. Of the three, only Magennis lived to learn that he had won the Cross and to receive it. He was also the only one of the trio – and of all the war's Irish VCs – to come from Northern Ireland.

Born in Belfast in 1919, **James Joseph Magennis** joined the Royal Navy as a teenager in 1935 and was a highly-experienced veteran by July 1945. He had seen active service on surface vessels, large and small, and beneath the waves and had been sunk off Tripoli in HMS *Kandahar* in Mountbatten's 5th Flotilla in December 1941. Mick Magennis, as he was known in the service, trained as a diver, the role in which he won his Victoria Cross. In its efforts to devise a weapon to strike at the German battleship *Tirpitz* in a Norwegian fjord, and inspired by the Italian Navy's successes with human torpedoes in the Mediterranean, the Royal Navy developed similar underwater vehicles, or Chariots, before producing a four-man midget submarine. These X-Craft were 'undoubtedly one of the most potent and versatile vessels ever constructed for the Royal Navy', able to be used for striking at targets such as *Tirpitz* in heavily defended harbours, or enemy strategic communications, and for beach reconnaissance prior to amphibious landings. They could even be deployed as navigational beacons.[99]

X-Craft were first used in Operation SOURCE in September 1943 when six vessels set off to attack *Tirpitz*, *Scharnhorst* and *Lützow* in Kaafjord.* Magennis was in the crew of X7, which was towed by HM Submarine *Stubborn* to the release point off Sorøy Sound. X6 and X7 were the only two to penetrate the defences around *Tirpitz* and X7 was the sole vessel to return. However, *Tirpitz* was rendered incapable of sailing operationally and repairs would have to be carried out in Norway since the Luftwaffe could no longer mount an air operation such as had covered *Scharnhorst*, *Gneisenau* and *Prinz Eugen* on their dash from Brest in February 1942.[100]

---

* Kaafjord is a branch of Altenfjord. Some sources record *Tirpitz* as being tied up in the latter but all three ships did move from one anchorage to the other from time to time.

The subsequent sinking of *Tirpitz* by Bomber Command, and the destruction of *Scharnhorst* at the battle of North Cape, left few targets for X-Craft in Europe. A decision was taken to deploy them against the Japanese in the Far East but there was a reluctance on the part of the US Navy to have the little vessels in an operational role. However, a task was eventually assigned to them: the cutting of submarine telegraph cables linking Japanese forces in Hong Kong, Saigon and Singapore. Admiral James Fife, the US Seventh Fleet's Commander Submarines, decided that the British midget submarines could undertake an operation against two Japanese cruisers, *Myoko* and *Takao* which were anchored in the Johore Strait.[101]

Takao had been severely damaged by bombing in February and both ships were moored in the strait as floating anti-aircraft batteries although the US Navy believed both to be seaworthy and a danger to Allied shipping. And so it was decided to deploy the X-Craft to neutralize that danger. (In fact, the vessels of 14th Submarine Flotilla were XE-Craft, a tropical development of the original vessel.)

The plan was that XE1 and XE3 would attack the cruisers on the night of 31 July while XE4 and XE5 would cut undersea cables from Saigon to Hong Kong and Hong Kong to Singapore respectively. James Magennis was to sail in XE3, under command of Lieutenant Ian Fraser and towed by HM Submarine *Stygian*. As the diver, it was Magennis' job to leave the XE-Craft and attach mines to the hull of *Takao*, XE3's target. At 1 p.m. on 30 July the XE-Craft slipped their tows at the eastern end of the Singapore strait to cover the final forty miles alone.[102]

Fraser had little difficulty in locating *Takao* and XE3 passed through the open gate of the protective boom at about 9 a.m. on the 31st to make its way up channel to *Takao*, which was close inshore on the north end of Singapore Island, stern towards the island and well camouflaged. After allowing his three crew members to observe *Takao* through the periscope, Fraser brought XE3 under the cruiser's hull. XE3 had two cargo carriers: a container with six limpet mines on her port side and one large side charge on the starboard.

As Magennis tried to leave XE3 to place the mines, he found that the hatch would open only to a quarter of the normal distance. The tide was falling and *Takao* was settling on the submarine but the Belfastman escaped by deflating his breathing apparatus and squeezing and wriggling through the restricted gap. His problems did not end there for it was not easy to fix six limpet mines in a forty-five-foot line along the cruiser's hull. Both the hull's curvature and its barnacle-encrusted state meant that Magennis had to scrape clear an area on which to place his mines. Securing them meant tying them in pairs with a line that passed under the hull. Although this was physically exhausting work, Magennis persevered where 'a lesser man would have been content to place a few limpets and then to return to the craft. Magennis, however, persisted until he had placed his full outfit [of mines] before returning to the craft in an exhausted condition.'[103]

A steady leakage of oxygen from his breathing apparatus further handicapped Magennis. The leaking oxygen rose to the surface in bubbles and presented the danger of being spotted by an alert sentry. Even when he had returned to XE3's wet and dry chamber, his work was not over. Fraser released the starboard charge before trying to manoeuvre his vessel out from under *Takao*, which was finally achieved after twenty nerve-wracking minutes of applying full ahead and then full astern, as well as blowing and filling tanks. When XE3 eventually got free, it shot to the surface less than fifty yards from *Takao*. Fraser took it to the bottom again immediately.

XE3 was very difficult to manoeuvre because the port-side mine carrier had not released. Although physically exhausted from his earlier efforts, Magennis volunteered to don his diving suit again and went out with a sledgehammer, crowbar and chisel. He succeeded in freeing the recalcitrant container and Fraser then set a course for the Horsburgh Light, and the rendezvous with *Stygian*, which was reached at 3.30 a.m. on 1 August. XE3's crew had been on duty, without sleep, for fifty-two hours, sixteen of which had been underwater. The coxswain had spent more than thirty hours at the helm without relief.

XE1, forced to abandon the attack on *Myoko*, had placed another side charge under *Takao* on her way out. At 9.30 p.m. on 31 July the charges exploded, although XE3's main charge, a half-ton of amatol, did not detonate. Some limpets did explode and a large hole, over twenty feet by ten feet, was blown in *Takao*'s hull, damaging fire control instruments and distorting the roller paths for the main gun turrets. Although *Takao* did not sink fully, settling on the seabed with its upper deck above water, the ship's useful days for the Japanese Navy were over.[104]

An explosion heard by Fraser and his crew was later discovered to be an aircraft crashing at Changi and not *Takao* blowing up.[105] The cruiser had been cleared of ammunition and only a small care and maintenance party was aboard, which probably explains why Magennis' activities went undetected.[106] But the risks taken by the crew of XE3 were very great and were recognised by awards of the Victoria Cross to Ian Fraser and to James Magennis. Two DSOs went to the XE1's crew, while the total of awards to the two cable-cutting vessels and the pair that had entered the Johore strait included another DSO, six DSCs, a Conspicuous Gallantry Medal, two DSMs, two OBEs and eleven Mentions in Despatches.[107]

Although plans were made to return to the Johore strait to finish off the cruisers, the dropping of atomic bombs on Hiroshima and Nagasaki brought the war to an end. James Magennis had played a central role in one of the Royal Navy's final operations of the Second World War and, with his XE-Craft comrades, had also earned the admiration of Admiral James Fife, who described their flotilla as 'the little guys with a lotta guts'.

With the end of the Second World War the story of Ireland and the Victoria Cross comes to an end. It is impossible to tell whether that is a temporary situation or whether further Irish names may some day be added to the list of Victoria Cross winners. When the war ended there were only three surviving Irish VC laureates of that conflict: Harold Marcus Ervine Andrews, Richard Kelliher and James Magennis. With the death of Andrews in 1995 there were, for the first time since 1856, no living Irish holders of the Victoria Cross.

Since 1945 eleven VCs have been won in places as far apart as Borneo, Vietnam and the Falkland Islands as well as in the Korean War. None of those post-war winners has been Irish. It is to be hoped that never again will situations arise in which Victoria Crosses may be won, as that would mean that man had again resorted to violence to resolve issues of international dispute. But the lessons of recent years do not indicate that man has learned to live without conflict. When NATO troops entered Kosovo in June 1999, there were two Irish battalions included in the force – 1st Irish Guards and 1st Royal Irish Regiment – and many other Irishmen, and women, were to be found within the ranks of other units. The uncertainties that have replaced the certainty of the Cold War mean that there may be more Kosovo-type situations and this brings the possibility that the *London Gazette* may yet carry further announcements of the award of the Victoria Cross.

8 Recommendation Rejected

Ever since its inception the Victoria Cross has been a prized award, as was indicated by Colonel Daubeney of the 55th Regiment's efforts to obtain the medal for himself and some thirty of his regiment.[1] Those efforts were unsuccessful and they were among the first recommendations for the Victoria Cross that were rejected. Such rejections have been an integral part of the story of the VC and the two world wars of this century have seen further examples. Inevitably a number of Irishmen feature in these rejections. It would be impossible to unearth all the stories of rejected recommendations and there were certainly many that did not justify the premier award for valour. In other cases, where the facts are known, it is difficult to understand why the individual did not receive a Victoria Cross. To illustrate this point, the stories of six individuals – three each from the Great War and the Second World War – follow.

Captain Henry Gallaugher, from Manorcunningham, near Letterkenny in County Donegal, was a member of the Donegal and Fermanagh Volunteers, which became 11th Royal Inniskilling Fusiliers, who was killed during the battle of Messines on 7 June 1917. He was subsequently recommended for a posthumous Victoria Cross, but the recommendation was rejected.[2] Gallaugher earned the DSO for his actions on 1 July 1916 in the opening day of the battle of the Somme. On that day his battalion suffered the seventh-highest casualty rate of all the British battalions engaged in the assault. With 589 killed, wounded or missing – twelve officers and 577 men – the battalion's losses were also the second-highest in 36th (Ulster) Division; only the County Down Volunteers, with 595 casualties, fared worse.[3]

The award of the Distinguished Service Order to Lieutenant Henry Gallaugher on that day is indicative of actions that were close to meriting a Victoria Cross; it is generally agreed that the award of the DSO to a junior officer is a gallantry decoration second only to the Victoria Cross, and there are those who refer to such awards as 'failed VCs'. It is clear from the official history of the Ulster Division that Gallaugher's actions that day were outstanding.

> Lieutenant H. Gallagher [sic], 11th Inniskillings, was the sole officer of his battalion to cross the German front line. With his orderly's rifle he killed six Germans holding up the advance, and then, at the Cruci-

174

fix, organized the resistance, being one of the last to quit the German trenches at night.[4]

When the Ulster Division moved to the attack at Messines, Gallaugher was already well known for his courage and leadership in the battalion. Early in the action he was badly wounded when a piece of shrapnel left his right arm useless. He was urged to return for medical treatment but refused to do so. Unable to use the rifle he was carrying he threw that weapon down and drew his revolver with his left hand, telling his men that 'this will do me rightly'. He led his company on to its objective, supervised the consolidation of the positions they had taken and then set out to have his arm tended to. At that stage he was struck by a shellburst and was killed instantly.[5]

Gallaugher had shown both outstanding personal bravery and inspiring leadership. The battalion commander, Lieutenant-Colonel A.C. Pratt, a fellow Donegal man, wrote a citation for Gallaugher's Victoria Cross. Pratt's submission was unsuccessful, as much because of the lacklustre and pedestrian style of the citation, as any doubt that there may have been about Gallaugher's courage.[6] The story of Henry Gallaugher emphasizes the importance of the citation being written in such a fashion that there can be no doubt about the achievements of the recommended individual.

Another Royal Inniskilling Fusiliers' officer to display outstanding bravery on 1 July 1916 was Lieutenant Ernest McClure, of the Derry Volunteers – 10th Inniskillings. In much the same manner as Henry Gallaugher, he led his platoon in an advance that successfully penetrated the German lines. Later, as the pressure of the enemy counter-attacks told on the Derrys, he gathered the shattered remnants of his company and organized a last stand. McClure fell, fighting to the very end, and his name became a legend for courage among the survivors of the Derrys. Yet it appears that he was never recommended for the Victoria Cross. The reason for that was that there were simply not enough witnesses to the heroism shown by the young Derryman.[7]

Lieutenant-Colonel Donagh McCarthy-O'Leary, of the Royal Irish Fusiliers, was commanding a battalion of Royal Irish Rifles in 36th (Ulster) Division in March 1918 when the Germans launched Operation MICHAEL. In the course of the bitter fighting that followed the seven units that made up 107 Brigade were so badly mauled that they had to be re-organized into three groups, the largest of which, consisting of the survivors of the three infantry battalions, was placed under Donagh McCarthy-O'Leary's command. That re-organization took place on 26 March, five days after the opening of the German offensive.[8]

McCarthy-O'Leary's group of exhausted soldiers was put into the line to close a gap by linking up with the remnants of 108 Brigade. Throughout that night the group was engaged in action with McCarthy-O'Leary constantly encouraging and inspiring his men. He seemed to have limitless energy and refused to leave his soldiers when he was wounded. His inspiring leadership was a vital factor in the stand made by what was left of 107 Brigade. Late the following morning Donagh McCarthy-O'Leary was wounded a second time and was evacuated for treatment. Although he had done all that was required to earn a Victoria Cross, no award was ever made to him and there is no surviving evidence to suggest that a citation was even written.[9] A native of Glasnevin, Dublin Donagh McCarthy-O'Leary later commanded the Royal Irish Fusiliers in India where the father of one of the authors served under him.

Lieutenant-Colonel Maurice French, of Newbay, County Wexford, was commanding 2nd Royal Irish Fusiliers when a British force was sent to occupy the island of Leros in the Dodecanese in September 1943. Although suffering from sandfly fever, Colonel French spared no effort in making preparations to defend the sector of the island allocated to his battalion against a possible German attack.[10] That attack finally came on 12 November following the German capture of the islands of Cos, Levita and Calinos and a lengthy aerial bombardment of Leros – something with which the Faughs were quite familiar as they had been part of the garrison of Malta during the siege of that island.[11]

German landings were made at small bays in the north of Leros and also at Appetici, on the north side of Pandeli Bay. The seaborne landings were followed by a parachute assault by some 700 Fallschirmjäger and, by evening, the invaders, in spite of heavy casualties, had made significant progress, cutting the island in half by establishing themselves in the narrow neck of land between Alinda and Gurna Bays. A counter-attack was planned, but was not delivered that night and enemy reinforcements strengthened the German position the following day.[12]

Another counter-attack was planned, with Maurice French leading four companies – B and C Companies of the Faughs plus two companies of the King's Own – against the enemy lodgement in the small Appetici peninsula; this attack was timed for the early hours of 14 November. In their attack the infantrymen were to have the support of a Royal Navy bombardment from offshore. But everything that could go wrong with the plan did so: B and C Companies were unavailable; the threat of an attack on the brigade headquarters meant the redeployment of some of the King's Own; and the destroyer bombardment did not happen.[13]

Faced with such problems a lesser man might have baulked but Maurice French's sense of duty was too strong: with one and a half companies of the

King's Own, he led the assault. As dawn's light crept over the island, however, they were still short of their objective and the Germans

> Realising the unhappy position of the attackers, counter-attacked down the hill at dawn, inflicting severe casualties. Lieutenant Ardill ... and Fusilier Hardy ... were the only Faughs with Colonel French during this night; they returned to Battalion H.Q. to tell how a gallant soldier, and true Faugh, met his death, with a rifle to his shoulder, in the face of the enemy counter-attack; he had no thought of withdrawing. From our arrival in Leros Maurice French had given 24 hours of his day to the Island's defence, finally laying down his life to the cause; no man could do more.[14]

Eventually the Germans gained the upper hand and took control of Leros, taking prisoner most of the survivors of 2nd Royal Irish Fusiliers. The brigade commander, Brigadier Robert Tilney, a new arrival on Leros, had relied heavily on Maurice French's advice on many aspects of his command and later wrote that 'we lost the battle when we lost Maurice'. In the aftermath of the battle, Maurice French was awarded a posthumous Mention in Despatches. Tilney wrote: 'I recommended him for a posthumous MID which is the utmost one can do for one who died in circumstances when the award of a Victoria Cross is only foregone for the lack of positive evidence to support it – I believe he probably earned it.'[15]

As the Faughs on Leros were fighting their desperate battle against the German invaders, the soldiers of the Irish Brigade were engaged in another grim struggle in the Italian peninsula. The Brigade included 6th Royal Inniskilling Fusiliers, 2nd London Irish Rifles and 1st Royal Irish Fusiliers. All three battalions had already seen much hard fighting in Italy as the Allied advance came to a halt against the German fortifications of the Gustav line. Not until May 1944 would the Allied armies in Italy succeed in breaking through that line, the best-known feature of which was Monte Cassino, on which stood the ancient monastery of Saint Benedict.[16]

Operation DIADEM was the overall plan to smash through the German defences south of Rome. Eighth Army's part in the attack was code-named Operation HONKER and the Irish Brigade played a vital part as HONKER unfolded. Following the creation of a bridgehead by 4th British and 8th Indian Divisions, 78th (The Battleaxe) Division was to push out of the bridgehead and continue Eighth Army's attack. In the van of 78th Division was the Irish Brigade, led by 6th Inniskillings. The Inniskillings were the first of the three Irish battalions to be committed to the assault and they fought their way to the line of the road from Cassino to Pignataro, which was code-named Grafton, thrusting a salient into the Gustav line.[17]

It was essential that the Inniskillings' gains be supported and built upon and 2nd London Irish were to be part of that building programme. The battalion's advance was delayed when the commanding officer, Ion Goff, was killed by German shellfire, and there was a further delay to allow 2nd Lancashire Fusiliers, of 11 Brigade, to prepare for their advance on the right of the London Irish. Finally, the advance got underway at 9a.m. on 16 May with three companies of the battalion forward and one in reserve. The attacking companies were E on the left, H in the centre and G on the right.[18]

H Company was commanded by Major Desmond Woods MC and, as his company moved forward, Major Woods wondered how any German could live under the bombardment that the British guns were putting down. But the German artillery was still active and their guns soon found the range of the advancing Irishmen. H Company lost two platoon commanders to shellfire: Lieutenant Michael Clark MC was killed and Lieutenant Geoffrey Searles, an American, was wounded. The infantry were supported by the tanks of a squadron of 16th/5th Lancers who moved off behind the foot soldiers. It was the movement of the tanks that had signalled the start of the German bombardment.[19]

As the Rifles approached Sinagoga village there was fierce close-quarter fighting as they engaged the defenders of the village. Then the tanks supporting H Company ran into German anti-tank guns which claimed several of the Shermans. Although the infantry had penetrated the village, most of the leading tanks had been knocked out as they approached Sinagoga. It was at this point that one of Desmond Woods' NCOs, Corporal Jimmy Barnes, from Keady in County Armagh, took a hand.[20]

Jimmy Barnes' platoon commander was down, seriously wounded, as was the platoon sergeant. The platoon's strength was no greater than that of a section – about a dozen men – but Barnes took command and led his men in an attack on a well-dug-in 88mm gun that had been doing most of the damage.

> one by one the men were cut down by machine-gun fire on their left flank until Corporal Barnes remained alone. He went on by himself and then he fell dead, cut [down] by a machine gun, but by then the crew of the 88mm had baled out and the tanks were able to get forward once again.[21]

In his final dash towards the gun, Barnes had lobbed a grenade at its emplacement, thus making the gun crew's mind up to abandon their weapon. His sacrifice made possible the advance of the Lancers' tanks and before long H Company was on its objective and Sinagoga was in the hands of the London Irish.[22]

Major Desmond Woods was awarded a Bar to his MC that day. He wrote a citation for a posthumous Victoria Cross for Corporal Barnes but the recommendation was not accepted and the gallant young corporal – 'the very best kind of young NCO' – was not even recognized with a posthumous Mention in Despatches.[23] There can be no doubt, however, that Jimmy Barnes had performed a feat worthy of the Victoria Cross. It is worth contrasting his actions with those of a soldier of 2nd Lancashire Fusiliers, who were advancing on the right flank of the London Irish.

At much the same time as the advance of H Company, 2nd London Irish was being held up by anti-tank guns, C Company, 2nd Lancashire Fusiliers, also supported by tanks of 16th/5th Lancers, met stubborn opposition and were also counter-attacked by enemy tanks supported by infantry. A tank deadlock developed with opposing tanks on either side of a rise in the ground and with a sunken lane preventing an outflanking move. But the presence of two German Panzer Mk IVs threatened the Lancashires' advance until Fusilier Francis Jefferson, a company runner, stepped into the picture.[24]

Jefferson saw the enemy tanks approach, seized a PIAT, or Projector, Infantry Anti-Tank – a spring-loaded anti-tank weapon – and dashed forward under machine-gun fire to take up a position under cover. Since he could not see properly, he left cover, moved into the open and, ignoring a hail of bullets, fired at the leading tank. The PIAT round struck the tank, which was almost immediately engulfed in flames, its crew trapped inside. As Jefferson began to reload, the crew of the second tank decided to withdraw. The way was clear for the Lancashires to resume their advance.[25]

No one could deny the courage of either Jimmy Barnes or Francis Jefferson. But the question must be posed: why award the Victoria Cross to Jefferson but not to Barnes? The answer may lie in what appears to be a cynical soldiers' view of the award of gallantry decorations – that there was a rationing system. In the battles fought by Eighth Army to smash the Gustav line, three divisions from the British XIII Corps played the major part in breaching the enemy defences, while II Polish Corps assaulted Monte Cassino. Each of the divisions of XIII Corps was awarded a Victoria Cross: on 12 May Sepoy Kamal Ram of 8th Punjab Regiment earned the Cross that went to 8th (Indian) Division; on 12 May Captain Richard Wakeford of 2/4th Hampshire Regiment won the Cross that went to 4th Division while Jefferson won 78th Division's Cross on 16 May.[26] In an earlier Eighth Army battle, at Wadi Akarit in Tunisia in April 1943, three Victoria Crosses were also won with one going to each of the three assaulting divisions.[27] Could it therefore be that

Jimmy Barnes was denied the recognition that his gallantry deserved because someone far from the scene of the battle decided, arbitrarily, that only one VC would be awarded to each division? The story of Major Desmond Whyte of the Royal Army Medical Corps would suggest that such an attitude was not restricted to the Italian campaign.

Desmond Whyte, a County Down man, had already received a Mention in Despatches for his work in Burma in 1943. In 1944 he was the senior medical officer of 111 Brigade, which was taking part in the second Chindit expedition.[28] The Chindits operated behind enemy lines and attempted to disrupt the communications of, and supplies to, the Japanese forces engaged in the attacks on the Indian frontier. As the expedition was due to be withdrawn the brigades were ordered to remain in Burma and 111 Brigade was deployed to take up a blocking position, known as Blackpool, on the Japanese lines of communication.[29]

A hospital was set up within the Blackpool block and Desmond Whyte and his doctors were soon busy, for many of the soldiers were suffering from various illnesses due to their already lengthy spell behind the lines. It was not long before the Japanese began attacking Blackpool and battle casualties were added to the workload on Whyte and his doctors. The nature of the battle meant that the hospital itself was not immune: many enemy shells and mortar rounds fell in and around it and the work of the doctors was made so much more difficult. Desmond Whyte was himself wounded in the back during one attack but continued to give all his attention to his patients.[30]

Eventually the order was given to evacuate Blackpool and 111 Brigade, now totally exhausted, moved off into the jungle to continue its operations against the Japanese. The wounded were transported to a large lake where flying-boats flew them out to safety. Major Whyte remained with the main body of the brigade and his work was now even more tiring as soldiers who were completely physically worn out died from such minor ailments as scratches and slight infections.[31]

At the end of the operation, Desmond Whyte's brigade commander – John Masters, later to become famous as a novelist – wrote a citation for the Victoria Cross for his senior doctor. It was a citation that was supported by the four battalion commanders of the brigade. However, the citation was unsuccessful. Desmond Whyte was awarded the DSO and John Masters was furious. He later wrote that Desmond was the

> man, who, above all others, has kept the brigade going... but Desmond has not dashed out and rescued one wounded man under fire, he has only saved two hundred, over a hundred days, calm and efficient and cheerful while shells blast the bodies to pieces under his hands. The

Cross is refused and he gets a Distinguished Service Order instead. This is not good enough.[32]

Masters had written one successful citation for the Victoria Cross, for Major Frank Blaker who, when his Gurkhas had faltered in the face of fire from well dug in Japanese machine guns, had charged the Japanese positions in spite of intense fire and had inspired his soldiers to continue, successfully, with their attack. Blaker had died as a result of his deed.[33] Masters was convinced that Desmond Whyte was equally deserving of the Victoria Cross and there is no logical reason to argue with him. It is interesting to note that no British Army doctor was awarded the Victoria Cross in the Second World War, although one medical orderly was so decorated and one doctor did receive the George Cross.

The treatment of Desmond Whyte and other doctors during the Second World War also points the way to another noteworthy absence from the Victoria Cross Roll. Although a handful of chaplains have received the VC, no Irish Catholic chaplain was ever awarded it. In fact, it has never been awarded to a Catholic chaplain. This was in spite of there being a number of men who were obvious candidates. Perhaps the most surprising exclusion, in the eyes of his contemporaries, was the legendary Father Willie Doyle MC.

Willie Doyle was the Catholic chaplain, at various times, to several of the battalions that made up 16th (Irish) Division, although his career as a chaplain began with 8th Royal Irish Fusiliers. He was killed in August 1917 during the disastrous battle of Langemarck while helping the wounded on the battlefield, even though he had been ordered, by the commanding officer of 8th Royal Dublin Fusiliers to stay back.[34] The action that cost him his life was typical of Willie Doyle; he had brought comfort and the Last Rites of his Church to many wounded and dying soldiers in that terrible stretch of tortured earth that lay between the opposing lines. His commanding officer, his brigade commander and his divisional commander recommended him for the Victoria Cross but no award was ever made, although he had been awarded the MC for his service on the Somme in 1916. The divisional commander, Major-General William Hickie, later wrote that Father Doyle was

one of the bravest men who have fought or worked out here. He did his duty, and more than his duty, most nobly, and has left a memory and a name behind him that will never be forgotten. On the day of his death, 16th August, he had worked in the front line, and even in front of that line, and appeared to know no fatigue – he never knew fear.

He was killed by a shell towards the close of the day, and was buried on the Frezenberg Ridge.[35]

Tributes to Willie Doyle came not only from Catholic soldiers of 16th (Irish) Division, but also from Protestant soldiers of 36th (Ulster) Division. Among the latter was this tribute from a Belfast Orangeman published in the *Glasgow Weekly News*

> Fr Doyle was a great deal among us. We couldn't possibly agree with his religious opinions, but we simply worshipped him for other things. He didn't know the meaning of fear, and he didn't know what bigotry was. He was as ready to risk his life to take a drop of water to a wounded Ulsterman as to assist men of his own faith and regiment. If he risked his life in looking after Ulster Protestant soldiers once, he did it a hundred times in the last few days. ... The Ulstermen felt his loss more keenly than anybody, and none were readier to show their marks of respect to the dead hero priest than were our Ulster Presbyterians. Fr Doyle was a true Christian in every sense of the word, and a credit to any religious faith.[36]

Father Doyle's biographer suggested that it was 'the triple disqualification of being an Irishman, a Catholic and a Jesuit' that prevented his being gazetted as a VC winner.[37] The charge has been repeated in more recent times by the historian of 16th (Irish) Division.[38] However, there had already been many Irish and Catholic VC winners and it seems unlikely that such considerations would have swung the balance against him. Nor should his being a Jesuit have been an influence. Had that been so, would the Victoria Cross have been awarded to officers such as Maurice Dease, who had been educated at Stonyhurst, a Jesuit public school that produced no less than seven winners of the VC? Such an explanation for Doyle not being awarded the VC is too simplistic and was made at a time when Irish nationalistic feelings were running very high. The authors of the seminal work on Catholic chaplains in the forces – *The Cross on the Sword* – suggest that the truth will never be discovered but add that

> It is interesting, nonetheless, taking account of relative military achievement and losses of each division, to compare Victoria Crosses awarded to 16th Irish Division, and 36th Ulster Division. Having carefully examined the circumstances of each award and the numbers involved, it is difficult not to accept that there was discrimination against 16th Division. Fr Doyle may have been a victim.[39]

He may equally have been a victim of a 'rationing' policy. The same authors also note that Father Luke Bellanti, a Stonyhurst priest, was recommended for a VC, but was awarded the MC instead, 'as the unit had just received a VC'.[40]

In the Second World War another Irish priest achieved a reputation similar to that of Willie Doyle. Father Dan Kelleher, from County Kerry, was referred to by an English officer of the Irish Brigade as the 'Willie Doyle of our war'.[41] In April 1944 Father Dan, as he was affectionately known to all in the Irish Brigade, was awarded the MC for rescuing wounded men during the shelling of 1st Royal Irish Fusiliers' positions in Cairo village near Monte Cassino in Italy.[42]

Father Dan performed many similar acts on other occasions and, as with Willie Doyle, ministered to Catholic and Protestant alike. The letter written by the Belfast Orangeman as a tribute to Father Doyle could equally have been written by a Second World War Orangeman about Dan Kelleher.

The citation for Kelleher's Military Cross was written by the adjutant of the Irish Fusiliers, Captain Brian Clark, who was also to earn the MC. Almost fifty years later Brian Clark suggested to one of the authors that, had Father Dan been serving in an English battalion in an English brigade, he might well have received a periodic Victoria Cross, in the same manner as Leonard Cheshire earned his VC. Brian Clark's reasoning for this suggestion was not that higher authority was discriminating in any way against Irishmen but that a Catholic chaplain serving in an Irish Brigade, the majority of whose members were Irishmen, and largely Catholic, was ministering in a situation where his courage was not seen as exceptional but as the norm for the role that he played. In an English battalion the expectations of a Catholic padre would not have been as high as in an Irish unit and courage such as that shown by Dan Kelleher may well have been rewarded with a VC, provided, of course, that the rationing system did not rule out such an award. It is an interesting theory that may go some way towards explaining the absence of Irish Catholic priests from the roll of VC winners.[43]

In the final analysis neither Willie Doyle nor Dan Kelleher would have sought such rewards. They sought only to answer their vocations, and to minister as best they could to men who lived close to death. No one can doubt that they did so; and that their ultimate reward was greater than any temporal decoration.

8   Postscript

The aim of this book is to tell the story of those Irishmen who have won the Victoria Cross since the institution of the medal in the middle of the nineteenth century. When the authors began their research there was an accepted total of 166 Irish-born winners. However, both authors were aware that many other VC winners were Irish: some of these latter were born of Irish parents outside Ireland, but who retained a home here, such as the Gough family, or were the first generation born outside Ireland of a family that had emigrated in search of a better life for their children. Some also were the sons of an Irish mother and a father who was from one of the other nations of the British Isles, or vice versa.

By checking the roots of the parents of many VC winners the authors were able to establish that over 200 of those men were Irish. This makes the story of the Irish Victoria Cross winners even more fascinating than ever; it means that 16.5 per cent of all VC winners have been Irish, a remarkable statistic for a small nation. And as most of the Irish VCs were won in the nineteenth century, when, generally one had to survive in order to earn the medal, it indicates just how significant was the Irish contribution to the British forces in the Victorian era. The Irish percentage of VC winners in the British forces actually increases when one removes from the equation the number of VCs that have been won by Commonwealth and Imperial soldiers, sailors and airmen. It is a truly remarkable story.

And yet there may still be omissions in this work. There are a number of other VC laureates whom the authors suspect may have an Irish connection, but we have been unable sufficiently to prove that connection for this book. Examples include Edward Dwyer, who was born in Fulham, London in 1895 and won the VC while serving with 1st East Surreys on 21 April 1915 at Hill 60. His surname is obviously Irish; and he was baptized a Catholic and attended a Catholic school.[1] To date, however, it has not been possible to prove whether Dwyer senior was Irish-born.

Another Dwyer appears on the register of VC winners in the Great War. John James Dwyer was born in Tasmania in 1890 and won the Cross at Zonnebeke in Belgium on 26 September 1917 when serving with 4th Company, Machine Gun Corps of the Australian Imperial Force. In later life he was prominent in politics in Tasmania.[2]

Edward Donald Bellew was born in India into an old military family in 1882. He was commissioned into the Royal Irish Regiment in May 1901, which indicates that his family regarded itself as Irish. He served with the Royal Irish for two years before leaving the Army. In 1907 he emigrated to Canada and on 10 August 1914 he was commissioned into the 11th Irish Fusiliers of Canada, again a strong indication of Irishness. His may be the family that gave its name to Bellewstown. He won the VC near Kerseleare in Belgium on 24 April 1915.[3]

In May 1945 Private Edward Kenna of 2/24th Bn (New South Wales) Australian Imperial Force won the VC in New Guinea when he was responsible for the capture of a Japanese bunker that had been holding up the advance of his company. Kenna had been born in Victoria in 1919 and may have been the son or grandson of Irish immigrants.[4]

The name Kenny has already appeared twice in this book; but a total of six Victoria Crosses went to men of that clan. The first was won by Private James Kenny of the 53rd Regiment at the Secundra Bagh, Lucknow in 1857 during the Indian Mutiny. No definitive information has been found on Kenny's date and place of birth.[5] All that is known is that he was born in the mid-1820s and it is possible that he was born in Ireland.* In November 1915 Private Thomas Kenny, 13th Bn, Durham Light Infantry, won the VC near La Houssoie in France. He had been born in South Wingate, County Durham, in 1882.[6] Kenny, or Kenney, is just one of many Irish names that can be found in the north-east of England and it appears on the nominal rolls of battalions of the Tyneside Irish, who were recruited from the area's large Irish immigrant population, and from the sons and grandsons of Irish immigrants.[7] Thus Thomas Kenny VC, may have regarded himself as one of the North-East's Irish community. The final Kenny to win the Victoria Cross was another member of the Australian Imperial Force: Private Thomas James Bede Kenny, 2nd Bn, (New South Wales) AIF, won his Cross on 9 April 1917 at Hermies in France.[8]

Another Great War VC winner who was of Irish descent was Sub-Lieutenant Arthur Walderne St Clair Tisdall, who earned a posthumous award while serving with the Anson Battalion of the Royal Navy Division at Gallipoli. Tisdall was born in Bombay, India, the second son of the Reverend William St Clair Tisdall, MA, DD, who was at one time vicar of St George's, Deal. The Reverend Tisdall was one of a family noted in Burke's Landed Gentry of Ireland, the Tisdalls of Charlesfort.[9]

* Another Indian Mutiny VC went to Private Charles Anderson, 2nd Dragoon Guards. Born in Liverpool, Anderson was the son of parents from Dublin. He won his VC at Sundeela, Oudh, on 8 October 1858.

There is one VC winner who was long considered Irish but who was English-born. Lance-Corporal John Patrick Kenneally, of the Irish Guards, who won the VC in Tunisia in April 1943, had enlisted in the Irish Guards using the identity of an Irishman with whom he had worked on building sites in wartime Britain. Kenneally was really Leslie Robinson, born in Birmingham, who had previously deserted from the Royal Artillery but wanted to return to the Army. The real Kenneally had returned to Ireland to avoid being called up.[10] For many years after the war it was firmly believed that Kenneally VC was an Irish-born soldier and he was included in many listings of the Irish Victoria Cross winners of the Second World War.

On 19 August 1942, British and Canadian forces undertook Operation JUBILEE, better known as the Dieppe raid. Although the raid was a disaster, it provided many lessons for future amphibious operations and it also brought many displays of gallantry. Three Victoria Crosses were won that day, two of which went to Canadian officers. One of the two Canadians was a Presbyterian chaplain, the Reverend John Weir Foote. During the battle Foote collected wounded and saved many lives as well as inspiring others with his example. As the Canadians were being evacuated, he climbed from the relative safety of the landing craft and walked into the German positions to be made a prisoner of war so that he could continue to help the men in captivity. He did this until he was liberated in 1945 and he was shocked to discover that he had been recommended for the Victoria Cross. His award was gazetted on 14 February 1946.[11] Foote was descended from Irish immigrants into Canada.[12]

One other VC winner had an Irish connection. The improbably named Frederick Whirlpool, an Indian Mutiny winner, was actually born Frederick Conker in Liverpool.[13] His father was, at one time, the postmaster in Dundalk. There can have been little love between father and son, for the latter ran off to join the Army, using the aliases Frederick Humphrey James and Frederick Whirlpool. His father's position in Dundalk is, however, Whirlpool's only known connection with Ireland, although his regiment – 3rd Bombay Europeans – later became the Leinster Regiment.

No woman has ever won the Victoria Cross although there is nothing in the warrant to preclude women receiving the distinction. In part, that is a product of the era in which the Cross was instituted when no-one would have considered the possibility of a woman being in a situation in which a VC might be won. It is all the more interesting, therefore, to note that the officers of a largely-Irish regiment – the 104th Bengal Fusiliers, later Royal Munster Fusiliers – presented a gold replica of the Victoria Cross, without the words 'For Valour' to a woman in 1859. That woman was Mrs Webber Harris, wife of the commanding officer of the battalion, and she was given the award 'for her indomitable pluck in nursing the men during an outbreak of cholera in 1859 (27 men died in one night)'.[14] Mrs Harris' personal courage stands comparison with that of any VC winner and she may be considered an honorary VC.

It may well be that a future edition of this book, or the work of other researchers, may add some of the names mentioned above to the list of Irish Victoria Cross winners. Whether the figure stands at 166, or 207 or even higher, it represents a story of which all of Ireland, of whatever religious persuasion or political belief, can be proud. Those who won the Victoria Cross deserve to be remembered and if this book has helped that remembrance in any way it has served its purpose.

Appendix One: Alphabetical List of Irish VC Winners

*Entries with * appear in the photograph section*

Name	Adams, James William, MA
Rank	Reverend
Unit	Bengal Ecclesiastical Department
Action	Afghanistan, 11 December 1879
Gazette	26 August 1881
Born	Cork, 24 November 1839
Died	Ashwell Rectory, near Oakham, Rutland, 20 October 1903
Mem.	Stow Bardolph Church, Norfolk
Remarks	First clergyman to be awarded the Victoria Cross

Name	Agar, Augustine William Shelton
Rank	Lieutenant
Unit	Royal Navy
Action	Kronstadt, Russia, 17 June 1919
Gazette	22 August 1919
Born	Kandy, Ceylon, 4 January 1890
Died	Alton, Hampshire, 30 December 1968
Mem.	Alton Cemetery, Hampshire
Remarks	Also awarded DSO, author of *Footprints in the Sea* (autobiography) *Showing the Flag*, *Baltic Episode*. Family from County Kerry. VC at: Imperial War Museum, London.

Name	Alexander, Ernest Wright
Rank	Major
Unit	119 Battery Royal Field Artillery
Action	Elouges, Belgium, 24 August 1914
Gazette	18 February 1915
Born	Liverpool, 2 October 1870
Died	Kingsbridge, Devon, 24 August 1934
Mem.	Putney Vale Cemetery, London
Remarks	Mother from Belfast. VC at: Royal Artillery Institution, London.

Name	Alexander, John
Rank	Private
Unit	2nd Bn, 90th Perthshire Light Infantry
Action	The Crimea, 18 June and 6 September 1855
Gazette	24 February 1857
Born	Mullingar, County Westmeath, date unknown
Died	Killed in action at Alum Bagh, India, 24 September 1857

Mem.   No memorial
Remarks   Buried near where he fell. VC at: Scottish United Services Museum, Edinburgh Castle

Name   Anderson, Charles
Rank   Private
Unit   2nd Dragoon Guards (Queen's Bays)
Action   Sundeela, Oudh, India, 8 October 1858
Gazette   11 November 1862
Born   Liverpool, 1826
Died   Seaham Harbour, Sunderland, 19 April 1899
Mem.   No memorial
Remarks   Parents from Dublin.

Name   Aylmer, Fenton John
Rank   Captain
Unit   Royal Engineers
Action   Hunza campaign, India, 2 December 1891
Gazette   12 July 1892
Born   Hastings, Sussex, 5 April 1862
Died   Wimbledon, Surrey, 3 September 1935
Mem.   Golders Green, London, Kilcock Church, County Kildare
Remarks   County Kildare family, related to Coghill VC. VC at: Royal Engineers Museum.

Name   Barry, John
Rank   Private
Unit   1st Bn, Royal Irish Regiment
Action   Monument Hill, South Africa, 7/8 January 1901
Gazette   8 August 1902
Born   St Mary's Parish, Kilkenny, 1 February 1873
Died   Belfast, South Africa, 8 January 1901
Mem.   Irish Regiments' Museum, Sandhurst
Remarks   Died of wounds received on Monument Hill, first VC of 20th century

Name   Bell, David
Rank   Private
Unit   2nd Bn, 24th (2nd Warwickshire) Regiment
Action   Andaman Islands, 7 May 1867
Gazette   17 December 1867
Born   County Down, 1854
Died   Gillingham, Kent, 7 March 1920
Mem.   Woodlands Cemetery, Gillingham, Kent
Remarks   Peacetime award. VC at: Royal Regiment of Wales Museum

Name   Bell, Edward William Derrington
Rank   Captain
Unit   23rd (Royal Welch Fusiliers) Regiment
Action   The Alma, Crimea, 20 September 1854

Gazette	24 February 1857
Born	Kempsey, Worcestershire, 18 May 1824
Died	Lisbreen, Fortwilliam Park, Belfast, County Down, 10 November 1879
Mem.	Kempsey Churchyard, Worcestershire
Remarks	Also awarded French Legion d'Honneur and Turkish War Medal. VC at: Royal Welch Fusiliers

Name	Bell, Eric Norman Frankland
Rank	T/Captain
Unit	9th Bn, Royal Inniskilling Fusiliers
Action	The Somme, 1 July 1916
Gazette	26 September 1916
Born	Enniskillen, County Fermanagh, 28 August 1895
Died	Killed in action, Somme, 1 July 1916
Mem.	Listed on the Thiepval Memorial
Remarks	Attached to 109th Light Mortar Battery at the time of his award

Name	Beresford, Lord William Leslie de la Poer
Rank	Captain
Unit	9th Queen's Royal Lancers
Action	Zululand, 3 July 1879
Gazette	23 August 1879
Born	Mullaghbrack, County Armagh, 20 July 1847
Died	Deepdene, Dorking, Surrey, 28 December 1900
Mem.	Clonagam Churchyard, Curraghmore, County Waterford
Remarks	Third son of the Reverend John de la Poer, 4th Marquis of Waterford

Name	Bergin, James
Rank	Private
Unit	33rd (Duke of Wellington's) Regiment
Action	Magdala, Abyssinia, 13 April 1868
Gazette	28 July 1868
Born	Killbricken, Queen's County (Leix) 29 June 1845
Died	Poona, India, 1 December 1880
Mem.	No memorial
Remarks	Later served in the 78th Highlanders. *See also* Magner, Michael. VC at: Duke of Wellington's Regiment Museum.

Name	Bingham, Edward Barry Stewart, the Hon
Rank	Commander
Unit	HMS *Nestor*, Royal Navy
Action	Jutland, 31 May 1916
Gazette	15 September 1916
Born	Bangor, County Down, 26 July 1881
Died	London, 24 September 1939
Mem.	Bangor Castle, County Down
Remarks	Also awarded OBE and Order of St Stanislaus (Russia). VC at: North Down Museum, Bangor

Name   Boulger, Abraham
Rank   Lance Corporal
Unit   84th (York and Lancaster) Regiment
Action   Indian Mutiny 12 July to 25 September 1857
Gazette   18 June 1858
Born   Kilcullen, County Kildare, 4 September 1835
Died   Ireland, 23 January 1900
Mem.   Roman Catholic Churchyard, Ballymore, County Westmeath
Remarks   Severely wounded at the relief of Lucknow, fought at Tel-el-Kebir. VC
            at: York & Lancaster Regiment Museum

Name   Boyd-Rochfort, George Arthur
Rank   Second Lieutenant
Unit   1st Bn, Scots Guards
Action   La Bassée, France, 3 August 1915
Gazette   1 September 1915
Born   Middleton, County Westmeath, 10 January 1880
Died   Dublin, 11 August 1940
Mem.   No memorial
Remarks   First Guards' VC since Crimean War. VC at: Scots Guards

Name   Bradshaw, Joseph*
Rank   Private
Unit   2nd Bn, Rifle Brigade
Action   Crimea, 22 April 1855
Gazette   24 February 1857
Born   Pettigreen, Dromkeen, County Limerick, 1835
Died   Woolwich, London, 21 March 1875
Mem.   Rifle Brigade memorial, Winchester Cathedral
Remarks   Awarded Medaille Militaire by France. VC at: Royal Green Jackets

Name   Bradshaw, William
Rank   Assistant Surgeon
Unit   90th Perthshire Light Infantry
Action   Indian Mutiny, 26 September 1857
Gazette   18 June 1858
Born   Thurles, County Tipperary, 12 February 1830
Died   Thurles, County Tipperary, 9 March 1861
Mem.   St Mary's Church, Thurles, County Tipperary
Remarks   Also awarded Turkish Crimea Medal, Crimea Medal

Name   Bromhead, Gonville
Rank   Lieutenant
Unit   24th (2nd Warwickshire) Regiment
Action   Rorke's Drift, Natal, 22 January 1879
Gazette   2 May 1879
Born   Versailles, France, 29 August 1844

Died   Allahabad, India, of typhoid, 10 February 1891
Mem.   Name inscribed on the Colour pole of the 24th
Remarks   Irish mother. VC at: Royal Regiment of Wales Museum

Name   Brooke, James Anson Otho
Rank   Lieutenant
Unit   2nd Bn, Gordon Highlanders
Action   Gheluvelt, Belgium, 29 October 1914
Gazette   18 February 1915
Born   Newmills, Scotland, 3 February 1884
Died   Killed in action 29 October 1914
Mem.   Attached to captured German field gun, Regimental Museum, Ennis-
            killen and Zantvoorde British Cemetery, Belgium
Remarks   County Fermanagh family. VC at: Gordon Hldrs Museum

Name   Brown, Edward Douglas, later Browne-Synge-Hutchinson
Rank   Major
Unit   14th King's Hussars
Action   Geluk, South Africa, 13 October 1900
Gazette   15 January 1901
Born   Kassouli, Dagshai, India, 6 March 1861
Died   London, 3 February 1940
Memorial   No memorial
Remarks   Family from Castle Sallagh, County Wicklow. VC at: 14th/20th Hussars
            Museum

Name   Brown, Francis David Millest
Rank   Lieutenant
Unit   1st Bn, Bengal European Fusiliers (later Royal Munster Fusiliers)
Action   Narnoul, India, 16 November 1857
Gazette   17 February 1860
Born   Bhagalpur, Bengal, India, 7 August 1837
Died   Sandown, Isle of Wight, 21 November 1895
Mem.   Royal Munster Fusiliers memorial, Winchester Cathedral
Remarks.   Irish family

Name   Burgoyne, Hugh Talbot
Rank   Lieutenant
Unit   Royal Navy
Action   Aboard HMS *Swallow* in the Crimea, 29 May 1855
Gazette   24 February 1857
Born   Dublin, 17 July 1833
Died   At sea, near Finisterre, 7 September 1870.
Mem.   St Paul's Cathedral; His name is listed on the plaque in Westminster
            Abbey which commemorates the 471 officers and men lost on HMS
            Captain. Family grave at Brompton Cemetery, London.
Remarks   Son of Field Marshal Sir John Fox Burgoyne.

Name	Burslem, Nathaniel
Rank	Lieutenant
Unit	67th (South Hampshire) Regiment
Action	Taku Forts, China, 21 August 1860
Gazette	13 August 1861
Born	Limerick, 2 February 1838
Died	1865
Mem.	No memorial
Remarks	Drowned in the Thames River, New Zealand. VC at: Royal Hampshire Regiment Museum. *See also* Lane, T.

Name	Byrne, James
Rank	Private
Unit	86th (Royal County Down) Regiment
Action	Jhansi, India, 3 April 1858
Gazette	11 November 1859
Born	Newtownmountkennedy, County Wicklow, 1882
Died	North Dublin, 6 December 1872
Mem.	No memorial
Remarks	VC at: Royal Ulster Rifles Museum.

Name	Byrne, John
Rank	Private
Unit	68th (Durham – Light Infantry) Regiment
Action	Crimea, 5 November 1854 and 11 May 1855
Gazette	24 February 1857
Born	Castlecomer, Kilkenny, September 1832
Died	Caerleon, Monmouthshire, 10 July 1879
Mem.	St Woolo's Cemetery, Newport, Monmouthshire
Remarks	Also awarded the DCM. On 4 November 1985 a headstone to his grave was erected and dedicated.

Name	Byrne, Thomas
Rank	Trooper
Unit	21st Lancers
Action	Khartoum, 2 September 1898
Gazette	15 November 1898
Born	St Thomas, Dublin, December 1866
Died	Canterbury, Kent, 14 March 1944
Mem.	No memorial
Remarks	Winston Churchill witnessed his act of winning the VC. Of the three VCs awarded to the Lancers on this date only Byrne died of natural causes

Name	Caffrey, John
Rank	Private
Unit	2nd Battalion York and Lancaster Regiment

Action   La Brique, France, 16 November 1915
Gazette   22 January 1916
Born   Birr, King's County (Offaly) 23 October 1891
Died   Derby, 26 February 1953
Mem.   No memorial
Remarks   Also awarded the Cross of the Order of St George (4th Class) by Russia.
              VC at: York & Lancaster Regiment Museum

Name   Cambridge, Daniel
Rank   Sergeant
Unit   Royal Regiment of Artillery
Action   Crimea, 8 September 1855
Gazette   23 June 1857
Born   Carrickfergus, County Antrim, 1820
Died   London SE18, 12 June 1882
Mem.   No memorial
Remarks   Confusion with regard to date of death. VC at: Royal Artillery
              Institution.

Name   Carlin, Patrick
Rank   Private
Unit   1st Bn, 13th Regiment (1st Somersetshire) (Prince Albert's Light
              Infantry)
Action   Indian Mutiny
Gazette   26 October 1858
Born   Belfast, County Antrim, 1832 (Belfast was not a county borough at this
              time.)
Died   Union Infirmary, Belfast, 11 May 1895
Mem.   No memorial
Remarks   VC at: Somerset LI Museum.

Name   Carton de Wiart, Adrian
Rank   T/Lieutenant Colonel
Unit   4th (Royal Irish) Dragoon Guards, attached to 8th Bn Gloucestershire
              Regt.
Action   La Boiselle, France, 2/3 July 1916
Gazette   9 September 1916
Born   Brussels, 5 May 1880
Died   Killinardrish, County Cork, 5 June 1963
Mem.   *Happy Odyssey*, autobiography
Remarks   Irish grandmother. VC at: National Army Museum.

Name   Cather, Geoffrey St George Shillington*
Rank   Lieutenant
Unit   9th Bn, Princess Victoria's (Royal Irish Fusiliers)
Action   Hamel, France, 1 July 1916
Gazette   9 September 1916

Born   Streatham Hill, London, 11 October 1890
Died   Killed in action, Hamel, 1 July 1916
Mem.   Thiepval Memorial, France
Remarks   Mother from Portadown, County Armagh. VC at: Royal Irish Fusiliers
           Museum.

Name   Coffey, William
Rank   Private
Unit   34th (Cumberland) Regiment
Action   Crimea, 29 March 1855
Gazette   24 February 1857
Born   Knocklong, County Limerick, 5 August 1829
Died   Sheffield, 13 July 1875
Mem.   No memorial
Remarks   Was also awarded the DCM and Medaille Militaire. Died by shooting
           himself at the Army Drill Hall, Sheffield. Buried in Spittal Cemetery,
           Chesterfield, Derbyshire. VC at: King's Own Royal Border Regiment
           Museum.

Name   Coghill, Nevill Josiah Alymer
Rank   Lieutenant
Unit   24th (2nd Warwickshire) Regiment (later South Wales Borderers)
Action   Isandhlwana, 22 January 1879
Gazette   2 May 1879 and 15 January 1907
Born   Drumcondra, County Dublin, 25 January 1852
Died   22 January 1879
Mem.   Name inscribed on the Colour Pole of the 24th Regiment
Remarks.   Portrait in the chapel of Haileybury College. VC at: Royal Regiment of
           Wales Museum.

Name   Colvin, Hugh
Rank   Second Lieutenant
Unit   9th Bn, Cheshire Regiment
Action   Belgium, 20 September 1917
Gazette   8 November 1917
Born   Burnley, Lancashire, 1 February 1887
Died   16 September 1962
Mem.   Family plot Carnmoney Cemetery
Remarks   Died in England, body brought home by his sister. VC at: Cheshire
           Regiment Museum.

Name   Conker, *see* Whirlpool

Name   Connors, Joseph
Rank   Private
Unit   3rd (East Kent – The Buffs) Regiment
Action   Crimea, 8 September 1855

Gazette   24 February 1857
Born   Davaugh, Listowel, County Kerry, October 1830
Died   Corfu, 22 August 1858
Mem.   No memorial
Remarks   Died of disease. VC location not known; the medal may have been destroyed.

Name   Connolly, John Augustus
Rank   Lieutenant
Unit   49th (Princess of Wales's Hertfordshire) Regiment
Action   Crimea, 26 October 1854
Gazette   5 May 1857
Born   Cliff, Ballyshannon, County Donegal, 30 May 1829
Died   Magistrate's House, Curragh, County Kildare, 23 December 1888
Mem.   Mount Jerome Cemetery, Harold's Cross, Dublin
Remarks   Served in the Dublin Metropolitan Police 1877-83. VC at: Coldstream Guards.

Name   Cosgrove, William
Rank   Corporal
Unit   1st Bn, Royal Munster Fusiliers
Action   V Beach, east of Cape Helles, Gallipoli, 26 April 1915
Gazette   23 August 1915
Born   Upper Aghada, County Cork, 1 October 1888
Died   Millbank, London, 14 July 1936, in hospital from an old wound
Mem.   No memorial
Remarks   Also awarded the MSM.

Name   Costello, Edmond William*
Rank   Lieutenant
Unit   22nd Punjab Infantry, Indian Army
Action   With the Malakand Field Force, 26 July 1897
Gazette   9 November 1897
Born   Sheikhbudia, North West Frontier, 7 August 1873
Died   Eastbourne, Sussex, 7 June 1949
Mem.   St Mark's Church, Hadlow Down, Sussex; Stonyhurst College, Clitheroe, Lancashire
Remarks   Irish parents. Served in Great War. VC at: National Army Museum.

Name   Coughlan (or Coughlin), Cornelius
Rank   Colour Sergeant
Unit   75th Regiment
Action   Indian Mutiny, 8 June 1857
Gazette   11 November 1862
Born   Eyrecourt, County Galway, 27 June 1828
Died   Westport, County Mayo, 14 February 1915
Mem.   No memorial
Remarks   VC at: Scottish United Services Museum.

Name	Creagh, Sir O'Moore
Rank	Captain
Unit	Bombay Staff Corps, Indian Army
Action	Kabul river, Afghanistan, 22 April 1879
Gazette	17 November 1879
Born	Cahirbane, County Clare, 2 April 1848
Died	65 Albert Hall Mansions, South Kensington, London, 9 August 1923
Mem.	East Sheen Cemetery, Surrey
Remarks	Also awarded GCB, GCSI, Order of the Rising Sun (Japan). Knight of Grace of St John of Jerusalem Compiler and editor (with EM Humphris) of *The VC* and *DSO*. VC at: National Army Museum, London.

Name	Crean, Thomas Joseph FRCSI
Rank	Surgeon Captain
Unit	1st Imperial Light Horse (Natal)
Action	Tygerkloof, South Africa, 18 December 1901
Gazette	11 February 1902
Born	Northbrook Road, Dublin, 19 April 1873
Died	London, 25 March 1923
Mem.	St Mary's Roman Catholic Cemetery, Kensal Green, London
Remarks	Also awarded the DSO and two MiDs. VC at: Royal Army Medical Corps.

Name	Crichton, James
Rank	Private
Unit	2nd Battalion Auckland Infantry Regt, New Zealand Expeditionary Force
Action	Crevecoeur, France, 30 September 1918
Gazette	15 November 1918
Born	Carrickfergus, County Antrim, 15 July 1879
Died	Auckland, New Zealand, 22 September 1961
Mem.	Soldiers' Cemetery, Waikumete, Auckland
Remarks	Constant refusal by local council to erect memorial in Carrickfergus

Name	Crimmin, John
Rank	Surgeon
Unit	Bombay Medical Services attached to 27th Bombay Infantry
Action	Lwekan, Eastern Karenni, Burma, 1 January 1889
Gazette	17 September 1889
Born	Dublin, 19 March 1859
Died	Wells, Somerset, 20 February 1945
Mem.	No memorial
Remarks	Also awarded CB, CIE, VD, KHP, IMS

Name	Cunningham, John
Rank	Corporal
Unit	2nd Bn, Leinster Regiment (The Prince of Wales's Royal Canadians)
Action	Bois-en-Hache, Barlin, France, 12 April 1917

Gazette   8 June 1917
Born   Hall St, Thurles, County Tipperary, 22 October 1890
Died   Died of wounds near Barlin, 16 April 1917
Mem.   St Mary's, Thurles
Remarks   Buried in Barlin Cemetery, plot 1, row A, grave 39

Name   Danaher, John
Rank   Trooper
Unit   Nourse's Transvaal Horse
Action   Elandsfontein, South Africa, 16 January 1881
Gazette   14 March 1882
Born   Limerick, 25 June 1860
Died   Ireland 9 January 1919
Mem.   No memorial
Remarks   Educated at Christian Brothers School, Edward St, Limerick. His six
             sons served in the 1914-18 War. VC at: National Army Museum.

Name   Dease, Maurice James*
Rank   Lieutenant
Unit   4th Bn, Royal Fusiliers
Action   Mons canal, France, 23 August 1914
Gazette   16 November 1914
Born   Gaulstown, Coole, County Westmeath
Died   Killed in action, 23 August 1914
Mem.   St Symphorien Military Cemetery, Nimy Bridge, Westminster Cathedral
             (twice); Stonyhurst College, Clitheroe, Lancashire
Remarks   First Victoria Cross awarded in First World War. VC at: Royal Fusiliers
             Museum.

Name   Dempsey, Denis
Rank   Private
Unit   1st Bn, 10th (North Lincolnshire) Regiment
Action   Indian Mutiny, 1857/8
Gazette   17 February 1860
Born   Rathmichael, Bray, County Wicklow, 1826
Died   Toronto, Canada, 10 January 1896
Mem.   No memorial

Name   De Wind, Edmund
Rank   Second Lieutenant
Unit   15th Bn, Royal Irish Rifles
Action   Race Course Redoubt, Groagie, France, 21 March 1918
Gazette   15 May 1919
Born   Comber, County Down
Died   Killed in action 21 March 1918
Mem.   De Wind Drive, Comber County Down, Pozieres, France and Mount
             De Wind, Alberta, Canada.

Name   Diamond, Bernard
Rank   Sergeant
Unit   Bengal Horse Artillery
Action   Indian Mutiny, 28 September 1857
Gazette   24 April 1858
Born   Portglenone, County Antrim, 1827
Died   Masterton, New Zealand, 24 January 1892
Mem.   No memorial
Remarks   VC at: Queen Elizabeth II Army Memorial Museum, New Zealand.

Name   Divane *see* Duane, John

Name   Donohoe, Patrick
Rank   Private
Unit   9th Queen's Royal Lancers
Action   Indian Mutiny, 28 September 1857
Gazette   24 December 1858
Born   Nenagh, County Tipperary, 1820
Died   Ashbourne, County Meath, 1876
Mem.   No memorial

Name   Doogan, John
Rank   Private
Unit   1st King's Dragoon Guards
Action   Lang's Nek, South Africa, 28 January 1881
Gazette   14 March 1882
Born   Aughrim, County Galway, March 1853
Died   Folkestone, Kent, 24 January 1940
Mem.   Military Cemetery, Shorncliffe, Kent
Remarks   VC stolen during the 1956 Centenary Exhibition, now held by a collec-
            tor in America

Name   Dowling, William
Rank   Private
Unit   32nd (Cornwall) Regiment
Action   Lucknow, Indian Mutiny, 4 and 9 July 1857
Gazette   21 November 1859
Born   Thomastown, County Kilkenny, 1825
Died   Liverpool, 17 February 1887
Mem.   No memorial
Remarks   VC at: Duke of Cornwall's LI Museum.

Name   Downie, Robert
Rank   Sergeant
Unit   2nd Bn, Royal Dublin Fusiliers
Action   Lesboeufs, France 23 October 1916
Gazette   25 November 1916

Born　　　Glasgow, 12 January 1894
Died　　　Glasgow, 18 April 1968
Mem.　　　No memorial
Remarks　　Parents from Dublin

Name　　　Doyle, Martin
Rank　　　Company Sergeant Major
Unit　　　1st Bn, Royal Munster Fusiliers
Action　　Reincourt, France, 2 September 1918
Gazette　　31 January 1919
Born　　　New Ross, County Wexford, 25 October 1891
Died　　　Dublin, 20 November 1940
Mem.　　　No memorial
Remarks　　Also awarded the Military Medal; posthumously decorated by Irish government for services to IRA during war of independence

Name　　　Duane, John, listed as Divane*
Rank　　　Private
Unit　　　1st Bn, 60th, or The King's Royal Rifle Corps
Action　　Indian Mutiny 10 September 1857
Gazette　　20 January 1860
Born　　　Canavane, Loughrea, County Galway, November 1828
Died　　　1 New Street, Penzance, Cornwall, 1 December 1888
Mem.　　　Memorial on pauper's grave erected by Royal Green Jackets, August 1995
Remarks　　Elected by the regiment

Name　　　Duffy, James*
Rank　　　Private
Unit　　　6th Bn, Royal Inniskilling Fusiliers
Action　　Kereina Peak, Palestine, 27 December 1917
Gazette　　28 February 1918
Born　　　Thor, Gweedore, County Donegal, 17 November 1889
Died　　　Letterkenny, County Donegal, 8 April 1969
Mem.　　　Conwal Cemetery, Letterkenny
Remarks　　Buried in Conwal Cemetery, Letterkenny. VC at: Royal Inniskilling Fusiliers Museum

Name　　　Duffy, Thomas
Rank　　　Private
Unit　　　1st Bn, Madras Fusiliers (later Royal Dublin Fusiliers)
Action　　Lucknow, Indian Mutiny, 26 September 1857
Gazette　　18 June 1858
Born　　　Caulry, Athlone, County Westmeath, 1805
Died　　　Dublin, 23 December 1868
Mem.　　　No memorial

Name　　　Dunlay, John (or Dunlea)
Rank　　　Lance Corporal

Unit   93rd Highlanders
Action   Lucknow, Indian Mutiny, 16 November 1857
Gazette   24 December 1858
Born   Douglas, County Cork, 1831
Died   Douglas, County Cork, 17 October 1890
Mem.   No memorial

Name   Dunn, Alexander Roberts
Rank   Lieutenant
Unit   11th Prince Albert's Own Hussars
Action   Charge of the Light Brigade, Balaclava, 25 October 1854
Gazette   24 February 1857
Born   Dunstable, York, (now Toronto), Canada
Died   Senafe, Abyssinia, 25 January 1858
Mem.   Military Cemetery, Senafe; Regimental memorial, York Minster
Remarks   Irish parents. Was he murdered? VC at: Upper Canada College.

Name   Dunville, John Spencer
Rank   Second Lieutenant
Unit   1st (Royal) Dragoons
Action   24/25 June 1917
Gazette   2 August 1917
Born   Marylebone, London, 7 May 1896
Died   Died of wounds, 26 June 1917
Mem.   Holywood, County Down
Remarks   Member of the Dunville's Whiskey family. Only VC of this regiment.
            VC at: Household Cavalry Regiment

Name   Dynon, Denis
Rank   Sergeant
Unit   53rd (Shropshire) Regiment
Action   Chota Behar, Indian Mutiny, 2 October 1857
Gazette   25 February 1862
Born   Kilmannon, Queen's County (Leix), September 1822
Died   Dublin, 16 February 1863
Mem.   No memorial

Name   Edwards, Frederick Jeremiah
Rank   Private
Unit   12th Bn, Middlesex Regiment (Duke of Cambridge's Own)
Action   Thiepval, France, 26 September 1916
Gazette   25 November 1916
Born   Queenstown (Cobh), County Cork, 3 October 1894
Died   Richmond, Surrey, 9 March 1964
Mem.   Richmond Cemetery, Richmond, Surrey
Remarks   VC at: National Army Museum

Name   Emerson, James Samuel*
Rank   T/Second Lieutenant
Unit   9th Bn, Royal Inniskilling Fusiliers
Action   Hindenburg Line, north of La Vacquerie, France, 6 December 1917
Gazette   13 February 1918
Born   Collon, Drogheda, County Louth,
Died   Killed in action, 6 December 1917
Mem.   Church of Ireland, Collon. Cambrai Memorial, France

Name   English, William John*
Rank   Lieutenant
Unit   2nd Scottish Horse
Action   Valkfontein, South Africa, 3 July 1901
Gazette   4 October 1901
Born   Cork, 6 October 1882
Died   At sea near Egypt, 4 July 1941
Mem.   Maala Military Cemetery, Aden
Remarks   Served in Great War in the RASC and in Second World War with the
          Royal Ulster Rifles

Name   Ervine-Andrews, Harold Marcus*
Rank   Captain
Unit   1st Bn, East Lancashire Regiment
Action   Dunkirk, France, 31 May/1 June 1940
Gazette   30 July 1940
Born   Keadue, County Cavan, 29 July 1911
Died   30 March 1995
Mem.   Stonyhurst College, Clitheroe, Lancashire
Remarks   Last Irish VC holder to die. VC at: Blackburn Museum

Name   Esmonde, Eugene*
Rank   Lieutenant Commander
Unit   825 Squadron, Fleet Air Arm
Action   Straits of Dover, attacking *Prinz Eugen*, 12 February 1942
Gazette   3 March 1942
Born   Yorkshire, 1 March 1909
Died   Killed in action 12 February 1942
Mem.   Woodlands Cemetery, Gillingham, Kent
Remarks   Tipperary family, great-nephew of Thomas Esmonde VC; also awarded
          DSO for attack on *Bismarck* and Mention in Despatches for services on
          HMS *Ark Royal.*

Name   Esmonde, Thomas
Rank   Captain
Unit   18th (Royal Irish) Regiment
Action   Crimea, 18 and 20 June 1855
Gazette   25 September 1857
Born   Pembrokestown, County Waterford, 23 August 1829

Died   Bruges, Belgium, 14 January 1873
Mem.   No memorial
Remarks   Great uncle of Eugene Esmonde. Assistant Inspector General RIC 1865-67

Name   Farrell, John
Rank   Quartermaster Sergeant
Unit   17th Lancers
Action   Crimea, 25 October 1854
Gazette   20 November 1857
Born   Dublin, March 1826
Died   Secunderabad, India, 31 August 1865
Mem.   No memorial
Remarks   VC awarded for his action in the Charge of the Light Brigade

Name   Fegen, Edward Stephen Fogarty*
Rank   A/Captain, Royal Navy
Unit   HMS *Jervis Bay*
Action   North Atlantic, 5 November 1940
Gazette   22 November 1940
Born   Southsea, Hampshire, 8 October 1891
Died   Killed in action, 5 November 1940
Mem.   Chatham Naval Memorial; sundial at Hamilton, Bermuda; column in
           grounds of hospital, St John, New Brunswick, Canada; Seamen's
           Institute, Wellington, New Zealand
Remarks.   Family from County Tipperary; Also awarded Dutch Life Saving Medal.
           VC at: Royal Naval Museum

Name   Fitzclarence, Charles
Rank   Captain
Unit   Royal Fusiliers, attached Protectorate Regiment
Action   South Africa, 14 and 27 October, 26 December 1899
Gazette   6 July 1900
Born   Bishopscourt, County Kildare, 8 May 1865
Died   Killed in action Polygon Wood, France, 12 November 1914
Mem.   Menin Gate, Ypres
Remarks   Transferred to Irish Guards on their formation in 1900, killed in action
           commanding 1 Guards Brigade at Polygon Wood

Name   Fitzgerald, Richard
Rank   Gunner
Unit   Bengal Horse Artillery
Action   Indian Mutiny, 28 September 1857
Gazette   23 February 1880
Born   St Finbar's, Cork, December 1831
Died   India, 1884
Mem.   No memorial
Remarks   VC destroyed by German bombing

Name	Fitzgibbon, Andrew
Rank	Hospital Apprentice
Unit	2nd Bengal Artillery
Action	Taku Forts, China,
Gazette	13 August 1861
Born	Goojerat, India, 13 May 1845
Died	7 March 1883
Mem.	No memorial
Remarks	Irish parents from Tipperary; one of the two youngest VCs. VC believed buried with holder

Name	Fitzpatrick, Francis
Rank	Private
Unit	94th Regiment
Action	Zulu War, South Africa, 28 November 1879
Gazette	23 February 1880
Born	Tullycorbet, County Monaghan, 1859
Mem.	No memorial
Died	Glasgow, 10 July 1933
Remarks	VC at: National Army Museum

Name	Flinn, Thomas
Rank	Drummer
Unit	64th (2nd Staffordshire) Regiment
Action	Indian Mutiny, 28 November 1857
Gazette	12 April 1859
Born	Athlone 1842
Died	Athlone, 10 August 1892
Mem.	Garrison Church, Whittington Barracks, Lichfield
Remarks	One of the two youngest VC winners

Name	Foote, John Weir
Rank	Hon. Captain
Unit	Canadian Chaplains Service
Action	Dieppe, 19 August 1942
Gazette	14 February 1946
Born	Madoc, Ontario, Canada, 5 May 1904
Died	
Mem.	No memorial
Remarks	Member of the Orange Order, believed to have Irish parents

Name	Forrest, George
Rank	Lieutenant
Unit	Bengal Veteran Establishment
Action	Indian Mutiny, 11 May 1857
Gazette	18 June 1858
Born	St Michael's, Dublin, 1800
Died	Dehra Dun, India, 3 November 1859

Mem.   Tablet over gateway in Delhi
Remarks   Medals sold by Phillips in 1996 for £31,050

Name   Fowler, Edmund John
Rank   Private
Unit   90th Perthshire Light Infantry
Action   Zululand, 28 March 1879
Gazette   5 April 1882
Born   Waterford, 1861
Died   Colchester, Essex, 26 March 1926
Mem.   No memorial
Remarks   Medal sold by Sotheby's in February 1906 for £42. VC at: Cameronians
             Museum

Name   Gardiner, George
Rank   Sergeant
Unit   57th (West Middlesex) Regiment
Action   Crimea, 22 March and 18 June 1855
Gazette   2 June 1858
Born   Glenwallen, Warrenpoint, County Down
Died   Lifford, County Donegal, 17 November 1891
Mem.   Lifford Cemetery
Remarks   Also awarded Distinguished Conduct Medal. VC at: Princess of Wales's
             Royal Regiment (Queen's and Royal Hampshire)

Name   Garland, Donald Edward*
Rank   Flying Officer
Unit   No. 12 Squadron, Royal Air Force
Action   Albert canal, Belgium, 12 May 1940
Gazette   11 June 1940
Born   Ballinacor, County Wicklow, 28 June 1918
Died   Killed in action, 12 May 1940
Mem.   Heverlee War Cemetery, Louvain, Belgium
Remarks   First RAF VC of Second World War. Second VC awarded in war. VC
             at: Royal Air Force Museum, Hendon

Name   Garvin, Stephen*
Rank   Colour Sergeant
Unit   60th, or The King's Royal Rifle Corps
Action   Indian Mutiny, 23 June 1857
Gazette   20 June 1860
Born   Cashel, County Tipperary, 1826
Died   Chesterton, Oxfordshire, 23 November 1874
Mem.   No memorial

Name   Gill, Peter
Rank   Sergeant Major
Unit   Loodiana Regiment, Indian Army

Action	Indian Mutiny, 4 June 1857
Gazette	23 August 1858
Born	St Paul's, Dublin, September 1831
Died	Morar, Central India, 26 July 1868
Mem.	No memorial

Name	Gore-Browne, Henry George
Rank	Captain
Unit	32nd (Cornwall) Regiment
Action	Indian Mutiny, 21 August 1857
Gazette	20 June 1862
Born	Newtown, Roscommon, 30 September 1830
Died	Shanklin, Isle of Wight, 15 November 1912
Mem.	Brook Cemetery, Isle of Wight
Remarks	Buried in Brook Cemetery. He was the great-grandson of Arthur Browne, in whose arms Wolfe died at Quebec. VC at: Duke of Cornwall's LI Museum

Name	Gough, Charles John Stanley
Rank	Major
Unit	5th Bengal European Cavalry
Action	Khurkowdah, India, 15 August 1857
Gazette	21 October 1859
Born	Chittagong, India, 28 January 1832
Died	Clonmel, County Tipperary, 6 September 1912
Mem.	Plaque and memorial window in St Patrick's Church, Innislonagh, Clonmel
Remarks	Brother of H.H. Gough VC and father of J.E. Gough VC

Name	Gough, Hugh Henry
Rank	Lieutenant
Unit	1st Bengal European Light Cavalry
Action	Alumbagh, India, 12 November 1857
Gazette	24 December 1858
Born	Calcutta, India, 14 November 1833
Died	London, 12 May 1909
Mem.	Kensal Green Cemetery, London
Remarks	Brother of C.J.S. Gough VC and uncle of J.E. Gough VC

Name	Gough, Sir John Edmund*
Rank	Brevet Major
Unit	The Prince Consort's Own (Rifle Brigade)
Action	Daratoleh, Somaliland, 22 April 1903
Gazette	15 January 1904
Born	Muree, India, 25 October 1871
Died	Estaires, France, 22 February 1915
Mem.	Estaires Communal Cemetery, France and Rifle Brigade Memorial, Winchester Cathedral
Remarks	Son of C.J.S. Gough VC and nephew of H.H. Gough VC

Name   Grady, Thomas*
Rank   Private
Unit   4th, or The King's Own Regiment
Action   Crimea, Sebastopol, October and November 1854
Gazette   23 June 1857
Born   Cheddah, County Galway, 18 September 1835
Died   Australia, 18 May 1891
Mem.   Australian War Memorial, Canberra
Remarks   First VC of the Regiment, Also awarded the Distinguished Conduct
            Medal. VC at: Australian War Memorial

Name   Graham, Patrick
Rank   Private
Unit   90th Perthshire Light Infantry
Action   Indian Mutiny, 17 November 1857
Gazette   24 December 1858
Born   St Michael's, Dublin,
Died   Dublin, 3 June 1875
Mem.   No memorial
Remarks   Elected by the regiment. VC at: Cameronians Museum

Name   Grant, Peter
Rank   Private
Unit   93rd Highlanders
Action   Indian Mutiny, 16 November 1857
Gazette   24 December 1858
Born   Ireland 1824
Died   Dundee, Scotland, 10 January 1868
Mem.   No memorial
Remarks   Elected by the regiment

Name   Green, Patrick
Rank   Private
Unit   75th Regiment
Action   Indian Mutiny 11 September 1857
Gazette   26 October 1858
Born   Ballinasloe, County Roscommon, 1842
Died   Cork, 19 July 1889
Mem.   No memorial
Remarks   Medal sold to an unknown buyer in May 1926 for £26

Name   Griffiths, William
Rank   Private
Unit   24th (2nd Warwickshire) Regiment
Action   Andaman Islands, 17 December, 1867
Gazette   17 December 1867
Born   Roscommon, 1841

Died	Battle of Isandhlwana, 22 January 1879
Mem.	Regimental Memorial, Isandlwana
Remarks	Peace time award; see Bell, David. VC at: Royal Regiment of Wales Museum

Name	Hackett, Thomas Bernard
Rank	Lieutenant
Unit	23rd (Royal Welch Fusiliers) Regiment
Action	Indian Mutiny 18 November 1857
Gazette	12 April 1859
Born	Riverstown, County Tipperary, 15 June 1836
Died	Arrabeg, King's County, 5 October 1880
Mem.	Marshall family vault, Lockeen Churchyard, Borrisokane, Co. Tipperary
Remarks	Killed in a shooting accident when the breech of his gun exploded

Name	Hall, Frederick William
Rank	Company Sergeant Major
Unit	8th Manitoba Regiment, Canadian Expeditionary Force
Action	Ypres, Belgium, 24 April 1915
Gazette	23 June 1915
Born	Kilkenny, 8 February 1885
Died	Died of wounds, Gravenstafel, Ypres, 25 April 1915
Mem.	'Valour Road', Winnipeg, Canada; Menin Gate, Ypres, Belgium
Remarks	Two brothers also served in Great War; both were killed in action. VC at: Winnipeg Rifles Museum, Canada

Name	Hamilton, Thomas De Courcy
Rank	Captain
Unit	68th (Durham - Light Infantry) Regiment
Action	Crimea, 11 May 1855
Gazette	24 February 1857
Born	Stranraer, Scotland, 20 July 1825
Died	Cheltenham, Gloucestershire, 3 March 1908
Mem.	Cheltenham Cemetery and Garrison Church, Whittington Barracks, Lichfield
Remarks	Family from Ballymacoll, County Meath

Name	Hamilton, Walter Richard Pollock
Rank	Lieutenant
Unit	Bengal Staff Corps/ Corps of Guides
Action	Afghanistan, 2 April 1879
Gazette	1 September 1879
Born	Inistigoe, Kilkenny, 18 August 1856
Died	Defending Kabul Residency, 3 September 1879
Mem.	Horse Show Hall, Ballsbridge, Dublin; Sanctum Crypt, St Luke's Church, Chelsea, London
Remarks	Family connections with County Down and County Monaghan

Name	Hanna, Robert Hill
Rank	Company Sergeant Major
Unit	29th Bn, British Columbia Regiment, CEF
Action	Lens, France, 21 September 1917
Gazette	8 November 1917
Born	Kilkeel, County Down, 6 August 1887
Died	Mount Lehman, British Columbia, 15 June 1967
Mem.	Masonic Cemetery, Burnaby, BC, Canada; Kilkeel, Co. Down
Remarks	Member of Vancouver LOL No. 2226

Name	Harrison, John
Rank	Leading Seaman
Unit	HMS *Shannon*, Royal Navy
Action	Indian Mutiny, 16 November 1857
Gazette	24 December 1858
Born	Castleborough, County Wexford, 24 January 1832
Died	London, 27 December 1865
Mem.	No memorial
Remarks	Buried in Brompton Cemetery, London, in an unmarked grave. VC at: National Maritime Museum

Name	Hart, Reginald Clare
Rank	Lieutenant
Unit	Corps of Royal Engineers
Action	Afghanistan, 31 January 1879
Gazette	10 June 1879
Born	Scarriff, County Clare, 11 June 1848
Died	Bournemouth, Hampshire, 19 October 1831
Mem.	Roll of Honour, Cheltenham College
Remarks	Also awarded GCB, KCVO, Royal Humane Society Silver Medal

Name	Hartigan, Henry
Rank	Pensioned Sergeant
Unit	9th Queen's Royal Lancers
Action	Indian Mutiny 8 June and 10 October 1857
Gazette	19 June 1860
Born	Drumlea, Enniskillen, County Fermanagh, March 1826
Died	Calcutta, India, 29 October 1886
Mem.	No memorial
Remarks	VC at: Newcastle-under-Lyme Museum

Name	Harvey, Frederick Maurice Watson,
Rank	Lieutenant
Unit	Lord Strathcona's Horse, Canadian Expeditionary Force
Action	Guyencourt, France, 27 March 1917
Gazette	8 June 1917
Born	Athboy, County Meath, 1 September 1888

Died   Calgary, Canada, 24 August 1980
Mem.   No memorial
Remarks   Also awarded the Military Cross

Name   Hawthorne, Robert*
Rank   Bugler
Unit   52nd (Oxfordshire Light Infantry) Regiment
Action   Indian Mutiny, 14 September 1857
Gazette   27 April 1858
Born   Maghera, County Londonderry, 1882
Died   Manchester, 2 February 1879
Mem.   Ardwick Cemetery, Manchester
Remarks   VC at: Royal Green Jackets Museum

Name   Hill, Samuel
Rank   Sergeant
Unit   90th Perthshire Light Infantry
Action   Indian Mutiny, 16 November 1857
Gazette   24 December 1858
Born   Glenavy, County Antrim, 1826
Died   Meerut, India, 21 February 1863
Mem.   No memorial
Remarks   Elected by the regiment. VC at: Tolson Mem. Museum, Huddersfield

Name   Holland, Edward James Gibson
Rank   Sergeant
Unit   Royal Canadian Dragoons
Action   South Africa, 7 November 1900
Gazette   23 April 1901
Born   Ottawa, Canada, 2 February 1878
Died   Coblat, Ontario, Canada, 18 June 1948
Mem.   Island 17, Lake Temagami, Ontario
Remarks   Family from Athy, County Kildare. VC at: Royal Canadian Dragoons
             Museum

Name   Holland, John Vincent*
Rank   Lieutenant
Unit   3rd Bn, Leinster Regiment (Prince of Wales's Royal Canadians)
Action   Guillemont, France, 3 September 1916
Gazette   26 October 1916
Born   Athy, County Kildare, 19 July 1889
Died   Hobart, Tasmania, 27 February 1975
Mem.   Cornelian Bay Cemetery, Hobart, Tasmania
Remarks   Related to Holland, E.J.G.

Name   House, William
Rank   Private

Unit   2nd Bn, Royal Berkshire Regiment (Princess Charlotte of Wales's)
Action   Mosilikatse Nek, South Africa, 2 August 1900
Gazette   7 October 1902
Born   Thatcham, near Newbury, Berkshire, 7 October 1879
Died   Dover, Kent, 28 February 1912
Mem.   St James's Cemetery, Dover
Remarks   Irish family

Name   Hughes, Thomas
Rank   Private
Unit   6th Bn, Connaught Rangers
Action   Guillemont, France, 3 September 1916
Gazette   26 October 1916
Born   Coravoo, Castleblaney, County Monaghan, 30 May 1885
Died   Carrickmacross, County Monaghan, 8 January 1942
Mem.   No memorial
Remarks   Decorated by the King. VC at: National Army Museum

Name   Irwin, Charles
Rank   Private
Unit   53rd (Shropshire) Regiment
Action   Indian Mutiny, 16 November 1857
Gazette   24 December 1858
Born   Manorhamilton, County Leitrim, 1824
Died   Newtownbutler, County Fermanagh, 8 April 1873
Mem.   No memorial
Remarks   Elected by the regiment. VC at: King's Shropshire LI Museum

Name   Jackman, James Joseph Bernard*
Rank   T/Captain
Unit   1st Bn, Royal Northumberland Fusiliers
Action   El Duda, near Tobruk, 25 November 1941
Gazette   31 March 1942
Born   Dublin, 19 March 1916
Died   Died of wounds, El Duda, Tobruk, 26 November 1941
Mem.   Tobruk War Cemetery; Stonyhurst College, Clitheroe, Lancashire. VC
              at: Stonyhurst College

Name   Jennings, Edward
Rank   Rough Rider
Unit   Bengal Artillery
Action   Indian Mutiny, 14 to 22 November 1857
Gazette   24 December 1858
Born   Ballinrobe, County Mayo, 1815
Died   North Shields, Northumberland, 10 May 1889
Mem.   Preston Cemetery, North Shields
Remarks   After his military service worked as a Corporation street labourer. VC
              at: Royal Artillery Institution

Name   Johnston, Robert
Rank   Captain
Unit   Imperial Light Horse
Action   Elandslaagate, South Africa, 21 October 1899
Gazette   12 February 1901
Born   Laputa House, Ballyshannon, County Donegal, 13 August 1872; 1901
              census records show his birthplace as Kingstown, County Dublin.
Died   Kilkenny, 24 March 1950
Mem.   No memorial
Remarks   In Great War commanded the PoW Camp at Oldcastle, County Meath

Name   Jones, Henry Mitchell
Rank   Captain
Unit   7th (Royal Fusiliers)
Action   The Quarries, Sebastopol, 7 June 1855
Gazette   25 September 1857
Born   Dublin, 11 February 1831
Died   Eastbourne, Sussex, 18 December 1916
Mem.   No memorial
Remarks   Also awarded the Legion d'Honneur. VC at: Victoria Barracks, Sidney,
              Australia

Name   Kavanagh, Thomas Henry
Rank   Civil Servant
Unit   Bengal Civil Service
Action   Indian Mutiny, 9 November 1857
Gazette   5 July 1859
Born   Mullingar, County Westmeath,
Died   Gibraltar, 11 November 1882
Mem.   North Front Cemetery, Gibraltar
Remarks   One of only four civilians awarded the VC

Name   Keatinge, Richard Harte
Rank   Major
Unit   Bombay Artillery
Action   Indian Mutiny, 17 March 1858
Gazette   25 February 1852
Born   Dublin, 17 June 1825
Died   Horsham, Sussex, 25 May 1904
Mem.   No memorial
Remarks   CSI

Name   Kelliher, Richard*
Rank   Private
Unit   2/25th Battalion (Queensland) A.I.F
Action   New Guinea, South West Pacific, 13 September 1943
Gazette   30 December 1943
Born   Ballybeggan, Tralee, County Kerry, 1 September 1910

Died   Melbourne, Australia, 28 January 1963
Mem.   Springvale Lawn, Cemetery, Melbourne and Australian War Memorial,
            Canberra
Remarks   VC at: Australian War Memorial

Name   Kelly, Henry*
Rank   T/Second Lieutenant
Unit   10th Bn, Duke of Wellington's Regiment
Action   Le Sars,
Gazette   25 October 1916
Born   Rochdale Road, Manchester, 10 July 1887
Died   Prestwich, Lancashire, 18 January 1960
Mem.   No memorial
Remarks   One of ten children to Charles and Jane Kelly, Dublin. Served in Irish
            Army. Fought in the Spanish Civil War. Also awarded the Military
            Cross. VC at: Duke of Wellington's Regiment Museum

Name   Keneally, William*
Rank   Private
Unit   1st Bn, Lancashire Fusiliers
Action   W Beach, Gallipoli, 25 April 1915
Gazette   24 August 1915
Born   38 Parnell Street, Wexford, 26 December 1886
Died   Killed in action on W Beach
Mem.   Lancashire Landing Cemetery, Gallipoli
Remarks   One of the 'six VCs before breakfast'

Name   Kenna, Paul Aloysius*
Rank   Captain
Unit   21st Lancers
Action   Khartoum, 2 September 1898
Gazette   15 November 1898
Born   Everton, Liverpool, 2 February 1862
Died   Mortally wounded Scimitar Hill, Gallipoli, 21 August 1915
Mem.   Lala Baba Cemetery, Gallipoli; Stonyhurst College, Clitheroe, Lancashire
Remarks   Irish military family. VC at: Queen's Royal Lancers Museum

Name   Kenny, Henry Edward*
Rank   Private
Unit   1st Bn, Loyal North Lancashire Regiment
Action   Loos, France, 25 September, 1915
Gazette   30 March 1916
Born   Hackney, London, 27 July 1888
Died   St Peter's Hospital, Chertsey, Surrey, 6 May 1979
Mem.   St John's Cemetery, Woking, Surrey
Remarks   Parents from County Limerick

Name   Kenny, William
Rank   Drummer
Unit   2nd Bn, Gordon Highlanders
Action   Ypres, Belgium, 23 October 1914
Gazette   18 February 1915
Born   Malta, 24 August 1880
Died   London, 10 January 1936
Mem.   Brookwood Cemetery, Woking (dedicated 1999)
Remarks   Parents from Drogheda, County Louth; awarded Freedom of Drogheda.
            VC at: Gordon Hldrs Museum

Name   Kenny, William David
Rank   Lieutenant
Unit   4/39th Garwhal Rifles
Action   Kot Kai, North West Frontier, 2 January 1920
Gazette   9 September 1920
Born   Saintfield, County Down, 1 February 1899
Died   Killed in action on 2 January 1920
Mem.   Delhi Memorial, Donaghadee War Memorial
Remarks   VC sold 6 May 1998 for £59,000

Name   Lambert, George
Rank   Sergeant Major
Unit   84th (York and Lancaster) Regiment
Action   Unao, India, 29 July 1857
Gazette   18 June 1858
Born   Markethill, County Armagh, December 1819
Died   Sheffield, 10 February 1860
Mem.   Mullaghbrack Church, County Armagh
Remarks   Buried in Wardsend Cemetery. VC at: York & Lancaster Regiment
            Museum

Name   Lane, Thomas
Rank   Private
Unit   67th (South Hampshire) Regiment
Action   Taku forts, China, 21 August 1860
Gazette   13 August 1861
Born   Cork, May 1836
Died   Kimberley, South Africa, 13 April 1889
Mem.   No memorial
Remarks   VC forfeited 7 April 1881. VC at: Royal Hampshire Regiment Museum

Name   Laughnan, Thomas
Rank   Gunner
Unit   Bengal Artillery
Action   Indian Mutiny, 14 November 1857
Gazette   24 February 1858

Born	Kilmadaugh, Gort, County Galway, August 1824
Died	County Galway, 23 July 1864
Mem.	No memorial
Remarks	Name may also be spelt Laughlin. VC at: Royal Artillery

Name	Lawrence, Samuel Hill
Rank	Lieutenant
Unit	32nd (Cornwall) Regiment
Action	Indian Mutiny, 7 July and 26 September 1857
Gazette	21 November 1859
Born	Cork, 22 January 1831
Died	Montevideo, Uruguay, 17 June 1868
Mem.	No memorial
Remarks	Cousin of Lieutenant T. Cadell VC. VC at: Duke of Cornwall's LI Museum

Name	Leach, Edward Pemberton
Rank	Captain
Unit	Corps of Royal Engineers
Action	Afghanistan, 17 March 1879
Gazette	6 December 1879
Born	Londonderry, 2 April 1847
Died	Caddenabbia, Lake Como, Italy, 27 April 1913
Mem.	No memorial
Remarks	Also awarded KCB, KCVO

Name	Leet, William Knox
Rank	Major
Unit	13th (1st Somersetshire) (Prince Albert's Light Infantry)
Action	Zululand, 28 March 1879
Gazette	17 June 1879
Born	Dalkey, County Dublin, 3 November 1833
Died	Great Chart, Kent, 29 June 1896
Mem.	Great Chart (St Mary the Virgin) Churchyard, Kent
Remarks	Also awarded the CB. VC at: Somerset LI Museum

Name	Lendrim, William James
Rank	Corporal
Unit	Royal Engineers
Action	Crimea, 14 February; 11 and 20 April 1855
Gazette	24 February 1857
Born	Ireland, 1 January 1830
Died	Camberley, Surrey, 28 November 1891
Mem.	Camberley Churchyard
Remarks	Also awarded Legion d'Honneur and Medaille Militaire. VC at: Royal Engineers Museum

Name   Lloyd, Owen Edward Pennyfather, LRCS, LRCP, LM
Rank   Surgeon
Unit   Royal Army Medical Corps
Action   Burma, 6 January 1893
Gazette   2 January 1894
Born   County Roscommon, 1 January 1854
Died   St Leonards-on-Sea, Sussex, 5 July 1941
Mem.   Kensal Green Cemetery, London
Remarks   Also awarded the KCB. VC at: Royal Army Medical Corps

Name   Lord, David Samuel Anthony*
Rank   Flight Lieutenant
Unit   271 Squadron, Royal Air Force
Action   Arnhem, 19 September 1944
Gazette   13 November 1945
Born   Cork, 18 October 1913
Died   Killed in action
Mem.   Oosterbeek War Cemetery, Holland; St Mary's R.C. Pro-Cathedral,
            Wrexham; Down Ampney Church, Gloucestershire; and Cork
Remarks   Also awarded the Distinguished Flying Cross

Name   Lucas, Charles Davis
Rank   Mate
Unit   HMS *Hecla*, Royal Navy
Action   Crimea, 21 June 1854
Gazette   24 February 1857
Born   Druminargale House, near Poyntzpass, County Armagh, 19 February 1834
Died   Great Culverden, Kent, 7 August 1914
Mem.   St Lawrence's Church, Mereworth, Maidstone, Kent
Remarks   First ever winner of the VC. Place of birth may have been Clontibret,
            Co Monaghan. VC at: National Maritime Museum

Name   Lucas, John
Rank   Colour Sergeant
Unit   40th (2nd Somersetshire) Regiment
Action   New Zealand, 18 March 1861
Gazette   17 July 1861
Born   Glasgomy, Bagenalstown, County Carlow, 1827
Died   Dublin, 29 February 1892
Mem.   No memorial
Remarks   VC at: South Lancashire Regiment Museum

Name   Lyons, John
Rank   Private
Unit   19th (1st Yorkshire, North Riding) Regiment)
Action   Crimea, 10 June 1855
Gazette   24 February 1857

Born   Carlow, 1823
Died   Naas, County Kildare, 20 April 1867
Mem.   No memorial
Remarks   Also awarded Legion d'Honneur. VC at: Green Howards Museum

Name   Lyster, Harry Hamilton
Rank   Lieutenant
Unit   Bengal Native Infantry
Action   Indian Mutiny, 23 May 1858
Gazette   21 October 1859
Born   Blackrock, County Dublin, 24 December 1830
Died   London, 1 February 1922
Mem.   No memorial
Remarks   Also awarded the CB. Uncle of Captain H.L. Reed VC

Name   McCorrie (or McCurry) Charles
Rank   Private
Unit   57th Regiment
Action   Crimea, 23 June 1855
Gazette   24 February 1857
Born   Killeard, County Antrim, 1830
Died   Malta, 19 April 1857
Mem.   No memorial

Name   McCourt, Bernard (listed as McQuirt)
Rank   Private
Unit   95th Regiment
Action   Indian Mutiny, 6 January 1857
Gazette   11 November 1859
Born   Donacloney, County Armagh, 1829
Died   Ireland, 5 October 1888

Name   McCudden, James Thomas Byford
Rank   T/Captain
Unit   56 Squadron, Royal Flying Corps
Action   Western Front, August 1917 to March 1918
Gazette   2 April 1918
Born   Gillingham, Kent, 28 March 1895
Died   Marquise, France, 9 July 1918
Mem.   Wavans British Cemetery, France; Sheerness Parish Church; War
               Memorial, Gillingham, Kent
Remarks   Irish family. VC at: Royal Engineers Museum

Name   McFadzean, William Frederick
Rank   Private
Unit   14th Bn, Royal Irish Rifles
Action   Somme, 1 July 1916

Gazette	8 June 1917
Born	Lurgan, County Armagh, 9 October 1895
Died	Killed in action, 1 July 1916
Mem.	Thiepval, France; Newtownbreda Presbyterian Church, Belfast.
Remarks	VC at: Royal Ulster Rifles Museum

Name	McGovern, (or McGowan) John
Rank	Private
Unit	1st Bn, Bengal European Fusiliers (later Royal Munster Fusiliers)
Action	Indian Mutiny, 23 June 1857
Gazette	18 June 1859
Born	Templeport, County Cavan, 16 May 1825
Died	Hamilton, Ontario, Canada, 22 November 1888
Mem.	No memorial
Remarks	VC at: National Army Museum, London

Name	McGuire, James
Rank	Sergeant
Unit	1st Bn, Bengal European Fusiliers (later Royal Munster Fusiliers)
Action	Indian Mutiny, 14 September 1857
Gazette	24 December 1858
Born	Enniskillen, County Fermanagh, 1827
Died	Not known
Mem.	No memorial
Remarks	VC rescinded 22 December 1862, VC at: National Army Museum, London

Name	McHale, Patrick*
Rank	Private
Unit	1st Bn, 5th or Northumberland Fusiliers
Action	Indian Mutiny, 22 October 1857
Gazette	19 June 1860
Born	Killala, County Mayo, 1826
Died	Shorncliffe, Kent, 26 October 1866
Mem.	Shorncliffe Military Cemetery, Kent
Remarks	VC at: Fusiliers Museum of Northumberland

Name	McManus, Peter*
Rank	Private
Unit	1st Bn, 5th or Northumberland Fusiliers
Action	Indian Mutiny,
Gazette	18 June 1858
Born	Tynan, County Armagh, March 1829
Died	Allahabad, India, 27 April 1859, of smallpox
Mem.	No memorial
Remarks	*See also* John Ryan, Private. VC at: Fusiliers Museum of Northumberland

Name   McMaster, Valentine Munbee
Rank   Assistant Surgeon
Unit   78th (Highland) Regiment, or Ross-Shire Buffs
Action   Indian Mutiny, 25 September 1857
Gazette   18 June 1858
Born   Trichinopoly, India, 16 May 1834
Died   Belfast, Ireland, 22 January 1882, (heart attack)
Mem.   Belfast City Cemetery, St Columb's Cathedral, Londonderry
Remarks   Irish family. VC at: Scottish United Services Museum

Name   McQuirt, *see* McCourt, Bernard

Name   McWheeney, *see* Mawhinney, William

Name   Madden, Ambrose
Rank   Sergeant
Unit   41st (The Welsh) Regiment
Action   Crimea, 26 October 1854
Gazette   24 February 1857
Born   Cork, 1820
Died   Jamaica, 1 January 1863
Mem.   No memorial
Remarks   VC held in the Welch Regiment Museum, Cardiff.

Name   Magennis, James Joseph*
Rank   Leading Seaman
Unit   Royal Navy
Action   Johore Straits, 31 July 1945
Gazette   13 November 1945
Born   Belfast, 27 October 1919
Died   Halifax, Yorkshire, 12 February 1986
Mem.   Belfast City Hall, War Memorial Building, Belfast and Halifax, Yorkshire
Remarks   Biography. Last Irishman to win the VC

Name   Magner, (Barry) Michael
Rank   Drummer
Unit   33rd (Duke of Wellington's) Regiment
Action   Abyssinia, 13 April 1868
Gazette   28 July 1868
Born   Fermanagh, 21 June 1840
Died   Melbourne, Australia, 6 February 1897
Mem.   Melbourne General Cemetery, Victoria, Australia
Remarks   VC at: Museum of Victoria, Australia

Name   Mahoney, Patrick
Rank   Sergeant
Unit   1st Bn, Madras Fusiliers (later Royal Dublin Fusiliers)
Action   Indian Mutiny, 21 September 1857

Gazette   18 June 1858
Born   Waterford, 1827
Died   Killed in action at Lucknow, 30 October 1857
Mem.   No memorial
Remarks   VC at: India Office Library

Name   Manley, William George Nicholas
Rank   Assistant Surgeon
Unit   Royal Artillery
Action   Tauranga, New Zealand, 29 April 1864
Gazette   22 September 1864
Born   Dublin, 17 December 1831
Died   Cheltenham, 16 November 1901
Mem.   Cheltenham Cemetery
Remarks   Holder of the Iron Cross for service in the Franco-Prussian War

Name   Mannock, Edward
Rank   Major
Unit   85 Squadron, Royal Air Force
Action   Western Front, 1918
Gazette   18 July 1919
Born   Brighton, Sussex, 24 May 1887
Died   Near Lille, France, 26 July 1918
Mem.   Arras Memorial, France; Canterbury War Memorial; Canterbury Cathedral; Mannock House, Military Road, Canterbury
Remarks   Irish family

Name   Masterson, James Edward Ignatius*
Rank   Lieutenant
Unit   1st Bn, Devonshire Regiment
Action   Wagon Hill, Ladysmith, South Africa, 6 January 1900
Gazette   4 June 1901
Born   Ireland, 20 June 1862
Died   Waterlooville, Hampshire, 24 December 1935
Mem.   Exeter Cathedral
Remarks   Enlisted Princess Victoria's (Royal Irish Fusiliers) at Armagh, 1881; great-nephew of Masterson, the 'Eagle' taker of Barrosa. VC at: Devonshire Regiment Museum

Name   Maude, Sir Frederick Francis
Rank   Brevet Lieutenant Colonel
Unit   3rd (East Kent – The Buffs) Regiment
Action   Crimea, 5 September 1855
Gazette   24 February 1857
Born   Lisnadill, County Armagh, 20 December 1821
Died   Torquay, Devon, 20 June 1897
Mem.   Brompton Cemetery, London
Remarks   Inspector General of Irish Militia. Cousin of Captain F.C. Maud VC

Name   Mawhinney, William (listed as McWheeney)
Rank   Sergeant
Unit   44th (East Essex) Regiment
Action   Crimea, 20 October 1854
Gazette   24 February 1857
Born   Bangor, County Down, 1837
Died   Dover, Kent, 17 May 1866
Mem.   St James's Cemetery, Dover
Remarks   Medal sold in 1911 for £95. VC at: Essex Regiment Museum

Name   Moffatt, Martin
Rank   Private
Unit   2nd Bn, Leinster Regiment
Action   Ledgehem, Belgium, 14 October 1918
Gazette   26 December 1918
Born   Sligo, 15 April 1884
Died   Sligo, 5 January 1946
Mem.   No memorial
Remarks   Enlisted in Connaught Rangers

Name   Moore, Arthur Thomas
Rank   Lieutenant
Unit   3rd Bombay Light Cavalry
Action   Persia,
Gazette   3 August 1860
Born   Carlingford, County Louth, 20 September 1830
Died   18 Waterloo Place, Dublin, 25 April 1913 (heart failure)
Mem.   No memorial
Remarks   Also awarded the CB

Name   Moore, Hans Garrett
Rank   Major
Unit   88th (Connaught Rangers) Regiment
Action   South Africa, 29 December 1877
Gazette   27 June 1879
Born   Richmond Barracks, Dublin, 31 March 1834
Died   Drowned in rescue attempt, in Lough Derg, Tipperary, 6 October 1889
Mem.   No memorial
Remarks   Military family going back to the time of Henry VIII. VC at: Africana
            Library, South Africa

Name   Morrow, Robert*
Rank   Private
Unit   1st Bn, Princess Victoria's (Royal Irish Fusiliers)
Action   Messines, Belgium, 12 April 1915
Gazette   22 May 1915
Born   Coalisland, Dungannon, County Tyrone, 7 September 1891
Died   St Jan, Ypres, Belgium, 26 April 1915
Mem.   White House Cemetery, Belgium
Remarks   VC at: Royal Irish Fusiliers Museum

Name   Moyney, John
Rank   Lance Sergeant
Unit   2nd Bn, Irish Guards
Action   Broembeek, Belgium, 12/13 September 1917
Gazette   17 October 1917
Born   Rathdowney, Queen's County (Leix), 8 January 1895
Died   Roscrea, Tipperary, 10 November 1980
Mem.   No memorial
Remarks   VC at: Irish Guards

Name   Moynihan, Andrew
Rank   Sergeant
Unit   90th Perthshire Light Infantry
Action   Crimea, 8 September 1855
Gazette   24 February 1857
Born   Wakefield, Yorkshire, 8 September 1831
Died   Malta, 19 May 1867
Mem.   No memorial
Remarks   Died from drinking diseased milk. VC at: Cameronians Museum

Name   Mullane, Patrick
Rank   Sergeant
Unit   Royal Horse Artillery
Action   Maiwand, 27 July 1880
Gazette   16 May 1881
Born   Ahmednuggar, Deccan, India, October 1858
Died   Plaistow, Sussex,
Mem.   No memorial
Remarks   Irish parents

Name   Murphy, Michael
Rank   Farrier
Unit   2nd Bn, Military Train
Action   Indian Mutiny, 15 April 1858
Gazette   27 May 1859
Born   Cahir, County Tipperary, 1831
Died   Ireland, 15 April 1893
Mem.   Troop of Junior Leaders named after him
Remarks   VC rescinded by Royal Warrant in 1872. VC at: Royal Logistic Corps Museum

Name   Murphy, Thomas
Rank   Private
Unit   2nd Bn, 24th (2nd Warwickshire) Regiment
Action   Andaman Islands, 7 May 1867
Gazette   17 December 1867
Born   Dublin, 1839
Died   Philadelphia, USA, 22 March 1900
Mem.   No memorial
Remarks   Peace time award; *see also* Bell, D. and Griffiths, W.

Name	Murray, James
Rank	Lance Corporal
Unit	2nd Bn, Connaught Rangers
Action	South Africa, 16 January 1881
Gazette	14 March 1882
Born	St Michael's Parish, Cork, February 1859
Died	Dublin, 19 July 1942
Mem.	No memorial
Remarks	VC at: National Army Museum

Name	Murray, John
Rank	Sergeant
Unit	68th (Durham – Light Infantry) Regiment
Action	New Zealand, 21 June 1864
Gazette	4 November 1864
Born	Birr, King's County (Offaly), 1837
Died	Derrinlogh, King's County, 7 November 1911
Mem.	No memorial
Remarks	VC at: Durham Light Infantry Museum

Name	Mylott, Patrick
Rank	Private
Unit	84th (York and Lancaster) Regiment
Action	Indian Mutiny, 12 July 1857
Gazette	24 December 1858
Born	Hollymount, near Clanmorris, County Mayo,
Died	Liverpool, Lancashire, 22 December 1878
Mem.	No memorial
Remarks	Elected by the regiment, under Rule 13 of the VC Warrant

Name	Nash, William*
Rank	Corporal
Unit	2nd Bn, Rifle Brigade
Action	Indian Mutiny, 11 March 1858
Gazette	24 December 1858
Born	Newcastle, County Limerick, 23 April 1824
Died	Hackney, Middlesex, 29 April 1875
Mem.	Rifle Brigade Memorial, Winchester Cathedral

Name	Nelson, David
Rank	Sergeant
Unit	L Battery, Royal Horse Artillery
Action	Nery, France, 1 September 1914
Gazette	16 November 1914
Born	Deraghland, County Monaghan
Died	Killed in action, as a Major, 8 April 1918
Mem.	Lillers Communal Cemetery, France
Remarks	VC at: Imperial War Museum

Name   Nunney, Claude Joseph Patrick
Rank   Private
Unit   38th Bn, Canadian Expeditionary Force
Action   Vis-en-Artois, France, 1 and 2 September 1918
Gazette   14 December 1918
Born   Dublin, 24 December 1892
Died   18 September 1918, of wounds
Mem.   Claude Nunney Memorial Branch, Canadian Legion
Remarks   Also awarded DCM and MM. VC at: Cornwall Armouries, Ontario, Canada

Name   Nurse, George Edward
Rank   Corporal
Unit   66 Battery, Royal Field Artillery
Action   South Africa, 15 December 1899
Gazette   2 February 1900
Born   Enniskillen, County Fermanagh, 14 April 1873
Died   Liverpool, 25 November 1945
Mem.   No memorial
Remarks   Born in Enniskillen while parents were on holiday. VC at: Royal Artillery Institution

Name   O'Connor, Sir Luke
Rank   Sergeant
Unit   23rd (Royal Welch Fusiliers) Regiment
Action   Indian Mutiny, 20 September 1854
Gazette   24 February 1857
Born   Elphin, Roscommon, 21 January 1831
Died   London, 1 February 1915
Mem.   St Mary's RC Cemetery, Kensal Rise, London. Portrait in Regimental Museum
Remarks   First Army VC. Also awarded KCB. VC at: Royal Welch Fusiliers

Name   O'Hea, Timothy*
Rank   Private
Unit   1st Bn, Prince Consort's Own Rifle Brigade
Action   Canada, 9 June 1866
Gazette   1 June 1867
Born   Skull, Bantry, County Cork, 1846
Died   Sturt's Desert, Queensland, Australia, November 1875
Mem.   Danville Town Hall, Quebec, Rifle Brigade memorial, Winchester Cathedral
Remarks   Peace time award for extinguishing a fire on an ammunition train. Died during a rescue attempt in the desert, Australia. VC at: Royal Green Jackets

Name   O'Leary, Michael
Rank   Lance Corporal
Unit   1st Bn, Irish Guards

Action   Cuinchy, France, 1 February 1915
Gazette   18 February 1915
Born   Macroom, Inchigeela, County Cork, 28 September 1888
Died   London, 2 August 1961
Mem.   Paddington Cemetery, Mill Hill, London
Remarks   Served in North West Mounted Police and in Second World War. VC
             at: Irish Guards

Name   Olpherts, William ('Hell-fire Jack')
Rank   Captain
Unit   Bengal Artillery
Action   Indian Mutiny, 25 September 1857
Gazette   18 June 1858
Born   Dartrey, County Armagh, 8 March 1822
Died   Upper Norwood, London, 30 April 1902
Mem.   Richmond Cemetery, London
Remarks   Biography. Also awarded GCB. VC at: National Army Museum, London

Name   O'Meara, Martin
Rank   Private
Unit   16th Bn, (SA and WA) Australian Imperial Force
Action   9/12 August 1916
Gazette   5 September 1916
Born   Curcragha, Terryglass, County Tipperary, 31 December 1882
Died   Claremont, Perth, Australia, 20 December 1935
Mem.   Karrakatta Cemetery, Perth and Australian War Memorial Canberra
Remarks   Left a sum of money to go towards the restoration of Lorrha Abbey,
             County Tipperary. VC at: Army Museum of Western Australia

Name   O'Rourke, Michael James
Rank   Private
Unit   7th Bn, British Columbia Regiment CEF
Action   Hill 60, France, 15/17 August 1917
Gazette   8 November 1917
Born   Limerick, 19 March 1878
Died   Vancouver, BC, Canada, 6 December 1957
Mem.   Forest Lawn Burial Park, North Burnaby, B.C., Canada
Remarks   VC at: British Columbia Regiment, Canada

Name   O'Sullivan, Gerald Robert*
Rank   Captain
Unit   1st Bn, Royal Inniskilling Fusiliers
Action   Suvla Bay, Gallipoli, 21 August 1915
Gazette   1 September 1915
Born   Frankfield, Douglas, County Cork, 8 November 1888
Died   Killed in action, 21 August 1915
Mem.   Helles Memorial, Gallipoli

Name   Owens, James
Rank   Corporal
Unit   49th (Princess of Wales's Hertfordshire) Regiment
Action   Crimea, 30 October 1854
Gazette   24 February 1857
Born   Killane, Baileyboro, County Cavan, 1829
Died   Romford, Essex, 20 August 1901
Mem.   No memorial
Remarks   VC sold in London on 15 October 1902. VC at: Royal Gloucestershire,
           Berkshire and Wiltshire Regiment

Name   Park, John
Rank   Sergeant
Unit   77th (East Middlesex) Regiment
Action   Crimea, 20 September and 5 November 1854
Gazette   24 February 1857
Born   Londonderry, 1835
Died   Allahabad, India, 18 May 1863
Mem.   No memorial
Remarks   VC at: Leicester Museum & Art Gallery

Name   Pearson, James
Rank   Private
Unit   86th (Royal County Down) Regiment
Action   Indian Mutiny, 3 April 1858
Gazette   28 April 1860
Born   Rathdowney, Queen's County (Leix), 2 October 1822
Died   India, 23 January 1900
Mem.   Memorial Park, Lion's Head, Ontario, Canada
Remarks   Reported to have ridden in the Charge of the Light Brigade

Name   Probyn, Dighton
Rank   Captain
Unit   2nd Punjab Cavalry
Action   Indian Mutiny, 1857-8
Gazette   18 June 1858
Born   London, 21 January 1833
Died   Sandringham, Norfolk, 20 June 1924
Mem.   Kensal Green Cemetery, London; Sandringham Church, Norfolk
Remarks   Irish mother

Name   Prosser, Joseph*
Rank   Private
Unit   2nd Bn, 1st or Royal Regiment (The Royal Scots)
Action   Crimea, 16 June 1855
Gazette   24 February 1857
Born   Monegal, King's County (Offaly), 1828
Died   Tipperary, 1869
Mem.   No memorial
Remarks   VC at: Royal Scots Museum

Name   Purcell, John
Rank   Private
Unit   9th Queen's Royal Lancers
Action   Indian Mutiny, 19 June 1857
Gazette   15 January 1858
Born   Kilcommon, Oughterard, County Galway, 1814
Died   Delhi, 19 September 1857
Mem.   No memorial

Name   Quigg, Robert
Rank   Rifleman
Unit   12th Bn, Royal Irish Rifles
Action   Hamel, France, 1 July 1916
Gazette   9 September 1916
Born   Ardihennon, Giants Causeway, County Antrim, 28 February 1885
Died   Ballycastle, 14 May 1955
Mem.   Billy parish Churchyard, County Antrim
Remarks   Also awarded Medal of the Order of St George, 4th Class (Russia). VC
            at: Royal Ulster Rifles Museum

Name   Raymond, Claude*
Rank   Lieutenant
Unit   Royal Engineers
Action   Talaku, Burma, 21 March 1945
Gazette   28 June 1945
Born   Mottistone, Isle of Wight, 2 October 1923
Died   Talaku, 22 March 1945, of wounds
Mem.   Taukkyan War Cemetery, Burma
Remarks   Irish parents. Family was from County Kerry. VC at: Royal Engineers Museum

Name   Reed, Hamilton Lyster
Rank   Captain
Unit   7 Battery, Royal Field Artillery
Action   Colenso, South Africa, 15 December 1899
Gazette   2 February 1900
Born   Dublin, 23 May 1869
Died   London, 7 March 1931
Mem.   No memorial
Remarks   Nephew of Lieutenant H.H. Lyster VC

Name   Reynolds, James Henry
Rank   Surgeon Major
Unit   Army Medical Department (later Royal Army Medical Corps)
Action   Rorke's Drift, Zululand, 22/23 January 1879
Gazette   17 June 1879
Born   Kingstown, County Dublin, 3 February 1844
Died   London, 4 March 1932
Mem.   St Mary's RC Cemetery, Kensal Rise, London
Remarks   One of the two Irish VCs awarded for this action. VC at: Royal Army
            Medical Corps. *See also* Bromhead, Gonville

Name	Richardson, George
Rank	Private
Unit	34th (Cumberland) Regiment
Action	Indian Mutiny, 27 April 1859
Gazette	1 November 1859
Born	Derrylane, Killeshandra, County Cavan, 1 August 1831
Died	Westminster hospital, London, Ontario, Canada, 28 January 1923
Mem.	Veterans Section, Prospect Cemetery, Toronto, Canada
Remarks	VC held by private collector in Canada

Name	Ridgeway, Richard Kirby
Rank	Captain
Unit	Bengal Staff Corps attached to 44th Gurkha Rifles
Action	India, 22 November 1879
Gazette	11 May 1880
Born	Oldcastle, County Meath, 18 August 1848
Died	Harrogate, Yorkshire, 11 October 1924
Mem.	No memorial
Remarks	Also awarded CB

Name	Roberts, The Hon. Frederick Hugh Sherston*
Rank	Lieutenant
Unit	The King's Royal Rifle Corps
Action	Colenso, South Africa, 15 December 1899
Gazette	2 February 1900
Born	Umballa, India, 8 January 1872
Died	Chieveley, Natal, South Africa, 17 December 1899, from wounds
Mem.	Rifle Brigade Memorial, Winchester Cathedral
Remarks	Son of Earl Roberts VC. VC at: National Army Museum

Name	Roberts, Frederick Sleigh
Rank	Lieutenant
Unit	2nd Troop, 3rd Brigade, Bengal Horse Artillery
Action	Khodagunge, Indian Mutiny, 2 January 1858
Gazette	24 December 1858
Born	Cawnpore, India, 30 September 1832
Died	54 rue Carnot, St Omer, France, 14 November 1914
Mem.	St Paul's Cathedral; Horse Guards Parade; St Luke's Church, London
Remarks	Father of Lieutenant The Hon. F.H.S. Roberts VC (*see* above). VC at: National Army Museum

Name	Roddy, Patrick
Rank	Ensign
Unit	Bengal Army
Action	Indian Mutiny, 27 September 1858
Gazette	12 April 1859
Born	Elphin, Roscommon, 17 March 1827
Died	Jersey, Channel Islands, 21 November 1895
Mem.	No memorial
Remarks	Believed to have refused Bar to VC in preference to promotion.

Name	Rogers, Robert Montresor
Rank	Lieutenant
Unit	44th (East Essex) Regiment
Action	Taku Forts, China, 21 August 1860
Gazette	13 August 1861
Born	Dublin, 4 September 1834
Died	Maidenhead, Berkshire, 5 February 1895
Mem.	No memorial
Remarks	Also awarded CB, later served in 90th Foot

Name	Roupell, George Rowland Patrick
Rank	Lieutenant
Unit	1st Bn, East Surrey Regiment
Action	Hill 60, 20 April 1915
Gazette	23 June 1915
Born	Tipperary, 7 April 1892
Died	Shalford, Surrey, 4 March 1974
Mem.	Regimental Chapel and Parish Church, Kingston-on-Thames, Surrey
Remarks	Croix de Guerre, Order of St George 4th Class (Russia)

Name	Ryan, John
Rank	Private
Unit	1st Bn, Madras Fusiliers (later Royal Dublin Fusiliers)
Action	Indian Mutiny, 26 September 1857
Gazette	18 June 1858
Born	Kilkenny, 1823
Died	Cawnpore, India, 4 March 1858
Mem.	No memorial
Remarks	VC at York & Lancaster Regiment Museum

Name	Ryan, John
Rank	Lance Corporal
Unit	65th (2nd Yorkshire – North Riding) Regiment
Action	New Zealand, 7 September 1863
Gazette	16 January 1864
Born	Borrisoleigh, Tipperary, 1839
Died	Tuakan, New Zealand, 29 December 1863, drowned during a rescue attempt
Mem.	No memorial
Remarks	VC sold in London 17 April 1902 for £58

Name	Ryan, Miles
Rank	Drummer
Unit	1st Bn, Bengal European Fusiliers (later Royal Munster Fusiliers)
Action	Kabul Gate, Delhi, India, 14 September 1857
Gazette	24 December 1858
Born	Londonderry, 1826
Died	Bengal, India, January 1887
Mem.	No memorial

Name   Scott, Robert*
Rank   Private
Unit   1st Bn, Manchester Regiment
Action   Caesar's Camp, Natal, South Africa, 6 January 1900
Gazette   26 July
Born   Haslingden, Lancashire, 4 June 1847
Died   Downpatrick, County Down, 22 February 1961
Mem.   Kilkeel, County Down
Remarks   Parents from Downpatrick. Served in both world wars. VC at: Manchester Regiment Museum

Name   Sinnott, John
Rank   Lance Corporal
Unit   84th (York and Lancaster) Regiment
Action   Indian Mutiny, 6 October 1857
Gazette   24 December 1858
Born   Wexford, 1829
Died   Clapham London, 20 July 1896
Mem.   No memorial
Remarks   Elected by the regiment. VC at: York & Lancaster Regiment Museum

Name   Sinton, John Alexander
Rank   Captain
Unit   Indian Medical Services
Action   Orah Ruins, Mesopotamia,
Gazette   21 June 1916
Born   British Columbia, Canada, 2 December 1884
Died   Cookstown, County Tyrone, 25 March 1956
Mem.   No memorial
Remarks   Born in Canada of Irish parents. VC at: Royal Army Medical Corps

Name   Sleavon, Michael
Rank   Corporal
Unit   Royal Engineers
Action   Indian Mutiny, 3 April 1858
Gazette   11 November 1859
Born   Magheraculmoney, County Fermanagh, 1827
Died   Ederney, County Fermanagh, 14 August 1902
Mem.   No memorial
Remarks   VC sold in London 22 January 1903 for £53. Friend of J. McGuire VC

Name   Smith, Frederick Augustus*
Rank   Captain
Unit   43rd (Monmouthshire Light Infantry) Regiment
Action   New Zealand, 21 June 1864
Gazette   4 November 1864
Born   Dublin, 18 November 1826
Died   Duleek, County Meath, 22 July 1887

Mem.   No memorial
Remarks   VC received through the post on 31 January 1865

Name   Smith, Philip
Rank   Corporal
Unit   17th (Leicestershire) Regiment
Action   Crimea, 18 June 1855
Gazette   24 February 1857
Born   Lurgan, County Armagh, 1825
Died   Harold's Cross, Dublin, 16 January 1906
Mem.   British Legion Hall, Lurgan, County Armagh
Remarks   Subject of a Terence Cuneo painting. VC at: Royal Leicestershire
            Regiment Museum

Name   Somers, James*
Rank   Sergeant
Unit   1st Bn, Royal Inniskilling Fusiliers
Action   Gallipoli, 1 and 2 July 1915
Gazette   1 September 1915
Born   Belturbet, County Cavan, 12 June 1884
Died   Cloughgordon, Tipperary, 7 May 1918
Mem.   Modreeny Church of Ireland, County Tipperary

Name   Stagpoole, Dudley
Rank   Drummer
Unit   57th (West Middlesex) Regiment
Action   New Zealand, 2 October 1863
Gazette   22 September 1864
Born   Killunan, County Galway, 1838
Died   Ware, Herefordshire, 1 August 1911
Mem.   Hendon Park Cemetery, London
Remarks   Also awarded DCM. VC at: Princess of Wales's Royal Regiment

Name   Sullivan, John
Rank   Boatswain's Mate
Unit   Naval Brigade
Action   Crimea, 10 April 1855
Gazette   24 February 1857
Born   Bantry, County Cork, 10 April 1830
Died   Kinsale, County Cork, 28 June 1884
Mem.   No memorials
Remarks   Also awarded Legion d'Honneur, Al Valori Militari, CGM, RHS (Silver)

Name   Temple, William
Rank   Assistant Surgeon
Unit   Royal Regiment of Artillery
Action   New Zealand, 20 November 1863
Gazette   22 September 1864
Born   Monaghan, County Monaghan, 7 November 1833

Died	Tunbridge Wells, Kent, 13 February 1919
Mem.	No memorial

Name	Travers, James
Rank	Colonel
Unit	2nd Bengal Native Infantry
Action	Indian Mutiny, 1 July 1857
Gazette	1 March 1861
Born	Cork, 6 October 1820
Died	Italy, 1 April 1884
Mem.	No memorials
Remarks	Also awarded CB

Name	Traynor, William Bernard
Rank	Sergeant
Unit	2nd Bn, West Yorkshire Regiment
Action	Bothwell Camp, South Africa, 6 February 1901
Gazette	17 September 1901
Born	29 Moxon Street, Hull, 31 December 1870
Died	Dover, Kent, 20 October 1956
Mem.	Charlton Cemetery, Kent
Remarks	Son of Francis Traynor of County Monaghan

Name	Walker, Mark (Sir)
Rank	Lieutenant
Unit	30th (Cambridgeshire) Regiment
Action	Crimea, 5 November 1854
Gazette	2 June 1858
Born	Gore Port, Finca, County Westmeath
Died	Arlington, Devon, 18 July 1902
Mem.	Cheriton Road Cemetery, Folkestone, Kent; Canterbury Cathedral, Kent
Remarks	Also awarded KCB. Fought in China. VC at: Buffs Museum

Name	Ward, Joseph
Rank	Sergeant
Unit	8th (The King's Royal Irish) Hussars
Action	Indian Mutiny, 17 June 1858
Gazette	28 January 1859
Born	Kinsale, County Cork, 1832
Died	Longford, 23 November 1872
Mem.	No memorial
Remarks	Elected by the regiment

Name	Whirlpool, Frederick
Rank	Private
Unit	3rd Bn, Bombay European Regiment (later Leinster Regiment)
Action	Jhansi, 3 April 1858 and Lohari, 2 May 1858, Indian Mutiny
Gazette	21 October 1859
Born	Liverpool, 1829

Died   McGrath's Hill, near Windsor, NSW, 24 June 1899
Mem.   Presbyterian Cemetery, McGrath hill, New South Wales
Remarks   Son of Major Conker, Postmaster, Dundalk. Assumed name of Frederick
           Humphrey James in Australia. Served as Whirlpool, enlisting in Glasgow

Name   White, George Stuart
Rank   Major
Unit   92nd (Gordon Highlanders) Regiment
Action   Afghanistan, 6 October 1879
Gazette   2 June 1881
Born   Ballymena, County Antrim, 4 July 1835
Died   Chelsea, London, 24 June 1912
Mem.   Statue in Portland Place, London; Tablet, RMA Sandhurst; Broughshane
           Presbyterian Church, County Antrim. Originally commissioned in 27th
           (Inniskilling) Regiment
Remarks   GCB, OM, GCSI, GCMG, GCIE, GCVO. VC at: Gordon Hldrs
           Museum

Name   Wright, Alexander
Rank   Private
Unit   77th (East Middlesex) Regiment
Action   Crimea, 22 March and 19 April and 30 August 1855
Gazette   24 February 1857
Born   Ballymena, County Antrim, 1826
Died   Calcutta, India, 28 July 1858
Mem.   No memorial
Remarks   VC at: Princess of Wales's Royal Regiment

Name   Young, Alexander
Rank   Sergeant Major
Unit   Cape Police, South African Forces
Action   South Africa, 13 August 1901
Gazette   8 November 1901
Born   Ballinona, Clarinbridge, County Galway, 27 January 1873
Died   The Somme, 19 October 1916
Mem.   Pier and Face 4C, Thiepval Memorial, France
Remarks   During First World War held the rank of Lieutenant in the 4th
           Regiment S.A Infantry

All other Victoria Crosses are held privately, either by the families of the VC winners or by collectors.

Appendix Two: Forfeited Awards

In the history of the Victoria Cross there have been eight instances where the winner of the award has subsequently been deprived of his distinction. This penalty was exacted under Clause 15 of the original warrant as a punishment for anyone who brought shame on the Cross by being convicted of treason, cowardice, felony or any 'other infamous crime'[1] and the men thus penalized have included three Irishmen: Sergeant **James McGuire**, 1st Bengal European Fusiliers; Private **Michael Murphy**, 2nd Bn, Military Train; and Private **Thomas Lane**, 67th (South Hampshire) Regiment.[2]

One other soldier to forfeit the VC served in an Irish regiment after winning his award. Private **Valentine Bambrick**, 1st Battalion, 60th Rifles, won his Cross on 6 May 1858 at Bareilly during the Indian Mutiny.[3] Bambrick transferred to the 87th (Royal Irish Fusiliers) in 1860 and served with them until 1863. (Also serving with the Faughs at that time was another Mutiny VC-winner, Charles Irwin.) After a series of misdemeanours, Bambrick was convicted and imprisoned in 1863 for assaulting another soldier during a fracas in a brothel and stealing the other man's medals.[4] In court, Bambrick pleaded guilty to the charge of assault but maintained that there were extenuating circumstances and that he had been protecting a woman whom the other soldier was attempting to murder. He denied the charge of theft. Nonetheless he was found guilty and sentenced to imprisonment. His sentence was to be carried out at Winchester and Pentonville Gaols and in those places Bambrick found unusual allies in his attempts to clear his name. Both prison governors considered him to be an innocent man and petitioned for his release. The two officials expected their petitions to be successful but Bambrick pre-empted any attempt at release: he committed suicide by hanging himself in Pentonville on 1 April 1864, five months after the announcement that his VC had been forfeited.

After Bambrick's death the editor of the *United Service Gazette* called attention to the case in the editions of 9 and 16 April. He considered that Bambrick had suffered an injustice. The VC warrant also allows the Sovereign to restore a VC that has been forfeited but this prerogative has never been exercised. Perhaps it is now time for all eight forfeitures to be rescinded.

The last forfeiture of a Victoria Cross took place in 1908 and, although the authority for forfeiture remains, the practice was ended effectively by King George V in 1920 when he stated that even if a Victoria Cross winner were to be convicted of murder he was still entitled to mount the scaffold wearing his VC.

THE IRISH FORFEITURES

Name, rank, unit and date of award	*Date of warrant authorizing forfeiture*
James McGuire, Sergeant, 1st Bengal European Fusiliers; 14 September 1857	22 December 1862*
Michael Murphy, Private, 2nd Bn, Military Train; 15 April 1858	5 March 1872
Thomas Lane, Private, 67th (South Hampshire) Regiment; 21 August 1860	7 April 1881

* This is the date that is wrongly quoted as McGuire's date of death in many publications.

Appendix Three: Irish VCs and Poetry

At least two Irish Victoria Cross winners have inspired poems about their deeds. The first of these was Thomas Grady, only the twelfth man, and the fourth Irishman, to win the Cross. A member of the 4th King's Own Royal Regiment, Grady gained the award for his courage on two occasions during the Crimean war. The ballad-style poem about Grady appeared in the 1988 edition of *The Lion and the Dragon*, the journal of the King's Own Royal Border Regiment, the successor to Grady's regiment. Written about 1905 by Ellis Williams, a former colour-sergeant in the King's Own, it is very much a poem to celebrate a regimental hero. By contrast the anonymous ballad-style poem about Martin Moffatt VC, extolls the heroism of a local lad and is very much a celebration by Sligo of its VC-winning son.

How Tom Grady Cleared the Gun
A true story of the King's Own, or 4th Regiment of Foot.

We have read of deeds of daring done for dear old England's sake,
Of the glorious death of Nelson, of the pluck of gallant Drake;
Of Wellington and duty, we have often talked before,
And the schoolboy knows the story of Corunna and of Moore;
Still ring from Heights of Abraham, Wolfe's dying words, 'They fly!'
Words just as fresh today as then. Such memories never die.
Then the names of Clive and Campbell, of Havelock, Lawrence, Neill,
Remind us but of victories won by British pluck and steel.

The world was taught how heroes die when the *Birkenhead* went down;
And on those Balaclava slopes, of Light Brigade renown,
That ride into the jaws of death filled Europe with amaze:
Subject for painter's canvas – fit theme for poet's praise!
Now, comrades, I'll tell ye a story; 'tis not of a victory won,
But the deed of a lowly private, yet a deed right nobly done;
How, face to face with death, he stood, unaided and alone,
And we claim him as a comrade: he was one of the old King's Own.

'Twas a bleak October morning, and the British forces lay
Entrenched round grim Sevastopol, with the Russians held at bay.
Cold, hunger, fever, wounds, and death had thinned that gallant band;
Yet once again, 'mid frost and snow, those gunners take their stand.
From the early grey of morning, till the day fades into night,
For weary months those gunners had stood steadfast in the fight.

With fusillade of shot and shell the fortress answered back,
As the thunder of our batteries rolled along the left attack.

But of all those guns that volley forth along the British Line,
None speak so sharp, or speak so true as gallant Number Nine,
Oft had the foeman marked this gun; its frequent battery smoke:
This morn a Russian chieftain to his willing gunners spoke:
'Bring your guns to bear together on that hornet over there;
That British bulldog barks too loud, bring four or five to bear.'
So Number Nine stands silent now, and answereth not at all,
Helpless, with choked embrasure and broken battery wall;
All torn and rent with Russian shell, the pride of the left attack
Is useless now in the British line and sends no answer back.

Yet now one notes its silence; a chief there in command,
And, turning to the gunners, says, 'Come, lads, who'll bear a hand?
Who'll clear the gun?' he cried aloud; but the bravest hold their breath;
Full well they know those words imply a task of life or death.
'Who'll clear the gun, I say?' he cries a second time;
Then one stands forth, no gunner he, but a private of the line.

So, silent, face to face with death, he mounts the battery slope;
He springs up single-handed with those Russian guns to cope.
With his own stout heart and willing hand, a pickaxe and a spade _
A breach in the shapeless battery wall he very soon hath made.
Now he grasps his spade in a firmer grip, and his pick deals a heavier blow,
For every moment his last may be – he works under fire from the foe;
Five minutes more – and the battery stands all shapely, firm, and sound.
And he leaps back safe, whilst Number Nine hurls forth her hindered round.
'Right nobly done', cries Lushington, as the hero's hand he rings,
'Your name, and corps?' 'I'm Grady, sir – Tom Grady, Fourth o' King's!'

By many a Christmas fireside bright this tale was told I ween;
It was told in the cot of the lowly, it was told to England's Queen.
Aye! told to the Queen he served so well: and it was not told in vain,
For she pinned on his breast that priceless gift – the Cross which bears her name.
I've read the Regiment's story, its leaves turned o'er and o'er;
But Tom's is the bravest deed I find in the records of our corps;
So, when ye hear folks talk of heroes, or a deed of daring done,
Tell this, your Regiment's Story – How Tom Grady cleared the gun.

Martin Moffatt, VC

From old Sligo, where beauty and nature so grand,
And a cottage in Knappagh, where the hero was born,
For his King and his country, unfettered and free,
Went forward to battle, Martin Moffatt, VC.

'O'er the top' was the order, and the boys to a man,
With a true Irish cheer, it was he led the van.
And with a few bombs round the hut he leaped free,
And captured thirteen, Martin Moffatt, VC.

When the war it broke out, says he 'I'm out for fun,
And with rifle and bayonet for the land of the Hun.'
When he landed in France 'twas a sight for to see
The brave lad from Knappagh, Martin Moffatt, VC.

When the news it reached Sligo, the land of his birth,
They loudly proclaimed that the lad proved his worth,
And brought honour to Sligo, so gallant and free,
Loyal and brave, Martin Moffatt, VC.

For brave deeds old Sligo has well done her share,
All military honours are recorded there,
And the highest that's given for brave deeds, I see
The cream of the lot is Martin Moffatt, VC.

May long he enjoy the honours he's won,
At the risk of his life in the land of the Hun,
May the parents that nursed him be long spared to see
Their son Martin enjoy his well earned VC.

When home he returns for a well earned rest,
Prepare to receive him, he's one of the best,
For the name of the hero the Huns dread to see,
May God bless you and keep you, Martin Moffatt, VC.

Notes

Biographical notes on individuals are taken from the relevant Lummis File held by the Military Historical Society at the National Army Museum and are not included in the following chapter notes.

1   A New Military Order

1 Stonyhurst College.
2 Ibid., Order of service, Memorial Mass for Harold Marcus Ervine-Andrews.
3 PRO, Kew, WO98/2.
4 Clark, B.D.H., 'The Victoria Cross: a register of awards to Irish-born officers and men', *Irish Sword*, vol. xvi, no. 64, p. 187.
5 PRO, Kew, WO98/1.
6 Royal archives, G4/65.
7 PRO, Kew, WO98/1.
8 Ibid.
9 Medal of Honor Historical Society.
10 *Register of the Victoria Cross*, pp 345 & 351.
11 Hancocks, letter to Doherty, May 1999.
1 Ibid.
13 *Times*, 28 June 1857.
14 Ibid.
15 PRO, Kew, WO98/3, p. 435.
16 Ibid., pp 169-171.
17 Duncan, J., & Walton, J., *Heroes for Victoria*, p. 92.
18 *Proceedings of the Royal Ulster Constabulary Historical Society*, spring 1999, p. 7.

2   The Crimea

1 *London Gazette*, 5 Feb 1856.
2 Young, P., & Lawford, J.P., *History of the British Army*, pp 152-3.
3 Ibid., p. 153.
4 Ibid.
5 Ibid., Lummis File, L. 43.
6 Woodward, *The Age of Reform, 1815-1870*, p. 271.
7 Young & Lawford, op. cit., p. 152; Messenger, C., *For Love of Regiment*, vol. I, p. 169.
8 Messenger, op. cit., p. 170.
9 Young & Lawford, op. cit., p. 153.
10 Ibid.
11 Hill, J.R., *The Oxford Illustrated History of the Royal Navy*, pp 171-3.
12 Lummis Files, L. 43.
13 Hill, op. cit., pp 172-3.
14 Ibid., pp 173-4.
15 Ibid.
16 PRO, Kew, WO98/3.
17 Ibid.
18 Smyth, J., *The Story of the Victoria Cross*, p. 27.
19 Young & Lawford, op. cit., pp 153-4.
20 Ibid., p. 154.
21 Ibid.
22 *Newtownards Chronicle*, 25 Feb 1911.
23 Young & Lawford, op. cit., pp 154-155.
24 Ibid., p. 155.
25 Ibid.
26 Brereton, J.M., & Savory, A.C.S., *The History of the Duke of Wellington's Regiment (West Riding), 1702-1992*, p. 186.

27 Young & Lawford, op. cit., p. 156.
28 Ibid., p. 158.
29 Ibid., pp 159-60.
30 PRO, Kew, WO98/2.
31 Ibid.
32 Ibid.

3 The Indian Mutiny

1 Hibbert, C., *The Great Mutiny India 1857*, pp 391-3.
2 Young & Lawford, op. cit., pp 162-4.
3 Ibid., p. 164; Messenger, op. cit., p. 182.
4 Young & Lawford, op. cit., p. 164; Messenger, op. cit., p. 183.
5 Young & Lawford, op. cit., p. 164; Hibbert, op. cit., pp 68-9.
6 Young & Lawford, op. cit., p. 164; Messenger, op. cit., p. 183.
7 Hibbert, op. cit., pp 209-15.
8 Young & Lawford, op. cit., p. 165.
9 Ibid., p. 166.
10 Ibid., pp 166-8.
11 Ibid., p. 168.
12 PRO, Kew, WO98/2.
13 Ibid.
14 Ibid.
15 PRO, Kew, WO98/3, pp 410-12.
16 PRO, Kew, WO32/7359.
17 Hibbert, passim.
18 Ibid., pp 253-4.
19 Ibid., pp 254-5.
20 *The Sheffield & Rotherham Independent*, 18 Feb. 1860.
21 Collister, P., *'Hellfire Jack!' VC*, pp 1-10 & 52-5.
22 Saint Columb's Cathedral records; PRO, Kew WO16/237.
23 PRO, Kew WO98/3, p. 414.
24 Ibid., p. 278.
25 Forrest, G., *The Life of Lord Roberts*, pp 1-12.
26 PRO, Kew, WO32/7323.
27 Gaylor, J., *Sons of John Company*, pp 68-70 & 299.

28 PRO, Kew, WO98/1.
29 PRO, Kew, WO98/3, pp 543-4.
30 PRO, Kew, WO98/4, pp 80-2.
31 Ibid., pp 161-2.
32 Ibid., p. 412.
33 Ibid., pp 185-7 .
34 Harris, R.G., *The Irish Regiments 1683-1999*, pp 210, 226, 128 & 196.

4 The Small Wars of Empire

1 Duncan & Walton, op. cit., p. 67.
2 Haythornthwaite, op. cit., p. 155.
3 Ibid., pp 146-7.
4 Ibid., p. 147.
5 Ibid., p. 148.
6 Ibid.
7 Ibid.
8 Ibid., p. 137.
9 Ibid.
10 Langrishe, Henry H., 'Lieutenant W.R.P. Hamilton, VC', *Irish Sword* i, no. 4, pp 354-5.
11 Haythornthwaite, p. 237.
12 Ibid., pp 239-40.
13 Ibid., pp 240-1.
14 Duncan & Walton, op. cit., pp 28-9.
15 Ó Snodaigh, P., 'The use of the title "I.R.A."', *Irish Sword* xvi, no. 64, pp 226-7.
16 Haythornthwaite, op. cit., p. 263.
17 *London Gazette*, 17 Dec 1867.
18 Haythornthwaite, op. cit., p. 114.
19 Ibid.
20 Smyth, op. cit., pp 116-17.
21 Haythornthwaite, op. cit., p. 114.
22 Kirby, S.L. & Walsh, R.R., *The Seven V.C.s of Stonyhurst College*, pp 11-12.
23 Ibid., pp 12-13.
24 Ibid.
25 Ibid.
26 Ibid., pp 13-15.
27 Ibid., p. 15.
28 Ibid.
29 Ibid., p. 18.

30 Ibid., p. 19.
31 Ibid.
32 Ibid., p. 21.

5   *The Dark Continent*

1 Haythornthwaite, op. cit., p. 159.
2 Ibid.
3 Ibid.
4 Ibid., pp 159-60.
5 Ibid., p. 186.
6 Ibid., p. 187.
7 Ibid.
8 *London Gazette*, 17 Jun 1879 .
9 *London Gazette*, 2 May 1879.
10 Haythornthwaite, op. cit., p. 188.
11 Ibid.
12 Ibid., p. 189.
13 Ibid., p. 193.
14 Ibid., p. 194.
15 Ibid.
16 Messenger, op. cit., pp 198-9.
17 Ibid., p. 206.
18 Ibid.
19 Ibid., pp 206-10.
20 Ibid., pp 215-16.
21 Ibid.
22 Ibid., p. 217.
23 Ibid.
24 Kirby & Walsh, op. cit., p. 43.
25 Ibid., p. 45.
26 Ibid., p. 48.
27 Ibid., pp 50-9.
28 Messenger, op. cit., p. 218.
29 Ibid.
30 Smyth, op. cit., p. 130.
31 Ibid.
32 Messenger, op. cit., p. 218.
33 Holmes, R., *The Little Field Marshal*, p. 62.
34 Smyth, op. cit., pp 132-3.
35 Messenger, op. cit., p. 221.
36 Haythornthwaite, op. cit., p. 198.
37 Gretton, G.L.E.M., *Campaigns and History of The Royal Irish Regiment*, p. 355.

38 PRO, Kew, WO98/3 & WO32/7498. The latter file relates to the bestowal of the VC on deceased officers and men, and especially Lieutenant Neville Coghill. When Sir John Brodrick announced the government's intention to award posthumous VCs to those killed in South Africa 'in the performance of acts of gallantry which would have entitled them to such decorations had they survived' this led to pressure from Lord Rathmore (brother-in-law of Sir John Coghill, and Lord Roberts to award the VC to those listed in the *London Gazette* as potential VC recipients had they lived. The *London Gazette* of 2 May 1879 had so listed Coghill and Melvill. The award of the VC to both men was approved in October 1902.
39 Beckett, Ian, *Johnnie Gough, V.C.*, pp 2-8.
40 Ibid., pp 85-7.
41 Ibid., pp 91-101.
42 Ibid., p. 100.
43 Ibid., p. 145.
44 Ibid., pp 173-207.

6   *1914-19*

1 Harris, op. cit., p. 32.
2 Dungan, M., *Distant Drums*, p. 55.
3 Kirby & Walsh, op. cit., pp 61-2.
4 Ascoli, D., *The Mons Star. The British Expeditionary Force 1914*, pp 57-60.
5 Ibid., p. 61 (map).
6 Ibid., p. 62; Kirby & Walsh, op. cit., p. 66.
7 Kirby & Walsh, op. cit., pp 66-7.
8 PRO, Kew, WO32/3422.
9 Kirby & Walsh, op. cit., p. 67 .
10 *Register of the Victoria Cross*, p. 121.
11 Ascoli, *The Mons Star*, op. cit., p. 133; Farndale, M., *History of the Royal Regiment of Artillery. Western Front 1914-18*, p. 56.

12 Farndale, op. cit., pp 56-7.
13 Farrar-Hockley, A., *Death of an Army*, pp 73-105 passim.
14 Kipling, R., *The Irish Guards in the Great War. The First Battalion*, p. 77.
15 The *Times*, 22 Jun 1915.
16 Cunliffe, M., *The Royal Irish Fusiliers 1793-1968*, p. 283.
17 Ibid., p. 284.
18 Burrowes, A.R., *The 1st Battalion Faugh-A-Ballaghs in the Great War*, p. 30.
19 *Journal of the Queen's Royal Surrey Regiment*, Nov. 1963, p. 475.
20 *Daily Telegraph*, 25 Aug. 1915.
21 Messenger, *For Love of Regiment*, vol. 2, 1915-94, p. 28.
22 Johnstone, T., *Orange, Green and Khaki*, pp 102-9.
23 McCance, S. *History of the Royal Munster Fusiliers*, vol ii, p. 212.
24 *Daily Mail*, 2 Sep 1915.
25 Batchelor, P. F. & Matson, C., *VCs of the First World War. The Western Front 1915*, pp 157-8.
26 Smyth, op. cit., pp 209-11.
27 Ibid., p. 210.
28 *Daily Mail*, 25 May 1926.
29 *London Gazette*, 9 Sept. 1916.
30 Ibid., 25 Nov. 1916.
31 *London Gazette*, 25 Nov. 1916.
32 Portora Royal School, letter to Truesdale.
33 *London Gazette*, 25 Nov. 1916.
34 Kipling, *The Irish Guards. The Second Battalion*, pp 148-9.
35 *Irish Times*, March 1999.
36 Register of the Victoria Cross, p. 67.
37 Cheshire Regiment Museum.
38 Falls, C., *History of the Ulster Division*, pp 170-1.
39 Ibid., pp 172-3.
40 Ibid., pp 173-4.
41 Johnstone, op. cit., pp 318-23.
42 *London Gazette*, 25 July 1918.
43 *The Irish Soldier*, no. 2, p. 16.
44 *London Gazette*, 30 Oct. 1918.
45 Smyth, op. cit., p. 292.

46 Information from Medal Society of Ireland.
47 Bowyer, C., *For Valour. The Air VCs*, pp 156-62.
48 Ibid., pp 121-31.
49 *The Irish Soldier*, no. 1, p. 5.
50 Smyth, op. cit., p. 302.
51 Ibid., pp 302-3.

7   *1920-45*

1 Smyth, op. cit., p. 328.
2 Ibid., p. 327.
3 Ibid., p. 328.
4 Ibid.
5 Ibid.
6 Ibid., pp 328-9.
7 From *The Young British Soldier*.
8 Smyth, op. cit., p. 329.
9 Ibid., p. 328.
10 Kenny family to Truesdale.
11 Bowyer, op. cit., p. 216.
12 Ibid., p. 215.
13 Ibid.
14 Doherty, R., *Irish Men and Women in the Second World War*, pp 98-9.
15 Ibid., p. 99.
16 Bowyer, op. cit., pp 216-17.
17 Ibid., p. 217.
18 Ibid.
19 Ibid.
20 Ibid.
21 Ibid.
22 Ibid., pp 217-18.
23 Doherty, op. cit., p. 101.
24 Ibid.
25 Kirby & Walsh, op. cit., pp 105-8.
26 Ibid.
27 Ibid.
28 Smyth, op. cit., p. 343.
29 Kirby & Walsh, op. cit., p. 110.
30 Ibid.
31 Smyth, op. cit., p. 343.
32 Doherty, op. cit., p. 79.
33 Ibid., pp 79-80.
34 Turner, John F., *VCs of the Royal Navy*, pp 55-6.

35 Doherty, op. cit., p. 80.
36 Ibid., pp 80-1.
37 Ibid., p. 81.
38 Turner, op. cit., pp 56-7.
39 Doherty, op. cit., p. 81.
40 Turner, op. cit., p. 57.
41 Ibid., pp 57-8.
42 Ibid., p. 58.
43 Ibid., pp 58-9.
44 Doherty, op. cit., p. 82.
45 *Wexford People*, 19 May 1945.
46 Turner, op. cit., p. 61.
47 Kirby & Walsh, op. cit., pp 121-3.
48 Ibid., p. 123.
49 Ibid., pp 123-6.
50 Myatt, F., *The British Infantry 1660-1945*, p. 206.
51 Doherty, *A Noble Crusade*, pp 14-31.
52 Ibid.
53 Ibid.
54 Doherty, *Irish Men and Women*, p. 73.
55 Ibid., pp 73-4.
56 Barclay, *The History of the Royal Northumberland Fusiliers in the Second World War*, p. 61.
57 Doherty, *Irish Men and Women*, p. 74.
58 Ibid.
59 Royal Northumberland Fusiliers' (RNF) Museum, notes by Fus. R.J. Dishman.
60 Barclay, op. cit., pp 62-3.
61 Humble, R., *Crusader*, p. 145.
62 RNF Museum, notes by Fus. Dishman, op. cit.
63 Kirby & Walsh, op. cit., pp 133-4; Doherty, *Irish Men and Women*, p. 75.
64 *London Gazette*, 31 March 1942.
65 Bowyer, op. cit., p. 271; Bowyer, *Eugene Esmonde*, p. 17.
66 Bowyer, *For Valour*, pp 271-2.
67 Ibid., p. 273; PRO, Kew, ADM1/11260.
68 Bowyer, op. cit., pp 273-4; *London Gazette*, 20 Jan. 1942; Doherty, *Irish Men and Women*, p. 88.
69 Bowyer, *Eugene Esmonde*, p. 108.

70 Ibid., pp 110-14.
71 Doherty, op. cit., pp 89-90.
72 Bowyer, *Eugene Esmonde*, pp 117-19.
73 Ibid., pp 120-2.
74 Ibid., pp 124-34.
75 Ibid., pp 140-5.
76 Ibid., pp 148-50.
77 Ibid., 150-1.
78 Ibid., pp 152-3.
79 Ibid., pp 166-7; *London Gazette*, 3 March 1942.
80 Bowyer, *For Valour*, p. 278.
81 Bowyer, *Eugene Esmonde*, pp 170-4.
82 Wigmore, L., *They Dared Mightily*, p. 154.
83 Pitt, B., *The Military History of World War II*, p. 164.
84 Ibid.
85 Ibid.
86 Wigmore, op. cit., p. 155.
87 *London Gazette*, 30 Dec. 1943.
88 *Reconquest*, p. 49.
89 Ibid., pp 48-50.
90 Bowyer, *For Valour*, pp 405-6.
91 Ibid., pp 409-10.
92 Royal Engineers' (R.E.) Museum to Truesdale.
93 Ibid.
94 Smyth, op. cit., pp 424-5.
95 R.E. Museum.
96 Ibid.
97 Ibid.
98 *London Gazette*, 28 June 1945.
99 Kemp, P., *Underwater Warriors*, p. 128.
100 Ibid., pp 176-8.
101 Ibid.
102 Ibid., pp 178-9.
103 *London Gazette*, 13 Nov. 1945.
104 Kemp, op. cit., p. 180.
105 Ibid.
106 p. 182.
107 Ibid., pp 181-2.

8 Recommendation Rejected

1 PRO, Kew, WO98/2.
2 Royal Inniskilling Fusiliers Museum, war diary 11th Inniskillings.
3 Middlebrook, M., *The First Day on the Somme*, p. 330.
4 Falls, C., *History of the Ulster Division*, p. 60.
5 Ibid., p. 101.
6 War diary, op. cit.
7 Mitchell, G., *Three Cheers for the Derrys*, pp 104-5.
8 Falls, op. cit., p. 222.
9 Ibid., p. 226.
10 Cunliffe, op. cit., p. 412.
11 Ibid.
12 Ibid., pp 413-14.
13 Ibid., p. 415.
14 Ibid.
15 Johnson, E.B.W., *Island Prize*, pp 62-4.
16 Doherty, *A Noble Crusade*, pp 203-23.
17 Ibid.
18 Doherty, *Clear the Way!*, pp 136-7.
19 Woods, Col A.D., *A personal account of his service with 2 LIR in Italy*.
20 Ibid.
21 Ibid.
22 Ibid.
23 Ibid.
24 Ford, K., *Battleaxe Division*, p. 167.
25 Ibid.
26 Doherty, *A Noble Crusade*, p. 348.
27 Ibid.
28 Doherty, *Irish Men and Women*, p. 158.
29 Ibid., p. 162.
30 Ibid., pp 163-4.
31 Ibid., pp 164-5.
32 Masters, J., *The Road past Mandalay*, p. 278.
33 I bid.
34 Denman, T., *Ireland's Unknown Soldiers*, p. 123.
35 O'Rahilly, A., *Father William Doyle, S.J.*, p. 554.

36 Ibid., pp 556-7.
37 Ibid., p. 555.
38 Denman, op. cit., p. 123.
39 Johnstone & Hagerty, *The Cross on the Sword*, p. 163.
40 Ibid., p. 162.
41 Colin Gunner, letter to Doherty.
42 Doherty, *Clear the Way!*, p. 124.
43 Lt-Col. B.D.H. Clark, interview with author Oct. 1991.

Postscript

1 Batchelor & Matson, *VCs of the First World War. The Western Front 1915*, pp 58-9.
2 Buzzell, *Register of the Victoria Cross*, p. 99.
3 Batchelor & Matson, op. cit., pp 71-2.
4 Buzzell, op. cit., p. 176.
5 Ibid., p. 178.
6 Ibid.
7 Sheen, J., *Tyneside Irish*, pp 207-64.
8 Buzzell, op. cit., p. 178.
9 Lummis.
10 Kenneally, J.P., *Kenneally, VC*, passim.
11 Buzzell, op. cit., p. 112, Lummis.
12 Orange Order website.
13 Buzzell, op. cit., p. 332.
14 Clark, B.D.H., 'The Victoria Cross A register of awards to Irishborn officers and men', *Irish Sword* xvi, no. 64, p. 186.

Appendix Two: Forfeited Awards

1 PRO, Kew, WO98/1. The Victoria Cross warrant.
2 Smyth, op. cit., pp 462-3.
3 Ibid., p. 88.
4 Tambling, V.R.S., 'The Bambrick Brothers. Life after Waterloo', *The Waterloo Journal*, vol. xxi, no. 2, p. 28.

Bibliography

Adkin, Mark, *The Charge*, London 1996

Ascoli, David, *The Mons Star. The British Expeditionary Force 1914*, London 1981

—, *A Companion to the British Army 1660-1983*, London 1984

Barclay, Brigadier C.N., *The History of the Royal Northumberland Fusiliers in the Second World War*, London 1952

Barnett, Correlli, *Engage the Enemy More Closely – The Royal Navy in the Second World War*, London 1991

Barthorp, Michael, *The Zulu War*, London 1980

—, *War on the Nile*, London 1984

Batchelor, Peter F. & Matson, Christopher, *VCs of the First World War. The Western Front 1915*, Stroud 1997

Beckett, Ian, *Johnnie Gough, VC. A biography of Brigadier-General Sir John Edmond Gough, VC, KCB, CMG*, London 1989

Bowyer, Chaz, *Eugene Esmonde, VC, DSO*, London 1983

—, *For Valour. The Air VCs*, London 1992

Bredin, Brigadier A.E.C., DSO, MC, DL, *History of the Irish Soldier*, Belfast 1987

Brereton, J.M. & Savory, A.C.S., *The History of the Duke of Wellington's Regiment (West Riding), 1702-1992* (Halifax, 1993)

Burrowes, Brig-Gen A.R., CMG, DSO, *The 1st Battalion Faugh-A-Ballaghs in the Great War*, Aldershot (nd)

Buzzell, Nora (ed.), *The Register of the Victoria Cross*, Cheltenham 1988

Carton de Wiart, Sir Adrian, *Happy Odyssey*, London 1950

Collister, Peter, *'Hellfire Jack!' VC. General Sir William Olpherts, 1822-1902*, London 1989

Cooper, Bryan, *The Tenth Irish Division at Gallipoli*, London 1918 (reprint Dublin 1993)

Creagh, General Sir O'Moore, VC & Humphris, Miss E.M. (ed.), *The Victoria Cross*, London 1924

Cunliffe, Marcus, *The Royal Irish Fusiliers, 1793-1968*, Oxford 1970

Denman, Terence, *Ireland's Unknown Soldiers. The 16th (Irish) Division in the Great War*, Dublin 1992

Doherty, Richard, *Clear the Way! A History of the 38th (Irish) Brigade, 1941-47*, Dublin 1993

—, *A Noble Crusade The History of Eighth Army, 1941-45*, Staplehurst 1999

—, *Irish Men and Women in the Second World War*, Dublin 1999

Dooner, Mildred G., *The Last Post*, London 1980

Dudgeon, James M., *'Mick'. The Story of Major Edward Mannock, VC, DSO, MC, RFC, RAF*, London 1981

Duncan, John & Walton, John, *Heroes for Victoria*, Tunbridge Wells 1991

Dungan, Myles, *Distant Drums. Irish Soldiers in Foreign Armies*, Belfast 1993

Eastwood, Stuart, *Lions of England*, Kettering 1991

Falls, Cyril, *History of the Ulster Division*, Belfast 1922

—, *The History of the Royal Irish Rifles*, Aldershot 1925

Farndale, *General Sir Martin, KCB, History of the Royal Regiment of Artillery. Western Front 1914-18*, London 1986

Farrar-Hockley, Anthony, *Death of an Army*, London 1967

Farrington, Anthony, *Casualty Roll, Second Afghan War*, London 1986

Farset Youth and Community Development Ltd, *Ireland's VCs*, Belfast (no date)

Fleming, George, *Magennis VC*, Belfast 1997

Ford, Ken, *Battleaxe Division. From Africa to Italy with the 78th Division, 1942-45*, Stroud 1999

Forde, Frank, *The Long Watch*, Dublin 1991

Forrest, Sir George, *The Life of Lord Roberts, VC*, London 1914

Fox, Sir Frank, *The Royal Inniskilling Fusiliers in the Great War*, London 1928

Geoghegan, S., *Campaigns and History of the Royal Irish Regiment (2 volumes)*, Edinburgh 1927

Gilbert, Adrian (ed.), *The Imperial War Museum Book of the Desert War*, London 1992

Gliddon, Gerald, *V.C.s of the Somme – a biographical portrait*, Norwich 1991

Glover, Michael, *Rorke's Drift*, London 1997

Gretton, Lt-Col. G.L.E.M., *Campaigns and History of the Royal Irish Regiment*, London 1911

Harris, Henry, *The Irish Regiments in the First World War*, Cork 1968

Harris, R.G., *The Irish Regiments, 1683-1999*, Staplehurst 1999

Harrison, A.T., *The Graham Indian Mutiny Papers*, Belfast

Harvey, David, *Monuments to Courage. Victoria Cross headstones and memorials*, London, 1999

Haythornthwaite, Philip J , *The Colonial Wars Source Book*, London 1995

Heathcore, T.A., *The Afghan Wars, 1839-1919*, London 1980

Hibbert, Christopher, *The Great Mutiny India, 1857*, London 1978

Hill, J.R. (ed.), *The Oxford Illustrated History of the Royal Navy*, Oxford 1995

Holmes, Richard, *The Little Field Marshal. Sir John French*, London 1981

Humble, *Richard, Crusader. The Eighth Army's Forgotten Victory November 1941- January 1942*, London 1987

Jervis, Lt-Col. H.S., *The 2nd Munsters in France*, Aldershot 1922

Johns, W.E., *The Air VCs*, London 1935

Johnson, Edward B.W., *Island Prize. Leros, 1943*, Kemble 1992

Johnston, Peter, *Front Line Artists*, London 1978

Johnstone, Tom, *Orange Green and Khaki. The Story of the Irish regiments in the Great War, 1914-18*, Dublin, 1992

— & Hagerty, James, *The Cross on the Sword. Catholic Chaplains in the Forces*, London 1996

Jourdain, H.N.F., *History of the Connaught Rangers* (3 volumes) London 1925-28

Kemp, Paul, *Underwater Warriors*, London 1996

Kenneally, John Patrick, VC, *Kenneally VC*, Huddersfield 1991

Kipling, Rudyard, *The Irish Guards in the Great War. The First Battalion*, Staplehurst 1997 (reprint)

—, *The Irish Guards in the Great War. The Second Battalion*, Staplehurst 1997 (reprint)
Kirby, H.L. & Walsh, R.R., *The Seven VCs of Stonyhurst College*, Blackburn 1987
Knight, Ian, *Brave Men's Blood*, London 1980
— and Laband, John, *The Anglo-Zulu War*, Stroud 1996
Laffin, John, *British VCs of World War 2*, Stroud 1997
Lloyd, Alan, *The Zulu War*, London 1973
McAughtry, Sam, *The Sinking of the Kenbane Head*, Belfast 1977
McCance, Captain S., *History of the Royal Munster Fusiliers* (2 volumes), Aldershot 1927
McDonagh, M., *The Irish at the Front*, London 1916
Malleson, G. B., *The Indian Mutiny of 1857*, London 1892
Masters, John, *The Road past Mandalay*, London 1961
Messenger, Charles, *For Love of Regiment, Volume One, 1660-1914*, London 1994
—, *For Love of Regiment, Volume Two, 1915-1994*, London 1996
Middlebrook, Martin, *The First Day on the Somme*, London 1971
Mitchell, Gardiner S., *Three Cheers for the Derrys. A History of the 10th Royal Inniskilling Fusiliers in the 1914-18 War*, Derry 1991
Moorehead, Alan, *Gallipoli*, London 1956
Morris, Donald R., *The Washing of the Spears*, London 1965
Myatt, Frederick, *The British Infantry 1660-1945. The evolution of a fighting force*, Poole 1983
O'Rahilly, Alfred, *Father William Doyle S.J.*, London 1932
Pakenham, Thomas, *The Boer War*, London 1979
Pillinger, Dennis & Staunton, Anthony, *Victoria Cross Locator*, Maidenhead 1997
Pitt, Barrie (ed., *The Military History of World War II*, London 1986
Powell, Geoffrey, *The History of the Green Howards*, London 1992
Sheen, John, *Tyneside Irish. A history of the Tyneside Irish Brigade raised in the North East in World War One*, Barnsley 1998
Smith, Peter C., *Victoria's Victories*, Tunbridge Wells 1987
Smyth, Sir John, VC, *The Story of the Victoria Cross*, London 1963
Sutherland, Douglas, *Tried and Valiant. The Border Regiment, 1702-1959*, London 1972
Swettenham, H., *Valiant Men: Canada's VC and GC Winners*, Toronto 1973
Tavender, I.T., *Casualty Roll for the Zulu and Basuto Wars, 1877-79*, London 1985
—, *Casualty Roll for the Indian Mutiny, 1857-59*, London 1985
Turner, John Frayn, *VCs of the Royal Navy*, London 1956
Whitehouse, Howard, *A Widow Making War*, London 1995
Whitton, F.E., *The History of the Prince of Wales's Leinster Regiment* (2 volumes), Aldershot 1926
Wigmore, L. & Harding, B., *They Dared Mightily*, Canberra 1963
Wilkins, P.A., *Heroes of the Victoria Cross*, London 1904
Williams, W. Alister, *The VCs of Wales and the Welsh Regiments*, Wrexham 1984
Wilkins, Philip A., *The History of the Victoria Cross*, London 1904
Winton, J., *The Victoria Cross at Sea*, London 1978
Woodward, Sir Llewellyn, *The Age of Reform, 1815-1870*, Oxford 1938
Wylly, H.C., *Crown and Company (2nd Bn Royal Dublin Fusiliers)*, Aldershot
—, *Neill's Blue Caps (1st Bn Royal Dublin Fusiliers)*, Aldershot 1925
Young, Peter & Lawford, J.P. (eds), *History of the British Army*, London 1970

Reconquest – An Official Record of the Australian Army's Successes in the Offensives ...
   Sept 1943-June 1944 (Australian Forces' official publication, n.d.)
Volunteers from Éire who have won distinctions serving with the British Forces, Dublin
   1943 (revised edition, 1944, supplement to mid-1944)

ARTICLES

Blacker, S., 'A Great Irish soldier: Lieutenant W.R.P. Hamilton, VC', *Irish Sword*
   (hereinafter *IS*), I, no. 3, p. 231
Boyce, P.J., 'A Victoria Cross', *IS*, IX, no. 36, p. 242
Clark, B.D.H., 'The Victoria Cross: a register of awards to Irishborn officers and
   men', *IS*, XVI, no. 64, pp 185-207
Forrester, H., *Royal Irish Constabulary Victoria Cross Holders, Proceedings of the Royal
   Ulster Constabulary Historical Society*, spring 1999
Langrishe, H.H., 'Lieutenant W.R.P. Hamilton, VC', *IS*, I, no. 4, pp 354-5
Mullen, T.J., '"Mick" Mannock – the forgotten ace, *IS*, X, no. 39, pp 77-86
Tambling, V., 'The Bambrick Brothers. Life after Waterloo', *Waterloo Journal*, XXI,
   no. 2, p. 27
Whyte, Desmond, 'A Trying Chindit (in "Medicine and War")', *British Medical
   Journal*, no. 285, pp 18-25, December 1982

UNPUBLISHED PAPERS

Military Historical Society
The Lummis Files. Held in the Reading Room, National Army Museum, London

Public Record Office, Kew
ADM1/17330. Correspondence relating to the loss of HMS *Jervis Bay*
ADM1/11260. Correspondence relating to the hunt for the German battleship
   Bismarck
WO32/3422. The First VC – war 1914-21
WO32/7323. On Patrick Roddy's VC
WO32/7498. Bestowal of VCs on deceased officers and men: Case of late Lieut.
   Coghill
WO98/1. The original Victoria Cross warrant
WO98/2. Papers and letters relating to recommendations for the award of the Victoria
   Cross
WO98/3 and 4. The register of the Victoria Cross

Index

Bold entries refer to VC winners

Abduallah el-Taaishi, the Khalifa, 87
Aberdeen, 106
Aberdeen, Lord, 23
Abyssinia, 31, 81, 87
Adams, James William, 71, 189
Adams, John Henry, 141
Admiralty, 24, 148, 150, 160
Advanced Air Striking Force (AASF),
  143, 146
Afghanistan, 42, 68
Afghan War, second, 68, 113
Africa, North, 154
Agar, Augustus, 139, 140, 189
Aghada, 111, 112
Agra, 45, 63
Ahmed, Mohammed, *see also* Mahdi, the,
  87
Aisne, the, 114, 133
Alambagh, the, 52, 57, 62
Åland islands, 24
Albert canal, 144
Albert, Prince, 16, 19
Alberta, 125, 133
Albuoys' Point, 153
Albrecht, Herman, 95, 96
Alexander, Annie, 104
Alexander, Ernest Wright, 104, 189
Alexander, John, 38, 189-190
Alexander, Robert, 104
Ali Masjid, 68
Allahabad, 36, 53, 60
Alma, battle of, 26, 27, 33, 36
Alma, river, 26, 29
Altenfjord, 170n
Alton, 140
Alum Bagh, 38
Amballa, 44
American Civil War, 40, 75
Amifontaine, 144, 145
Andaman island, Little, 76
Anderson, Charles, 186, 190

Andrews, Harold Marcus Ervine, 15,
  146, 147, 148, 154, 173, 203
Anson, Major O. H. St George, 57
Anson Battalion, 186
Anstruther, Lieutenant-Colonel, 86
Anstruther, Lieutenant, 26
Antrim, county, 34, 38, 53, 56, 71, 118,
  137
Appetici, 176
Arakan, 67, 168
Ardill, Lieutenant, 177
Armagh, 51, 95, 118
Armagh, county, 25, 37, 50, 51, 53, 58,
  85, 117, 178
Army, British, 15, 16, 17, 18, 63, 65, 91,
  95, 124, 136
Army Cadet Force, 84
Army, Eighth, 154, 155, 177, 179
Army Hospital Corps, 84
Army Pioneer Corps, 107
Army Service Corps, 61, 98
Arnhem, 12, 167, 168
Arnold, Captain, 53
Arrabeg, 57
Arrah, 50
Ashanti expedition, 27
Ashburner, Captain, 103
Ashton-in-Makerfield, 110
Assam, 67
Atbara, river, 88
Athboy, 125
Athlone, 52, 58
Athy, 96, 122
Atlantic, the, 153, 154, 160, 160
Aubigny-en-Artois, 135
Auckland, 137
Aughnahoory, 127
Australia, 28, 76, 120, 164, 165
Australian Imperial Force, (AIF), 120,
  164, 185
Australian War Memorial, 167

Austria, 21
Auxiliary Division, RIC, 20
Avion, 135
Aylmer, Fenton John, 77, 78, 131, 190
Azimgurh, 60, 61
Azov, sea of, 34

Badcock, Lieutenant, 78
Badli-ki-Serai, 44, 45
Baileyboro', 32
Baillie Guard Gate, 62
Bairnsfather, Bruce, 103
Balaclava, 30
Balaclava Cove, 29
Balaclava Day, 31
Balikpapan, 167
Ballachulish Corps, 25
Ballinacorr, 143
Ballinakill house, 89
Ballinasloe, 47
Ballinlanty, 149
Ballinona, 99
Ballinran, 95
Ballinrobe, 55
Ballybeggan, 164
Ballycastle, 118
Ballyconnell house, 51
Ballymacoll, 36
Ballymena, 35, 71
Ballymore, 49
Ballyragget, 97
Ballyshannon , 31, 92
Baltic sea, 19, 23
Bambrick, Valentine, 235
Bangor, 28, 116, 128
Bank of Commerce, 133
Bank of Ireland, 133
Bantry, 76
Bareilly, 52, 235
Barlin, 125
Barnard, Sir Henry, 44
Barnes, Jimmy, 178, 179, 180
Barnett, Major, 44
Barrosa, 95
Barry-au-Bac, 143, 144
Barry, Mrs Catherine, 97
Barry, John, 96, 97, 190
Battersby, Captain, 27
Battye, Major Wigram, 69
Beaumont Hamel, 119

Becke, Major A. F., 103
Beersheba, 130
BEF, 101, 102, 104, 143, 147
Belfast, 29, 38, 52, 61, 98, 104, 110n, 117, 118, 119, 128, 131
Belfast Newsletter, the, 52
Belgium, 38, 92, 105, 120, 137, 144, 184, 185
Bell, David, 77, 190
Bell, Captain E. H., 117
Bell, Edward William Derrington, 27, 190-1
Bell, Eric Norman Frankland, 117, 191
Bell, E. W., 27
Bellanti, Father Luke, 183
Bellew, Edward Donald, 185
Bellewstown, 185
Belturbet, 113
Benares, 44
Ben Bulben, 137
Bengal, 42, 48
Bengal Army, 42, 45, 62
Bengal Artillery, 51, 55, 58, 62, 63, 73
Bengal Ecclesiastical Dept, 71
Bengal Horse Artillery, 53, 62
Bengal Staff Corps, 77
Bengal Veteran Establishment, 44
Bengal, bay of, 76
Beni Madhu, 62
Bennett, Sergeant-Major, 112
Berber, 88
Berbera, 100
Beresford, Lord William Leslie de la Poer, 85, 191
Bergin, James, 82, 191
Bergues, canal de, 146, 147, 148
Berkshire, 73
Bermuda, 153
Berryman, Sergeant Major, 31
Bethune, 106
Bhopal Levy, 50
Bingham, Edward Barry Stewart, 116, 191
Birmingham, 187
Birr, 75, 115, 120n
Bishopscourt, 91
Bithur, 50
Black and Tans, 20
Blacker-Douglass, Lieutenant, 106

Blackpool block, 180
Blackrock, 61
Black Sea, 22
Blackwatertown, 51
Blaker, Major Frank, 181
Blamey, Sir Thomas, 165
Board of Ordnance, 40
Boer War, 11, 86, 90, 100, 105, 120, 125, 136
Bois-en-Hache, 125
Boisragon, Lieutenant, 78
Bolandshahr, 53
Bomarsund, 24, 25
Borrisokane, 57
Bombay, 42, 66, 185
Bombay Army, 66
Bombay Artillery, 59
Bombay Staff Corps, 70
Bombay-Burma Trading Company, 67
Bomber Command, 160, 161, 171
Booker, Alfred, 76
Borneo, 167, 173
Borrisoleigh, 149
Bothnia, Gulf of, 24
Boulger, Abraham, 49, 192
Bournemouth, 69
Bowyer, Chaz, 162
Boyd-Rochfort, George Arthur, 113, 114, 192
Boyd-Rochfort, Colonel H., 114
Boyd-Rochfort, Major R. H., 114
Boyle, 27
Boyne, the, 154n
Bradshaw, Joseph, 36, 192
Bradshaw, William, 52, 192
Bray, 50, 154
Brennan, Patrick, 65
Brentwood, 32
Brest, 160, 161, 170
Bridle Drift, 93
Brigades:
  British
    2nd, Central Indian Field Force, 59
    Heavy (cavalry), 30
    1 Cavalry, 104
    32 Army Tank, 155, 156
    2 Infantry, 93
    9 Infantry, 102
    11 Infantry, 178
    20 Infantry, 105

21 Infantry, 105
22 Infantry, 105
23 Infantry, 155
38 (Irish), 177, 183
43 Infantry, 141, 142
54 Infantry, 122
57 Infantry, 120
107 Infantry, 175
108 Infantry, 119, 175
111 (Chindit), 180
126 Infantry, 147
127 Infantry, 147
Highland, 30
Irish (Hart's), 93
Light (cavalry), 30, 31
Naval, 34, 56, 81
  Royal Artillery
    59th, 105
  Indian
    4th Infantry, 168
  other
    Mid-Clare (IRA), 136
Brighton, 138
Bristol, 53
Britain, 21, 22, 23, 40, 80, 81, 92, 132, 148, 149
Britain, battle of, 148
British Ambulance Corps, 75
British Columbia, 126, 127, 131
British Expeditionary Force, *see* BEF
Broembeek, the, 127, 128
Bromhead, Gonville, 84, 192-193
Brooke, James Anson Otho, 106, 193
Broughshane, 71
Brown, Captain, 44
Brown, Edward Douglas, later Browne-Singe-Hutchinson, 96, 193
Brown, Francis David Millest, 193
Browne, Arthur, 51
Browne, Sam, 68
Brownlow, Major, 87
Bruce, Captain C. M., 101
Bruges, 38
Brussels, 90
Buckingham palace, 17, 109, 112, 113, 114, 115, 116, 117, 119, 121, 122, 125, 126, 127, 128, 130, 133, 134, 136, 137, 146, 153, 161, 164
Buckley, Captain, 38
Buckley, John, 44

Buckley, Lieutenant, 34
Buffalo river, 83, 84
Bulford, Private, 74
Buller, Redvers, 92, 93, 94
Buna, 165
Bunagee, 131
Burgoyne, Hugh Talbot, 34, 35, 193
Burgoyne, Field-Marshal Sir John Fox, 34
Burma, 51, 67, 76, 85, 167, 180
Burmese war, 25, 67
Burnaby, 127
Burnett, Father T. H., 32
Burnley, 129
Burns, Private Michael, 60
Burslem, Nathaniel, 72, 73, 194
Burroughs, Captain, 55
Bushire, 66
Bushmills, 118
Butler, Charlotte, 82
Butler, Ronnie, 150
Byford, Amelia, 138
Byrne, Bridget, 89
Byrne, James, 60, 194
Byrne, John, 32, 194
Byrne, Thomas, 89, 90, 194

Cadell, Thomas, 49
Caerleon, 33
Caernarvon, 27
Caesar's Camp, 95
Caffrey, John, 115, 194
Cahir, 61
Cahirciveen, 64
Cairo, 87
Cairo village, Italy, 183
Calcutta, 35, 43, 44, 45
Calgary, 125
Calinos, 176
Calpee, 60, 61
Camberley, 109
Cambrai, 130
Cambridge, 168
Cambridge, Daniel, 34, 194
Cambridge, Duke of, 29
Cambrin, 113
Cameron, 74
Cameron, Captain, 81
Campbell, Sir Colin (*see also* Baron
    Clyde), 27, 30, 48, 51, 54, 60, 61
Campbell College, Belfast, 98, 133

Canada, 31, 37, 46, 50, 63, 76, 81, 96,
    107, 110, 125, 127, 131, 133
Canadian Expeditionary Force, 109, 120,
    125, 126, 127
Canning, Lord, 44
Canterbury, 33, 89
Canton, 71
Cape Colony, 98
Cape Helles, 111
Cape Mounted Police, 99
Cape Town, 92
Cardinal Vaughan School, 143
Carlin, Patrick, 60, 61, 195
Carlingford, 66
Carlisle, 36
Carnmoney, 128
Carlow, County, 30, 37, 74
Carrickfergus, 137
Carrickmacross, 122
Carton, CQMS, 107
Cashel, 46
Cassino, 178
Castleblaney, 121
Castleborough, 56
Castlereagh Borough Council, 117
Castle Shane, 25
Castletown, 114
Cather, Captain Dermot, 119
**Cather, Geoffrey St George
    Shillington**, 119, 195
Catholic Soldiers Association, 27
Cavagnari, Sir Louis, 69, 70
Cavan, 133
Cavan County, 32, 46, 62, 113, 146, 147
Cawnpore, 50, 52, 53, 54
Cemetery, the, 28
Central Indian Field Force, 59
Ceylon, 139
Chakdara pass, 79, 80
Chandairee, 59
Changi, 172
Chapman, Sir Thomas, 27
Charasiah, 70
Charity, the Sisters of, 27
Charlesfort, 185
Chatham, 164
Chavasse, Noel Godfrey, 12, 132
Cheape, Colonel H., 114
Cheape, Major Leslie, 114
Chelmsford, Lord, 82, 83, 84, 85

Chelsea, 80
Chelsea, Royal Hospital, 63, 71
Cheltenham, 29, 75, 133
Cheshire, Leonard, 183
Chester, 129
Chesterfield, 36
Chesterton, 46
China, 29, 33, 71, 72, 78
Chindit expedition, second, 180
Chindits, 180
Chitral, 79
Chittagong, 67
Chota Belhar, 53
Churchill, Winston, 89, 138
Ciliax, Admiral Otto, 160, 161, 162, 164
Clare, County, 69, 70
Claremont, 121
Clares, the Poor, 27
Clare, Viscount, 154n
Clarinbridge, 99
Clark, Brenda, 9
Clark, Captain (later Lt-Col) Brian, 12,
    183
Clark, Michael, 178
Clark, Shanny, 9
Cliff, 31
Clinton, Jack, 163
Clitheroe, 15
Clongowes Wood College, 99, 122
Clonmel, 58
Clontibret, 25
Cloughjordan, 113
Clyde, the, 153
Clyde, Baron (*see also* Campbell, Sir
    Colin), 60, 61
Coastal Command, 161
Cobbe, Captain A. S., 100
Cobo hotel, 11
Coffey, William, 35, 196
Coghill, Sir John Joscelyn, 83
Coghill, Neville, 83, 132, 196
Cogwell, W. H.L., 52
Colenso, 92, 93
Collegians RFC, 117
Collon, 130
Colvin, Hugh, 128, 129, 196
Comber, 133
Conker, Frederick, *see* Whirlpool,
    Frederick
Connolly, Edward Michael, 31n

Connolly, Augustus John, 31, 32, 197
Connors, Joseph, 39
Convoys:
    HX 84, 149, 150, 151, 153
    HX 89, 153
Cookstown, 132
Coole, 102
Copenhagen, 23
Coravoo, 121
Corbett, Private, 46
Corfu, 39
Cornkirk, 117
Cork, 12, 29, 34, 48, 49, 53, 55, 62, 72,
    73, 98, 107, 108, 167
Cork, County, 32, 71, 76, 111, 112, 120,
    123, 132
Coronel, battle of, 115
Corps:
    British
    II, 102
    III, 129
    XIII, 179
    XX, 130
    XXX, 167
    Polish
    II, 179
    German
    XXVII, 105
Corps of Commissionaires, 106
Cornwall, 47
Cos, 176
Cosgrove, William, 111, 112, 197
Costello, Bessie, 78
Costello, Charles Peter, 78
Costello, Edmund William, 78, 79, 80,
    197
Coughlan, Cornelius, 45, 46, 197
County Down Volunteers, 174
Courcelles, 133, 134
Courtney, Corporal, 28, 29
Creagh, O'Moore, 61n, 70, 198
Crean, Thomas Joseph, 99, 198
Crean, Thomas, 99
Crevecoeur, 136
Crichton, James, 136, 137, 198
Crimea, the, 42, 51, 75
Crimean War, 15, 16, 17, 21–41, 42, 63,
    66, 113, 159
Crimmin, John, 67, 68, 198
Crolly Bridge, 131

Cuinchy, 106
Cunningham, John, 125, 198
Cuneo, Terence, 38
Curragh, 40
Cyprus, 21

D Force, 168
Daily Express, 114
Daily Telegraph, 148
Dakka, 70
Dalkey, 85
Dalriada Hospital, 118
Danaher, John, 86, 199
Danville, 76
Dardanelles, 110
Darlington, 61
Daratoleh, 101
Dartry Lodge, 51
Daubeney, Colonel C. B., 40, 41, 174
Davy, Pilot Officer T.D. H., 145
Dease, Edmund Fitzlawrence, 102, 182
Dease, Katherine, 102
Dease, Maurice James, 102, 103, 104, 199
Dehra Dun, 44
Delhi, 43, 44, 45, 46, 47, 48, 49, 73, 132
Delhi Lancers, 53
Delville Wood, 119
Dempsey, Denis, 50, 199
Denmark, 144
Denmark Strait, 150
Deraghland, 104
Derby, 115
Derbyshire, 36
Derry, 52, 113
Derry Volunteers, 175
Derrylane, 62
Devon, 38
Dewar, Lieutenant, 86
De Wet, 100
De Wiart, Adrian Carton, 120, 199
De Wind, Edmund, 132, 133, 199
De Wind, Mount, 133
Diamond, Bernard, 53, 200
Dieppe, 186
Dillon, John, 64
Dishman, Fusilier R. J., 157
Divane, John, *see* Duane, John
Divisions:
  Australian
    2nd, 120

4th, 120
6th, 165
7th, 165, 166
British
  7th Armoured, 155
  1st Infantry, 146
  3rd Infantry, 102
  4th Infantry, 177, 179
  7th Infantry, 105
  10th (Irish), 130
  11th Infantry, 122
  16th (Irish), 181, 182
  18th Infantry, 122
  36th (Ulster), 119, 129, 132, 174, 175, 182
  42nd (Lancashire), 147
  46th Infantry, 146
  70th Infantry, 155, 156
  78th (The Battleaxe), 177, 179
  1st Airborne, 167
Indian
  8th Infantry, 177, 179
Dodecanese, 176
Dogger Bank, battle of, 115
Donaghadee, 142
Donegal, County, 31, 35, 51, 92, 131, 174
Donegal and Fermanagh Volunteers, 174
Donegan, Lieutenant-Colonel, 107
Dongola, 88
Donohoo, Patrick, 53, 200
Donohue, Dan, 41
Doogan, John, 87, 200
Dorchester, 113
Dorking, 85
Dorset, 69
Douglas, Assistant Surgeon, 77
Douglas, 112
Dover, 29, 98, 148, 158, 161, 170
Down, County, 28, 35, 77, 95, 116, 127, 128, 133, 141, 180
Down, Ensign, 74
Downing, W. McCarthy, 65
Dowling, William, 49, 200
Downie, Robert, 124, 125, 200
Doyle, Martin, 20, 135, 136, 201
Doyle, Father Willie, 181, 182, 183
Drogheda, 11, 105, 106, 107, 130
Drogheda Independent, 11
Drominagh, 159
Dromkeen, 36

Drum, 82
Drumcondra, 83, 132
Druminargal, 25
Druminargal House, 25n
Drumlea, 44
Duane, John, 46, 54, 201
Dublin, 27, 30, 34, 37, 40, 44, 52, 56, 59,
  60, 62, 64, 67, 73, 75, 77, 81n, 82, 87,
  94, 98, 99, 123, 125, 126n, 134, 136,
  175
Dublin, County, 61, 83, 84, 89
Dublin Metropolitan Police, 32
Dufferin Hall, 116
Duffy, James, 130, 131, 201
Duffy, Thomas, 52, 201
Duleek, 75
Dunalley, Lord, 113
Dundee, 56
Dundalk, 187
Dundonald, Lord, 93
Dungannon, 51, 109
Dunkirk, 147, 148
Dun Laoghaire, 84, 154
Dunlay, John, 55, 201
Dunlea/Dunley, John, *see* Dunlay, John
Dunn, Alexander Roberts, 31, 81, 202
Dunn, James, 41
Dunville, John Danville, 126
Dunville, John Spencer, 126, 202
Dunville Park, 126
Durand, A.G.A., 77, 78
Durham, County, 185
Dwyer, Edward, 184
Dwyer, John James, 184
Dynan, Denis, *see* Dynon, Denis
Dynon, Denis, 54, 202

Eastbourne, 37
East India Company, 19, 42, 46, 51, 59,
  63, 65, 72
East Sussex, 134
Edinburgh, 46, 68
Edward VII, King, 92, 100
Edwards, Frederick Jeremiah, 122,
  123, 202
Egan, John, 41
Egypt, 21, 87, 90, 98, 114, 118
El Adem, 156
El Duda, 156, 157, 158
Elandsfontein, 86

Elandslaagte, 92, 99
Elcock, Luke J., 106
Elouges, 104
Elphin, 27, 62n
Emerson, James Samuel, 129, 130, 203
England, 37, 47, 77, 81, 87, 110, 115, 137
English channel, 160, 162
English, William John, 98, 203
Ennis, 136
Enniskillen, 11, 38, 44, 93, 117, 125
Erasmus, Commandant, 99
Erie, Fort, 76
Eritrea, 87
Erskine, Ensign, 50
Ervine-Andrews, *see* Andrews
Eshowe, 84
Esmonde, Revd Donald, 164
Esmonde, Eily, 164
Esmonde, Eugene, 12, 158, 159, 160,
  161, 162, 163, 164, 170, 203
Esmonde, John, 159
Esmonde, Owen, 164
Esmonde, Patrick, 164
Esmonde, Thomas, 38, 159, 203
Essex Regimental Gazette, 29
Essigny, 132
Estaires, 101
Evans, Private, 26
Eyre, Canon Richard Booth, 133
Eyre, Sara, 133
Eyrecourt, 45, 133

Fakir, Mad, 79, 80
Falkland Islands, 115, 173
Far East, 171
Farrell, John, 30, 31, 204
Fauqissart, 101
Fegen, Edward Stephen Fogarty, 149,
  150, 151, 152, 153, 154, 170, 204
Fegen, Miss M. C., 153
Fenian Brotherhood, 75
Fenwick, Sir John, 154n
Fermanagh, County, 44, 48, 56, 60, 82,
  93, 106, 133
Fermoy, 65, 68
Ferozopore, 47
Fianna, 75
Fife, Admiral James, 171, 173
Finch, Private George, 29
Fingoes, 82

Finisterre, Cape, 35
Finland Gulf of, 23
First World War, 141
Fisher, John, 40
Fitzclarence, Charles, 91, 92, 204
Fitzgerald, Richard, 53, 204
Fitzgibbon, Andrew, 73, 205
Fitzgibbon, Elizabeth, 73
Fitzgibbon, William, 73
Fitzmaurice, Sergeant, 85
Fitzpatrick, Francis, 85, 205
Flawn, Private, 86
Fleet Air Arm, 12, 159, 160
Flinn, Thomas, 58, 73, 205
Folkestone, 33, 87
Foote, John Weir, 187, 205
Forsyth, Mr J., 29
Forrest, George, 44, 205
Fort McLeod, 125
Fowler, Edmund, 85, 206
France, 21, 22, 35, 36, 37, 40, 100, 101,
    107, 113, 120, 121, 123, 124, 127, 132,
    133, 136, 138, 143, 144, 148, 161, 185
Franco-Prussian war, 75
Fraser, Ian, 171, 172
Freemantle, 120
French, Major-General Johnnie, later
    Lord French, 92
French, Maurice, 176, 177
Frezenberg Ridge, 182
Frontier Armed Mounted Police, 82
Frontier Light Horse, 85
Fugitives' Drift, 83
Fulham, 185
Furphy, Colour Sergeant, 41
Futterbad, 69

Galekas, 82
Galghoek, 146
Gallaugher, Henry, 174, 175
Gallipoli, 90, 110, 111, 112, 113
Gandhi, Mohandas K., 94
Galway, County, 27, 39, 45, 47, 55, 87,
    99, 133
Gardiner, George, 35, 206
Gare, Corporal, 157
Garland, Donald Edward, 143, 144,
    145, 146, 153, 206
Garvin, Stephen, 46, 206
Gaulstown, 102

Gaza, 130
Gdansk/Gdynia, 150
Geluk, 96
George V, King, 12, 103, 109, 112, 114,
    115, 118, 119, 121, 122, 125, 126, 127,
    128, 133, 136, 138, 235
George VI, King, 15, 146, 153
Germany, 139, 140, 143, 144
Gheluvelt, 105
Ghlin bridge, 102
Giant's Causeway, 117, 118
Gibaut, Lieutenant, 54
Gibraltar, 55, 159
Gibraltar Chronicle, 55
Giese, Private, 82
Gill, Peter, 44, 206-7
Gillingham, 164
Gladstone, W. E., 87
Glasgow, 106, 124, 125
Glasgow Weekly News, 182
Glasnevin, 175
Gleave, Tom, 163, 164
Glenageary, 154
Glenavy, 56
Glinn, Sergeant, 54
Godley, Sidney Frank, 103
Goff, Ion, 178
Gorakphur, 61
Gordon, Charles 'Chinese', 87
Gore Browne, Henry George, 51, 207
Gort, 55
Gorteen la Poer, 58
Gough, Charles John Stanley, 57, 58,
    100, 207
Gough, Hubert, 100
Gough, Hugh, 57, 58, 70, 100, 207
Gough, John Edmund, 58, 100, 101,
    207
Grady, Thomas, 27, 28, 207, 237-8
Graham, Sir James, 24
Graham, Patrick, 56, 208
Grant, Sir Hope, 72
Grant, Peter, 56, 208
Gravenstafel, 110
Gray, Sergeant Thomas, 145, 146
Great Battery, the, 29
Great Chart, 85
Great Culverden, 25
Great War, 17, 90, 102-140, 143, 148,
    149, 174

Green, Patrick, 47, 48, 60, 208
Greenhill Battery, 34
Grenfell, Lieutenant, 90
Griffin, Second-Lieutenant, 147
Griffiths, William, 77, 208
Groagie, 132
Grogan, George William St George, 133
Guerin, Eileen, 124
Guernsey, 11, 93
Guillemont, 121, 122
Gulf War, 94
Gurna Bay, 176
Gustav line, 178, 179
Guyencourt, 125
Gwalior, 61
Gweedore, 131

Hackett, Robert Henry, 57
Hackett, Thomas Bernard, 57, 209
Hackett-Payne, Brigadier, 130
Hackney, 59, 114
Halifax, 149, 153
Hall, Captain, 24
Hall, Frederick, 109
Hall, Frederick William, 109, 110, 120, 209
Hall, Mary Ann, 110
Hamble, 143, 168
Hamilton, 46
Hamilton Harbour, Bermuda, 153
Hamilton, James John, 36
Hamilton, Lieutenant, 61
Hamilton, Thomas de Courcy, 36, 209
Hamilton, Walter Richard Pollock, 69, 70, 209
Hampshire, 149
Hancock, Trooper, 45
Hancocks, 18
Hanks, Tom, 118
Hanna, Robert Hill, 127, 210
Hardcastle, Ian, 63
Hardy, Fusilier, 177
Harold's Cross, 37
Harris, Mrs Webber, 186-7
Harrison, John, 56, 210
Harrogate, 77
Hart, Major-General, 93
Hart, Reginald Clare, 69, 210
Hartigan, Henry, 44, 45, 210
Harvey Grammar School, Folkestone, 98

Harvey, Reverend David, 125
Harvey, Frederick Maurice Watson, 125, 126, 210-11
Haslingen, 95
Hassan, Mohamed-bin-Abdullah, 101
Hastings, 78, 134n
Havelock, Sir Henry, 49, 50, 61
Hawkes, Private, 59
Hawthorne, Robert, 48, 211
Hearn, Olive Margaret, 167
Heart, Afghanistan, 66
Heath's plantation, 165, 166
Helstone, Sergeant, 44
Henry VIII, King, 82
Herefordshire, 74
Hermies, 185
Highland Ridge, 129
Hickie, William, 181
High Seas Fleet, 115
Hildyard, Major-General, 93
Hill, Samuel, 56, 211
Hindu Kush, 79
Hiran Khana, 50
Hiroshima, 172
Hitler, Adolf, 140, 143, 160
Hlangwane, Mount, 93
Hlobane, 84
Hobart, 122
Holland, Edward James Gibson, 96, 211
Holland, John Vincent, 122, 211
Hong Kong, 147, 171
Holy Places, 21
Holywood Parish Church, 126
Holy Rosary Cathedral, 127
Home Guard, 114
Home Park, 47
Home, Surgeon, 52
Horse Guards, 40
Horsham, 60
House, William, 211-12
Hughes CSM, 157
Hughes, Thomas, 121, 122, 212
Huirangi Bush, 74
Hull, 97
Hume, Andrew, 76
Hunza, 77, 78
Hyde Park, 18, 25, 29, 122

Imperial Airways, 159
Imperial Japanese Army, 165

Imperial Order of Daughters of the
  Empire, 63
Inchigeela, 107, 108
India, 31, 36, 42, 44, 47, 48, 53, 56, 58,
  65, 68, 71, 72, 77, 80, 82, 89, 92, 94, 96,
  100, 110, 112, 136, 141, 167, 175, 185
Indian Army, 67, 78, 122, 141
  Army Service Corps, 98
  Empire, 21
  Expeditionary Force, 131
  Medical Estab/Service, 73, 78, 131, 141
  Mutiny, 19, 27, 36, 38, 39, 42-65, 66,
  100, 186, 187, 235
Indore, 50
Inislonagh, 58
Inkerman, 32, 33, 36
Inkson, Edgar Thomas, 113n
International Brigade, 124
IRA, 20, 131, 136
Irby, Captain, 56
Ireland, 37, 47, 49, 52, 60, 65, 75, 80, 86,
  87, 89, 92, 99, 117, 124, 131, 154, 167,
  173, 185
Irish Free State Army, 124, 136
Irish Republican Army, 75
Irish Soldier, 133
Irish Sword, 12
Irrawaddy Flotilla Company, 67
Irwin, Charles, 56, 212, 235
Isandhlwana, 77, 83, 84, 85
Isle of Wight, 51, 54, 168
Italy, 69, 123, 177, 183

Jackman, James Joseph Bernard, 154,
  155, 156, 157, 158, 212
Jackman, Dr J. J., 154
Jackman, Mrs, 154
Jamaica, 32
James II, King, 154n
James, Frederick Humphrey, 186
Jameson Raid, 90
Jammu, 73
Japan, 165, 170
Jefferson, Fusilier Francis, 179
Jellallabad, 57
Jellicoe, Admiral, 115
Jennings, Edward, 55, 212
Jensen's plantation, 165
Jerome, Captain, 60
Jerusalem, 114

Jhansi, 60
Johnston, Robert, 92, 213
Johore strait, 19, 170, 171, 172
Jones, Henry Mitchell, 37, 212
Jones, Robert James Thomas Digby, 95,
  96
Jugdispore, 50
Jumna river, 43
Jutland, battle of, 115, 116

Kaafjord, 170
Kabul, 68, 69
Kabul gate, 48
Kaipakopako, 74
Kakamega, 164
Kam Dakka, 70
Kandahar, 68, 71
Kandy, 139
Karachi, 58
Karenni, 67
Kashkai Regiment, 66
Kashmir, 77
Kashmir Gate, 48
Kassala, 81, 88
Kavanagh, Thomas Henry, 19, 54, 55,
  213
Keadue, 146
Keady, 178
Keane, John, 28
Keatinge, Richard Harte, 59, 60, 213
Kelleher, Father Dan, 183
Kelliher, Richard, 164, 165, 166, 167,
  173, 213-14
Kellon, James, 64
Kelly, Charles, 123
Kelly, Henry, 123, 214
Keneally, John, 110, 214
Keneally, William, 110, 111
Kenna, Edward, 185
Kenna, James, 89
Kenna, Paul Aloysius, 89, 90, 214
Kenneally, John Patrick, 186
Kennedy, Charlotte, 136
Kenny, Henry Edward, 114, 115, 214
Kenny, James, 185
Kenny, Thomas, 185
Kenny, Thomas James Bede, 185
Kenny, William, 11, 12, 105, 106, 107, 215
Kenny, William David, 141, 142, 143,
  215

Kensal Rise, 27, 84, 100
Kensington, 143
Kent, 25, 27, 85, 89, 138, 161, 164
Kenya, 164
Kereina peak, 130
Kerr, John C., 127
Kerry County, 39, 88, 124, 139, 164, 168, 183
Kerseleare, 185
Kewanie, 63
Khalifa, the (*see also* Abdullah el-Taaishi), 87, 88, 89
Khan, Nazim, 78
Khan, Roopur, 45
Khan, Safdar Ali, 78
Khan, Zafar, 78
Khartoum, 87, 88
Khodagunge, 59
Khurkowdah, 57
Khyber pass, 68, 73
Kilcock, 78
Kildare County, 37, 49, 78, 91, 96, 122
Kilkeel, 127
Kilkenny, 32, 53, 92, 97, 109, 136
Kilkenny County, 49, 69
Killa Kazi, 71
Killala, 54
Killashandra, 62
Kilmannon, 54
Kimberley, 91, 93
King, Harry, 168
King's County, 37, 57, 115
Kingsmill, Charles, 162, 163
Kingstown, 84
Kinsale, 34, 109
Kipling, Rudyard, 67
Kippax, Herb, 63
Kitchener, General Herbert, 88, 89, 90
Knocklong, 35
Kokoda trail, 165
Komgha, 82
Konoma, 77
Koodsia Bagh, the, 47
Kooer Singh, 61
Koosh-ab, 66
Kordofan, 89
Korean War, 173
Kosovo, 173
Kot Kai, 141
Krancke, Theodor, 150, 151, 153

Kriegsmarine, 160, 164
Kronstadt, 23, 139
Kruiseecke, 105
Kumaon Battalion, 73
Kurram valley, 68
Kut el Amara, 131
Kuthirga, 62
Kyleballuhue House, 30

La Bassée canal, 106, 113
La Brique, 115
La Houssoie, 185
La Pallice, 161
Ladysmith, and siege of, 91, 92, 94, 95, 99
Lae, 165, 166
Laing's Nek, 86, 87
Lambert, George, 50, 215
Lancashire, 15, 95, 110
Lancaster, 89
Lancaster Priory, 28
Lane, Able Seaman, 151
Lane, Thomas, 72, 215, 235, 237
Langemarck, battle of, 181
Laois County, 128
Laputa house, 92
Laughlin, Thomas, *see* Laughnan, Thomas
Laughnan, Thomas, 55, 215-16
Lawrence, Sir Henry, 54
Lawrence, Samuel Hill, 49, 216
Leach, Edward Pemberton, 69, 216
Leach, James, 20
Ledgehem, 137
Lee, Edgar, 163
Lee-on-Solent, 159, 164
Leeds, 77
Leet, William Knox, 85, 216
Lehman, 127
Leichardt expedition, 76
Leitrim County, 56
Lendrim, William James, 33, 216
Lens, 127
Le Pontchu, 132
Leros, 176, 177
Le Sars, 123
Lesboeufs, 124
Leslie, Sir Shane, 25
Letpan, 168
Le Transloy, 124

Letterkenny, 130, 131, 174
Levita, 176
Lewin, Lieutenant F. R. A., 94
Libya, 154, 155
Lichfield, 58
Liffey, river, 90
Lifford, 35
Limerick, 59, 72, 86, 126
Limerick County, 35, 36, 114
Lion and The Dragon, The, 237
Lisburn, 34, 131
Lisnadill, 38
Listowel, 39
Liverpool, 37, 49, 117, 122, 131, 186
Lloyd, Captain Derek, 157
Lloyd, Owen Edward Pennefather, 68, 217
London, 18, 27, 29, 32, 34, 35, 38, 40, 61, 71, 88, 98, 103, 106, 112, 114, 116, 119, 128, 131, 136, 150, 167, 184
London, Ontario, 63
Londonderry, 36, 52, 69
Londonderry County, 48, 52
London Gazette, 17, 21, 40, 47, 60, 63, 77, 80, 95, 100, 105, 116, 122, 128, 130, 132, 137, 139, 146, 153, 164, 167, 173
Long, Colonel C. J., 93
Longford, 62, 65, 84
Loos, 114
Lord, David, 12, 167, 168, 217
Lorrha, and abbey, 120, 121
Louth County, 11, 66, 105, 130
Lower Rhine, 167
Lucas, Charles Davis, 15, 18, 19, 24, 25, 217
Lucas, John, 74, 217
Lucknow, 19, 27, 49, 49, 50, 51, 52, 53, 54, 55, 56, 57, 59, 62, 167, 185
Lucknow Residency, 50, 51
Luftwaffe, 148, 164, 170
Lummis, Canon E. M., MC, 13
Lurgan, 37, 117
Lushington, Captain, 28
Luxembourg, 144
Lwekaw, 67
Lydenburg, 86
Lyons, John, 37, 217-18
Lyster, Harry Hammond, 61, 218

McCarthy-O'Leary, Donagh, 175, 176
McClure, Ernest, 175
McConaghy, David, 118
McCorrie, or McCurry, Charles, 38, 218
McCourt, Bernard, 58, 218
McCudden, James Thomas Byford, 138, 218
McCudden, William Henry, 138
Macdiarmid, Hugh, 138
McFadzean, William Frederick, 117, 218-19
McFadzean, William, 117
McGarry, Jane, 123
McGovern, John, 46, 219
McGowan, John, *see* McGovern, John
McGuire, James, 48, 219, 235, 237
McHale, Patrick, 54, 219
McIntosh, Pilot Officer I. A., 145
McKay, Sergeant D., 156, 157
McLaughlin, Daniel, 64
McManus, Peter, 53, 219
McMaster, Valentine Munbee, 51, 220
McNaghten, 63
Macnaghten, Douglas, 119
Macnaghten, Sir Harry, 118, 119
McNamara, Frank Hubert, 138
McQuirt, Bernard, *see* McCourt, Bernard, 58, 220
McWheeney, *see* Mawhinney
McWhiney, *see* Mawhinney
Macroom, 107
Madden, Ambrose, 32, 220
Madras, 42
 Army, 45
Mafeking, 91, 100
Magdala, 81
Magennis, James Joseph, 19, 170, 171, 172, 173, 220
Maghera, 48
Magner, Michael, 82, 220
Magwe Battalion, 68
Mahdi, the, 87
Mahoney, Patrick, 52, 53, 220-1
Mahsuds, 141, 142
Maidanah, 69
Maidstone, 25
Maiwand, 71
Majuba Hill, 86
Malakand, 78, 79, 80

Malakand Field Force, 80
Malakoff redoubt, 30, 39
Malcolmson, Lieutenant, 66
Malone, Trooper, 31
Malone, Riding Master, 52
Malta, 11, 38, 39, 105, 111, 159, 176
Maltby, Admiral, 149
Manchester, 123, 124
Manitoba, 110
Manley, William George Nicholas, 75, 221
Mannock, Edward 'Mick', 137, 138, 221
Manorcunningham, 174
Manorhamilton, 56
Manston, 161
Maori war, 73, 74
Marcoing, 129
Mardan, 70
Markethill, 50
Markham Point, 167
Marland, Sergeant Fred, 145
Marlborough, duke of, 26
Marne, the, 114
Marquise, 138
Martin, Rowland Hill, 88
Massawa, 81
Masters, John, 180, 181
Masterson, James Edward Ignatius, 95, 96, 221
Masterson, Sergeant Patrick, 95
Maude, Francis Cornwallis, 38
Maude, Frederick Francis, 38, 221
Maude, Sir Stanley, 38
Mawhinney, William, 28, 29, 222, *see also* McWheeney
Maxwell, Colonel, 122
Mayo County, 46, 54, 55
Meath County, 36, 75, 77, 89, 125
Medway, 164
Meeangunge, 57
Meerut, 43, 56
Meiklejohn, Brigadier-General, 80
Melbourne, 82, 167
Melvill, Teignmouth, 83
Menin Gate, 92
Menin Gate Memorial, 110
Menin Road, 105
Menschikoff, Prince, 25, 26, 29
Merchant Navy, 98
Mereworth, 25

Merrion, 27
Merritt, C. C., 127
Mesopotamia, 38, 118, 131, 141
Messines, 108, 174, 175
Mhow, 52
Middle East, 164, 165
Midleton Park, 114
Milan, 30
Military Historical Society, 13
Military History Society of Ireland, 12
Milne Bay, 165
Milner, Sir Alfred, 99
Mindon, King, 67
Minha, 67
Mirat, 50
Modreeny, 113
Moffatt, Martin, 137, 222, 237, 239
Moldavia, 21, 23
Molyneux, the Hon. R. F., 89
Monaghan County, 25, 75, 86, 97, 104, 121
Monegal, 37
Monmouth's rebellion, 154n
Monmouthshire, 33
Mons, 102, 103, 104, 114
Montauban, General de, 72
Monte Cassino, 177, 179, 183
Montevideo, 49
Montmorency, Lieutenant de, 90
Montreal, 37, 76
Monument Hill, 96
Moore, Arthur Thomas, 66, 222
Moore, Garrett, 82
Moore, Hans Garrett, 82, 222
Moore, Ross, 66
Morar, 44
Morrow, Mrs Margaret Jane, 109
Morrow, Robert, 108, 109, 222-3
Morton, Captain, 68
Mottistone, 168
Mouquet Farm, 121
Moyney, John, 127, 128, 223
Moynihan, Andrew, 39, 223
Mullaghbrack, 50, 85
Mullah, Mad, the, 101
Mullane, Patrick, 71, 223
Mullingar, 19, 54
Mullins, Captain, 92
Mullins, Sergeant, 54
Mullins, Private, 54
Mungulwar, 52

Murree, 100
Murphy, Michael, 61, 223, 235, 237
Murphy, Thomas, 77, 223-4
Murray, James, 86, 87, 224
Murray, John, 33
Murray, Sergeant John, 75, 224
Musicians' Company, 106
Mylott, Patrick, 49, 224

Naas, 37
Nadzab, 165
Nagar, 77, 78
Nagasaki, 172
Napier, Sir Charles, 23, 24, 25
Napier, Sir Robert, 81
Napoleon, Emperor, 22, 27
Napoleon III, Emperor, 21, 22
Nash, William, 59, 224
Natal, 83, 84, 86, 91, 92, 94
National Army Museum, London, 13, 80, 122
National University of Ireland, 124
National Volunteers, 107
NATO, 173
Nazi party, 143
Neder Rijn, 167
Nelson, David, 104, 105, 224-5
Nelson, Lord, 23
Nenagh, 102
Nery, 104, 105
Netherbury, 69
Netherlands, the, 144, 154n
Newbay, 176
New Guinea, 164, 165, 185
New Mills, 109
New Ross, 135, 136, 146
Newton Abbot, 105
Newtownards, 28, 95
Newtownbreda Presbyterian Church, 117
Newtownbutler, 56
New York, 23
New York Herald, 81
New Zealand, 32, 53, 73, 74, 76
New Zealand Expeditionary Force, 136
Ney Copse, 127
Niagara river, 76
Nicholas, Czar, 21, 23
Nicholson Memorial School, 131
Nijmegen, 167
Nile, river, 88

Nilt, 78
Nimy bridge, 102, 103
Nolan, Babington, 30
Nolan, Captain Lewis Edward, 30
North Cape, battle of, 171
Northern Ireland, 132, 170
North Queen Street Barracks, 52
North Shields, 55
North-West Frontier, 77, 78, 141, 147
Norway, 144, 160, 170
Nottingham, 115
Notting Hill, 27
Nourse's (Transvaal) Horse, 86
Nunney, Alfred, 135
Nunney, Claude Joseph Patrick, 134, 135, 225
Nurse, Charles George Colenso, 94
Nurse, George Edward, 11, 12, 93, 94, 225
Nurse, Stuart Colenso, 94

Oakfield house, 89
Oakham, 71
O'Brien, Daniel, 154n
O'Connor, Luke, 18, 25, 26, 27, 225
Offaly County, 75, 120n
O'Hea, Timothy, 76, 225-6
Olander, Sven, 152
Oldcastle, 77
O'Leary, Michael, 107, 226
Olpherts, Henry, 51
Olpherts, William, 51, 226
Olpherzen, General, 51
Omdurman, 88, 89, 90
O'Meara, Martin, 120, 121, 226
O'Moore, Rory, 82
Omdurman, 88
O'Neill, Captain John, 150, 152
O'Neill, John, 76
Onions, George, 20
Ontario, 46, 63, 96
Oosterbeek, 167
Operations:
    CEREBUS, 160, 161
    CRUSADER, 154, 156
    DIADEM, 177
    HONKER, 177
    JUBILEE, 187
    MARKET GARDEN, 167
    MICHAEL, 132, 175

NICKEL, 144
SICHELSCHNITT, 144
SOURCE, 170
Opium War, 72
Orah ruins, 131, 132
Orange Free State, 91, 93
Orange Order, 127
Orange River Colony, 100
O'Rourke, Michael James, 126, 226
Osman Digna, 87, 88
O'Sullivan, Gerald Robert, 112, 113, 226
Ottoman empire, 21
Ottawa, 96
Oudh, 52, 61, 62, 185
Oughterard, 45
Outram, Sir James, 52, 62, 66
Owens, James, 32, 227
Owen Stanley mountains, 165
Oxfordshire, 46

Pagan, King, 67
Palestine, 21, 130
Palmerston, Lord, 22
Pandeli Bay, 176
Pandy, Mangal, 43
Panmure, Lord, 16
Papua, 165
Paris, 39, 84, 104
Park, John, 36, 227
Pearson, James, 60, 227
Pearl Harbor, 164
Peel, Captain, 56
Pegu, 67
Peiho river, 72
Peirse, Sir Richard, 160
Peiwar Kotal, 68
Peninsular War, 33
Pentonville Gaol, 235
Penzance, 47
Persia, and Shah of, 66
Persian War, 52, 66
Perth, 121
Peshawar, 45, 69, 79
Phillips auctioneers, 44
Pickard, A.F., 74
Pignataro, 178
Pillinger, Dennis, 13
Plaistow, 71
Plumstead, 34
Plunket, John, third Baron, 83

Polygon Wood, 92
Pomeroy-Colley, Sir George, 86
Pontoko, 74
Poona, 82
Portadown, 119
Port Neuf, 39
Portora Royal School, 125
Portsmouth, 34
Potchefstroom, 86
Power, Harriette, 58
Poyntz Pass, 25n
Pozieres, 120, 133
Pratt, Colonel A. C., 175
Prendergast, Major-General Harry, 67
Pretoria, 86, 91
Probyn, Dighton McNaghten, 63, 227
Prosser, Joseph, 37, 227
Prut, river, 23
Pryne Street School, 97
Pullein, Henry, 83
Purcell, John, 45, 228
Pyper, Mary Isabel, 98

Quarries, the, 28, 36, 37
Quebec, 51, 76
Queen's College, Belfast, 131
Queen's County, 54, 60, 82
Queensland, 164
Queenstown, 123
Quetta, 68
Quigg, Robert, 117, 118, 228

Racecourse Redoubt, 132
Raeder, Admiral, 160
Raglan, Lord, 22, 26, 30, 32
Ram, Dowlut, 69
Ram, Sepoy Kamal, 179
Rampore Kussiah, 36
Ramsay, Bertram, 161, 162, 163, 164
Ramsgate, 161, 162
Ramu valley, 167
Rangiriri, 74
Rangoon, 76
Rathdowney, 128
Rathronan House, 58
Rawalpindi, 69, 100
Raymond, Claud, 168, 169, 228
Raynor, William, 44
Redan, the, 27, 30, 34, 35, 36, 37, 38, 39
Red Fort, the, 43

Red Sea, 81, 100
Reed, Sir Andrew, 94
Reed, Andrew Patrick, 94
Reed, Hamilton Lyster, 61, 94, 228
Regan, Michael, 28n
Regan, Patrick, 28n
Rees, Lieutenant, 74
Regiments:
British
2nd Life Gds, 122
1st R. Dgns, 126
Household Cavalry Regt, 126
1st Dgn Gds, 86, 87, 155
2nd Dgn Gds (Queen's Bays), 98, 104, 185
Carabiniers, 43
4th (R. Irish) Dgn Gds, 102
4th Queen's Own Lt Dgns, 30
5th Dgn Gds, 92, 104, 137
5th (R. Irish) Lancers, 92
6th (Inniskilling) Dgns, 52
7th Hussars, 61
8th (King's R. Irish) Hussars, 30, 61, 62, 89, 129
9th (Queen's R.) Lancers, 44, 45, 53, 71, 85, 104
11th Prince Albert's Own Hussars, 30, 31, 104
13th Lt Dgns, 30, 31
14th Lt Dgns/King's Hussars, 66, 96
15th Hussars, 114
16th/5th Lancers, 178, 179
17th Lancers, 30, 31, 61
18th Hussars, 31
21st Hussars/Lancers, 88, 89, 90
Queen's R. Lancers, 90
North Irish Horse, 133
Scottish Horse, 98
Warwickshire Yeo, 114
101st Regt, R. Arty, 55
Coldstream Gds, 32, 106, 107
Scots Fus Gds/Scots Gds, 38, 113
Irish Gds, 94, 106, 107, 127, 128, 173, 186
1st, or Royal, 37, 75
3rd (East Kent - The Buffs), 38, 39
4th (King's Own), 28
King's Own, 176, 177, 237, 238
King's Own R. Border Regt, 237
Monk's/5th Regt, 154n

Northumberland Fusiliers (later R. Northumberland Fus), 53, 54, 112, 154, 155, 158
Tyneside Irish, 185
R. Regt of Fus, 103
7th (R. Fus), 37
R. Fus, 91, 102, 103, 119, 123
8th (The King's), 39
10th (N. Lincolnshire), 50, 65
Devonshire Regt, 95, 96
13th (1st Somersetshire) (Prince Albert's LI), 60, 85
Somerset LI, 85
W. Yorkshire Regt, 78, 97, 115
17th (Leicestershire), 37
18th (R. Irish), 38,
R. Irish Regt, 85, 96, 97, 110, 136, 185
19th (1st Yorkshire, N Riding), 37
Lancashire Fus, 110, 111, 178, 179
21st (R. Scots Fus), 86
R. Scots Fus, 102
Cheshire Regt, 124, 129
23rd (R. Welch Fus), 25, 27, 57
R. Welsh Fus, 167
24th (2nd Warwickshire), 76, 77, 83, 84, 85
King's Own Scottish Borderers, 111
27th (Inniskilling), 113n
R. Innisk Fus, 65, 112, 113, 117, 129, 130, 131, 137, 174, 175, 177, 178
R. Irish Regt, 173
Gloucestershire, 120
30th (Cambridgeshire), 33, 39
E. Lancashire, 146, 147
E. Surrey, 109, 184
32nd (The Cornwall), 49, 51
33rd (Duke of Wellington's), 81, 82
Duke of Wellington's, 123, 124
34th (Cumberland), 35, 36, 63
37th (N. Hampshire), 44
Hampshire, 111, 179
38th, 82
40th (2nd Somersetshire), 74
S. Lancashire, 109
41st (The Welsh), 32
Black Watch, 155
43rd (Monmouthshire LI), 75
44th (E. Essex), 28, 72
Essex, 156, 157
Loyal N. Lancs, 114

49th (Princess of Wales's)
Hertfordshire, 31, 32
52nd (Oxfordshire LI), 48
53rd (Shropshire), 53, 54, 56, 185
55th, 40, 41, 174
57th (W. Middlesex), 35, 38, 74
Middlesex, 35, 102, 107, 122, 123
58th (Rutlandshire), 86
60th Rifles, 43, 46, 235
Manchester Regt, 95, 124
64th (2nd Staffordshire), 58
65th (2nd Yorkshire, N. Riding), 74
67th (S. Hampshire), 72, 73, 235, 236
68th (Durham LI), 32, 33, 36
Durham LI, 185
75th, 36, 45, 46, 47, 75
77th (E. Middlesex), 35, 36
78th (Highland), also Ross-Shire Buffs, 51, 52
82nd (Prince of Wales's Volunteers), 35, 36, 64
84th (York and Lancaster) 49, 50, 54
York and Lancaster, 115, 156
Cameron Hldrs, 124
86th (R. County Down), 60, 65
R. Irish/R. Ulster Rifles, 94, 98, 117, 129, 132, 133, 175
87th (R. Irish Fus), 56, 95, 235
Princess Victoria's (R. Irish Fus), 95, 108, 109, 119, 120, 132, 175, 181
R. Irish Fus, 176, 177, 183
88th (Connaught Rgrs), 86
Connaught Rgrs, 82, 107, 121, 122, 137
89th, 40
90th Perthshire LI, 38, 39, 51, 52, 56, 57, 85
92nd (Gordon Hldrs), 70, 113n
Gordon Hldrs, 11, 105, 113n
93rd Highlanders, 30, 55, 56
94th, 82, 85, 86
95th (Derbyshire), 58, 62
99th (Lanarkshire), 28n
Leinster Regt, 65, 108, 122, 125, 128, 137, 186
104th Bengal Fus, 186
R. Munster Fus, 65, 111, 135, 136, 186
R. Dublin Fus, 65, 111, 124, 136, 181
Rifle Brigade, 36, 59, 76, 100, 119
R. Green Jackets, 47
Liverpool Scottish, 132

London Irish Rifles, 177, 178, 179
Westmeath Militia, 100
Donegal Militia, 31n
2nd Bn, Military Train, 61, 235, 236
Canadian
R. Can Dgns, 96
Lord Strathcona's Horse, 125
8th Manitoba Bn, 110
31st Bn (Calgary Regt), 133
38th Bn (Eastern Ontario Regt), 134, 135
80th Bn, 135
106th Bn, CEF
British Columbia Regt, 126, 127
Irish Fus of Canada, 185
Australian
2nd (New South Wales) Bn, 185
16th (S. Australia and W. Australia) Bn, 120, 121
2/12th, 164
2/24th (NSW) Bn, 185
2/25th (Queensland) Bn, 164, 165, 166, 167
New Zealand
2nd Bn, Auckland Infantry, 136
East India Company/Indian
Central India Horse, 50
2nd Light Cavalry, 31
2nd Punjab Cavalry, 63
3rd Bengal European Cavalry, 90n
3rd Light Cavalry, 43
3rd Bombay Light Cavalry, 66
3rd Sikh Cavalry, 61
4th Irregular Cavalry, 45
10th Bengal Lancers, 70
13th Bengal Lancers, 69
Guides Cavalry, 57, 69, 70
Hodson's Horse, 57
Mead's Horse, 45
Poona Irregular Horse, 66
Probyn's Horse (5th King Edward VII's Own Horse), 63
Scinde Irregular Horse, 66
1st Bengal Fus, 46, 48, 235, 236
1st Madras Fus, 52, 53
1st Native Infantry, 52
2nd Bengal Native Infantry, 50
3rd Bombay Europeans, 186
3rd Gurkha Rifles, 73
4th Madras Rifles, 60

Regiments: *Indian (continued)*
8th Native Infantry, 62
15th Ludhiana Sikhs, 44
19th Infantry, 43
22nd Punjab, 78
24th Punjab, 79
27th Infantry, 44
27th Bombay Infantry, 67
34th Infantry, 43
39th Garhwal Rifles, 141, 142
44th Gurkha Rifles, 77
45th Sikhs, 69
Ramgurh Bn, 53
Pakistan Army
5th Horse, 63
Others
Imperial Light Horse, 92, 95, 96, 99
Protectorate Regt, 91
S. African Scottish Regt, 99
West India Regt, 89
Reincourt, 135
Renmore Barracks, 99
Revel, 23, 24
Rewa, 58
Reynolds, James, 84, 228
Reynolds, Leading Aircraftman L. R.,
145, 146
Richards, Corporal W. H., 166
Richardson, Anne, 62
Richardson, George, 62, 63, 229
Richardson, John, 62
Richmond, 123
Ridgeway, Richard Kirby, 77, 229
Rigby, Maurice, 37
Ripon, Marquess of, 71
Robarts, Gunner, 34
Roberts, Sir Abraham, 59
Roberts, Frederick Sleigh, later Field
Marshal Earl Roberts of Kandahar and
Waterford, 58, 68, 69, 91, 93, 97, 229
Roberts, Lieutenant Freddy, 93, 94,
229
Roberts, John, 58, 59
Robinson, Leslie, 186
Roddy, Patrick, 62, 229
Rogers, Robert Montressor, 72, 73, 230
Rohilcund, 52
Rohtuk, 57
Rolland, Captain George, 101
Romania, 21n

Rorke's Drift, 84
Roscrea, 128
Roscommon County, 25, 62n, 68, 77, 95n
Rose, Sir Hugh, 50
Rosses Point, 137
Ross-Shire Buffs, the, *see* 78th (Highland)
Regiment
Roupell, George Patrick Rowland,
109, 230
Royal Air Force (RAF), 15, 17, 94, 95,
143, 146, 148, 159, 168
Royal Army Medical Corps (RAMC), 84,
99, 115, 132, 180
Royal Artillery, 51, 55, 74, 75, 93, 94,
103, 186
Royal Belfast Academical Institution, 131
Royal College of Surgeons, Dublin, 99
Royal Corps of Transport, 61
Royal Engineers, Corps of, 33, 69, 77, 95,
126, 168
Royal Field Artillery, 11, 93, 104, 105
Royal Flying Corps, 138
Royal Garrison Artillery, 123
Royal Hibernian Military School, 123
Royal Horse Artillery, 71, 104, 114
Royal Irish Constabulary, 20, 38, 94
Royal Irish University, 68
Royal Logistic Corps Museum, 61
Royal Marines, 19, 115
Royal Military College, Sandhurst, 89,
100, 102, 154
Royal Naval College, Greenwich, 140
Royal Navy, 15, 16, 17, 18, 19, 27, 28,
34, 56, 63, 107, 115, 139, 153, 160, 162,
163, 170, 176
Royal Navy Division, 185
Royal North-West Mounted Police, 107,
125
Royal Regiment of Artillery, also Royal
Artillery, 34
Royal Sappers and Miners, Corps of, 33,
48, 60
Royal School, Dungannon, 51
Royal Signals, 94
Royal Society, the, 132
Royal Star and Garter Home, 123
Royal Victoria Hospital, Belfast, 126, 131
Ruiters' Kraal, 99
Rutlandshire, 71
Russell, William Howard, 40

Russia, 21, 22, 132
Ryan, James, 41
Ryan, John, 53, 230
Ryan, John, 74, 230
Ryan, Mike, 84
Ryan, Miles, 48, 230

Saigon, 171
Sailors' Battery, 28
Saint Arnaud, General, 26
Saint Benedict, monastery of, 177
Saint Columb's cathedral, Londonderry, 52
Saintfield, 141
Saint Gerard's School, Bray, 154
Saint Helena, 27
Saint Helen's, 110
Saint James's Palace, 92, 100
Saint Julien, 110
Saint Lawrence's church, Merewath, 25
Saint Leonard's-on-Sea, 68
Saint Mary's Cathedral, Hobart, 122
Saint Mary's Cathedral, Wrexham, 12, 167
Saint Mary's church, Thurles, 52
Saint Nazaire, 161
Saint Patrick, Order of, 16
Saint Patrick's School, Manchester, 124
Saint Paul's Cathedral, 35
Saint Petersburg, 23
Saint Pius X's church, 164
Saint Symphorien, 103
Salkeld, Lieutenant, 48
Sammy House, the, 46
Sanctuary Wood, 109, 110
Sandhurst, 100, 106, 122
Sandringham, 118
Sandyford, 123
Sangor, 50
Sardinia, 34
Scarriff, 69
Scheer, Admiral, 115, 116
School of Gunnery, 104, 105
Scobie, Major-General, 155
Scotland, 25, 36
Scott, Robert, 20, 95, 231
Scott, Major, 45
Scottish National Museum, 46
Searles, Geoffrey, 178
Second World War, 12, 64, 120, 132, 141, 146, 148, 167, 173, 174, 181, 183, 186

Secunderabad, 31
Secundra Bagh, the, 55, 56, 57, 185
Sedd-el-Bahr, 111
Sekukuni, King, 86
Senafe, 31
Sevastopol, 18, 25, 26, 28, 29, 30, 31, 33, 34, 35, 37, 39, 40, 41, 238
Sewell, Lieutenant, 60
Shah Nujeff mosque, 56
Shahpuri Island, 67
Shalford, 109
Shanghai, 147
Shankland, Robert, 127
Sheffield, 50
Shell Hill, 36
Sherrard, Rev. William, 65
Ship Street Barracks, 40
Ships:
Australian
  HMAS *Ajana*, 120
British
  HMS *Ardent*, 34
  HMS *Ark Royal*, 159
  HMS *Captain*, 35
  HMS *Cornwall*, 139
  HMS *Daedalus* (shore base), 164
  HMS *Dorsetshire*, 139
  HMS *Emerald*, 149
  HMS *Hecla*, 24
  HMS *Jervis Bay*, 149, 150, 151, 152, 153, 170
  HMS *Kandahar*, 170
  HMS *Laforey*, 159
  HMS *Miranda*, 34
  HMS *Nestor*, 116
  HMS *Nicator*, 116
  HMS *Nomad*, 116
  HMS *Odin*, 24
  HMS *Shannon*, 56
  HMS *Shikari*, 148
  HMS *Swallow*, 34
  HMS *Valorous*, 24
  HMS *Victorious*, 159
  HM *Coastal* Motor-Boat No. 4, 139
  HM Sub. *Stubborn*, 170
  HM Sub. *Stygian*, 171, 172
  X6, 170
  X7, 170
  XE1, 171, 172
  XE3, 171, 172

Ships: *British (continued)*
  XE4, 171
  XE5, 171
German
  Admiral Scheer, 150, 151, 153
  Bismarck, 159, 161
  Gneisenau, 12, 160, 170
  Lutzow, 170
  Prinz Eugen, 12, 158, 160, 162, 163,
  170
  Scharnhorst, 12, 160, 161, 170, 171
  Tirpitz, 170, 171
Japanese
  Myoko, 171, 172
  Takao, 171, 172
Russian
  Andrei Pervozzani, 139
  Oleg, 139
  Petropavlosk, 139
Merchant
  Assam Valley, 76
  Beaverford, 153
  Cornish City, 149, 150, 152
  Empire Penguin, 149
  Fresno City, 153
  Kenbane Head, 153
  Khedive, 55
  Maidan, 153
  Mopan, 150
  Puck, 153
  River Clyde, 111
  San Demetrio, 153
  Stureholm, 152
  Trewellard, 153
Shoeburyness, 104
Shooja-ool-Moolk, 66
Shumshabad, 57
Sima post, 68
Simla, 44, 71
Sinagoga, 178, 179
Singapore, 19, 165, 170, 171
Singh, Subadar Matab, 68
Sinnott, John, 54, 231
Sinope, 22
Sinton, John Alexander, 131, 132, 231
Sinton, Isabella, 131
Sinton, Walker, 131
Sleavon, Michael, 60, 232
Sligo, 137, 237, 239
Smith, Frederick Augustus, 75, 231

Smith, Lieutenant, 85
Smith, Ernest, 127
Smith, Philip, 37, 38, 232
Smith-Dorrien, General, 97
Smithfield Market, Belfast, 29
Smyth, Sir John, 25, 141, 142, 147
Somaliland, 58, 100
Somers, James, 113, 232
Somerset, 68
Sorøy Sound, 170
Somme, battle of, 116, 119, 121, 174
Sotheby's, 29, 34, 61, 85, 92
South Africa, 73, 82, 87, 91, 92, 97, 98, 99
South African War, 113n, 133
South Wingate, 185
Spanish Civil War, 124
Spinks, 89
Squadrons:
RFC/RAF
  No. 1, 145
  No. 12, 143, 144, 146
  No.56, 138
  No. 72, 161
  No. 150, 144
  No. 271, 167
Fleet Air Arm
  No. 825, 159, 160, 162, 163, 170
Staff College, 40, 109
Stagpoole, Dudley, 74, 232
Stanley, Henry Morton, 81n
Star Fort, the, 30
Stewart, Sir Donald, 68
Stirk, Corporal, 115
Stoney, Captain, 111
Stonyhurst College, 14, 78, 80, 89, 102,
  103, 147, 154, 182, 183
Strachan, Harcus, 127
Stranraer, 36
Stubbs, Private, 111
Suakin, 87
Subzee Mundee, 46
Sudan, 81, 87
Sullivan, John, 34, 232
Sundeela, 185
Surgham, 88
Surrey, 11, 84, 85, 109, 115, 123
Sussex, 37, 60, 68, 71, 78
Suvla Bay, 90, 113
Swarbrick, Corporal, 90
Swat valley, 79, 80

Sweaborg, 23
Sweden, 23
Swift, Captain, 39, 74
Syria, 164

Ta Braxia, 39
Takapuna, 137
Taku forts, 29, 72
Talaku, 169
Talbot, Private, 74
Tank Corps, 133
Taranto, 161
Tarbert Fort, 34
Tasmania, 122, 185
Taungup, 168
Tauranga, 75
Temple, William, 74, 75, 232
Templemore, 39
Te Ranga, 32
Territorial Force, 124
Thames river, 73
Theodore III, King, 81
Thibaw, King, 67
Thiepval, 99, 117, 122
Thinganet chaung, 169
Thomas, Corporal Edward, 102
Thomas, Flying Officer Norman, 144
Thomastown, 49
Thompson, Lewis, 76
Thorr, 131
Thurles, 52, 125
Tighe, Lieutenant, 67
Tigris, river, 131
Tilney, Robert, 177
Times, The, 18, 19, 25, 107, 152, 153
Tipperary, 12, 37, 38, 53, 74
Tipperary County, 39, 46, 52, 57, 61, 82,
    100, 102, 109, 113, 120, 121, 125, 128,
    149, 159
Tisdall, Arthur Walderne St Clair, 185
Tisdall, Revd William St Clair, 185
Tobruk, 154, 155, 156, 158
Todleben, 29, 30
Tolstoy, Leo, 30
Toronto, 50, 63
Torquay, 38
Toronto Star, 63
Tralee, 164
Trans-Gogra, 63
Train, Charles, W., 127

Transport Command, 12, 167, 168
Transvaal, 86, 90, 92, 100
Travers, James, 50, 233
Traynor, Frances, 97
Traynor, Rebecca, 97
Traynor, William Bernard, 97, 98, 233
Trigh Capuzzo, 157
Trinchinopoly, 51
Tripoli, 170
Tuakan, 74
Tugela river, 92
Tula, 30
Tullamore, 54
Tullycorbet, 86
Tunbridge Wells, 75
Tunisia, 179, 187
Turkey, 21, 35, 110
Tygerskloof, 100
Tynan, 53

Ulster Special Constabulary, 20, 95
Ulundi, 83, 84
Unao, 50
United Kingdom, 11, 22, 148
United Service Gazette, 235
United States, 15, 23, 73, 75
units, miscellaneous:
    D Bty, 105
    L Bty, 104
    N Bty, 83
    7 Bty, 93, 94
    14 Bty, 93
    66 Bty, 93
    119 Bty, 104
    148 (Meiktila) Bty, 55
    58 Coy, D Force, 168
    No. 58 Casualty Clearing Station, 105
    No. 2 Flying Trg School, RAF, 143
    4th Coy, Machine Gun Corps, AIF, 184
Uruguay, 49
U.S. Air Force, 17
U.S. Navy, 171
U.S. Seventh Fleet, 171
Ushant, 161
Uthman Diqna, *see* Osman Digna

V Beach, 111
Valkfontein, 98
Varna, 22, 23, 25
Vaulx Vraucourt, 133

Veldwezelt, 144, 145, 146
Verdun, 129
Versailles, 140
·Vichy French, 164
Victoria, 126, 185
Victoria, Queen, 15, 16, 17, 25, 29, 32,
    40, 47, 48, 69, 80, 81, 85, 92, 94
Vietnam, 173
Villers Faucon, 126
Vimy Ridge, 135
Vittoria, 27
Vroenhoven, 144, 145

W Beach, 111
Wadi Akarit, 179
Waggon Hill, 95, 96
Wakefield, 39
Wakeford, Captain Richard, 179
Wales, 12
Walker, Alexander, 33
Walker, Mark, 33, 233
Walker, William, 101
Wallachia, 21, 23
Wanderers RFC, 15, 92, 99, 125
Ward, 2/Lieut F., 156, 157
Ward, Joseph, 62, 233
War Office, 18, 40, 53, 54, 124
Warrenpoint, 35
Waterford, 85, 154
Waterford County, 58, 59
Waterloo, battle of, 22
Waziristan, 141, 147
Wellington, duke of, 22, 26, 81n
Wellington College, 106, 168
Wells, 68
Welsh Ridge, 129
West, Augustus George, 133
West, Gertrude Annesley, 134
West, Maud Ethel, 134
West, Richard Annesley, 133, 134
West, Sara, 133
Western Front, 132, 137, 139
Western Queensland, 76
Westmeath County, 27, 33, 49, 54, 102,
    114
Westminster Cathedral, 103
Westminster Hospital, 63
Westminster Township, 63
Westport, 46
Wexford, 54, 110, 146, 150

Wexford County, 56, 135, 176
Wexford People, 152
Whelan, Jeremiah, 41
Whirlpool, Frederick, 186, 233
White Park, 133
White, George Stuart, 70, 91, 113n, 234
Whitehall, 46
White Umvolosi river, 85
Whittaker's plantation, 165
Whittington Barracks, 58
Whitworth hall, 130
Whyte, Desmond, 180, 181
Wicklow, county, 50, 60, 143, 154
Wigan, 110
William of Orange, 154n
Williams, Ellis, 237
Williams, William Henry, 163
Willoughby, Lieutenant, 43
Wilmott, Captain, 59
Wilson river, 76
Winchester Cathedral, 36
Winchester Gaol, 235
Windsor, 47, 80, 85
Windsor Castle, 69, 114
Winnipeg, 110
Woking, 106, 115
Wolfe, 51
Wood, Evelyn, 84
Wooden, Quartermaster, 52
Woods, Major Desmond, 178, 179
Woolwich, 36
Woodmount, 139
Woronzoff road, 36
Wrexham, 12, 167
Wright, Alexander, 35, 234
Wyndham, Major Crole, 90

Xaverian Brothers College, Manchester, 124

York Cottage, 118
Yorkshire, 12, 39, 77, 158
Young, Alexander, 99, 234
Younghusband, Major, 59
Ypres, and battles of, 11, 92, 105, 109,
    110, 129

Zandvoorde, 105
Zonnebeke, 92, 183
Zululand, 82, 84, 85
Zulu War, 57